# NAKED TRUTH

# NAKED TRUTH

Strip Clubs, Democracy, and a Christian Right

JUDITH LYNNE HANNA

University of Texas Press · Austin

Requests for permission to reproduce material from this work should
be sent to:
  Permissions
  University of Texas Press
  P.O. Box 7819
  Austin, TX 78713-7819
  www.utexas.edu/utpress/about/bpermission.html

⊚ The paper used in this book meets the minimum requirements of
ANSI/NISO Z39.48-1992 (R1997) (Permanence of Paper).

Library of Congress Cataloging-in-Publication Data

Hanna, Judith Lynne.
    Naked truth : strip clubs, democracy, and a christian right / by Judith
Lynne Hanna. — 1st ed.
        p.      cm.
    Includes bibliographical references and index.
    ISBN 978-0-292-72911-7 (cloth : alk. paper) — ISBN 978-0-292-73576-7
(pbk. : alk. paper) — ISBN 978-0-292-73575-0 (e-book)
    1. Striptease—United States.  2. Striptease—Social aspects—United
States.  3. Stripteasers—United States.  4. Sex in dance—United
States.  5. Christianity and politics—United States.  6. Dance—Political
aspects.  I. Title.
    PN1949.S7H36   2012
    792.7'8—dc23                                                    2011038890

To all those who believe
in the Constitution
and the civil liberties
it has bestowed upon us.

# CONTENTS

# Acknowledgments

My appreciation goes to Bruce McLaughlin, a certified planner, who learned about my work on dance as nonverbal communication through listings in *Books in Print* and introduced me to attorney Gil Levy. They set me on an adventurous, enlightening odyssey when they asked me to be an expert court witness in a First Amendment case on adult entertainment exotic dance in Seattle, Washington. This book about my discoveries along the way is not the product of my efforts alone but also those of uncountable others' time, energy, and generosity in sharing their knowledge. I could not begin to list them all. I am indebted to those authors listed in the references whose works provided insight and nuance.

I appreciate the exotic dance clubs that provided me the opportunity to visit, analyze activities on and offstage, and ascertain the implications of government restrictions on the dance content. Legislators, judges, and attorneys raising challenging questions led me down diverse paths of inquiry. Unless they appear in the public record—for example, former dancers who have written about their experiences—the real names of people are not used because of the unfortunate stigma attached to exotic dance.

I received no financial reward for writing this book. None came from the exotic dance industry because I did not want to give the appearance of being its hired hand. In fact, I have declined to testify for clubs and government when there was not relevant evidence. Furthermore, I have testified against a club in a sexual harassment case.

My gratitude goes to Dave Manack, ED (Exotic Dancer) Publications, whose *Exotic Dancer's Bulletin* (and subsequent *Exotic Dancer's Club Bulletin*) has kept me current with industry news since its beginning in spring 1996. Angelina Spencer, Jeff Levy, and Larry Kaplan have shared information from the Association of Club Executives and its affiliates.

The insightful comments of individuals who have read portions of this book during its evolution—Wayne B. Giampietro, Randall Tigue, Jack Nasar, Ben Blount, Larry Bledsoe, Marty Klein, David Brent, John Zelezny, Pamela Squires, Amy Gorelick, and William John Hanna—have contributed to its development. Anonymous peer reviewers' remarks on both research reports and this book were invaluable. To the lawyers with whom I have worked, especially Luke Lirot (thirty cases) and Michael Murray (fifteen cases), I thank you for the education you have given me. I am indebted to my colleague Katherine Frank for sharing her knowledge as a dancer and anthropologist and for offering invaluable criticism. I thank my editors, Allison Faust, for her steadfast support, and Sally Furgeson for her knowledge and research.

# NAKED TRUTH

# PRELUDE | Sparks Fly

## Church and State Conflict

When I saw the announcement for America's #1 Dancer Contest at the 2005 Exotic Dancer Expo in Las Vegas, I asked the sponsor, Jerry Reid of Pure Gold clubs, what criteria the judges would use. He said that in prior years he had sponsored bikini contests without specified standards. I shared the artistic criteria that evolved in 2002 when I was a judge at the Miss Exotic World Pageant, held at the Exotic World Burlesque Museum Hall of Fame in Helendale, California. In turn, he invited me to be a judge in Las Vegas.

My reason for being at Expo actually goes back to 1995 when a city/land use planner from Tampa, Florida, and an attorney from Seattle, Washington, asked me to be an expert court witness in a First Amendment case related to exotic dance. They wanted me to apply the same anthropological approach to studying adult entertainment dance that I used to study dance in African villages and cities and in US schools and concert theaters. Being a strong free speech advocate—and excited to apply my somewhat esoteric anthropological knowledge to a world I did not know—I agreed. This led to my becoming the world's only expert court witness on the dance itself—from ballet to stripping—as nonverbal communication. Other experts on exotic dance mainly testify on problems the clubs might cause or on zoning.

Under the authority of *Daubert v. Merrell Dow Pharmaceuticals, Inc.* (1993), I have been accepted as an expert court witness forty-six times in city, county, state, and federal courts; Alcohol Beverage Control/Liquor Commission hearings; and depositions nationwide. The law requires that my testimony be a product of principles and methods generally accepted as reliable by the social science discipline of anthropology and the humanities discipline of dance. In addition, I must qualify on the basis of knowledge, skill, experience, training, and education, and I must swear to tell the truth. I engage in a practicing and public interest anthropology that is committed to social justice by conducting research relevant to the facts of each case and the issue before the court.

## An Awakening

In the process of learning about exotic dance since 1995, I have worked with fifty-nine attorneys on 125 legal cases in twenty-nine states and the District of Columbia. I have observed no fewer than fifteen hundred dance performances and dancer-patron interactions. I have interviewed more than one thousand dancers, managers, owners, bartenders, disc jockeys, housemothers and house dads, and patrons in excess of 141 clubs. I have spoken with community members. My "classrooms" for learning about "Striptease 101," as a reporter called my court testimony, have been gentlemen's clubs and their surrounding communities, courtrooms, judges' chambers, city and county council meetings, and state hearings. Did my presence affect dancers, club management, patrons, and adversaries and supporters of exotic dance? I don't think so. In the clubs, stakeholders are accustomed to seeing mature females as house moms, managers, or costume salespersons. Some stakeholders also see mature women in legislative and court settings concerned with exotic dance. I identified myself as a dance writer, a researcher. Strangers sent me their stories. To try to catch what I missed firsthand, I read the *Washington Post, New York Times*, other media, and the scholarly literature. I checked the US Department of Justice reports on crime (National Criminal Justice Reference Service and Bureau of Justice Statistics); Human Trafficking web resource; trade publications, such as *Exotic Dancer*; American Planning Association reports; and several list-servs, websites, and chat rooms dealing with the subjects of sexuality in society, adult entertainment, Christianity, and civil liberties. I interviewed criminologists at several universities and police in their jurisdictions. These experiences certainly opened my eyes and I'd like to share them with you.

I realized that exotic dance (also called strip club, erotic, striptease, stripper, topless, titty bar, barroom, nude, go-go, sports bar, table, lap, friction, couch, gentlemen's club dance, and even pornography) is a form of dance, art, and theater that communicates within its own aesthetic. Dancers perform in licensed establishments and their performances are not visible to those outside. The popular industry boasts about four thousand adult cabarets nationwide; it claims employees directly or indirectly (independent contractors and auxiliary service providers), numbering more than five hundred thousand people. A single gentlemen's club in a major metropolitan area may gross $10–20 million per year. Some chains are traded on NASDAQ (National Association of Securities Dealers Automated) and the American Stock Exchange and even own clubs abroad.

## From Strip Club to Religion

I did not intend to explore the relationship of religion and the adult entertainment industry. But my first case in 1995 was the beginning of startling revelations. I had to break through "Washington Together Against Pornography!" demonstrators in Bellevue, Washington, to begin to discover what went on inside exotic dance clubs. Men, women and children picketing the club held screaming banners of denunciation. A Christian church was behind this opposition to the adult entertainment.

Since then, I have been involved in more than one hundred successive cases nationwide (Appendix 9 lists cases in which I provided sworn testimony) to prevent the enactment of laws or to challenge laws that infringe upon the First, Fifth, and/or Fourteenth Amendments to the US Constitution or to defend dancers against false charges of prostitution, lewdness, indecency, or obscenity. In nearly all those cases, a pastor or church group was spearheading efforts to wipe out the alleged "moral cancer" of "toxic" exotic dance. At first, it seemed to me that the religious groups that were attacking exotic dance were acting independently in the tradition of local control. Eventually I realized that many were part of a web of connection in a powerful Christian Right (CR) political alliance in which a segment politically and financially supports fighting the exotic dance industry.

In my "classrooms"—case after case—I began to watch this segment of a politically active Christian Right (I refer to this group as "CR-Activists"), which is not supported by many in the diverse Christian Right. I saw CR-Activists belligerently oppose exotic dance through street, legislative, and judicial means. Many recent books provide a contextual framework for understanding the assaults against exotic dance as a battle within a broader "war" against the separation of church and state.[1]

CR-Activists act overtly by picketing clubs and using other "street"-level tactics against clubs, dancers, and patrons. They are vocal at council meetings and hearings related to exotic dance. They lobby government through powerful organizations, covertly burrow into government, and get elected so they can legislate and adjudicate against exotic dance. In addition, they hire CR-Activist attorneys to help draft and defend restrictive laws. CR-Activists also unstintingly publicize the misconception that the clubs cause crime, property depreciation, and disease more than any other place of public assembly. In addition, CR-Activists stimulate independent churches across the country to fight exotic dance and support these churches in their opposition. Part of a clash between theocracy and democracy, the exotic dance conflict illuminates the intersection of religion, dance, and democracy as it affects our liberty and free enterprise and diverts resources from coping with issues related to health, education, crime, and homeland security, among others.

## Aftershock of Secularism and Sexual Revolution

In 1973, a small group of evangelical men had a design for the nation.[2] In a sense, the CR came out of mothballs. The early twentieth-century evangelical movement had split from Protestant churches that were embracing modernism and gradually adapting beliefs and traditions. A handful of fundamentalist organizations entered the political arena to mobilize against the teaching of evolution. After the John T. Scopes 1925 "monkey trial" in Dayton, Tennessee,[3] the fundamentalist movement retreated from the national public scene. It went into exile from what it saw as a corrupt and hostile world. The trial had garnered nationwide publicity, capturing the attention of such luminaries as George Bernard Shaw and Albert Einstein. Part of the prosecution team, William Jennings Bryan, former secretary of state under President Woodrow Wilson and onetime Democratic presidential candidate, represented the fundamentalist Christians. He described the contest between evolution and Christianity as "a duel to the death." Scopes's attorney, Clarence Darrow, a well-known avowed agnostic, viewed the contest as civilization on trial. Although Scopes lost, the case brought to public awareness the vulnerability of free speech and individual freedom in a democracy. Ridicule of the fundamentalists left them skeptical about being able to accomplish much through politics, and their activism was replaced by a benign and apolitical evangelism, later exemplified by Billy Graham, that was primarily interested in saving souls. But the rise of the Cold War motivated religious conservatives to political action. Reverend Billy James Hargis led a strenuous anti-Communist movement, the Christian Crusade, during the 1950s.

Changes in American society—the growth of secularism, the 1960s sexual revolution that challenged repression of expression, globalization, and other dramatic, rapid social transformations—appear to have catalyzed the emergence of CR-Activists. The 1973 legalization of abortion convinced conservatives that the country had strayed from traditional cultural moorings. Consequently, in the 1970s, the CR became an association of conservative preachers and politicians, along with their grassroots followers, determined to influence public policy. Jerry Falwell turned dispensational Bible prophecy from a rationale for separation from the world into a rhetoric of urgent engagement with the world.[4] By 1976, he was preaching, "This idea of 'religion and politics don't mix' was invented by the devil to keep Christians from running their own country." Epitomizing concern with the trampling of values held dear, Falwell founded the Moral Majority in 1979 to mobilize fundamentalists as voters and to enact cultural reform. A business elite and intellectuals in magazines, journals, and think tanks facilitated the success of CR politics. Widespread jeremiads (named for the Old Testament prophet Jeremiah) lamented the moral condition of the nation, foresaw cataclysmic consequences, and called for dramatic moral reform.

Rogers Smith says the CR movement owes it origins to Internal Revenue Service and court actions that seemed to threaten the tax-exempt status of Christian broadcasters and Christian private schools and universities. In the early 1970s, the IRS denied tax-exempt status to Christian schools perceived as engaging in racial discrimination. Because the CR feared losing tax-exempt status, the National Association of Evangelicals coalesced to preserve access to public airwaves and maintain policies that help them finance their schools and other CR institutions.

In Preston Shires's view, the CR was not just a reactionary movement fomented by enraged fundamentalists, but also an extension of the sixties counterculture. Youth participants who eventually joined the community brought their countercultural ideals. They rejected the modernist establishment, secular humanism, liberal theology, establishment trappings of conservative churches, and science-calibrated religion. Evangelism's activist fervor and rebellious spirit comes from the counterculture.

After the Moral Majority folded in the late 1980s, Dr. Pat Robertson, Phi Beta Kappa from Washington and Lee University and graduate of Yale Law School and New York Theological Seminary, founded the Christian Coalition. When it imploded with Dr. Ralph Reed's departure in 1997, Dr. James Dobson's Focus on the Family took the reins of political activism.[5] Focus on the Family contained a group of thirty-eight sister associations across the country known as the Family Policy Council or Citizens for Community Values or the Free Market Foundation. They also had "action arms" and political action committees under many names in all fifty states. In 2009, Dobson received the "Ronald Reagan Lifetime Achievement Award" from the secretive Council for National Policy, in part for his railing against the sexual revolution of the 1960s and the adoption of no-fault divorce laws. He has been a member of the Council since 1981.

Jon Shields argues that the CR organizations helped create a more participatory democracy by mobilizing conservative evangelicals, heretofore an alienated constituency in the United States, and that the majority of these groups inculcates norms of civility and respect and cultivates dialog. But good manners may be a cover for the pursuit of antidemocratic goals.

After a thirty-year effort through dynamic organizational momentum, a religious "fifth column" has infiltrated the public arena. CR-Activists have helped conservatives gain office at the local, state, and national levels; influenced Supreme Court nominations; taken control of Congress for the first time in forty years, and triumphantly and proudly put George W. Bush, a born-again evangelical, into the White House. Bush's Office of Faith-Based and Community Initiatives further linked church and state. Government-funded religious social service providers are allowed to discriminate, proselytize, and play by different rules than other charities receiving taxpayer dollars. Conservatives redirected the US Department of Justice civil rights mission away from challenging voting plans that dilute the strength of black voters and investigating hate crimes to considering discrimination against Christians. The department transferred or demoted some experienced civil rights litigators and replaced them with "holy hires." The Christian Right Regent University, founded by Pat Robertson, boasted placing one hundred and fifty of its graduates in the Bush administration. Senior officials of the Bush administration hired so-called "right-thinking Americans" for apolitical career positions.

Following the 2008 election of the Democratic presidential nominee, Barack Obama, several pundits—such as E. J. Dionne, *Washington Post* columnist and frequent radio and TV commentator, and David D. Kirkpatrick, *New York Times* writer—proclaimed the era of the CR dead, dying, or irrelevant. Several times this epitaph has been erroneously written. The CR forms the base of the Republican Party, which lost the presidency and congressional majorities in 2008 but resurged in 2010, gaining control of the US House of Representatives and many state governments.

CR-Activists continued their winning streak on the volatile question of same-sex marriage. More than one thousand ministers, mostly from evangelical congregations, but also Catholics and Mormons, united to pass Proposition 8, a ballot initiative to amend the California constitution to ban same-sex marriage. Rob Boston, writing for *Church & State*, suggests the CR-Activists are jumping into the issues of deficits and unions hoping to "forge an alliance with the Tea Party and create a right-wing phalanx so powerful no one can stand against it."[6] As in the battle against the exotic dance industry, the Proposition 8 strategy included input from lawyers and political consultants coupled with a campaign of misinformation. Media technologies, sermons to galvanize congregations to engage in well-organized grassroots activity, and, of critical importance, funding from prominent CR-Activist organizations infused the initiative campaign. On the other side, the secular and compassionate message centered on securing rights for gays and lesbians.[7] CR-Activists also enshrined discrimination through a constitutional amendment in Florida that eliminated marriage for same-sex couples, leading to a successful ballot initiative drive to ban same-sex marriage in Arizona. In Arkansas, CR-Activists succeeded in convincing voters to deny same-sex couples and most straight unmarried couples the right to adopt children or be foster parents. In 2010, some members of the CR aligned themselves with the emerging, dynamic Tea Party within the Republican Party to win congressional seats. The CR crusade to ban abortion, deny civil rights to gay Americans, inject religion into public education and other institutions remains in the public limelight.

The judiciary is not immune. CR-Activists targeted seated judges in California and Iowa. Vowing to be God's ambassadors on the bench, four San Diego Superior Court candidates were backed by pastors, gun enthusiasts, and opponents of abortion and same-sex marriages. "We believe our country is under assault and needs Christian values," said Craig Candelore, a family law attorney and one of the group's candidates. "Unfortunately, God has called upon us to do this only with the judiciary."[8]

Dagmar Herzog believes that CR-Activists achieve power in these different controversial political and judicial domains primarily through attempts to control sexuality. However, there is ambiguity about which behaviors constitute "sex," and what it means. Seen through different eyes, sex can be anything from looking at another human being to sexual intercourse. Sex can mean a pleasurable activity, a sacrament, a means to procreation, an ecstasy, a disappointment, or a source of shame.

President Barack Obama's choice of anti-gay, anti-abortion pastor Rick Warren to give the invocation at his inauguration reminds us that the CR is a steady force in the political and cultural arena. The economic downturn has hurt everyone, including the CR. But as in the big Christian revivals of the nineteenth century, known as the second and third Great Awakenings and prompted by economic panics, evangelicals are drawing big crowds in these stressful times.[9]

In July 2009, the Alliance Defense Fund, a CR-Activist organization, requested a meeting with Attorney General Eric Holder "at the earliest opportunity" to discuss, among other issues, the "illegal pornography [that] has flooded homes, businesses, public libraries, and even schools," which has been "devastating to America." The pro-censorship crowd devotes energy on all political levels. A group in Indiana, with affiliates nationwide, that aggressively targets exotic dance says on its website:

> Citizens for Community Values is an educational organization devoted to protecting families from the harms of the porn/sex industry in all of its forms. . . . We believe that there is a great culture war for the soul of our nation being waged by many kinds of sexual revolutionaries that oppose the principles governing human sexual relations established by God.

I can testify from the "trenches" in the exotic dance battle—a conflict of which most people are unaware—that CR-Activists continually flex their moral muscle at the state and local levels in a relentless drive to eliminate the adult entertainment industry. The ever-growing public sexual expression in television shows, films, the Internet, and advertising fuels CR actions, as does nudity on clothes-optional beaches, in college spring break sexual antics, and in the performing arts. Playboy's circulation has fallen from 7 to 3 million over the past quarter century thanks to the emergence of even more explicit media.

Exotic dance is merely one among several battle targets in a broader culture war. Moreover, words, themes, and images commonly broadcast are now being censored. Fines for violations, jeopardized licenses, and litigation ensue. Books are removed from libraries and school curricula are changed. Business advertising is constricted, and prescriptions, stem cell research, end-of-life decisions, and women's choice are denied. Instead, CR-Activists call for prayer in schools and the teaching of creationism and intelligent design. Marty Klein's America's War on Sex provides detailed illustrations of these diverse battles.

## More Surprises

The exotic dance court cases that I've worked on—from First Amendment to sexual harassment, employee-independent contractor labor relations, obscenity, wrongful arrest, prostitution, and even homicide and suicide—have astonished me. And they've astonished others, too. I have received diametrically opposed responses to my unique vantage as researcher.

Anonymous people have sent me religious tracts designed to save my soul. A woman at a public hearing yelled, "You ought to be ashamed of yourself!" Wrongly assuming that exotic dancer equals prostitute, a friend who became a Los Angeles assistant district attorney responded to my tales about exotic dance by describing a prostitution case she had just handled.

A former college roommate from the University of California, Berkeley, said, "I hope those sleazy club owners pay you." A former academic dean of a major university refused to sign off on a research proposal to the Law and Society Program of the National Science Foundation to explore why people are so vehemently against exotic dance. He admitted he was uncomfortable with the subject matter! He said planners weren't concerned with adult entertainment when, in fact, the American Planning Association has sent out related materials to planners, had panels on the subject, published a book on the theme, and filed court briefs in favor of government regulations of exotic dance. And I later published articles on exotic dance in the peer-reviewed *Journal of Planning Literature*. A National Science Foundation reviewer of a proposal to study exotic dance in a particular community worried that the study would subject NSF to publicity from the Golden Fleece Award, which is given to grants ridiculed as a waste of public money by the US Congress. My Middle Eastern dance teacher gasped, "Oh my God!" when she saw my *New York Times* article on exotic dance accompanied by a picture of a stripper, sandwiched between a piece on Middle East dance and a picture of a burlesque dancer. She didn't like being associated with the adult entertainment offshoots of her art form.

Yet along with these negative reactions to my research and court testimony on exotic dance, I've also received neutral responses, accolades, and invitations to write and speak about my work. Newspaper reporters have asked, "What is a person like you with 'impeccable credentials' doing studying nude dancing?" I answer, "Anthropologists study human behavior." When I have conducted door-to-door exotic dance club neighborhood surveys, respondents have mistaken me for a member of the CR. Dancers have called me "Dr. Ruth," after the sexologist. A Nevada prosecutor said to me after my testimony, "I wish I had had you on my side." After my testimony about how striptease is a form of dance, art, and communication, male exotic dancers in the court gallery stood up and applauded (a no-no). Strangers write to me in appreciation of my attempts to report what is really going on. Friends, too. Renowned modern dancer, two-time Tony Award winner, Broadway choreographer/director, recipient of a MacArthur "Genius" Award, and 2010 Kennedy Center Honoree, Bill T. Jones is glad I contest censorship:

> My jaw dropped when I saw the level at which the discourse around sexuality and individual freedom still labors and I am heartened, amused and inspired by your head-on confrontation of such ignorance. I thank you for the effort on behalf of all of us who would shake our bootie, grind our hips and caress another in public.[10]

The dramatic expansion in the numbers of exotic dance clubs and in the size of audiences since the 1980s, with the advent of the gentlemen's club supplanting the strip joint, threatens the CR. In this changing landscape, couples and women increasingly attend the cabarets. Attesting to the popularity of exotic dance is the "stripperization" of America—strip aerobics in gyms, pole dance parties in women's homes, and DVDs on stripping for the everyday woman. Wives and girlfriends are flocking to classes. Exotic dance has become a staple of American entertainment. In 2003, *Time* reported professional trend spotter Irma Zandl's forecast: "Strippers are really setting the trends right now."[11] In 2009, Gucci and Neiman Marcus stores featured the kind of shoes that I had seen only on exotic dancers a few years earlier.

## Why Christian Right Activists Attack Exotic Dance

So, why are CR-Activists targeting exotic dance in particular? CR acceptance of Biblical injunctions concerning the use of the body, modesty, a male-female polarity, and patriarchy, as well as beliefs about the inherent uncontrollable nature of men are part of the answer. In addition, unrealistic expectations about women created by beautiful nude dancers and jealousy of performers create opposition to exotic dance. Eroticism unleashes passions that defy the dictates of CR churches and their male leaders in a world of absolute right and wrong. More importantly, however, CR-Activists' behavior, according to some opponents, is that of "sexual jihadists" struggling to reorganize American life. The implications of the outcome of attacks on exotic dance are frightening for all kinds of dance, other performing arts, you, me and American democracy, as I will explain later.

Harnessing an organizational network fueled by technology, money, and lawyers, an emboldened division of the CR fights adult entertainment as part of Dominionism. This political religious movement has a grand design to supplant our constitutional democracy with a Bible-based, Christian, theocratic governing elite.[12] Obsessed with dominion over the nation, movement adherents believe that expansion of state control over sexuality is key to creating a salutary environment for their children and making way for their ideal state. Believing that it is God's will that the country be subject to literal Biblical rule, *some* zealous evangelicals (e.g., Baptists, the Pentecostal Holiness, Reformed-Confessions, and Anabaptists, many who worship at nondenominational megachurches), Charismatics, and conservative Catholics make up the "troops." Political activism is considered a duty. The Quiverfull movement advocates that parents should accept as many children as God gives them (based on Psalm 127) in a concerted effort to win the culture wars demographically. Women attempting to control their own bodies are viewed as seizing God's power. Emphasis is placed on militaristic imagery, particularly arrows. The children become the arrows of the parents, part of their tools of war against the enemy.[13]

The fact that exotic dance is under the umbrella of the US Constitution, with some measure of First Amendment free speech protection, constrains CR-Activists' use of government to ban exotic dance outright. So its leaders do an end run around the Constitution. For "the public good" and especially to "protect our children," CR-Activists enter or lobby government to enact regulations that censor exotic dance, harm the business by eating away at its essence, and trample many people's civil liberties. Not unlike some other political groups, the CR-Activists mobilize a "disinformation factory." Vociferously and persistently capturing media attention, CR-Activists unstintingly charge that the clubs attract prostitution, drugs, and other crime; spread disease; degrade women; depreciate property; and hurt a residential or business district or city image—the so-called adverse secondary effects legal doctrine. This doctrine emerged from court decisions that deferred to legislatures' intent to protect the public welfare, even though the asserted need was based on invalid, outdated "studies." Social scientists have recently disproved these reputed adverse secondary effects by calling into question the shoddy methods of the so-called studies and conducting consistently robust new research that has been published in scholarly journals since 2001.[14] No study shows a link between what exotic dance is—the dance movement, costume, props, and distance or touch between dancer and patron—and any negative effects.

Nonetheless, CR-Activists manipulate the public by adopting secular reasoning with corrupted democratic concepts and the adverse secondary effects myth—belief or camouflage for positions held on moral grounds. Recasting their religion-based moral objections honestly or disingenuously, the exotic dance adversaries read from a hymnal of spin and gain support for regulations to destroy the adult hospitality business. The adverse secondary effects doctrine acquires a cachet of truth and consequently provokes broad public denunciation that inadvertently supports CR-Activists' efforts to break down the walls separating church and state. Even some feminists, following the oppression paradigm of dancer exploitation and perpetuation of gender inequality in the Catherine MacKinnon/Andrea Dworkin mold,[15] aid CR-Activists' attempt to strip the First Amendment, corset the exotic dancer, and dismantle the industry.

Not surprisingly, some politicians of any religious persuasion periodically, especially at election time, exploit and reinforce stereotypes about the cabarets and assail female exotic dancers. Such a red herring diverts attention from government failure to cope with the real problems of education, crime, health, and traffic. Thus, the politicians show their constituents that they are working on their behalf and merit being returned to office—even if their jurisdiction doesn't have a club.

Ironically, youngsters and even pastors belie the proclaimed rationale of CR-Activists "to protect our children" by upholding family values and going after adult clubs to create a salutary puritanical environment. Coarse language and profanity have long been heard among kids, including on elementary school playgrounds. Middle school and high school students' incidences of booty dancing, oral sex, out-of-wedlock pregnancy, and transmission of venereal disease make a mockery of CR-Activists' efforts to ban fantasy in venues that only adult patrons may voluntarily enter. The booty dancing, or freaking, style (the female bends forward and rubs her buttocks against the male's groin) has been popular among African Americans since the late 1970s. Brought to public attention in Spike Lee's 1988 film *School Daze*, booty dancing shocked white parents nationwide when it reached their schools in the 1990s. I got lots of calls from radio shows and the press to comment on this development. Of course, home schooling and isolating one's children can somewhat shelter them. Also ironic is the fact that Catholics and Baptists established organizations to help victims of sexual predators in the churches.

Exotic dance is about fantasy, a common human phenomenon, not carnality and pedophilia. The exotic dance industry, civil rights groups, and even various religious denominations—armed with their lobbyists, lawyers, and expert court witnesses and free speech advocates—fight back against CR-Activists. Cases periodically reach the US Supreme Court. Only recently has the court put brakes on some legislative action based on the presumptive need to regulate exotic dance. Governments can now be challenged on the truth of their claims based on "studies." Unfortunately, not all lower courts pay heed.

## Full Disclosure

Awakened to the broadside against exotic dance as part of a larger war on democratic values, I am moved to offer an unprecedented look at the battle between a powerful minority group and a marginalized strip club industry, with a bit of titillation plus a large share of gravitas. Clearly, exotic dance is a lightning rod, indeed, a barometer, for a maelstrom of public discord. Yet, CR-Activists' insidious encroachment on civil liberties draws little notice.

Culture wars and male clergy contesting the female body and dance are nothing new in American history, as I discovered reading about dance in *New York Times* articles dating to the newspaper's inception in 1851. Some artists and dances now widely acclaimed were "morally offensive" in their time. While clergymen railed against "debauched" dancing, dancing masters fought licensing laws. For the most part, restrictions against dancers were unsuccessful or short-lived.

Recurring conflagrations over exotic dance differ from notorious First Amendment battles over Robert Mapplethorpe's photographic exhibits that displayed male genitalia, the explicit sex in the movie *Behind the Green Door*, and the breasts and vaginas portrayed in *Hustler* magazine and online. Unlike those arts that use paper, canvas, and film, exotic dance manifests itself through the live body—the instrument of dance and of sex. Exotic dance is palpable, a multisensory performance, a nonverbal "conversation" in which patrons may become active communicators. More importantly, the exotic dance conflict bears on women's choice, discrimination, economic survival, and social mobility in addition to men's well-being.

A comment on my perspectives is warranted. I am a former Los Angeles high school civics teacher with an MA in political science and a PhD in anthropology. I have been a long-time advocate of the First Amendment and empiricism. I couldn't believe that in this day and age there would be such an intense church-state conflict reflected in the fight against exotic dance. Following government orders to crack down on clubs, police have lied under oath, forged a dancer's name on a sign-in sheet and then denied it, or claimed a dancer was nude during an entire dance when nudity was only its climax. CR-Activists participate in drafting legislation, litigating challenges to the constitutionality of such legislation, and "street fighting" tactics in pursuit of substituting the Bible for the Constitution. Many judicial courts have been intentionally or unintentionally complicit. I am saddened by the public's stereotypes that ultimately harm many people's well-being. I must admit, I savor the courtroom's "improvisational theater dance"—the adrenaline rush of verbal challenge and the opportunity to educate and win over an audience mired in misconceptions.[16] And I'm driven to tell the naked truth about the conflict I have been learning about for many years.

To those unfamiliar with the history and beliefs of the CR and the methods of a segment of the politically active CR, this book may appear, at first blush, to be an unfounded diatribe and a brief for the clubs or dancers. But the unfolding saga of my on-site experience (ethnography), buttressed by the writings of current and former members of the CR, scholars, and journalists, all combine to suggest otherwise. Uncovering this knowledge certainly challenged my preconceptions. Although balance is commonly the norm in serious writing, balance presumes legitimacy on both sides. However, balance can also be a pernicious concept implying that all ideas are equally valid. I don't think so. Do we give equal time to creationism? Nazism? Government battles against sexuality eerily recall sequential acts of fascist and totalitarian countries that have eaten away at human rights. Recall, Adolf Hitler wanted theater, art, literature, cinema, press, posters, and window displays cleansed of all manifestations of sexual ideas and stimulations and placed in the service of a moral, political, and cultural idea. So, too, the Taliban permits neither any kind of dance nor women's freedom.

Naked Truth: Strip Clubs, Democracy, and a Christian Right follows in the tradition of Franz Boas, father of American anthropology. Skeptical of prevailing views about various subjects, he questioned common assumptions and emphasized being at the scene. In an attempt to popularize the new science of anthropology, Dr. Boas indirectly brought the immediate forerunner of exotic dance, the Middle Eastern belly dance, to US public attention for the first time at the 1893 Chicago World's Columbian Exposition. My efforts to demystify exotic dance in the public arena also follow in the tradition of Dr. Margaret Mead, a member the Columbia University anthropology faculty, who dispelled myths through ethnographic research.

Yes, there is a plethora of books on religion and books on "strippers" that suggests the intense interest in these areas. A continually growing body of literature analyzes the Christian Right's initial mobilization, subsequent growth, and related issues.[17] There are also many books on exotic dancers, their history, motivations, exploitation, objectification and agency, identity, self-esteem, and various experiences. A few books focus on exotic dance club customers.[18] After all, sex piques curiosity and sells. The risqué carries a magnetic mystique.

However, Naked Truth: Strip Clubs, Democracy, and a Christian Right looks at provocations to our Constitution through the eye of exotic dance and sorts out fiction, fantasy, and fact surrounding this adult entertainment. The book explores the prism of religion, law, and sexual fantasy undergirded by concepts of the First Amendment; religion as a crucible of meanings in discourse and action; and philosopher Michel Foucault's view of the body as a locus of power.

My observations of exotic dancers onstage and off in performer-patron connections, coupled with the voices and photographs of stakeholders, take the reader behind the closed doors of exotic dance clubs. Clubs have elements of carnival and tourism, a "transgressive" adventure for dancers, patrons, owners, and staff. Readers may want single-answer explanations for their questions: What is exotic dance, the battle target? Who are the dancers? Patrons? Club owners? What are the clubs like? But complexity and diversity intertwine with historical time, governments' regulations, and jurisprudence.

My experiences with communities, government meetings, public hearings, and court proceedings, buttressed by media reports, archives, and scientific studies, bring the reader outside the clubs and into their neighborhoods, counties, cities, and states. I have spoken with neighbors, both residents and businesspeople, about the clubs' impact on the neighborhood's quality of life (see Appendix 13). Voices of exotic dance adversaries and defenders, portraits of the arsenal of weapons used against clubs, the defense's responses, and case studies will illustrate the conflicts and raise issues of questionable citizen action, police tactics, and government practices.

## Itinerary

Chapter 1 describes the CR-Activists' reasons for hostility toward exotic dance and for their crusade against the adult entertainment industry. Challenges to traditions, Dominionism, interpretations of Scripture concerning patriarchy, the body, dance, nudity and lust, and the CR view of the nature of men are key reasons. The First Amendment constrains CR-Activists from completely obliterating exotic dance. But they are unrelenting in their goal to drive the exotic dance industry out of business. Chapter 2 gives a picture of their battle strategy. CR tactics are imbued with militaristic rhetoric, boss politics actions, multimedia campaigns, "street fighting," and psychological and legalistic approaches for moral reasons.

What is the "incendiary" exotic dance that consumes so much of CR-Activists' and governments' time, energy, and monetary expenditure? Chapter 3 defines exotic dance. What the CR fantasizes? Pornography? Women who take their clothes off for sex? Who is actually onstage? How did they get there? What makes exotic dance "speech" with "serious artistic merit" that exempts it from being obscene in the legal sense and losing First Amendment protection? Why do men go behind the closed doors of adult entertainment clubs? How does the "devil seduce" patrons in an illusionary playful world? Male fantasy and vulnerability are part of the play for pay. What is the dancer's cornucopia of ploys in the game? Are there any socially redeeming values to exotic dance?

Because exotic dance is not an isolated phenomenon but part of American culture, Chapter 4 addresses the issue of nudity and touch that CR-Activists single out. Are nudity and touch expressive elements found in past and contemporary mainstream arts? Theater? Musicals? Opera? Theater dance? Performance art?

CR-Activists' opposition to exotic dance clubs plays out in different dogged ways. I describe attacks on exotic dance and how they unfold in communities and courts. Chapter 5 discusses assaults on adult entertainment and the consequent bench (before the judge) trials that took place over an eight-year period in Maryland. Spurred by religious groups and legislators acting on behalf of their own morality or that of their constituents, the conflict centered on a club and Prince George's County's chief executive and council. The story began to unfold when a riot squad entered a family-owned club with weapons in full combat readiness—"Don't move or talk or we will use physical force and fuck you up," warned an officer. The saga progressed with no convictions but more harassment and restrictive county ordinance after ordinance, each followed by legal challenge and an ironical denouement.

Chapter 6 reports interrelated antagonistic actions against exotic dance and dancers in Minnesota. Once again, Christian morality was the prime mover. Dancers were charged with obscenity and had jury trials. What constitutes police "evidence"? Looking up nude dancers' crotches? How do expert court witnesses act? How does a trial progress, a jury arrive at its verdict? What do members of the community think?

The CR claims that exotic dancers are degraded and exploited. But are they? Do they need to, or want to, be saved? Are they subject to unique workplace experiences? Chapter 7 focuses on the dancers' working conditions, examining the kinds of clubs where they dance, from brand-name chains of gentlemen's clubs listed on stock exchanges to the sleazy strip joints of yore. The dancers' bosses make a difference. What are contentious issues between dancers and the clubs? Dancers as independent contractors or employees is a big one.

The CR and others believe that exotic dance clubs cause adverse secondary effects. Chapter 8 looks at the charges of terror and crime: murder, rape, other types of violence, property destruction and damage, prostitution, bribery, and drugs. If exotic dance clubs have these problems, are their numbers disproportionate compared to other places of public assembly? Who is doing what to whom? Where is the real harm? What is the role of stigma in the judicial system and society more broadly?

In light of the CR-Activist-initiated belligerent behavior toward exotic dance, Chapter 9 turns to how the industry defends itself. The First Amendment, Takings and Due Process Clauses of the Fifth Amendment, and Equal Protection Clause of the Fourteenth Amendment to the US Constitution plus case law, citizen action, and club proactive and reactive responses facilitate a defense. Key court decisions legally constrain CR-Activism and government battle tactics, although some judges ignore them. The adult cabaret industry gains inadvertent defense from a number of Christian and other religious denominations that resent those seeking to impose their own specific views on the nation. Dogma and pluralism clash, the separation of church and state is squeezed. After all is said, what is the significance of a war at the margins of society for mainstream American democracy?

Given the public's inherent interest in sex, religion, and the direction of this country, *Naked Truth: Strip Clubs, Democracy and a Christian Right* is directed to both liberal and conservative readers. I have been interviewed by the media from the *Washington Post* to the *Washington Times*, from National Public Radio to Laura Ingraham and Focus on the Family. I hope this book will enlighten localities concerned about the impact of exotic dance clubs on their quality of life; planners, police, legislators, lawyers, and judges involved in the regulation of adult businesses; members of the adult industry; and dancers' families, as well as people interested in anthropology, criminology, dance, jurisprudence, politics, religion, sexuality, and women's issues.

# Scripture and Hostility to Exotic Dance

As the vice regents of God we are to exercise godly dominion and influence over our neighborhoods, our schools, our government, our literature and arts, our sports arenas, our entertainment media, our news media, our scientific endeavors—in short, over every aspect and institution of human society.

DR. D. JAMES KENNEDY

Today's battle against exotic dance is as much about the belief that modern culture itself is toxic, rife with social decay, as it is about local contests over morality, taste, and decency. Exotic dance is a lightning rod for an effort to return to "traditional values" by imposing sweeping "decency standards" and censoring and criminalizing discussion, artistic depictions, and any kind of nonmarital consensual sexual activity. Attacks on exotic dance are enmeshed in the goal to shape public policy by undermining what a segment of the politically active Christian Right—that is, CR-Activists—regards as the institutional secular strongholds of modern American liberalism that have led to the degradation of culture by corrupt values.

## Reasons for Christian Right Opposition

After all, the dancing and patronage are voluntary for adults only behind closed doors. And striptease culture is spreading. Aerobic workouts incorporate elements of erotic dance. Women are going to clubs with significant male others and by themselves. There has always been opposition to some "sexual" dances in American history.[1] Railing against the immorality and indecency of dancing, including the waltz, Charleston, tango, twist, and freaking, is persistent in American culture. In 1923, a professor developed a spiked belt, called the "Prince Lily Girdle," to ensure modesty in cheek-to-cheek dancing. About this time, in Kalamazoo, Michigan, a local dancing ordinance prohibited dancers from looking into each other's eyes in order to avoid breathing into each other's faces in the interest of health. The Jackson County, Florida, school board opposed dancing as late as 1932 and ruled that any teacher who indulged in dancing during the school year would automatically forfeit his or her position. In 1986, dancing of any kind was still considered sinful in Purdy, Missouri, a town of 967 people, where social conservatism and fundamentalist Christianity are the accepted ways. And Baylor University, the world's largest Baptist institution of higher learning, made an unwritten policy against dancing official in 1990. In protest against 151 years of no dancing, the student body overwhelmingly voted in 1996 to hold organized dances on campus.

Interestingly, since many Christian churches branded dancing as sinful, certain behavioral patterns formerly called "dancing" were renamed and otherwise modified. In the South, the ring-shout was a substitute for the banned dancing common to African and West Indian religious ceremonies. Some churches believe that on the day of Pentecost the Holy Ghost descended to the apostles and gave them "quickening powers" with speaking in tongues, patterned movement, and other manifestations of spiritual possession. Dancing is referred to as "feeling the spirit."

## Dominionism

Contemporary adversaries of exotic dance are more powerful than earlier opponents of other dance forms. Exotic dance is a bump in the road toward Dominionism. Chris Hedges traces the roots of Dominionism[2] to Genesis 1:26–31—God gives human beings "dominion" over all creation—and says it emanates from a Christian reconstructionism. This is spelled out in Rousas John Rushdoony's 1973 book, *The Institutes of Biblical Law*. Dominionism calls for a harsh, unforgiving, and violent Christian society. Reconstructionists forthrightly espouse theocracy and the return to the Old Testament legal codes of death for gays, blasphemers, adulterers, incorrigible teenagers, practitioners of witchcraft, the unchaste, and those who spread false religions.

Rushdoony's nonprofit Chalcedon Foundation is the leading Christian reconstructionist organization and its monthly *Chalcedon Report* deals with the relationship of Christianity to the world. The motto of American Vision, another reconstructionist organization, is "Exercising Servanthood Dominion."[3] With its overtly radical theocratic agenda, it seeks to rewrite American history and dismantle secular democracy. Illustrative of the Dominionist creed, Dr. D. James Kennedy of Coral Ridge Presbyterian Church, with ten thousand congregants and weekly sermons broadcast to more than forty thousand cities and towns in the United States and more than two hundred nations, preached the need to exercise godly dominion and influence over all facets of human society.

## Soldiers of the Cross

Clergy are known to speak of themselves as "generals" or "admirals" and their evangelist followers as "soldiers." Christian men are portrayed as powerful warriors. Satan convinces believers not to take part in the battle. Casey Sanchez of the Southern Poverty Law Center describes Joel's Army as an apocalyptic movement prophesied to become an Armageddon-ready military force of young people with a divine mandate to physically impose Christian "dominion" on nonbelievers. Joel's Army eschews democracy, pluralism, and the political system.

Moreover, CR-Activists have made an imprint in the US military through proselytizing.[4] Michael Weinstein, who served in the US Air Force, writes that evangelicals have used the Air Force Academy as "a wedge to insert their people in place within the entire command structure of the armed forces. . . . [T]he attempt to use their influence within the military to effect political change has been part of the strategy from the beginning."[5] Film-maker Brian Hughes in 2008 took video footage in Afghanistan that documents heavy-handed evangelical influence in the military. In the footage, widely broadcast, Lt. Col. Gary Hensley tells soldiers they have a responsibility "to be witnesses for him [Christ]. The Special Forces guys, they hunt men basically. We do the same things as Christians, we hunt people for Jesus. We do, we hunt them down. Get the hound of heaven after them, so we get them into the kingdom. That's what we do, that's our business."

The Bible is rife with martial imagery, from the scorched-earth conquest of Canaan to David's stalwart stand against Goliath. Paul's familiar Ephesians metaphors for the well-equipped Christian—"the breastplate of righteousness," "the shield of faith," "the helmet of salvation," "the sword of the Spirit"—together compose "the whole armor of God." Believers would sally forth to do battle against "the rulers of darkness of this world and against spiritual wickedness in high places." In 1920, Curtis Lee Laws in the Baptist newspaper, *Watchman-Examiner*, described practitioners as willing to "do battle royal" for Christian fundamentals.[6] Recently, an anti-exotic dance website used the address www.war-line.org and encouraged citizens to "engage in the battle." The site states: "Uniontown Protest is an organization of active citizens dedicated to educating and helping people, organizations, churches, government and law enforcement to control and even rid porn from their neighborhoods and communities."

Military imagery pervades CR-Activists' rhetoric. "Troops against the enemy"—the enemy including the exotic dance industry, deemed "porn" by the CR—come from local churches and regional associations, along with a segment of feminists. Women are called to "put on the full armor of God" and "do battle" against the evil forces in the world. *Jesus Camp*, a documentary about a summer program, shows youngsters dressed in camouflage, their faces painted brown and green, enacting a warlike ritual, dedicating themselves to fighting for God. Counselors are seen goading their young charges into joining in chants like "This means war!" and smashing coffee cups that symbolize secularized government. Ron Luce, founder of the Teen Mania Youth Ministry, rails against sexually suggestive messages: "Corporate America is raping and pillaging American teenagers." The ministry held a two-day event in March 2007 called "Battle Cry." Ralph Reed, former head of the Christian Coalition, said, "I do guerrilla warfare, I paint my face and travel at night. You don't know it's over until you're in a body bag. You don't know till election night." But Reed later decided that using military metaphors had "allowed the media and the organized left to caricature our movement as intolerant and uncaring."[7] He told the Coalition's field staff to use sports metaphors instead and sought to broaden the CR-Activists' breadth to include reforming welfare and the tax code to strengthen the two-parent family.

*Money and Influence*

CR-Activists have also gone global, targeting NGO (non-governmental organization) caucuses for a takeover and advocating policies at the United Nations.[8]

According to Rob Boston's "The Billionaire Boys Club," in the May 2011 issue of *Church and State*, the publication for Americans United for Separation of Church and State, Dominionists and other CR-Activists are well armed with financial and communication resources. For example, tax documents for 2009–2010 show that the radio/publishing enterprise of Dr. James Dobson, founder of Focus on the Family, brought in $130,258,480. With a budget of $14,569,081, Tony Perkins's Family Research Council lobbied for the CR agenda in Washington. Pat Robertson has an empire. His Christian Broadcasting Network operated with $295,140,001; Regent University, with $60,093,298; American Center for Law and Justice, with $13,375,429; Christian Advocates Serving Evangelism, with $43,872,322. The radio network and other enterprises of Rev. Donald Wildmon's American Family Association showed revenues of $21,408,342. The Southern Baptist Convention, the largest Protestant denomination with about 16 million members, pushed the CR agenda with revenues of $205,716,834. Appendix 11 lists key CR-Activist leaders, organizations, and revenues for the period 1995–2010.

The influence of CR-Activists may not be broadly apparent. Jeff Sharlet describes an "invisible" association, known as the "Family," with a house in Washington, DC. The Family is organized around public men, conservative Republicans, would-be theocrats. Its director Doug Coe believes that influence accrues to the less visible. The organization works with the powerful where it can and builds relationships elsewhere. The Family has operated under many guises; its Fellowship Foundation alone has an annual budget of nearly $14 million. Moneys are often given to affiliates.

Elected judges often decide exotic dance cases in accord with the views of CR-Activists in their constituencies. Some are CR-Activists, such as Judge William Pryor, formerly the attorney general of Alabama, who was active on behalf of CR causes during his tenure. He defended Alabama Chief Justice Roy Moore's effort to erect a Ten Commandments monument in the state Judicial Building. During an April 1997 pro-Moore rally in Montgomery, Pryor told a raucous crowd, "God has chosen, through his son Jesus Christ, this time, this place for all Christians—Protestants, Catholic and Orthodox—to save our country and save our court."[9] Worrisome for advocates of the separation of church and state is the conservative near-lock on US courts. Republicans appointed five of the nine Supreme Court justices. President George W. Bush's legacy is a federal court system in which Republican-appointed judges represent about 59 percent of the federal appeals court bench, and the majority of sitting judges on the federal circuit courts of appeal. Many of Bush's appointees are among the youngest ever nominated.

### Challengers in Christian Right

It is important to note that Dominionists do not have unanimous support in the Christian Right. The CR is composed of fundamentalists—that is, Protestants who believe the Bible is literally true and is the anchor for fundamentals through which to view and understand one's life, as well as Pentecostals and Catholics. They demand a strict interpretation of the Bible. White evangelical Christians, who number about 50 million and outnumber mainline Protestants, compose the CR core. There are evangelical traditionalist, centrist, and modernist divisions of the CR that contest theology and politics. They embrace newcomers, provide a sense of belonging, and offer a social safety network. Lively church services with high emotion, leading people to ecstasy, attract congregants. Biblical rules provide a structure in a world of uncertainty.[10] Churches with different philosophies and extent of political engagement often oppose one another on various issues. Most megachurches and independent "Bible churches" believe in congregational autonomy. However, their members are united in their disapproval of exotic dance. Some unite against the clubs and draw upon the CR-Activists' organizations and their resources.

Yet, some members of the CR argue for staying out of politics. Megachurch pastor Gregory A. Boyd speaks for the apolitical: "The church should steer clear of politics, give up moralizing on sexual issues, stop claiming the U.S. as a 'Christian nation' and stop glorifying American military campaigns."[11] Pastor Joel C. Hunter stepped down as president-elect of the Christian Coalition because the group rejected an agenda that included reducing poverty and fighting global warming.[12] Dick Armey, former congressman from Texas and House majority leader, criticized the political CR, referring to Dobson and his "gang," and other "self-appointed Christian leaders," as "thugs" and "bullies" who have split the conservative Christian movement into those who want to "practice their faith independent of heavy-handed government" and "big government sympathizers who want to impose their version of 'righteousness' on others."[13] In this book, I spotlight CR-Activist leaders and followers engaged in aggressive politics both to promote their values of sexual expression and to bulldoze the wall separating church and state. They represent a vocal active minority in the United States with a disproportionate, pernicious, and powerful impact on public policy and law.

Religious history, belief, and symbolism are the crucible for understanding the CR attitude and CR-Activism toward exotic dance as a pestilence to be wiped out before it spreads. Further understanding comes from considering CR views that stem from Biblical interpretation of the body, dance in general, nudity, lust, patriarchy, male nature, expectations for marital partners, and deceit. Ironically, there are dozens of versions of the Bible in English. James L. Kugel leads us through the book as it is understood by modern scholars. Brian Malley shows that interpretations may be derived from the Bible or merely attributed to it. Moreover, despite proclamation to literalism, readers may engage in non-literalist practice, which leaves room for selectivity. For example, the text, "Greet one another with a holy kiss," is ignored as being cultural. A scholar and ordained American Baptist pastor, Jennifer Wright Knust writes in *Unprotected Texts: The Bible's Surprising Contradictions about Sex and Desire*, "The Bible does not offer a systematic set of teachings or a single sexual code, but it does reveal sometimes conflicting attempts on the part of people and groups to define sexual morality, and to do so in the name of God."[14] Peter Gomes observed the potential danger of the second verse of Romans 12: here, Saint Paul endorses thoughtful Christian nonconformity. Of course, the CR does not tout this.

## The Body and Dance

Because the body is the instrument of both dance and sex, Christianity's love-hate relationship with the body has led to both positive and negative attitudes toward dance.[15] Dance uses the signature key of sexuality, essential for survival and desirable for pleasure. In this way, dance resonates universal realities and particular concerns. Women's dancing is performed, observed, and evaluated through notions about women that are ensconced in religious canonical texts.

Yet, Christianity has also scorned flesh as a root of evil to be transcended, even mortified. Gnostic heretics deemed all flesh corrupt. The Apostle Paul viewed unrestrained sex as immoral (1 Corinthians 6:18). The 2008 New International Version of the Bible puts his view this way: "Keep on running away from sexual immorality. Any other sin that a person commits is outside his body, but the person who sins sexually sins against his own body." The CR guardians of "family values" target the body as a surveillance zone central to the operation of power and, in Michel Foucault's theory of control, a locus of struggles. Especially contested terrain is the female body as males impose control to perpetuate their lineage. Any glorification of the body outside of marriage is anathema. The CR fear such attention to the body would undermine faith and unsettle the hierarchic patriarchal status quo. However, sex within marriage is valued, and counseling and literature on the subject are promoted. The CR has incorporated insights of the New Age men's secular movement and adapted the language of psychological health and the ideal of self-esteem into its own program. Part of the fight for sexual control, this program is meant "to transform an Internet-ogling insecure bumbler into a virile he-man who is competent at male-male friendship and rivalry as well as hot heterosexual romance. The movement has been wildly successful in part because of its extraordinary ability to present its own program as therapeutic," says Dagmar Herzog. According to Stephen Arterburn and Fred Stoeker: "To attain sexual purity as we defined it, we must starve our eyes of the bowls of sexual gratification that come from outside our marriage. When you starve your eyes and eliminate 'junk sex' from your life, you'll deeply crave 'real food'—your wife."[16]

Because they consider sexuality outside of marriage threatening and sinful, evangelicals have "prudential" rules that interdict behaviors they believe might lead a person to perdition. They follow the Bible and also, considering humans' powerful sinful nature, they take on extra precautionary guidelines. Consequently, as noted earlier, even mainstream dance has been banned or held in disfavor in places such as Purdy, Missouri, and, until 1996, Baylor University. (The often-told joke among outsiders is, "Why don't Baptists have sex standing up? They might be accused of dancing.") Not surprisingly, the CR considers exotic dance toxic, and CR-Activists feel compelled to extirpate clubs, if only to prevent themselves from being able to go to them.

## The Uncovered Body and Lust

The Christian Right believes that God commands women to "adorn themselves in modest apparel" (1 Timothy 2:9). Of course, what is considered modest varies. Nowhere in the Bible do we read that nudity, by its very nature, is wrong. John Ince points out that Genesis repeatedly focuses on attitudes toward erotic organs but pays no similar attention to any other feature of human anatomy. Hiding certain parts of the body draws attention to them. The more we are exposed to genitals and breasts outside an erotic context, the less likely it is that the sight of them sexually excites us.[17] Aesthetic beauty receives little attention in the Bible. Sexuality has power to inspire fear of transgression and loss of control. After Adam's fall, nakedness became a biblical euphemism for reproductive organs and shameful sexual acts. Moreover, nakedness is associated with paganism and demon possession.

Early Christianity's textual and visual depictions of the naked female body reveal it as a symbol for sin, the material, evil, and the finite. The CR, implicitly recognizing that the key sexual organ is the individual's imaginative brain, believes that seeing a woman nude causes men to lust, to feel intense sexual excitement, and to relish a woman, which according to Matthew 5:28 is also sinful: "I tell you that anyone who looks at a woman lustfully has already committed adultery with her in his heart." For example, after providing live coverage of the Shenandoah County Fair in Woodstock, Virginia, for ten years, the Woodstock TV station refused to air a single minute when the fair added a "striptease-to-the-buff" tent show. The station owner said: "We felt that by encouraging attendance, we would be flying in the face of Scripture, which specifically states that looking on a woman with lust is the same as committing adultery."[18]

But theology professor J. G. Davies distinguishes between lust and looking for aesthetic pleasure:

The disciple is not to avoid adultery in order to preserve himself from impurity, but so that he may not harm a married union . . . . But if the desire aroused is not more, though no less, than a pleasurable and enjoyable sensation, it is difficult to see why it should be condemned. What is more natural than that the beauty of a human being should arouse some sexual feeling? Is not the natural given by God, according to the Christian doctrine of creation? There need be no infidelity here, when a person is not contemplating intercourse but simply experiencing some sexual pleasure.[19]

Attending adult nude dance clubs equals the sin of adultery, according to Dorn Checkley of the Pittsburg Coalition against Pornography and WholeHearted: The New Revolution for Sexual Wholeness. I met Checkley in the courtroom hearing for *Bottoms Up Enterprises and Island International Ventures v. Borough of Homestead, Pennsylvania*. Homestead had passed two ordinances to prevent the opening in a blighted area of an upscale Scores franchise cabaret with a four-star restaurant. The Borough Council president, Marvin Brown, supported the opening because it would catalyze needed development in the area. But Brown said that when "the ecumenicals," meaning CR-Activists, heard about the possible club, they not only took legislative action against it opening, they also voted him out of office, disregarding his six years of work bringing economic development to the borough. Checkley had been working against pornography (which for the CR includes exotic dance) for twenty years to prevent the degradation of healthy sexuality according to Scripture. Checkley distributed a sixteen-page pamphlet, "Walk in the Light," that lists sources for help, such as Sex and Love Addicts Anonymous, Pure Life Ministries, Christian Recovery Workshop, and Help from Dr. Dobson. In the pamphlet, Checkley writes, "God Allows Do-Overs . . . . To begin healing, confess your sins and/or the hurts committed against you to a pastor, a loved one, a confidant or a counselor."

According to CR testimony in public hearings, legislative predicates, and exotic dance litigation, the sight of nude, semi-nude or "simulated" nude bodies of females tempts men to assault women and children, inside or outside a club, or engage in prostitution and sexually transmit disease. An example comes from Lansing, Michigan, where, at a public hearing on an ordinance to ban nude dance, a resident said: "I rise to salute council member Sandy Allen. She wants a more moral city, a healthy and more appealing environment in which to raise a family. We must bring light to the world. God is calling for leadership to condemn that which is evil and uphold that which is good." In that hearing, Pastor Janet spoke of nude clubs attracting child molesters. The clubs "affect our children, the rights of children; we expose them to things they don't need to be exposed at this early age." Another preacher argued that nudity and semi-nudity be made illegal as "a reflection of our community standards." One speaker read from the Bible. A male teacher opposed the clubs because "I hear the way students talk about women." The most impressive spokesperson in favor of the clubs was Dionne Wethington, an African-American senior in criminology at Michigan State University, who talked about her life as a dancer and her professional parents' support of her work.

Concerning the issue of nudity, it's worth pondering the question of the award-winning philosopher Leszek Kolakowski: "In heaven will we be clothed or naked? I wonder whether any of the doctors of the Church have ever taken up this question when discussing the conditions surrounding the resurrection of Bodies."[20]

## Patriarchy Challenged

The Platonic antagonistic dualism of soul and flesh and the Cartesian mind/body distinction appear in CR belief. So too does a masculine/feminine polarity of male-mental activities/female-bodily functions. Sexual roles are clear and distinct. Men, the CR believes, were made in God's image, and He commanded them to rule wife and family to preserve social cohesion. History reflects the interest of patriarchy and capitalism to control the female body as a source of pleasure, reproduction, domestic work, and commodity. The CR expects women to stay home, be submissive and responsive to the husband, according to the commonly cited Saint Paul in Ephesians 5: 22–23, which exhorts women to "submit to your own husbands, as to the Lord." Women serve God by serving husbands. Both home and church are bastions of male privilege. Radical Christian conservatism, in its hyper-masculinity that portrays Christian men as powerful warriors fighting for dominion, crushes the independence and self-expression of women. They must obey a male-dominated authoritarian church. Men practice in the home the domination over women and children that reflects the domination the men endure outside of the home and under God.[21] Spousal abuse is not a good enough reason for divorce; women complete men, according to pastoral perspectives, including those of Rick Warren and his Saddleback Church.[22]

Biblical Womanhood in the Home, a CR book supportive of patriarchy, is waging a "countercultural" rebellion against what it sees as the feminist status quo. Thousands of women have signed the "True Woman Manifesto" because they believe today's culture has gone astray as a result of its egalitarian approach and insistence on personal rights. Signers are called to encourage Godly masculinity, honor the God-ordained male headship of their husbands and pastor, teach the ways of God to the next generation, and capture all kinds of battlefronts for Christ.[23]

Consequently, the CR views exotic dance as perilous to the patriarchal social order: the "ungodly" exotic dance clubs destroy femininity and undermine men because they draw women out of the home and into "demimonde" employment. Single dancers compete sexually with married women and economically with men, in effect, challenging their sense of masculinity. Thus the outrage when "passive," "modest" woman steps out of the domestic realm into the public arena where she shamelessly removes her clothing and moves her nude, or semi-nude, body for sexually enticing commercial purpose and economic independence. The existence of the exotic dancer signals the males' insufficient surveillance and weakened masculinity.

The dancer reinforces the male/female polarity as well as the good woman/bad woman: dressed/undressed, phallic/destabilizing, culture/nature, active/passive, aggressive/receptive, spiritual/carnal, and rational/emotional. Primarily, exotic dancers are female and the audience members are male, though increasingly also female.

## The Nature of Men

Accepting mainstream culture's view of men—"boys will be boys"—CR men and women believe that men lack self-mastery and are unable to act independently of their sexual and aggressive urges. A study of views of male sexuality found that men are seen as having greater sexual appetites than women.[24] Why? The middle class tends to believe social influences are the cause, whereas the poor and working class ascribe biological origins, and, like the CR, they describe men's sexual needs as physiologically irrepressible. However, many men do have self-mastery and researcher Jason Winters and his colleagues found that some men can even control feeling sensations.

Nonetheless, Baptist pastor and popular writer Tim LaHaye attributes men's nature to their constant production of sperm and seminal fluid. In his book, How to Be Happy Though Married, he posits that the male sex drive is almost volcanic in its latent ability to erupt at the slightest provocation. This concept of male lack of control allows men to shirk responsibility for their nature. Therefore, patriarchal strictures are necessary to control this male anarchic, destructive, and predatory sexuality. Conservatives warn women to beware of "scanty dress" and other provocation.[25] Men marry for sex; women, out of a desire for security and reproduction. Lacking other options for persuading their men to become responsible and faithful husbands and fathers, women may choose patriarchal family life, including having sex with their husbands whether they want to or not. The premise is that a wife's willing and joyous submission tames a man's naturally monstrous urges and his will to power, thus offering a woman a strategy for securing loyalty, supporting her family, and getting what she wants.

## Expectations

A Focus on the Family male radio broadcaster told me that exotic dancers created unrealistic expectations for what women should look like. Not all humans are bestowed with the potential for a naturally beautiful or cultivated dancer's body (e.g., through diet, exercise, and grooming). Men become disappointed with the appearance of their wives who then see themselves as lacking and devalued. A dancer (Mary) believes that the deprecation of exotic dance on moral grounds by some family women is "just an excuse for their becoming fat and unattractive; they're afraid to compete with lithe, well-groomed females. And the Christian Right women refuse to believe that men seek stimulation so they can perform the husband role."

## Deceit

Another religious objection to exotic dance is that it is theater—that is, deceit and pretense that bear false witness. Mimesis presumably links theater with sin and blasphemy in "mocking" nature and God. Spectacle calls the very nature of truth into question by exaggerating it. CR perception holds that it is a short step from selling one's body onstage to selling it offstage. For hundreds of years, theater has stimulated and satisfied men by revealing the female form.

## The First Amendment Umbrella

On moral grounds, the CR would like governments to ban exotic dance outright. However, this is not possible because the US Supreme Court has recognized exotic dance as expression, "speech," with First Amendment protection. Note that the Fourteenth Amendment was adopted to extend

First Amendment protections. Free speech has been a powerful force for the spread of equality—for example, the abolition of slavery—under the law.[26]

In one 1991 case (*Barnes v. Glen Theatre*), a fractured Supreme Court allowed exotic dance regulation on moral grounds. But that "morality" justification has since fallen by the wayside. An expression-restricting law based on public morality reflects a political consensus among a majority of elected representatives, not necessarily the moral preferences of a majority of citizens. Thus, the law violates two foundational principles embodied in the Constitution—limited government and residual individual sovereignty. In a more recent case (*City of Erie v. Pap's A.M.*, 2000), the court held that government could regulate adult entertainment clubs if the aim is to prevent crime, property depreciation, and sexually transmitted disease—the legal doctrine of "adverse secondary effects," more fully discussed in Chapter 2. Time, place, and manner regulations of exotic dance were permitted, the amount of regulatory control dependent upon whether or not alcohol was sold.

Key premises for First Amendment protection are to assure individual self-fulfillment, attain truth, secure participation in decision-making, and maintain a balance between stability and change.[27] An important assumption informing the underlying First Amendment jurisprudence is that expression as an abstract category is valued over its contents. In general, therefore, expression that aims to reconcile the individual's and society's interests must be justified by evidence that it creates a clear and present danger, or that it is "obscene" under the difficult three-pronged "Miller test" (*Miller v. California*, 1973), discussed in Chapter 2, or that the restrictions otherwise further a compelling government interest. Moreover, restrictions on expression generally must combat the danger by the least restrictive means. The secondary effects doctrine is an exception to these general rules, allowing government to impose restrictions on exotic dance under an easier-to-satisfy standard.

Law professor Amy Adler adds a unique perspective to restrictions on the First Amendment: when exotic dancers asked the court to categorize their stripping as speech, the demand violated the convention of woman as object for the projection of male fantasy rather than a subject who can imbue her body with meaning. In keeping with the traditional view that female speech emanates from the body and not the mind, the woman's genitals are viewed as like her mouth. The imposition of the G-string on the nude dancing women in the US Supreme Court *Pap's* and *Barnes* cases, she argues, becomes a gag, a way to silence the female dancers' disturbing, irrational, vaginal speech.

The CR is hostile to exotic dance for a number of reasons. Violation of scripture's mandate for modesty and the threat to patriarchy are primary. Many in the CR merely hold negative attitudes toward the adult entertainment industry. Others go to battle against the dancers, clubs, patrons, and other stakeholders.

# Fighting Exotic Dance

## Call to War

Notwithstanding the constraints of the First Amendment, judicial decisions, and other laws, CR-Activists speak of being at war against secular culture. "Life is not a playground," Reverend Rusty Lee Thomas rails. "It is a war zone—a clash of ideas, philosophies, values, and worldviews. It demands leaders who do not shrink back in [sic] the day of battle." He calls life "spiritual warfare" and repeatedly summons images straight out of the Middle Ages, with gallant knights protecting grateful maidens and courtliness trumping gender equity. His Elijah Ministries Kingdom Leadership Institute, a weeklong ideological boot camp for home-schooled Christians between fourteen and twenty-one years old, follows his 2009 book, *The Kingdom Leadership Institute Manual*, a road map for their training and a game plan for action.

## The Attack
### General Political Strategy

In 1997, CR-Activist leader Dr. Pat Robertson told followers to follow the rough-and-tumble tactics of both Tammany Hall in New York and the Chicago political machine in Illinois. These models of local government embody effective communication, bossism, and corruption. Robertson advocates merging politics and modern technology, fully harnessing Christian talk radio, satellite television broadcasts, direct-mail advertising, music, and hardwired networks of names, addresses, and telephone numbers of supporters for grassroots organizing. CR-Activists operate through highly organized cells in churches, manipulating emotions through a media empire. Part of the mobilization effort is an "electric church" network of TV preachers, who appear on some thirteen hundred radio and TV stations and claim audiences of up to 130 million and profits of $500 million to billions. An "e-army" inundates legislators with e-mails for or against proposed bills. Grassroots members go door-to-door with petitions to bring certain issues to a vote. CR-Activists also seek to impose their views through lobbying, voter guides, and organizational structures. Prayer-action groups transform into political action committees.[1] The CR-Activist strategy is a marathon, not a sprint.

Strongly erotophobic outside the marital bed, CR-Activists orchestrate attacks on the "poisonous" exotic dance, especially what they call the "petting zoos," "sexual assault parlors," and "rape cubicles." They try to suppress nearly all information and entertainment about "sex" apart from marital sex education through the church. Ironically, at the same time the CR as a whole argues for less government, CR-Activists push for expanding state control over sex and sexuality. Yet, a number of exotic dancers have told me they saw the very same man fighting exotic dance in the name of religion in one community ogling their dancing in another. Perhaps religious zealots who try to "clean up" this country understand that exotic dance can challenge sexual repression, a foundational tenet of fundamentalist Christianity. Believers might see that eroticism outside the marital bedroom is pleasurable and consequently become a little less believing upon experiencing fatal flaws in their core beliefs.

Many CR-Activist groups aid the anti-exotic dance cause, among them, the American Family Association; Charles Keating's Citizens for Decency through Law (changed to Children's Legal Foundation, then Child Welfare Foundation after he was convicted of fraud and racketeering); Focus on the Family; Community Defense Counsel (CDC, formerly National Family Legal Foundation); and Alliance Defense Fund (ADF), which fields attorneys across the nation with a $32 million annual budget. James Dobson, D. James Kennedy, and other powerful fundamentalist broadcasters founded ADF in 1994 because they wanted to make their cases in the courts. Some political actors offer foot soldier workshops, prepare model anti-exotic dance legislation, and provide litigators and other legal services to local and state governments. State affiliates of the powerhouse Focus on the Family offer special training for people aspiring to public office. Mark Montini, a Georgia-based political consultant, said, "We put too much emphasis on who wins or loses. But what we're really after is cultural change."[2]

The Community Defense Counsel—a resource of the Alliance Defense Fund, under Alan Sears, who is president, CEO, general counsel, and a founder of the CDC—was set up specifically to fight adult businesses. It has offered national legal conferences, prosecutor or city attorney training seminars, and workshops for church folk to teach people how to keep adult businesses out of neighborhoods. In addition, it has been available for statute or ordinance drafting and testimony, trial assistance, and appellate and *amicus curiae* briefs. CDC has a law library with "studies" of secondary effects, a legal manual, and model city ordinances. The organization has been training hundreds of attorneys to develop "secure cities" for "the quality of life" in their communities. CDC has published articles in law journals and the popular media and produces slick multicolored flyers featuring slogans and taglines such as:

> We can help you draw the line for decency.
> How can I get involved?
> There's no place like home . . . for pornography?
> You call this victimless?
> How to keep sex businesses out of your neighborhood.

This statement appeared on the CDC website: "Everyone knows that cases are decided not only in courts of law, but also in the court of public opinion. From a pro-community perspective, CDC presents the factual evidence of sex business harms and defends cities' rights to pass reasonable regulations to prevent those harms."

The *Personal Faith, Public Policy* handbook of religious activism explains to zealots how to insert their morality into government policy making. In 1971, Jerry Falwell founded Liberty University in Lynchburg, Virginia, to train more than twenty-three thousand students to be public policy analysts and professionals dedicated to protecting traditional family life. Liberty University Law School opened in 2004. Patrick Henry College, in Purcellville, Virginia, opened in 2000 to prepare students to directly translate the tenets of evangelical faith into political action "to aid in the transformation of American society." It is the first undergraduate institution designed to train home-schooled evangelicals for government and political careers. In Virginia Beach, Virginia, Robertson founded Regent University in 1978, and Regent University Law School opened in 1986. Dobson launched Focus on the Family Institute in 1995, a semester-long program designed to prepare college students to fight the culture war. Yet another evangelical program, the Family Research Council's Witherspoon Fellowship, founded in 1997, accepted fourteen students each semester and provided housing, a $1,800 stipend, weekly seminars, and field trips, in addition to in-house internships for each student.

Frequently, governments accept volunteers or employ various for-profit and/or not-for-profit CR-Activists to draft and defend sexually oriented business regulations. These are often borrowed verbatim from CR-Activist standard recommendations. I frequently see Scott Bergthold, the omnipresent CR-Activist attorney, in court with his clients, from Pasadena, California, to Daytona Beach, Florida, and points in between. After graduating from Pensacola Christian College in 1994, Bergthold received his law degree from the Robertson-founded Regent University Law School, graduating third out of 102 students. At law school, he became involved with the American Center for Law and Justice (ACLJ), also part of Robertson's empire. The ACLJ, with a more than $13 million budget, helped vet President George W. Bush's Supreme Court nominees. Bergthold ran the Community Defense Counsel, which is tied to the Alliance Defense Fund. According to his website, his practice is "the nation's only law firm focused exclusively on the drafting and defense of municipal adult business regulations." He has served local governments as a consultant, drafting ordinances and updating outdated regulations, and, as a "double-dipping" litigator and appellate counsel, defending zoning, regulations, or licensing restrictions in state or federal court. Bergthold going from city to county nationwide to sell anti-exotic dance ordinances has been likened to an old-time snake oil salesman riding the circuit. Knoxville City Council member Joe Bailey remarked, "To me, it seems like he's just a franchisee and goes around from city to city and sells these laws and municipalities pass them, and then we hire him to represent the city at $200 per hour."[3] In 2011, Bergthold agreed to draft an ordinance for the town of Eliot, Maine, for a cost of $7,500. Services such as litigation or travel to the town for presentations at town meetings incur additional charges at $225 per hour, plus expenses.[4] Bergthold's clients and more than thirty cases appear in *Westlaw*, the legal research service. He has coauthored two books and written articles. His annual *Local Regulation of Adult Businesses* sells for a hefty one hundred dollars plus. For groups interested in regulating exotic dance in Arizona, California, Kansas, Tennessee, and Texas, he has offered seminars.

To try to counter the methodologically sound, peer-reviewed, published studies conducted by psychology professor Daniel Linz and his colleagues, plus archival data that challenge the adverse secondary effects doctrine, Bergthold uses Professor Richard McCleary as his expert witness. (A First Amendment lawyer said McCleary offered to be a witness for the clubs!) With credible credentials in statistics, but no peer-reviewed publications on exotic dance, McCleary puts forth an untested theory (like how the leopard got its spots)—indeed, one that defies empirical analysis. His theory (illustrated with obtuse but impressive-looking charts) predicts crime: the average male customer carries a lot of cash to avoid a credit card record of his club attendance and therefore is a target for robbers; fear of disclosure makes it less likely he will report such crime; and his cash and interest in sexual entertainment increase the likelihood of his using the services of a prostitute.

However, facts undercut McCleary's theory. Clubs have gone some-what mainstream—men increasingly take wives and girlfriends to see nude dancers, so these men are not hiding their attendance. Businesspeo-ple meet in clubs to seal deals. Many organizations choose to hold their conventions in locales where there are clubs. Patrons use charge cards, and ATM machines are common in clubs (Saffire Club in Las Vegas has eight). Since 1993, ATM wholesaler Cabe and Cato alone has provided ATM machines and service in two hundred adult nightclubs nationwide.[5] Mc-Cleary's theory feeds on stereotypes. Cincinnati First Amendment attor-ney Lou Sirkin was doing a study of bank robberies with an eye toward offering the facetious premise (in zoning ordinance disputes) that banks ought to be zoned into the boonies or at least one thousand feet away from schools—that is, the same zoning ordinances applied to exotic dance clubs in different jurisdictions.

"City councils like being in court," said Christopher Luna, former Dal-las, Texas, city council member, addressing the adult entertainment club exposition in 2001:

> People that advocate for states' rights and local control are the first ones to hide behind judicial robes. . . . [T]hey don't have to make a decision themselves. What they say is, "That damn federal judge ordered those businesses to stay open. That damn federal judge ruled that our SEXU-ALLY ORIENTED BUSINESS ordinance was unconstitutional." They fund litigation with taxpayers' dollars, and they feel they have an endless stream of money to continue to fund the litigation. . . . [W]e could be in executive session and the city attorneys would say, "We are going to lose this lawsuit—if we appeal this lawsuit, we will not prevail." And still the council decided to continue the fight. It's not their money.

US Attorney General John Ashcroft used the Patriot Act in 2003 to enter the fray in "Operation G-String," an investigation of corruption allega-tions against a strip-club owner in Las Vegas. His successor in the Bush administration, Attorney General Alberto Gonzales made the war on por-nography, defined too broadly to include exotic dance, a top priority of his office. One FBI agent anonymously said, "I guess this means we've won the war on terror. We must not need any more resources for espionage."[6]

In many instances, it is unclear if CR-Activists are directly or indirectly responsible for government regulation of exotic dance. In the Ohio case described below, CR-Activists had a driving hand in lobbying, electing leg-islators, and hiring their own attorneys to draft legislation. CR-Activists also had an indirect hand through rallying the uninformed and average

John Doe to fight adult entertainment by promoting the secondary effects doctrine. Convinced of such mythical effects, my high school classmate, who was a city mayor, adamantly told me, "We won't have clubs here!"

## "Adverse Secondary Effects" Campaign

CR-Activists put forward a public front using the "adverse secondary effects" doctrine that masks a private agenda of Dominionism. This discourse code is an emotionally charged mental representation of "toxic" sin and secularism that motivates actions to wipe out the exotic dance industry. Using networks of people, organizations, and communities, CR-Activists unstintingly publicize allegations that exotic dance clubs cause harm. Manipulating the public through secular reasoning to support their cause, CR-Activists' repeated charges become beliefs as other factors commingle: the media search for the sensational, a purported history of gangster-run strip joints, generalizations about all exotic dance clubs without being familiar with any contemporary or representative club, and "not in my backyard" (NIMBY) attitudes. Thus, CR-Activists win broad backing for governmental regulation of exotic dance clubs—namely, driving them out of business or preventing them from opening—for "the public good." Yet, nearly every local government already has laws on the books to address the suppositional problems of prostitution, drugs, and other crime.

### Allegations Challenged

Unproved assertions are touted by CR-Activists, even though courts have ruled since 2000 that legislatures' shoddy data or reasoning can be challenged. At one time, the courts did not question legislatures' stated intentions to deal with the alleged "negative effects" of exotic dance. However, *City of Erie v. Pap's A.M.*, and subsequent cases, changed that: "shoddy" evidence or reasoning no longer suffices to justify regulations, the Supreme Court said in *City of Los Angeles v. Alameda Books* (2002). Now, for localities to justify a law (its legislative predicate, preamble, or recital of finding), they should have evidence related to their own communities and show that the merit of that evidence can be contested in court.

Social and behavioral scientists have critiqued outdated and sloppy "studies." Following science protocol, the researchers have offered evidence that repeatedly debunks the mythical predicate for government control of exotic dance clubs—that is, beyond regulation of businesses in general. The new research includes tabulations of government's own records of crime, property values, and transmission of disease. This research appears in peer-reviewed journals and/or court proceedings (e.g., see Appendix 9). Work by psychologists Daniel Linz and Randy Fisher; planner R. Bruce McLaughlin; criminologists Terry Danner, Kenneth Land, and Jeffrey Cancino; real estate appraiser Richard Schauseil; real estate analyst George McCarthy; and economist G. Hartley Mellish disproves CR-Activists' allegations of negative effects stemming from exotic dance clubs. In interviews with residents and business operators in the proximate neighborhoods of three exotic dance clubs in Charlotte, North Carolina, I asked if any business had a negative impact on the quality of life in their neighborhood. Exotic dance clubs were not mentioned. Respondents reported no problems as a result of the presence of these adult performing arts theaters (see Appendix 13).

Overlooking the fact that there is neither a scintilla of medical evidence nor proof of cause, CR-Activists have, for example, used the adverse secondary effects misinformation to hijack the coercive power of the government to mandate a distance of four or more feet between a nude or even clothed dancer and patron. Why? "To prevent the spread of hepatitis and AIDS," according to many legislative preambles (predicates). However, public health specialist J. R. Greenwood found no data to support regulating adult-oriented businesses as a method of controlling sexually transmitted disease (STDs). The Center for Disease Control reports that AIDS, HIV infection, and other STDs may be transmitted through sexual intercourse, intravenous drug abuse, and exposure to infected blood and blood components. Biologist Rebekah Thomas told legislators in Pinellas County, Florida, that risk for STDs comes from taking blood, semen, or vaginal secretions into the body. Risk involves direct contact with genital to genital, anus, or mouth; clothing is an impenetrable barrier. Is this what happens in clubs? The norm is erotic fantasy, as I explain in Chapter 3. Theater offers an arena for a transgressive journey never made in the real world. Some lawmakers assert, without documentation, that the burden of distance between dancer and patron prevents prostitution and drugs. Where does a nude dancer carry drugs or phone numbers to arrange an assignation? In fact, clothing handily permits secreting these.

The common sense view is that nudity and alcohol are a volatile mix. However, the Fulton County government in Georgia asked its police to conduct several studies. Ironically, when the first study showed that businesses offering alcohol and nudity had fewer problems than those offering only alcohol, the county officials were incredulous and asked for a second study. Same result this time—and a third! Moreover, the county's own appraiser found high property occupancy rates near the club.

Similarly, researchers found in Daytona, Florida; Charlotte, North Carolina; San Antonio, Texas; and Toledo, Dayton, Columbus, and Cleveland, Ohio, that exotic dance clubs serving alcohol were not the primary source of sex crimes, and in some instances, sex crime was inversely related with the presence of clubs in the community.[7] Paul Gruenewald and L. Remer looked at six years of data from 581 zip codes in California. Hospital admissions related to assaults showed that the more bars and liquor stores in a neighborhood, the higher the rates of assault.

As noted in Chapter 1, the CR views nudity as sinful, rather than sacred or natural. Women are thus seen as "candles among gunpowder" and must dress so as not to "blow up the fire of men's lust" and consequent rape. However, researchers have found that seeing nudity decreases men's aggressiveness.[8] Women's smooth baby faces evolved to elicit protective responses in males. The smooth body devoid of body hair, including pubic hair, renders women more youthful and similarly evokes male protectiveness.

People presume nightclubs in general cause noise, drunkenness, and litter. Yet, despite the intuitive appeal of these assumptions, there is a surprising absence of proof. NIMBY battles pit sexually oriented business stakeholders—exotic dance club owners, dancers, staff, food and beverage suppliers, patrons, and civil libertarians—against hostile community residents and city, county, and state governments.

In fact, exotic dance establishments often enhance the bottom line of neighboring businesses and attract new ones.[9] Since Twin Peaks opened in Charlotte, North Carolina, twelve hotels have opened nearby. The garage manager across the street said, "We love the exotic dance business. Its customers have a pleasant place to wait while their car is repaired." In Florida, the Gold Club and Loehmann's, a women's store, were located across the street from each other. In Washington DC's upscale residential and commercial Georgetown, two clubs were across the street from each other. Many years ago, private developers were unsuccessful in blocking the Lusty Lady in downtown Seattle. Thereafter, the Seattle Art Museum was built across the street and Harbor Steps, a very high-end condominium/business development, was constructed next door. In Oregon, where the state constitution forbids special zoning and licensing regulations from being imposed on sexually oriented businesses, several clubs in downtown Portland coexist harmoniously with their neighbors. A club named Teaser's sits on Sioux City, Iowa's Historic Fourth Street. The city renovated a slum area and a big law firm leased the entire building directly across the street from Teaser's. A dancer recalled, "I lived in an industrial/

residential area in Deerfield Beach, Florida, that was surrounded by five strip clubs. Property values went up."

Club-positive experience is not surprising if you consider that the clientele of upscale gentlemen's clubs tend to have discretionary income that other businesses want to attract. So these businesses open in close proximity to adult nightclubs: gas stations, convenience stores, liquor stores, beauty salons, dry cleaners, restaurants, hotels, to name a few. Another example of the positive impact on non-adult businesses is the "Combat Zone" in Boston, low-income areas that the city zoned for adult nightclubs. These clubs stimulated the redevelopment of rundown neighborhoods, and property values soared around the exotic dance establishments as a result. Boris Buzak, manager of the downtown Pizza Parma in Pittsburgh, which sits across Ninth Street from the Blush nightclub, warned: "If they closed down, it literally would hurt my business. It generates people coming down here."[10] Beggars and bums around his pizza parlor caused more problems than the Blush patrons, whom he described as mostly businessmen. The Pittsburgh School for the Creative and Performing Arts (CAPA) is down the block from Blush, which, unlike most other Pittsburgh clubs, opens at noon. In 2007, Ebony Pugh, spokeswoman for the Pittsburgh public schools, said that neither the club nor its clientele had bothered CAPA students or faculty in the five years since the school opened.[11]

### Criteria for Evidence

Knowing what constitutes evidence to justify a law is critical for elected officials, lawyers, and judges. Most "studies" relied upon for anti-exotic dance ordinances do not follow professional social and behavioral science standards of inquiry, nor do they meet the basic requirements for acceptance of scientific evidence prescribed in *Daubert v. Merrell Dow* (1993). *Daubert* also accepts evidence based on the product of principles and methods generally accepted as reliable by the discipline of the researcher.

The "studies" typically include these faults: no control site is matched with an exotic dance cabaret site to ascertain if the latter is different regarding negative behavior, such as crime. No determination is made as to what exists before and what exists after a cabaret is opened in a particular location. No data are collected over several years to distinguish between a relatively unstable situation or a one-time blip. Use of information from the 1970s in one specific site does not apply to gentlemen's clubs established in the next century and in other places. Studies focused on concentrations of a combination of different kinds of adult businesses—such as bookstores, peep shows, massage parlors—may not be applicable to cabarets. And there have been no studies examining the impact of a particular type of dance or kind of expression (whether nudity, semi-nudity, simulated nudity, stage design, or dancer-patron interaction) taking place inside an exotic dance business.

Although adult entertainment cabarets in poor neighborhoods have more crime than businesses in other neighborhoods, this doesn't prove that the clubs cause crime (correlation is not causation). Change in police surveillance may also account for crime rates. Police calls by a cabaret are often club policy to maintain a safe and lawful establishment, not to cope with a troublesome business. Some police reports are proven false in court or do not reflect convictions. Charges for prostitution are at times merely based on the perception of "sexy" dancing or "come on" fantasy talk. An awareness that all places of public assembly have calls for police service simply on the basis of routine activities, such as fights or thefts, has been lacking. The larger a crowd, the more likely there are to be problems. These are in no way remedied by micromanaging a business and restricting "the exposure of specified anatomical areas" and other such characteristics of exotic dance. Opinions of appraisers constitute speculation, not empirical evidence of a valid relationship between exotic dance cabarets and their actual impact on property values. A "potential" negative impact is not a real impact.

*City of Los Angeles v. Alameda Books* (2002) spelled out a procedure for testing enacted or sustained ordinances through burden-shifting legislation. First, the government must prove it relied upon substantial data. Second, if the government satisfies stage one, the opposition must cast direct doubt on the government's data or reasoning; if it fails, the ordinance stays. Third, if the opposition satisfies stage two, the government can rebut; only successful rebuttal saves the ordinance. It has become harder for governments to overcome the many hurdles to withstand First Amendment challenges to their ordinances.

If a law is successfully challenged, the government may have to pay court costs, the challenger's attorney fees, and often damages to plaintiffs. For example, a settlement for Anaheim's unconstitutional zoning ordinance cost the city $2 million (*Gammoh v. City of Anaheim*, 2004). A jury awarded a club owner $1.4 million for profits lost because the City of San Bernardino closed his club for four years, claiming the property was not located in an area zoned for adult cabarets (*People v. Manta Management*, 2004). The city was liable under the Federal Civil Rights Act.

## Disregard of Evidence

Yet in 2007, in spite of the Supreme Court rulings, two incredible decisions gutted and rendered meaningless precedent and standards of evidence: the Eleventh Circuit Court decision in *Daytona Grand, Inc. v. City of Daytona Beach, Florida*, in which the court accepted shoddy data as evidence of adverse secondary effects followed by Federal Judge Richard A. Lazzara upholding three extremely stringent ordinances governing adult businesses in *"Tootsies" v. Hillsborough County, Florida*. By granting summary judgment in favor of the county, he totally ignored compelling, credible evidence that the businesses studied are not more troublesome than other types of businesses, nowhere near as problematic as regular, rock 'n roll or hip-hop clubs or biker bars. That meant he considered there was no "genuine issue as to any material fact" in the clubs' case. The court not only followed the unbelievable *Daytona Grand* decision, but it also went even further in flouting Supreme Court rulings by suggesting that any adult business expert testimony is now irrelevant.

Apparently, from this judge's viewpoint, the government can impose any regulations short of "closing the businesses." In fact, it does close twenty-first-century exotic dance. Judge Lazzara disavowed even the opportunity to evaluate evidence challenging the county's evidence: "*Daytona Grand* made it clear that given the existence of different conclusions based on studies, either empirical or anecdotal, the Court may not substitute its judgment for the Board (of county commissioners)." First Amendment attorney Luke Lirot, representing the clubs, explained to me:

> The judge did not feel any judicial obligation to weigh the evidence and determine the constitutionality of the ordinances. . . . Under this judicial standard, there is no way to measure the quality of the government's evidence. . . . As long as they say "magic words" [like not intending to infringe upon the First Amendment when enacting the law], we can't refute any accusation . . . . That is simply not the law. I know of no acceptable reasoning that would justify the argument . . . that adult businesses are the only entities that can't use the judicial Rules of Evidence to protect themselves from governmental abuses, and require the court to weigh the evidence on those old scales of justice, to see who prevails. I will definitely file an appeal of this horrendous decision, and try to get adult businesses on an equal playing field with pharmaceutical companies, tire manufacturers, bakeries, doctors and every other litigant that can rely on the courts to listen to their experts and weigh the evidence.

What kind of data would judges want as the basis for making decisions related to their own financial well-being, family health, or national security?

The courts are not alone in disregarding evidence of the absence of adverse secondary effects. The American Planning Association (APA) aids CR-Activists by sending "studies" to local and state governments. The old studies date from the 1970s; more recent ones allege adverse secondary effects that are inapplicable to their jurisdiction's time, place, and circumstance. Governments rely on these materials to justify ordinances harmful to the exotic dance business. The APA also writes friend-of-the-court briefs against clubs. In addition, the association published a seriously flawed publication about regulating adult entertainment that I critiqued in the *Journal of Planning Literature.*

Perhaps CR-Activists are engaging in sophistry, deliberately using an invalid argument and displaying ingenuity in reasoning for moral intent. There appears to be faith in moral rationalization, that is, beginning with a conclusion that exotic dance is toxic and then working backward to a plausible justification. An alternative explanation may be, as researchers have found, that once an idea has been implanted in people's minds, it can be difficult to dislodge. And then denials that repeat the bad information may paradoxically reinforce it.[12] Every time we recall a falsehood, the hippocampus in the brain "writes" it down again, and it's also reprocessed! We forget the sources, and even whether a statement is true, and tend to remember news that fits into our worldview. To stop a falsehood, one should avoid repeating it.[13] Denials and clarifications of bad information, for all their intuitive appeal, can paradoxically contribute to the resiliency of popular myths.

Communication experts Kathleen Hall Jamieson and Joseph N. Cappella agree:

> In the complex dance that is the persuasion process, audiences enter the political arena with existing attitudes and preferences. Once there, they are . . likely . . . to seek out information that is compatible with these beliefs and to shun data that challenge them. . . . In short, selective exposure, selective perception, and selective retention pervade the process by which we make sense of who we are as political creatures.

Furthermore, people can come to believe what they tell someone.

Disinformation is not only spread by the CR-Activists, legislatures, media, courts, but also by some feminists (of the MacKinnon and Dworkin perspective) and born-again former dancers who had negative club expe-

44

riences, became antagonistic to exotic dance, and, perhaps inadvertently, spread disinformation. It is accepted, in part, because exotic dance goes against the grain of prescribed respectability, even though it is adult play, fantasy, entertainment, and a form of art. The exotic dance industry is accused of exploiting, humiliating, and degrading women, using their bodies as a commodity and object of the rapacious male gaze. As such objects, exotic dancers are considered collaborators with male dominance and the patriarchal view that women's bodies are erotic property that meet specific standards of what constitutes female beauty. Thus, the dancers harm themselves and all women. Observer Gina Arnold had no doubt that the women at Rockin' Rodeo in the San Francisco Bay area were being objectified when the DJ yelled, "Look at that, guys—USDA grade meat!" as a dancer, dressed like a nun, bent over and showed her butt cheeks. I never heard DJs utter such crude comments. I wonder how long this one kept his job.

Dr. Louann Brizendin, a clinical professor of psychiatry at the University of California, San Francisco, has studied the male visual brain circuit. She found that "men look at attractive women the way we look at pretty butterflies. They catch the male brain's attention for a second, but then they flit out of his mind."

## WHAT'S ON A MAN'S MIND

SIGMUND FREUD

What's On a Man's Mind, © Paul Van Ewijk, One Euro-cards.

Contrary to some feminists' negative views unsupported by evidence, nearly all of the hundreds of dancers I talked with, and more who wrote about their work experiences or shared them with other researchers, say they feel empowered (see Chapter 7). They enjoy artistic self-expression and the self-confidence they gain from successfully facing strangers and winning their appreciation. Women who think of themselves as unattractive get a self-esteem boost when men tell them they are beautiful and pay to ogle them. Moreover, dancers also gaze at patrons' bodies for clues to their money-spending interest and how they might seduce them in fantasy. The dancers say they use their bodies as a commodity no more than do athletes, actors, and others in various fields who rely upon their corporeal resources to navigate the political economy. Moreover, an essential ingredient of the performer's profession is another's gaze. Objectification can occur anywhere; it does not need a woman's sexy dance performance to posit her as the object of the male gaze, a subject of desire. Moreover, does the gaze overwhelm the subject and reduce the person to shame or to pride? Writer Wendy McElroy asks, "Why is a naked female body more of an 'object' than a clothed one? A dancer more an exhibitionist than a writer?"

Objectification refers to a person considered as a part rather than as a whole being. However, women and men both long to be admired and desired for their physical appearance. Brad Zambrello, writing in the University of Connecticut *Daily Campus* (2005), provides an important perspective on men taking interest only in a woman's physicality—not her whole being—in exotic dance clubs. He notes that, in our modern-day, trade-reliant, large-scale society, every human being has countless casual interactions with other human beings and cannot take interest in their wholeness. For example:

> The coffee drinker speaks to the clerk to get his desired coffee, whereas the clerk fulfills the customer's requests to earn a paycheck—which he can later use to buy goods and services that fulfill his wants and needs. In this exchange, both parties have objectified each other—the clerk is not a man but a way to fulfill a want, just as the customer is not a person but a way to get a paycheck. This objectification is temporary, and ends once the transaction is completed. Yet no one is offended by the transaction.

Zambrello continues:

> On campus, both men and women casually "check out" members of the opposite sex (and, in about 10% of the time, members of the same sex). This, too, is objectification, as the viewer often has no intent on pursuing

this person or getting to know the observed. (Rather, the viewer is simply minimally satiating his or her naturally existing sex drive in an extremely benign fashion.) . . . Why, then, is it objectionable to temporarily objectify a member of the opposite sex in the form of adult entertainment? Like the previously described coffee transaction and the casual "checking out" found on campus, the transactions of the sex trade are merely temporary objectifications of others designed to fulfill wants—typically, but not necessarily, the man's desire for some form of sexual stimulation and the woman's desire to earn a paycheck.

Some feminists reject the idea that the dancers, as most of them assert, are savvy entrepreneurs who are empowered, autonomous decision makers who control their bodies and perform with dignity. Dancers vehemently contend that they want the freedom to manage their own exotic dance business without state interference, police harassment, male dominance, or social criticism. Exotic dancers resent the feminists who infantilize them as hapless, exploited victims of patriarchy and unbridled male control, lust, and avarice. Indeed, feminists opposed to exotic dance overlook male legislators' regulatory assaults on exotic dancers as attempts to dominate women. Causes of women's oppression are rooted in the social structure of an inequitable patriarchal system.

Other female adversaries of exotic dance include some soccer moms who told me at public hearings why they object to exotic dance: nude females on exotic dance club signage. They recoil from talking to their youngsters about sexuality when they ask about the signage on the drive to a game. Of course, many clubs do not have signs that even indicate they are adult entertainment.

Today a variety of feminists write about sexuality, and there seem to be more feminists who support exotic dance.[14] They recognize that, in the burlesque tradition, exotic dancers take sexual stereotypes and objectification and choose which to exaggerate and parody. Defying prevailing male concepts of passive femininity, they control the play of senses through personal and economic power (see Chapter 3 and Chapter 7). Dancers decide to whom they will direct their gaze, manipulate the degree and length of exposure of parts of the body, and choose with whom they will sit and talk and to whom they will try to sell a dance. Receiving money for being ogled is, a dancer explained, like reparation for the times she has been stared at and touched without consent outside the club. Being subject to the gaze is not done against the dancer's will but, rather, is made possible through her willingness. Looking and gazing are part of our normal stimulus-seeking behavior.

## Indecent, Lewd, and Obscene

In addition to the adverse secondary effects doctrine, CR-Activists help local and state governments use the legal concepts of indecent, lewd, and obscene. Obscenity is one of the few categories of expression the First Amendment does not safeguard. However, the US Supreme Court in Miller v. California (1973) laid out guidelines for determining whether a work qualifies as legally obscene:

> (a) whether the average person, applying contemporary community standards *would find that the work, taken as a whole,* appeals to the prurient interest; (b) whether the work depicts or describes in a patently offensive way, sexual conduct specifically defined by the applicable state law; and (c) whether the work, *taken as a whole, lacks serious literary, artistic, political or scientific value.* (italics added)

Indecency and lewdness, whatever they mean, are banned in some localities. Government restrictions single out exotic dance for sexual expression that occurs unrestricted in other forms of theater dance, performing arts, and social dance (see Chapter 4). Usually someone in the community complains to the government, which responds. No surprise usually that someone tends to be involved in a church-related anti-exotic dance campaign, led by, for example, anti-porn crusaders Phil Burress or Dorn Checkley.

However, in Roanoke, Virginia, in 1997, a dancer's vengeful ex-boyfriend, who was a police officer, complained to the city, instigating Roanoke's first obscenity trial in more than twenty years. A police investigation resulted in fifteen dancers at Girls, Girls, Girls being secretly videotaped. At the trial, it made no difference to the jury that upon entering the club, patrons faced a posted sign that read: "These are original artistic productions that allow each dancer to create their own individual and special artistic dance." My testimony that the nude performances met the criteria of art was apparently irrelevant. I also testified that the touring Broadway show Oh! Calcutta! performed at three different times in Roanoke to sold-out 2,400-seat houses. The production features not only female nudity, but also male and female frontal nudity, heterosexual coupling, and group body contact so close that a cake knife would not fit between the bodies. By contrast, only females dancing alone performed in Girls, Girls, Girls. In court, the judge excused the jury and he permitted me to show him three minutes of Oh! Calcutta! on video. But he refused to let the jury see it.

The judge told the jury to use "contemporary community standards" to determine if the dances were obscene. This means they appealed to a prurient interest; described sexual conduct in a "patently offensive way"; and, taken as a whole, lacked serious literary, artistic, political, or scientific value; or showed nudity (acceptable if "artistic dancing not for commercial exploitation"). The judge gave the jury no method for determining community standards. How does one distinguish a healthy interest from a prurient interest in sex? Out of two-and-a-half hours of fuzzy, black-and-white videotapes the undercover videographer took at Girls, Girls, Girls, not one performance of any dancer was captured in its entirety—no complete dance, no music, no color. Moreover, the videographer, seated below the stage, pointed the camera upward to catch a shot of the genitalia. How does one define "commercial exploitation"? Professionals in all forms of dance perform for income.

During the trial, newspapers and local television were supportive of the dancers and club, as was a psychologist sitting in the gallery, watching the jury's body language. He said we should win, but wouldn't. The local Roanoke culture of conformity is such that if one person objects, the group will go along. The conservative jury of four women and three men—an accountant, an insurance analyst, a restaurant cook, city school administrator, an auditor, nurse, and sewer plant worker—speaking for a city of close to one hundred thousand unanimously found the club guilty on one count of obscenity and fourteen counts of indecent exposure (nudity and display of genitals). Moreover, the jury fined the club the maximum: forty thousand dollars. One juror said, "We just wanted to send a message."

A dramatic class bias appeared in this case. Nudity is okay when seen in mainstream theaters by wine-drinking quiche eaters but not in club theaters by Joe Six-Pack beer-drinking pretzel eaters. The attorney handling the case for the exotic dance club felt certain he'd win in an appeal. Alas, the club owner, afraid of competition from other clubs, talked to the Commonwealth Attorney three times behind closed doors and is said to have worked out some private deal with the prosecutor.

The *Roanoke Times* editorial headline read: "Staged Ridiculousness in the City Courthouse." The writer went on to ask: "Why have Roanoke police, prosecutors and courts been tied up this week with an obscenity trial? Couldn't they be doing something useful?" The editorial said:

> More than faintly ludicrous, too, is the notion of giving seven jurors the task of determining where Roanoke's community standards fall on the prurience scale. How the heck should they know? If they're supposed to be a random sample of the entire populace, seven is a number so tiny it

would shame any respectable pollster. Besides, isn't the point of the Bill of Rights, including the First Amendment, to protect individual liberties against majoritarian tyranny?

Arkansas judge Tom Smitherman booted charges against topless dancers arrested during a late-night raid by Hot Springs and Garland County law enforcement in May 2000. The dancers were charged with public indecency and/or public exposure. Judge Smitherman said breasts are not sex organs as defined in the Arkansas State Code. A dancer giving a lap dance in a separate room or area within which only the participants were present is an activity that did not occur in a public place. One of the dancers arrested, Asphasia, wrote to me:

> After all the local police manpower hours, money which was used to raid the clubs and, the charges were DISMISSED!!! I am amazed at the local law enforcement's hardworking efforts to come in undercover, pay for private dances, tip us on stage and raid all four clubs in town at the same night and hour!!! . . . On top of all that, the plain clothed officers took all of us to the station in late model Camaros, Corvettes and SUVs, fully equipped audio system with a CD player, music being played on a CD, air-conditioned . . . the late model auto I rode in played the hip-hop CD song, "Back that Ass Up" at taxpayers' expense. We were booked and released within three hours, all 26 dancers. We were back dancing the next night in a near-empty club—the patrons did not return for a long while for fear of the local law enforcement and TV cameras returning to the club. Our earnings dropped, as well as the festive atmosphere, but I hung in because the dance for me is my priority, not the money. All of our court costs, etc. were paid for by the owners.

Wasting taxpayer resources, vice squads often botch investigations of indecency, lewdness, and obscenity through incompetence or testifying to what they don't actually believe. A Florida law gave police officers the right to testify as the offended parties of the public on behalf of "the collective view of the community." In February 2006, Pasco County deputies arrested twenty-five dancers from seven clubs: Lollipops, Calendar Girls, Vegas Showgirls, Brass Flamingo, Bare Assets, Foxy Lady, and Club Exstasy. The dancers were charged with cocaine peddling, prostitution, lewdness, exposure of sexual organs, and the improper solicitation of alcohol sales. Jamal Thalji wrote in the January 28, 2007, *St. Petersburg Times*: "So far, state prosecutors: 2; strippers: 5. Exotic dancers' arrests during police raids aren't leading to much more." The sheriff initiated raids and arrests because of complaints from residents who live near adult businesses. He acknowledged that the people complaining do not visit the strip clubs but said it is his duty as sheriff to investigate all complaints. The defense couldn't find out who made the specific "complaints," so nothing was known about the complainants' credibility or their relationship to the sheriff and his church. "As long as the sheriff's vice squad brings criminal charges against nude dancers, the cases will be prosecuted," said attorney Mike Halkitis, west Pasco's top prosecutor.

The prosecutor had tried to establish that because a police officer lived all his life in Pasco County, he knew community standards for indecency, lewdness, or obscenity. There is no written statement of what the standards are. In the first case I testified in, the prosecutor contended that, since I did not live in the county, I didn't know what the community standards were. When I prepared for the next case, I read about the county on the Internet and toured the place. The likelihood of a collective community standard is truly remote: the county has an urban half and a rural half, a west *Pasco Times* and an east *Pasco Times*, ten different cities/towns, several colleges, and eight nudist resorts.

In 2001, in another part of the country, the *Dallas Morning News* ridiculed the Cabaret Royale sting operation: "Strip club tab for 2 whose sting netted nothing: $634." One of the undercover officers filed a public lewdness case against a dancer. Admitting he had six or seven alcoholic drinks, he couldn't remember much except that a dancer "touched him sexually" during a private dance. He was unaware of her obvious large tattoos.

Whether nudity or simulated sex in dance is indecent, lewd, or obscene is in the perception of the beholder. Sexologists and other psychologists find that the biggest sex organ is the mind. Views of parts of the body and how they move can be accepted as natural, beautiful, or God's gifts to humankind. Alternatively, they can be considered sinful, indecent, lewd, and obscene. Of course, the setting is critical. One expects to see nude dancers and eroticism in a club licensed to offer adult entertainment.

A Kansas law mandates a grand jury investigation if enough names (thirty-three hundred signatures) can be gathered on a petition. Thus, CR-Activists in several cities have forced grand jury investigations of exotic dance clubs. Anti-porn zealot Philip Cosby, head of the Kansas City chapter of the National Coalition for the Protection of Children and Families, enlisted the help of church leaders and community activists in a petition drive calling for grand jury investigations of thirty-two adult businesses in Kansas and Missouri for promoting obscenity. However, grand juries have thrown out cases because of improprieties in the petition-gathering process and refused to issue indictments in most cases. Tactics against obscenity include involving citizens. In 2008, in response to a grand jury request, the Wyandotte County, Kansas, district attorney asked neighborhood "leaders" to rat out fellow citizens and act as the eyes and ears of the police to help identify businesses that might be violating laws on obscenity.[15]

## Government Regulation under a Mythical Pretext

CR-Activists burrow into government in order to subvert it toward Dominionism and to use the coercive power of local and state regulations against exotic dance. City and county council meetings frequently begin with a local pastor's invocation. First Amendment lawyer Roger Diamond thinks local politicians use religious prayers so that they can claim divine guidance when they adopt ordinances.

As I mentioned earlier, at election time, government officials often support or pass legislation regulating clubs in response to a church constituency. Legislation in one jurisdiction may influence another, and some governments even copy legislation against exotic dance clubs that courts have overturned. (Perhaps they think that they'll be luckier with the legislation in their jurisdictions, that they will not be challenged, or that they will have favorable judges and juries.) Such action is described in Chapter 6.

Las Vegas attorney Clyde DeWitt, a veteran anti-censorship litigator, referred to some government tactics in Florida as "stealing in the name of the Lord." Casselberry City tried to eliminate Michael Pinter's Club Juana with the 1998 City and Seminole County's voter-approved Public Decency Ordinance, banning nudity in "adult entertainment" exotic dance clubs, but not in "bona fide performances." Challenging this, the club (in existence since the 1930s) gained fame in 1999 with its production of a variation of Shakespeare's play. "Macbeth in the Buff," cleverly arranged by attorney Steve Mason, was billed on the club marquee as "the play you've been waiting for." The forty-five-minute revue, Les Femmes Fatale, at Club Juana featured skits, including the witches' scene from Macbeth—"Double, double toil and trouble; Fire burn and cauldron bubble"—an adaptation of the Marquis de Sade's Philosophy in the Bedroom, and several short pieces by playwright Morris Sullivan, who also directed the play. Political parody and satire with sexy repartee, poking fun at the government, helped the club beat the obscenity charge. Sullivan reasoned that Shakespeare's witches might well have performed their rituals nude. During the opening scene, three dancers stood on stage wearing only witches hats as dry ice vapor billowed from a Halloween basket-sized cauldron on the floor. Applause exploded when the women bent over to stir the ingredients to cast a spell. A balletic performance by a nude dancer using a samurai sword and tai chi-like movements stunned the audience into reverent applause. A law enforcement officer, wearing a "crime scene unit" jacket, videotaped the performance. However, Circuit Court Judge O. H. Easton Jr. said political satire with sexy repartee is "in the best of American traditions," dating to King George's ouster from our shores. Pinter fought many legal battles throughout the years but ultimately was forced out through eminent domain. Florida's Department of Transportation purchased Club Juana for a road-widening plan. Why was only his side of the street targeted for the right of way?

Governments can deny potential or existing establishments sexually oriented business licenses to have exotic dance. Employing more than one hundred people and posting annual revenues of more than $2 million, the 1720 Club on H Street NW, Washington, DC, closed in 1998. When 1720's lease expired, the building owner decided to redevelop the property. The 1720 Club had been grandfathered in legislation banning the opening of new nude dance establishments and therefore was allowed to continue "at that establishment." A counsel assigned to advise the DC Alcoholic Beverage Control Board (ABC) said the establishment could be mobile, that is, a business could move. Thrilled about this interpretation, Ben Zanganeh, 1720's owner, found a location a block away on 1716 I Street NW. But clubs benefiting from the closure of 1720 apparently hired a lobbyist to convince the commercial interest in this block that 1720 would cause adverse secondary effects. The 1720 Club had had no problems during the five years of its existence, and businessmen on I Street were frequent patrons. So, the club's adversaries hired a detective to find problems with the exotic dance club Good Guys (located in Georgetown), also owned by Zanganeh. He feared a setup: for example, the opposition would pay a cop to dump a bag of cocaine in the club and then take a picture of it to discredit Zanganeh. But Good Guys management was alert to the possibility of planted drugs and the club passed muster.

Then an alliance of religious and business interests formally protested 1720's reopening to the ABC, which heard the case brought by the Downtown Cluster of Congregations and the Franklin Square Association. The 1720 opposition put the director of HIPS (Helping Individual Prostitutes Survive) on the stand. A recent DC arrival and not certified as an expert witness, she was, however, allowed to say that a large percentage of the prostitutes helped by her agency had danced. But she would not provide evidence or explain where and when the "dancer" performed, or if they were prostitutes who tried to dance and had failed. A long-time member

Gabrial and Janelle at 1720 Club, photographer Chris Dame.

Shelby at 1720 Club, photographer Chris Dame.

Shelby at 1720 Club, photographer Chris Dame.

Shelby at 1720 Club, photographer Chris Dame.

of the vice squad testified that dancing was an easy avenue to prostitution and that pimps recruited in the clubs. But he, too, offered no evidence.

I had visited the club on several occasions: in 1995, at night with a female friend; in 1996, during the day with a *Washington Post* reporter,[16] a 1720 dancer, and two dancers from other clubs; and in 1997, during a busy lunchtime with a photographer to do a photo shoot and interview dancers and staff. I continued to interview some of the dancers (including a law student, married women with children, and the daughter of a Pentecostal preacher—none of whom reported prostitution or pimps recruiting in the club). Before the ABC, I testified how well-managed upscale clubs operate to ensure a safe and legal business and that exotic dancing and prostitution are not the same.

Across the country jurisdictions may turn to discriminatory licensing of exotic dance clubs and managers, imposing yet additional restraints on what exotic dance clubs customarily do. Governments look for indications that any license applicant has been charged with or convicted of particular crimes that are associated with the fictitious harms the government seeks to prevent. Governments requiring only exotic dancers, and not other dancers, to get licenses may violate the equal protection clause of the Fourteenth Amendment. These regulations may violate the First Amendment and also due process, the Fifth Amendment.

A city department may follow an arbitrary approval process. Or, using another tactic, a city may not allow owners to transfer their sexually oriented business permit to a buyer. And by holding up permit transfers, lawyers have argued, cities take property illegally. In Detroit, Michigan, Robin Barnes, a community outreach liaison for the Rev. Marvin Winans's Perfecting Church, declared, "If you are going to change ownership, we are going to shut you down. I think it's worth the cost [of a lawsuit]. I don't mind paying you $500,000 if you aren't in my neighborhood." The Rev. Ronald Griffin of Rose of Sharon Church of God in Christ, located near several Detroit strip clubs, said he understands that "city leaders' hands are somewhat tied" and realizes there is a risk the city could lose lawsuits filed by strip clubs. He'd like to see the community take over the fight against clubs through grassroots protests, rather than just though city council actions.[17]

Licensing, often expensive and cumbersome to the licensee, enables a locality to set standards for refusing, suspending, or revoking a license. Jackson, Mississippi, requires club licenses. But when Babe's applied, the city did not respond and, without even holding a hearing, closed the club because it did not have a license! The club sought legal recourse, the judge ruled that the city violated Babe's due process, and the club reopened. Sham licensing revocations are not unheard of. A city attorney may have a contract on an hourly rate with a hearing officer, who is beholden to the attorney for further work. First Amendment Lawyer Brad Shafer points out that the courts require government to justify license fees, which must be commensurate with the cost of administering the licenses.

Another "money grab" to harm exotic dance clubs is the imposition of "sin" taxes. In 2004, Utah enacted a 10 percent tax on topless clubs to pay for treatment of sexual offenders. The lawmakers assume a connection between the clubs and sex offenses, but there is none. The same year, the Texas legislature considered a five dollar per capita tax on exotic dance clubs. About 165 cabarets in Texas offer exotic dance entertainment and serve alcohol. The sin tax money was designated for schools, but the lawmakers' idea was mocked as "Tassels for Tots" and that proposal died.

However, the five dollar per-customer fee, expected to generate about $44 million per year, went into effect in 2007 to pay for sexual assault prevention programs and health insurance for low-income Texans. At the same time they passed the bill imposing the fee, the legislators also commissioned a study on the adult entertainment industry. Researchers at the University of Texas at Austin found that the state's exotic dance clubs generate nearly $217 million in economic activity, pay close to $56 million in state and local taxes, and employ more than 8,000 people.[18] According to the survey of club owners, there are about 3,181 dancers who on average earn about $57,157 per year; the average patron spends about $45 per visit. To fight the fee, the Texas Entertainment Association, Inc. (TEA) initiated litigation, and the Fifty-third District Court, on March 2, 2008, ruled that the taxes represent an invalid, unconstitutional violation of First Amendment rights. The Texas Attorney General's Office filed an appeal on April 7, and in letters issued to adult cabaret businesses across the state, the Comptroller's Office stated that the appeal suspended both the court's judgment and injunction. However, on June 5, 2009, the appellate court (Third Circuit of Texas) upheld the district court judgment that the tax improperly singled out a form of expression. On 8/26/2011, the Texas Supreme Court upheld the tax. The sin tax was also under consideration in California, Kansas, Nevada, New York, Tennessee, and Washington.

Some governments impose requirements that clubs hire police for security. Sunnyvale, California, forces clubs that never had problems to pay for two undercover inspections per year at a cost of $3,058 per club, up from the $490 clubs paid the year before. Just when I thought I had heard it all, the State of New Jersey wants to require municipalities to station security personnel at clubs when children are somewhere near—and to require clubs to pay the bill. "Our industry has *never* caused harmful effects on society, which we proved in 'The Union, New Jersey Secondary Effects Study.' Now, the state is introducing a bill that has severe underlying connotations that WE, adult entertainment establishments, cause harm to children!" exclaimed Jeff Levy, Executive Director of the New Jersey Adult Cabaret Association and Pennsylvania Hospitality and Entertainment Association. Lobbying efforts have kept the bill at bay. Levy, who maintains an extensive archival database of sexual assaults in the United States, remarked:

> The data prove that clergy, teachers, coaches, politicians, trusted family members, Boy Scout leaders, day care center personnel, doctors and repeat offenders hurt children . . . . Residents in Bucks County will protest an adult nightclub, while the Assistant District Attorney raped, sexually assaulted three young boys, gave them illegal drugs—all at a church outing.

The Kinsey Institute at Indiana University and the Rick A. Ross Institute in New Jersey also have databases on sexual assaults that show similar findings.

Discriminatory building and operating regulations are often imposed on exotic dance clubs. Restrictions include setting hours of operation and requiring specific configurations of stage and seating. Mandating bright lighting, similar to a hospital operating room, and patron-dancer distance requirements supposedly facilitate law enforcement. According to a Fort Worth, Texas, ordinance, if an exotic dance club is to be painted, a single "achromatic" color with a single "achromatic trim" must be used. The fine for noncompliance is two thousand dollars per day.

Some localities impede dancers' creativity by specifying costume and body parts that can show skin, as well as determining exotic dance styles and movements and the use of self-touch. Exotic dance opponents try to regulate the manner in which patrons may tip dancers. Adversaries attempt to ban simulated nudity and simulated sex—whatever these terms mean—and even require dancers to cover more of the body than is seen at the beach. For one court case, I spent an hour with my camera photographing women's buttocks on the beach to prove the point. And mainstream dance, requiring no license, has nudity and simulated sex, and at many school dances, youngsters are booty dancing.

Another opponent tactic is to change the rules as soon as exotic clubs comply with an ordinance and still thrive, or the court overturns a restrictive ordinance. Refusing to take no for an answer, city government in Dallas has been notorious for fighting clubs for more than twenty years, egged on by CR-Activists. Dallas banned nudity, permitting skin-colored covering of the areola. Then the city redefined "simulated nudity" and required non-flesh-colored, opaque pasties. Next, the city larded it on: every part of the breast below the top of the areola should be covered and the buttocks, too. The US District Court ruled unconstitutional the city regulation that the bottom half of the female dancer's breast be opaquely covered because it was a content-based restriction of expression not shown to be related to adverse secondary effects. So Dallas then did a blatant end-run around the ruling. The city changed the classification of the exotic dance clubs from "dance halls" to "sexually-oriented businesses," with the very same breast-covering restrictions that the judge had ruled unconstitutional. Moreover, the city added further regulations on contact between dancer and customer. Through zoning, clubs had been separated from residences, churches, and schools. But then Dallas added historical districts, hospital zones, and child care facilities (these included registered and unregistered facilities interspersed throughout the city, including warehouses, commercial, and office building districts). Other jurisdiction have similar histories.

Having lost exotic dance cases in court, some local governments are becoming cautious about passing anti-exotic dance ordinances. The Black Hills Neighborhood Citizens for a Better Community pressured the City of Grand Rapids, Michigan, to pass a tough ordinance banning nudity and impose a six-foot distance between dancers and patrons in strip clubs. Aware that they would face a legal challenge, the commissioners told the group that it would first have to create a legal defense fund of one hundred thousand dollars to cover the expected cost. The group raised ninety-three thousand dollars, teaming up with the Michigan Decency Council, in hopes of blocking an all-nude nightclub that a businessman planned to open, and the ordinance passed. Litigation ensued.

If, during a court hearing, a government realizes a challenge to its ordinance will most likely succeed, it amends the ordinance to render the court case moot and avoid paying the challenger's attorney fees. The Borough of Homestead, Pittsburgh, Pennsylvania, put the plaintiffs (and the court) through the time and expense of an elaborate and time-consuming presentation of evidence and testimony in 2007 to support the plaintiffs' challenges to the Borough's *last* attempt to censor its proposed business operation through swiftly adopted ordinances. Then the Borough said that "Homestead has advertised an amendment to its adult entertainment ordinance . . . which would make most of the Plaintiffs' challenges to the current ordinance moot by the time of either appeal or trial."

CR-Activists fight against exotic dance clubs through the government to make penalties for a crime committed in a club greater than those for a crime committed outside. Jimmy, who worked his way up from doorman to club owner, said:

> When the police write a ticket for street prostitution, for actual sex going on in the open for everybody to see, it's a misdemeanor. When they come into our clubs and write a ticket for simulated sex to a dancer who's clothed, except for her top, rubbing against a fully-clothed customer behind closed doors, it's a felony . . . . You can get sexually transmitted diseases on the street, not in our clubs. When people see a street walker, they just drive by. When you put "topless entertainment" in a club, people picket you and try to shut you down.

Governments may root out, prosecute, and severely penalize violations of generally applicable laws at sexually oriented businesses.

## Other Government Actions

Government crusades against exotic dancers increase the stigma directed toward them. Dancers say stigmatization is their biggest problem. Asking inspectors from fire, health, building, alcohol, and public works agencies to single out exotic dance clubs to find any kind of code violation is another form of harassment. Occasionally, inspection can help the dancers. For example, a club had one usable bathroom for one hundred dancers and inspectors forced the club to fix the other toilets.

Governments may exacerbate the exotic dance controversy and raid clubs, often on false pretenses, to distract people from real issues. Club Exstasy in Prince George's County, Maryland, experienced four raids in thirty days, and customers received citations for jaywalking and not parking between the lines in a private parking lot. Police use intimidating threats of undercover operations and vice squad raids to exert control. In some localities, law enforcement has prevented entry into a club and deterred patrons under the pretext of protecting demonstrators against the club, all the while permitting the demonstrators to trespass.

Governments unable to drive out clubs by winning in court have literally bought them out. To get rid of the Peppermint Gardens Club in Pasadena, California, the city paid $4.8 million in 2007 to settle three lawsuits and buy the property the club occupies. The topless nightclub was only open for a few days. Attorney Roger Diamond said his client "did very little work and made a profit of about a million-and-a-half dollars." The same year, the City of La Habra, California, offered to pay Badi "Bill" Gammoh, owner of Taboo Gentlemen's Club, $5.2 million to get out of town. After almost a decade of court battles and unsuccessful attempts to shut down its only strip club, La Habra made the offer before Gammoh's attorneys finished making their case to the jury. The city chose to settle the lawsuit, filed in 1998, without laying out its case in court.

## Psychological and Physical Assault

Tactics against exotic dance also include psychologically seducing and attacking exotic dancers and patrons. James Dobson believes that it is never too late to reverse course and become a "secondary virgin."[19] People can sin and find redemption. As mentioned earlier, evangelists often target as potential born-again believers those individuals having life crises.

For example, New Friends New Life, a Dallas church group, tries to help dancers get out of the industry in a city where some thirty-five clubs dot the landscape. They claim the typical "client" has spent several years stripping only to see her life overtaken by nasty boyfriends, mounting debts, and substance abuse—certainly problems not exclusive to exotic dance. The church finds a few dancers who have problems and extrapolates to the whole industry. Women in any profession can have bad boyfriends, debt, and drug problems.

In Ohio, Citizens for Community Values (CCV), a sister association of Focus on the Family, reported in its December 2002 publication that Vickie Burress, the Victims Assistance coordinator, wants to deter women like Amy, who couldn't help but notice a bold print ad for "Exotic Dancers." Amy thought, "I like to dance and I'm in good shape." The ad promised "serious money," probably more than the mall jobs offered. Besides, "professional dancer" sure had a better ring to it than "retail clerk." She could do her thing, rake in the tips, and save up enough to get her own place. After all, her dad had said that it was time for her to stop "sponging." However, Burress wants potential dancers to hear "the ugly truth about strip bars and the adult entertainment industry" before they join the ranks of those who learned that "truth the hard way." The Victims Assistance program placed classified ads in local newspapers, providing a Dancer Hotline toll-free number. When a woman called, she was connected to a former dancer who told the caller about a side of adult dancing that she wouldn't hear from the manager who interviews and auditions her. All four of the women who spoke on Dancer Hotline were involved in dancer ministries. As of 2011, Vicki Burress said budget issues caused a cutback, although twenty ministries listed on victimsofpornography.org, of which she is national coordinator, were helping dancers.

CCV also uses another CR tactic: seduction with gifts. In 2001, a CCV Spokane website stated:

> After a time of orientation, preparation, and prayer, six women took flowers to the ladies who work at Dèjá Vu strip club, while three men remained outside to pray. These gifts were delivered with a message of grace in the hope of demonstrating the heart of the Father. It is sometimes difficult for the ladies to believe that anyone would love them without asking anything in return. A few of the ladies were perplexed as they received these gifts of love. Still others gently stroked their flowers, accepting hugs from the women.

In Los Angeles, Harmony Dust, a former stripper, heads her ministry, Treasures. She sends young women with fistfuls of flamingo pink gift bags to approach bouncers and offer them cookies to gain access to exotic dance clubs. Once inside, the women leave gifts of lip gloss, jewelry, and handwritten cards in dressing rooms. Just hours after the visit, the women follow up with phone calls, texts, or e-mails, in which they are "preaching the Word." An exotic dancer in the hospital accepted the roses a CR-Activist group of women brought her and agreed to let them continue to visit her. The women became friends and within a week the patient accepted Christ, and upon her release from the hospital, she decided she would not return to dancing.[20]

Another former stripper-turned-evangelical Christian, Heather Veitch, the Pussycat Preacher, visits one strip club per month, paying for lap dances so she can talk to the performers about God. Veitch's approach is based on what she claims is her experience: in the 1990s, she worked as a stripper and acted in a handful of soft-porn movies. She said she plays up her sex appeal because adult industry workers relate to it. "I understand the culture of these girls. They respect that," says Veitch. According to her ministry's website, she was a successful Las Vegas stripper but inwardly feared that her lifestyle was a ticket to hell. She began attending church, became a Christian, went to beauty school, and got married. As she began reaching out to sex industry workers, Veitch found an ally in Matt Brown, her pastor at Sandals Church of Riverside. The seventeen hundred-member Southern Baptist congregation contributed fifty thousand dollars to her ministry in 2006.[21]

The Putnam Values Family task force met at Lighthouse Baptist Church in Hurricane, West Virginia, to set up a trust fund to help exotic dancers change jobs. As with other dancers, who have the organization Career Transitions for Dancers, exotic dancers also need help transitioning when they are too old to work in the business, get hurt, or can't perform anymore for whatever reason. However, some groups aimed at exotic dancers promulgate the notion that the work itself is horrible and further stigmatize dancers.

Some exotic dance adversaries pursue club owners and customers. Maxine Pulse and Lori Hanson, who oppose the nude Racehorses Gentlemen's Club in McCook County east of Salem, South Dakota, were stalking the owner Bob Rieger and his customers in 2004. State's Attorney Roger Gerlach said five different law enforcement agencies and an undercover agent had entered the club since it opened in May 2003, and no illegal activities had been discovered. "I've harassed him legitimately to the extent that I can without getting carried away," Gerlach said.

When the University of Pittsburgh Women's Studies Program used public funds to show Live Nude Girls Unite, a documentary on the unionization of strippers, a Pennsylvania pro-family group said the university's action glorified the life of exotic dancers without also revealing the truth about them. Diane Gramley, president of the American Family Association, asserted, "When you talk to some who have been in the lifestyle, they find it very demeaning and humiliating to be stripping for money—and a lot of them have to rely on drugs and alcohol to just get them through the night." She expressed concern that the university chose Valentine's Day to show the film.[22]

CR-Activists picket exotic dance clubs, note patrons' license plate numbers, and phone their families and employers. In Florida, in 2006, some City of Flagler Beach families posted on a website: "We NEED YOUR HELP! Picketing is important because it shows visible opposition to the businesses." Anti–Semitic comments about the owners of Christina's also appeared on the website. The organization sent parents living within three blocks of the club a letter alerting them to the opening of the club and made negative allegations against the club owners and their wives. As a result, the club owners' children were harassed in school.

Seeking to oust adult businesses from Kennedale, Texas, in 2004, Pastor Jim Norwood of the Oakcrest Family Church and his church members sent postcards to customers of Fantasy Foxx Club. With license plate numbers, car owners' names and addresses can be found online. Each postcard featured a photo of the customer's car parked outside the club with the text, "Observed you in the neighborhood. Didn't know if you were aware there is a church in the area." Norwood apparently got the picture-taking idea from his work as a chaplain at the jail, where sex offenders told him that their problems may not have escalated if their wives or girlfriends had found out about their "addiction" to strip clubs. However, Dr. Marty Klein, a licensed marriage and family therapist and certified sex therapist, says, "There's no such thing as sex addiction. There are people making poor sexual decisions all over the place (there's big news!), but almost all of them could make different choices if they really, really wanted to. To indulge our cravings may not be wise, but it's rarely sick." Norwood acknowledged that pornography and drugs were part of his "wild days" in the 1960s and 1970s before he turned to Christianity.

In Sunny Valley, Oregon, American Family Association picketers photographed club patrons' faces and license plate numbers and then placed them on a website, www.seewhosthere.com. In Janesville, Wisconsin, Bill Sodemann, from the People Advocating Decency, videotaped patrons entering Screamin' MeeMees Club. His justification? "We just wanted to make people think twice before they go in. They might think, 'I don't want the world to know about this.'" Going further, the Carolina Family Alliance in Wellford, South Carolina, used the car tags posted on its website to track the vehicles' owners and contact them by phone or mail to encourage them to seek professional help, as well as to notify their family and friends of the potential "danger" they posed to loved ones.

When stymied in all other efforts, CR-Activists have tried praying away a strip club. Elder Ronald Wilkerson, pastor of Faith Temple Deliverance Church in Little Rock, Arkansas, moved his church to within about 750 feet of the Paper Moon in 2008. Then he contacted the city to see if he could get the club kicked out because of "the possibility of prostitution, drugs, married men going on and looking at women," he said. But the club was there first. Now his tactic is to live a life in such a way that the club stakeholders might "want to be saved."[23]

Exotic club opponents have also tried disruption, noise, and advertising in their efforts to close establishments. Set back from the public sidewalk, the Imperial Showgirls Theater in Pico Rivera, California, went to court and succeeded in stopping Rev. Richard Ochoa and his group from adversarial action on the club's private property. The protesters picketed and using bullhorns yelled, screamed, and blew whistles. In Mansfield, Ohio, the Family Coalition protested the Top Hat Club for more than a year with a billboard warning: "Pornography Breeds Rapists." They lamented the opening of a "sin place" in the neighborhood and believed it was just a matter of not growing weary of protesting, that they would ultimately succeed. Anti-club combatants also engage in physical threats and assaults on property, such as slashing tires in club parking lots. In Indianapolis, vandals struck Delilah's Gone Platinum twice. There were sledgehammer-sized holes throughout the building; smashed block-glass windows, mirrors, ceramic statues, and stereo systems; water-filled hallways and rooms; and a torn-up dance stage floor.[24] Adult entertainment adversaries even sent death threats to club owners about their kin. In a case I worked on in upstate New York, a couple who owned a club under bombardment sent their daughter to live with relatives after threats to her life.

## An Illustrative Case: Phil Burress and the Citizens for Community Values

The self-described recovering twenty-five-year sex addict Phil Burress, leader of Citizens for Community Values (CCV) in Sharonville, Ohio, has been at war with the adult industry since 2001.[25] Burress claims his addiction caused his two divorces, and he apparently committed adultery during his second marriage before marrying his third wife. He is now divorced from her. He also filed for bankruptcy twice. Drawing on the political skills he picked up as a union organizer for truck drivers in the 1970s, Burress's CCV gets credit for turning out the vote in Ohio, a pivotal state, which put George W. Bush in the White House in 2004. The CCV belongs to the Arlington Group, a secretive society of top Christian Right power brokers who meet to plan and coordinate strategy. The group, including Jerry Falwell, James Dobson, Donald Wildmon, D. James Kennedy, Paul Weyrich (co-founder of the Heritage Foundation, a conservative think tank), and Richard Land (president of the Ethics and Religious Liberty Commission), lobbied the Bush White House on a regular basis. Armed with a multimillion-dollar budget and determination to decimate exotic clubs nationwide, Burress met with US Attorney General Alberto Gonzales in 2005 to discuss the creation and implementation of the FBI's "Obscenity Prosecution Task Force" to focus not on child abuse but on consensual adult material the CCV believes is inappropriate.[26]

Burress is the twenty-first-century Anthony Comstock (1844–1915), whose forty-two-year anti-obscenity crusade capitalized on a growing fear of sex. Burress wants to censor exotic dance clubs because "they breed lust." "Lust defiles the body, debauches the imagination, corrupts the mind, deadens the will, destroys the memory, sears the conscience, hardens the heart and damns the soul."[27] Like Burress, Comstock held the conviction that it is the role of government to curb the behavior of naturally sinful men, and he persuaded Congress to strengthen the federal obscenity law known as the Comstock Act, which permits the US Post Office to confiscate mail "containing any obscene, lewd, and/or lascivious material" and arrest the senders.

After Burress's group had limited Cincinnati's adult entertainment to a single chain-owned club called Déjà Vu, Burress moved on to the state level. In fighting to cripple exotic dance club regulations in Ohio, Burress went so far as having his followers intimidate state legislators by stalking them and threatening to spend fifty thousand dollars to unseat opponents of his bill, The Community Defense Act (CDA). Burress's efforts eventually imploded. His actions angered the senate president, who tabled what he would have otherwise supported. The Buckeye Association of Club Executives (BACE) thought this would stop Burress. But he became so enraged that the bill wasn't passed that the CCV collected enough signatures to force the issue into lawmakers' laps. The group had threatened to take its proposed law directly to voters if lawmakers failed to act. The CDA, in the form of a ballot petition initiative, became Senate Bill (SB) 16. Its restraints on exotic dance are draconian: a six-foot buffer around dancers, whether or not they are performing, clothed or unclothed; no touch; adult entertainment stopping at midnight. A bikini-clad dancer who unintentionally brushes up against a customer—or vice versa—would be a criminal, guilty of a fourth-degree misdemeanor punishable by thirty days in jail and a $250 fine. If the touching involves a "specified anatomical area"— defined as genitals, the pubic region, buttocks, and a portion of the female breast—no matter how brief or inadvertent the touch is, the crime elevates to a first-degree misdemeanor—in the same league as negligent vehicular homicide or similar crimes—punishable by sixty days in jail and a $1,000 fine.

Barry Sheets, a CCV member, was the only person to testify for the bill at its hearing. He alleged the restrictions were needed because of the "negative secondary effects" of strip clubs. Specifically, he said the six-foot rule was "to protect female strippers from being pawed by patrons and to limit drug transactions between strippers and patrons. This is the final piece of the puzzle we need." The lone Democrat who voted against the bill in committee, Senator Shirley Smith of Cleveland, said the four strip clubs in her poverty-riddled district don't cause problems. "I have not, to my knowledge, received even one report of any problem at these places." Senator Tom Niehaus, a Cincinnati-area Republican, asked, "Why haven't I heard from any community in any part of the state asking me to pass this bill?" Senator Larry Mumper, a Marion Republican, complained that he didn't understand the pressing need for the bill since state lawmakers had the year before passed House Bill 23, which gives townships the authority to further regulate strip clubs.

Former dancer Angelina Spencer, owner of the Circus Club in Cleveland, Ohio, and executive director of the Association of Club Executives National, queried lawmakers if they would be issuing "double-length yardsticks" to police officers asked to enforce the six-foot rule. "We should not be exhausting ourselves—going around in circles—debating the issues of adult entertainment because one theocratic organization demands that you do their bidding, their way," she told the lawmakers. Spencer said of BACE, "We are David. The CCV is Goliath. We have sling shots. The CCV drives an armored tank. They have 30 years on us in fundraising, communication and politics." The clubs have spent $2.5 million fighting the CCV.

Certainly, not all Ohio citizens supported the SB 16 strip club bill. Here are some comments related to church and tax exemption, self-control, actual crime, and democracy from among the 110 respondents in the *Columbus Dispatch* poll:

> I think it's time for Churches to pay taxes. No more free ride! Pay for your beliefs. No more charitable donations for Phil and his CCV. Instead let's allow the strip clubs to be tax free . . . that should give Phil some heartburn.

> I don't go to strip clubs but I think there is more crime being committed under religious banners than the few strip clubs in the state. Stealing money, defrauding church members, rape, lying, these are just some of the crimes church members and church leaders commit every day in Ohio.

> Phil Burress has some lingering issues he needs to deal with. . . . The vast majority of people can control themselves enjoying porn/strippers just like the vast majority of people enjoy alcohol. . . . I am uncomfortable with the idea that the proposed Senate Bill implies that adults are not able to self-govern their actions.

> If you don't like the entertainment, don't go to the clubs!

> Last time I checked the State of Ohio hadn't put detour signs in front of these strip clubs forcing us to go inside. Please stop forcing us to think and live as you. Your values of fear are not part of my family values.

> What do Phil Burress, George Bush and Adolf Hitler have in common? They want your loyalty, money, power and your freedom.

CCV and their political machine are out to tell the voting adults what they can read, how they must think, what they can wear and when and where they can spend their money. Sounds familiar . . . Germany 1939!

I've visited clubs with friends several times over the last ten years. Never been involved in drugs, prostitution or other crime when there. Just a different form of entertainment and another manner in which Ohio will be losing business and revenue to other states.

SB 16 nonetheless passed in 2007. Hoping to shelve the law before it could take effect, BACE and their performers obtained the one thousand registered voter signatures needed to launch the process for repeal. They were working to place the repeal language before the voters at the next general election. The projected cost of the petition drive was more than $1 million. BACE created a political action committee called Citizens for Community Standards, a play on the name of their adversary, Citizens for Community Values. CCV complained and, to end the dispute, BACE changed the name to Vote No on Issue 1 Committee. The Dancers for Democracy Steering Committee formed. Joe Redner, owner of the Mons Venus in Tampa, Florida, contributed ten thousand dollars to the BACE referendum campaign. He reasoned: "This Community Defense Act has the potential to spread to other states. This is NOT just an Ohio fight. If adult business owners can help to stop it in Ohio, we should." Alas, the company BACE contracted to collect the signatures botched the job, and BACE successfully sued the company. BACE advisory attorney J. Michael Murray filed one lawsuit against SB16 with statewide defendants—sixty-eight city law directors and county prosecutors—to stop people in positions to enforce CDA from doing so, arguing that adult entertainment provides constitutionally protected expression. After losing in the 6th US Circuit Court of Appeals, as of 2011 Murray was asking for US Supreme Court review.

The CCV's goal is to take Ohio's Community Defense Act nationwide. One of the tools being used to promote censorship is a twelve-minute video, This Is Our Battle, that is being distributed to churches and organizations across the country. The video focuses on how sex businesses destroy lives, devastate marriages, and hurt families. "All around us men, women and children and entire families are suffering as victims of pornography, sexually oriented businesses and other distortions of God's plan for our sexuality and as members of His Body . . . supporting the work of the CCV is one of the action steps that folks can take to demonstrate such love," explained CCV on the video. Randall Wenger, chief counsel of the Independence Law Center, a CCV affiliate, has been pushing church groups to fund and support new sexually oriented business bills in Pennsylvania and New Jersey state and local government jurisdictions. Jeff Levy learned in November 2009 that the New Jersey Family Policy Council received nine hundred thousand dollars to pressure several state senators and assembly people to adopt more stringent laws against adult entertainment. So far Levy's lobbying against such laws has been successful.

In May 2010, Missouri passed the Community Defense Act, another draconian piece of legislation against exotic dance clubs. CR-Activist attorney Scott Bergthold drafted the Act on behalf of the CCV. Dancers must have a radius of six feet between them and patrons. Clubs may have no nudity, no alcohol, and must close at midnight. Violation is a first-degree misdemeanor punishable by six months in jail and/or a thousand dollar fine. Senator Matt Bartle tried for twelve years to get this bill passed. Dick Snow, Missouri Association of Club Executives president, said, "We're all sick that a woman can be arrested and jailed for something as simple as coming within six feet of a man. If I were a woman, I'd be outraged that our leaders felt it necessary to dictate mores and waste taxpayer money to promote a patriarchal law that harkens back to the Dark Ages." Across the country, conservative organizations are using copies of the Missouri legislation as models for their own states.[28] Kansas came close to passing such a bill.

Dave Manack, associate publisher of *Exotic Dancer's Club Bulletin*, said, "We've never seen a group as well-funded and well-organized as the CCV, a group that will clearly not stop until every state is presented with an ordinance similar to Ohio's 'Community Defense Act.'" Clearly, the CR opposes adult entertainment, and CR-Activists want to drive it out of business. But that still leaves open several questions. Is exotic dance "pornography" and the "devil's doing" as the CR asserts? Let's look at the target and address the evidence for the charges.

# Target of Attack

## Striptease 101 or Seduction by the Devil

Where is the love, beauty, and truth we seek,
But in our mind?
PERCY BYSSHE SHELLEY, "Julian and Maddalo"

There are short-cuts to happiness, and dancing is one of them.
VICKI BAUM

Illusion works impenetrable,
Weaving webs innumerable,
Her gay pictures never fail,
Crowd each on other, veil on veil,
Charmer who will be believed
By man who thirsts to be deceived.
RALPH WALDO EMERSON, "Maia"

Just what is a segment of the politically active Christian Right (CR-Activists) warring against with its battle plans and its tactics of working through government, organizations, and individual foot soldiers? Exotic dance is not all "tits and ass," as I learned. True, the very essence of adult entertainment clubs is temptation. But it's also an opportunity for exotic dancers to reclaim both personal and economic power by subverting and manipulating sexual stereotypes. So what does the exotic dancer, deemed the "incarnation of the devil," actually do, and how do the male patrons respond?

Because folks at the University of Maryland had heard about my work on adult entertainment exotic dance, the Student Union Theater manager asked me to be on the panel accompanying the screening of *Inside Deep Throat* (2005) and *Deep Throat* (1972). The assumption was that live adult dance was like film pornography. Both are constitutionally protected expression. Both are controversial. And both are believed to cause violence against women: to exploit, oppress, and degrade them. Both are accepted by many students.

71

But there are big differences. Adult film is a recording, whereas exotic dance is palpable theater. Adult film shows interpersonal sex, whereas exotic dance is a performance symbolic of sex and other kinds of social relations, ideas, and values. While some adult film stars are feature exotic dancers (also called "headliners") and some dancers (called "regulars" or "house dancers") become adult film stars, most dancers are not, or have never been, in adult films. Dancers are erotic, as Octavio Paz put it, a "representation" that diverts or denies sex in action. Eroticism "is sexuality transfigured, a metaphor."[1] Onstage is a make-believe world in which exotic dancers "express erotic emotions, such as sexual excitement and longing," wrote Judge Richard A. Posner.[2]

In 1995, when a city/land use planner asked me to be an expert court witness in a First Amendment case related to "table dance" in Seattle, I didn't know what the term "table dance" meant. I thought it was performing on tabletops, like in the film *Zorba the Greek*. An Internet search turned up little on table dancing. Oddly enough, there was a *Wall Street Journal* article on Japanese office workers who, in their leisure time, went to nightclubs and danced on tabletops, flipping their skirts up, flashing.

I arrived in Seattle and met the lawyer handling the case, Gil Levy. He escorted me to six clubs involved in the litigation. Club owners and exotic dancers in *Ino Ino v. City of Bellevue* (a Seattle suburb) were challenging the 1995 ordinance that required dancers who perform in costume and then strip to nudity to perform onstage no closer than eight feet from spectators and offstage no closer than four feet. The clubs were also required to have an illumination of 30 lux, similar to the light at a surgeon's operating table. One club I visited was markedly different in ambience, being a former family restaurant. All the establishments were small, bar-like clubs in comparison with the large upscale nightclub-type gentlemen's clubs, or what former dancer Tonya Dee calls "dance emporiums."

I was reminded of having seen my first striptease dance in 1956 at the Strip City Club, a large theater with an expansive stage on Sunset Boulevard in Hollywood, California. Showcasing for the motion picture industry, the dancers and the dancing were gorgeous. In the 1980s and 1990s, I had seen nude dancing at clubs in Paris, France, and in Bangkok, Thailand. Of course, I know males like to look at nude female bodies. My dad would sneak a glance at my brother's *Playboy* magazines when he wasn't home. At age fourteen, my oldest son, Shawn, wanted to subscribe to *Playboy*. That was okay with me and his dad. However, concerned that Shawn might just view women as objects, I also got him copies of *Playgirl*, which he threw away: "Mom, I'm not gay!" My husband continued the *Playboy* subscription when Shawn went off to college.

Striptease, according to *Webster's Ninth New Collegiate Dictionary*, is a noun meaning "a burlesque act in which a performer removes his or her clothing piece by piece." Some of the dancers in the Seattle clubs wore one-piece outfits, so the climax of exotic dance—stripping to nudity—was fast. Dancing here was not on tables, although in a few of the clubs I visited elsewhere, women did dance on tabletops or on a long bar at which patrons sat. Dancers in Seattle performed close to, often between the legs, and sometimes on the laps of patrons seated at a table or on a couch, thus the names "table dancing," "couch dancing," and "lap dancing."

Is it possible that exotic dance has a different purpose and effect than that attributed by the CR? Could exotic dance be a form of dance? Art? Communication? Performance art? Theater? Play? Fantasy? Tourism? What exotic dance is called certainly has implications for public perception, business, and governmental policy. Labels have connotations that can color, sharpen, and diffuse meaning. Many in the adult entertainment industry prefer the term "exotic dance" or "entertainer" to other terms.

For political reasons, the term "sex workers" (which, among the general public, commonly refers to prostitutes) has been coopted by some exotic dancers who have written about exotic dance. Sex workers has been redefined to refer to any sort of labor in which sexual pleasure or entertainment is provided in exchange for money. Workers with similarities are assumed to be stronger when they band together. Dave Manack, associate publisher of the industry's *Exotic Dancer's Club Bulletin*, says, "It seems doubtful that anyone in our industry would willingly identify themselves as working in the 'sex industry.' We've never referred to it that way in our magazines or at the Expo, ever. 'Sex worker' is a damaging term; it refers to a prostitute, not a dancer." In the hundred-plus clubs I visited, I never heard a dancer refer to herself as a sex worker nor have I heard patrons and club management use that label.

Furthermore, many mainstream entertainers in plays and dance offer sexual enjoyment onstage in exchange for money and would reject the label of sex worker. Some exotic dance club patrons interact with dancers for asexual reasons, such as having a nonjudgmental listener. Homosexual men and heterosexual women go to exotic dance establishments to have the aesthetic pleasure of seeing a healthy female moving rhythmically and with a sense of her own beauty.

## Roots

Historical perspective helps create the setting for understanding what exotic dance is today. Exotic dance is "naughty" but certainly not the first kind
of dance to challenge mainstream propriety. The waltz was scandalous in
its day—eighteenth to early twentieth century—as it was the first time a
man and woman danced in tight embrace, their bodies rubbing. Exotic
dance is rooted in burlesque and Middle Eastern belly dance (also known as
danse du ventre, cootch, hootchy-kootchy, and Oriental dance), both vilified
in their time. Originating in sixteenth-century Europe, burlesque pokes
fun at classic literature and theater and "virtuous" behavior. More recently,
turn-of-the-century burlesque in the United States featured striptease, an
act in which a dancer gyrates, shimmies, shakes her booty, and removes
clothing piece by piece, teasing the audience about what is to come.

The Middle Eastern forerunner of exotic dance was first seen publicly in
the Streets of Cairo and Algerian and Persian village exhibits of the 1893 Chicago World's Columbian Exposition. The dancers wore loose tunics and
moved hips and breasts at a time when Western women's corsets crunched
their innards. The Exposition's Board of Lady Managers objected to the
dancers' "indecent and immoral" exotic gyrations, considered inappropriate for family entertainment, and requested the exhibits be abolished.
Manager Sol Bloom took advantage of their protest to advertise the exhibits of what he called "belly dance." This term now encompasses solo dance
forms from Morocco to Uzbekistan that engage the hips, torso, arms, and
hands in undulations, shimmies, circles, and spirals.[3] Viewing the sexy
dancer as the exotic "ethnological other" defused the threat of her sexuality and drew crowds to the exhibits.

Nudity onstage, which became integral to contemporary exotic dance,
dates back to the 1840s live female nudity in legitimate "high art" theater
in the United States. Nudity and sexuality appeared in American theatrical performance in the twentieth century as a caricature of social mores,
a mockery of religious repudiation of the flesh, that played with cultural
constructions of gender and ambiguity. "Nude" refers to being unclothed
and the body being an aesthetic object, whereas "naked" implies being
defenseless or being oneself without disguise, which is not the way most
dancers describe themselves.[4]

Burlesque was more respectable in the cities than in the traveling carni-
vals in the rural South and Eastern Seaboard, which added stripping burlesque acts.[5] The men were often very crude, grasping women's body parts.
When dancers performed around the pole in the traveling show's central

tent beginning in the 1900s, their venue became known as the dance-pole tents.[6]

In the mid-twentieth century, burlesque lost its popularity. The remaining clubs were referred to as "varicose alley" because they featured has-been burlesque performers, often lacking a full set of teeth and dancing to jukeboxes in sleazy joints and carnival tents. There were "titty bars" and bars with such names as Pink Pussy. Some "strip joints" were considered to have attracted criminals, gamblers, and other disreputable nighttime denizens. Beautiful women found more respectable stages.

Then Michael J. Peter, who in 1973 earned an MA at Cornell University's School of Hotel and Restaurant Administration and a BS in Business Administration from Syracuse University, came on the scene. He is recognized as the founder of the gentlemen's club. Peter liked the Las Vegas showgirls' style of entertainment but felt that people yearned for human contact in the era of computerization. So he encouraged the popular, palpable interaction between dancer and patron. For a little while, dancer and patron can act as if they are connected, and connection, more than sex, he argued, is what is missing in our increasingly impersonal society.

In 1974, Peter began the Solid Gold, Pure Platinum, and Dollhouse chains. His upscale clubs have hairdressers, makeup artists, house moms, and DJs. Dancers wear gowns and have their own identification insignia or personal trademark: a hat, elbow-length gloves, or a scarf to wear, twirl, or jump over in the choreography. "Classy," for example, has a floor cane as her signature. Feature dancers peddle club merchandise. The clubs have businessmen's buffets, credit card service, ATMs, and "funny money"(purchased tickets that substitute for money). Male staff, floor hosts/managers, wear tuxedos; waitresses, sexy uniforms. Peter believes an overdressed staff imparts elegance to the patron.

The 1980s saw the beginning of clubs run by business people and operated with best practices and ethical standards. Before, according to Robert Watters, the industry had been dominated by thugs—biker gangs rife with criminal activity. Watters opened the first Rick's Cabaret in Houston in 1983, and the chain has since grown to twenty-two clubs. Today, clubs run the gamut from the neighborhood bar and dives with one or more dancers to the Morton's Steakhousization-type club—larger, bureaucratized with hierarchical organization, and typified by specific written rules, quantifiable tasks, and consistency. After all, modern capitalism advances commodification and bureaucracy.[7] Don Waitt, publisher of *Exotic Dancer Magazine*, views strip clubs as a classic piece of Americana: Norman Rockwell in a pair of Lucite heels.[8]

Solid Gold, photographer Judith Lynne Hanna.

Club Risqué, photographer Judith Lynne Hanna.

Diamond Dolls, photographer Judith Lynne Hanna.

## Who's Onstage?

Since the 1980s, exotic dance at its best has been a parade of young and beautiful dancers. Actress Demi Moore said she prepared for her role in the film *Striptease* (1996) by visiting exotic dance clubs around the country. "I found that a lot of these places are upscale and cater to businessmen and women. I think the bars have become more a place of entertainment than sleazy dives, which was my previous perception of them." Moore discovered that dancers were happy with their profession.

> The pay affords them the opportunity to go to college, provides a comfortable life-style for them and their children, and gives them more time to be with their kids. Unlike the common perception that these women are either drugged out or drunk to get through their work day, I want people to know that a lot of them are young women who are very present, and know exactly what they're doing. . . . And as a mother of three myself, I don't judge that as being any less a professional choice than any of us have opted for.[9]

Like Moore, I had misconceptions about the women who worked in exotic dance clubs. Influenced by media portrayals of and innuendos about strippers, I expected to find exploited "bimbos" and messed-up women. Of course, I met scatterbrains in the adult entertainment industry, as I do in most industries. And I met high school dropouts. One dancer told me she'd be a prostitute if she couldn't dance. Certainly, if women with problems enter the adult entertainment world, these problems are likely to come with them. The stigma of exotic dance may cause additional difficulties.

But contrary to what most people think, I found that the educational levels of dancers vary. Some are going to Ivy League and other colleges. Graduates have degrees in, among others, the fields of sociology, law, and nursing. I have met professionals, such as a certified public accountant, computer analyst, and stockbroker. Three dancers at Club Joanna's in Washington, DC, had masters degrees and full-time day jobs. They told me they danced to get exercise, have fun, and pick up some extra money. I met performers who taught dance to children at their local Y. A number of former exotic dancers who have shared some of their experiences with me also have shared those experiences in their own PhD dissertations in anthropology, drama/theater arts, social work, sociology, and women's studies. Craig Duling, general manager of the Crazy Horse in San Francisco, said:

I was shocked by what I learned about my own people. For instance, one has a graduate degree in math. Another one is a microbiologist for NASA in Mountainview. Phaj, who's from India, is a banking officer at Wells Fargo in the commercial lending department. . . . Sterling just passed her oral examination to be in the San Francisco Police Department, passed the agility test, passed the written test, passed every interview so far, and if she passes the polygraph examination, she's going into the police academy. Brittany just graduated with her master's degree in chemistry from UC-Berkeley. Boalt Hall Law School is one of the top five law schools in the nation; we just had Lola get accepted into Boalt Hall. We have another one, Sasha, who's in law school at the University of San Francisco. We have two registered licensed dental hygienists. These are no puny, Mickey Mouse jobs. I've got 80 of these that I've got written down, out of 109 dancers. . . . What [California Assemblyman Charles] Calderon said on TV, was that dancers come out of the industry, they end up either addicted to drugs or other substances and with no skill set whatsoever, and end up on Medicare, Medicaid, Medi-Cal, or other social programs that cost the state money and therefore the industry that causes them to be like this ought to pay for it. That's just flat-out wrong, and our dancers prove it.[10]

Dancers also vary physically and mentally. Dancers often write me because they learn of my interest in understanding exotic dance. One wrote:

I was just thinking of all the girls with handicaps I've worked with over 15 years. I've worked with two girls that were deaf; one was very popular with customers. They never noticed her hearing aid and when she spoke they thought she had a French accent. . . . Speaking of French girls, I actually did work with a black French girl who spoke no English. We had an awful time trying to let her know when it was her turn on stage. Luckily for her, several customers spoke French and they helped her a lot. I also worked with a girl who had been a thalidomide baby. She had a tiny little hand that stuck out of her shoulder. She had the most courage I've ever seen to get out there on stage. . . . I also worked with a girl with half a foot, the result of a lawn mower accident. She wore a prosthetic device in her boots. As she couldn't wear pumps, she was quite talented on the pole. Also there was the girl with club feet and no calf muscles, a tiny girl with a huge mass of curly hair. Although she walked with a limp, she managed to dance fairly well. One night I worked with two really big girls about 189 and 225 pounds, respectively, and I've worked with girls that had one breast a lot bigger than the other. They were very well liked and made just as many tips as the other girls. I've also worked with several girls with varying degrees of mental illness, ranging from talking to themselves

and hearing voices to nerve problems where they couldn't stop shaking
their legs and pulling out their eyebrows and hair. Also there have been
several girls that just went berserk and started fighting with other girls or
customers for no apparent reason.

## Getting There

How does a woman get into the stigmatized business of adult entertainment, an industry that is assaulted by CR-Activists? In her role as a dancer,
Katherine Frank found that patrons like to learn about how the dancers
became strippers and what their problems are. There are various routes to
walking onstage. Demi Moore's aggressive championing of *Striptease,* and
the display of her own body, which was at the film's promotional heart, not
only signaled a heightened mainstream interest in exotic dance but also
drew some women onstage. Others take up exotic dance as a lark, a dare,
out of a need for money, or as a rebellious act. Divorcees recovering from
economic diminution, single moms, and students need income with flexible hours. There are runaways from tedium; from dead-end, low-paying
jobs; and from dysfunctional families. Some are attracted by the money
and free time. Misty decided that if her body was marketable enough that
people would come to see it and pay money, then she was going to cash in
on that. Sarah Katherine Lewis felt poverty was objectifying and demoral-
izing, not stripping. A former public school teacher turned to dancing as a
way of "freeing up" her time so she could travel, make a film, and eventually go to graduate school. A dancer at Rachel's Club in West Palm Beach
remarked:

> Most people know this business is a huge cash machine, but most don't
> recognize its full potential powers. I was taught to believe that "strip-
> pers" or "entertainers" were desperate and on drugs, and also that the
> clubs were seedy and dirty. It was not until I was 33 that I actually visited
> a true strip club. . . . I was hooked. . . . In my eyes, nude beautiful women
> are works of art. Having the opportunity to watch dancers and have their
> company is a luxury and erotic treat. I personally think the "entertainer"
> is a service to society.[11]

A businesswoman, like Jane in Las Vegas, dances to earn quick money for
new capital investment. Angel was an anthropology student at Tulane on
a scholarship that didn't cover all her expenses. So she started tending bar
at an exotic dance club in New Orleans. Seeing that the dancers earned far
more, she became a dancer.

Some women, because of highly restrictive parents or religious upbringing, make a statement by choosing to dance. Others are drawn to the unconventional or risk-taking nature of the profession or need affirmation of their attractiveness. Aspasia wrote me that she found dancing "is sooo healing. . . . If naked women generate pleasure and happiness, we need more naked women, not less! Speaking from experience of dancing, naked women have a calming effect on men in our culture." She was a late bloomer, forty years old when she began to dance.

> I was always the oldest dancer at every club I danced in and sometimes the only African-American. . . . I took more risks, dramatically and emotionally, since I no longer needed to prove myself to anyone. I further proved to myself though exotic dance that aging is a process of change rather than deterioration.

Many contemporary exotic dancers agree with former dancer Coty Lees: "What I do is still an art. I'm up there because it's the closest I'll ever be to the theatre."[12] Some exotic dancers pay homage to the gods of love, Eros and Venus; they celebrate female beauty and fecundity in their performances. Jame said, "Striptease is the shrine to mere sexual feeling and is enjoyment and celebration."

In Washington, DC, I asked Gabrial how she became a nude dancer. Hers was a common path: knowing someone who dances. Gabrial was seventeen, working at Safeway market, and going to high school. "I just wasn't making it financially," she explains.

> A classmate, a boy in the ninth grade, said he had a sister working as a stripper and making a lot of money. I hooked up with her. I met my husband in a club. Because there is opposition to going out with patrons, I quit and then went to a new club. We dated for three years and have been married for two.

Yes, as the stereotype has it, there are dancers who were born into alcoholic and/or drug-addicted families, sexually abused, pushed into dance to support a boyfriend's drug habit, and who have few occupational skills. Some dancers are battered by their male companions and are forced to dance. Such dancers often find support among the CR-Activists, who exploit them in their campaign to eradicate exotic dance.

Clubs may have "feature" (headliner) dancers who can quadruple the regular dancer ("house girl") income. Features are the elite strata of the industry. A common route to becoming a feature dancer is to accumulate "credits" for appearing in adult magazine centerfold photograph spreads

Jade Simone St. Claire, represented by Pure Talent Agency, Inc., photographer Alfonso Moreno of Mad Creativity.

and/or in films, for which a dancer collects "scalps"—that is, her photo on video box covers. Taya Parker, *Exotic Dancer*'s Entertainer of the Year in 2007/2008, has appeared in the pages of *Penthouse*. Dancers may become features by winning dance, bikini, Ms. Nude, and similar competitions, as did Schevelle who earned a BA in dance at the University of Texas, Austin. Jade Simone St. Clair began dancing at age six and studied modern dance for fifteen years, attending New York University and Juilliard Conservatory for the Fine Arts. Her Off-Broadway credits include appearances with Bernadette Peters and Gregory Hines. She became a nude comedian and, most recently, CEO of the Mobile Broadcasting Group. Appearing in mainstream magazines is another route to becoming a feature.

Successful features tend to be highly professional, often bringing their own lights and sound equipment along with costumes, props, and entourage. A feature is usually a choreographer, makeup artist, costume designer, musical director, marketing expert, producer, and sometime agent and truck driver. Like the earlier burlesque stars, they put on a show and interact with the audience in illusion-filled performances with titles such as "Magic Show," "Mortal Kombat," "High Voltage," "Fan Dance," "Sword Fare," and "Cat Show." Through agents (there are several agencies, such as Continental and Pure Talent), features do guest appearances in clubs on nationwide circuits and are paid, for the most part, according to the "credits" they have accumulated. The nation's top five or six feature dancers earn fifteen thousand to twenty thousand dollars a week performing four twenty-minute shows each night. The next level earns between eight thousand and fifteen thousand dollars a week. Driven by the desire for more money in their G-strings, house dancers may grasp at fame and fortune by working in adult films.

## Serious "Speech"

Because exotic dance is under siege, I explain to communities and courts the elements that give this expression First Amendment protection, namely that it is dance, communication, and art. I use illustrations to help people understand information that is strange to them; not too many people have studied dance making and dance theory. Exotic dance rests upon four continua: dance, art, play, and sexuality. Some people consider exotic dance, if a dance art at all, to be "lowbrow art" (another example of lowbrow art is popular social dance) on a continuum reaching to "highbrow art" (such as ballet). The play continuum ranges from child and family play to adult pretend entertainment, like charades. The sexuality continuum goes from fantasy (exotic dance) to real sex.

Exotic "dance"? People commonly think of exotic dancers (strippers) as merely sexually flaunting their bodies. "Just gyrating." "Walking and bending over." "Only sex." The 1995 film *Showgirls*, portraying a stripper who works at a seedy club in Las Vegas, doesn't tell everything! Like all dance, exotic dance is mind driven. Many people cannot define dance, let alone exotic dance, which, however, meets the criteria of dance. It is composed of purposeful, intentionally rhythmical, and culturally influenced sequences of nonverbal body movements other than ordinary motor activities. Dance takes from the everyday and stylizes it. Walking? The trick is to turn a normal locomotion into a stylized walk that may not be timed to one's natural body rhythm but to an external source such as music. The motion of dance (in time, space, and with effort) has inherent and aesthetic value and symbolic potential. Cultural notions of appropriateness and competency determine aesthetic value. Obviously, the criteria for excellence in ballet or tap is different from the criteria for excellence in exotic dance. Purpose in dance is from the dancer's perspective, usually shared by the audience members of the dancer's culture; individual choice and social learning play a role.

Dance USA, an organization for major ballet, modern dance, and folk dance companies, puts it this way:

> Dance is an art form that links mind and body in a society that tends to view the body with distrust . . . an art form that empowers women in a society that tends to diminish the value of "women's work," and . . . an art form that affirms the essential function of kinesthetic [bodily] intelligence in a culture that tends to measure knowledge in words and numbers.[13]

Dance is a language in the sense of being a means of communicating ideas or feelings.[14] Music and costume, as well as pantomime and role-playing, may enhance the messages. Strange as it may seem to many people, we know now that dance requires the same underlying faculty in the brain for conceptualization, creativity, and memory as does verbal language in speaking and writing. Both forms have vocabulary (steps and gestures in dance), grammar (rules for putting the vocabulary together), semantics (meaning), and the social, economic, cultural, and historical context in which communication takes place. Dance, however, assembles these elements in a manner that more often resembles poetry, with its often multiple, symbolic, and elusive meanings. In much linguistic behavior, an individual creates sentences and others respond to them without being conscious of how it works. Similarly, an individual dances and a spectator watches usually without being aware of the vocabulary, grammar, and semantics of the dance.

People receive messages more readily when all the senses are involved. Dance can convey erotic and other emotional charges through the sight of bodies moving in time and space; the sounds of physical movement and breathing, and usually the accompanying music; the smell of the dancers' body odors and perfume; the tactile sense of body parts touching ground, other body parts, people, or props; the proxemic sense of distance between dancers and between dancers and spectators; and the kinesthetic sense (feeling of bodily movement and tension) experience or empathy with dancers.

A key element of any kind of dance is body motion in space. The meaning of the artistic messages of distance between a dancer and spectator comes from the use of space in everyday social relations as people send and receive messages. Physical proximity in a social interaction conveys a message and an expectation about the level of intimacy appropriate or desired.

Edward Hall reported on the meaning of the use of space in daily life: in American culture, *intimate* distance has a close phase (o to 6 inches, such as in lovemaking, wrestling, comforting, and protecting) and a far phase (6 to 18 inches for less intense but still intimate interaction). Hall also found that *personal* distance, the usual space we maintain between ourselves and others, also has a close phase (1/2 to 2 1/2 feet for people bonded in some ways, such as family members), as well as a far phase (2 1/2 to 4 feet for discussing subjects of personal interest and involvement). *Social* distance has a close phase of 4 to 7 feet, used for impersonal business, and a far phase of 7 to 12 feet for formal business, as in an office or home. Finally, *public* distance has a close phase of 12 to 25 feet, such as in a presentation to a small audience, and a far phase of 25 feet or more.

Since dance takes from the everyday and transforms it, the space between dancer and patron carries distinct meaning. For example, in the ballet *Romeo and Juliet*, when Juliet's parents are urging her to marry Paris, there's a moment when she is standing near him and, to a quickly rising scale heard from the orchestra woodwind instruments, her eyes take in Paris, coolly surveying him from toe to head. Then her eyes turn away, and, rising on pointe, she briskly travels away from him, conveying the feeling, "no, this is not the right man, and I cannot be his."

The meaning of touch in dance has biological roots in the mother and child connection and sense of security. Real and life-confirming, touch is one of the most basic and commanding forms of human communicative behavior.[15] Our sense of self is connected to the physical experience of touch with its power to establish boundaries of contact and separation, to stimulate and arouse, or to pacify and calm. The body is the location for physical sensations that trigger social memories. Touch is part of attentiveness that includes gaze, smile, direct face-to-face body orientation, forward lean, and significance in erotic fantasy.

A sophisticated signaling system, touch plays a central role in adulthood flirting, expressing power, soothing, and playing. Researchers found that a touch can be worth a thousand words. Fleeting physical contact can express specific emotions such as anger, fear, happiness, sadness, disgust, and love. Touch has a complex vocabulary: hold, shake, rub, pat, squeeze, the small changes in amount of press applied, the variations in the abruptness of the stroke, the changing rates at which the fingers move across the skin, the differences in location, and the duration of the contact.

## Exotic Dance Dialect

Dance is the body sounding off with feeling. Thus, exotic dance "speech" attracts patron attention. The exotic dancer's choreography has movements simulating cultural rhythms of lovemaking, from flirting and foreplay to intercourse. After all, exotic dance is supposed to be "naughty." A disc jockey plays recorded music to provide theme and beat for the dancer. Through a display of sensuality, the dancer's purpose is to entice a patron(s) to give tips and to buy a personal dance. Meaning in exotic dance lies in modest and immodest body disclosure; natural, deodorized, and odorized scent; proximity between dancer and patron; the touch of self-delineation; dancer-to-patron touch; and the *pas de deux* of the dancer's flesh and personality with the patron's gaze and fantasy. A patron "ocularly penetrates" a dancer. Her improvisation attempts to trigger in a patron's mind an elaborate story or fleeting thought of, for example, some romance, sex, or dominance-submissive identity. Merely ogling the beauty of the kinetic body or just talking with a dancer may suffice for a patron.

Exotic dance has given rise to its own special imprint of "eye candy" movements, highlighting the breasts, buttocks, and hips in addition to the genitals. "I accentuate certain parts of my silhouette," said Helen, an exotic dancer and stockbroker. It is noteworthy that neuroscientist Heather A. Rupp and psychologist Kim Wallen found that men and women showed different patterns of brain activity while viewing sexual stimuli. Men focused and lingered on women's faces, not their breasts and genitals, whereas women were more likely to focus on "private parts." Women can tell by looking at naked men whether they are aroused, Wallen said, but female bodies don't reveal much. Facial expression does show interest in and enjoyment of sex.

Exotic dancers' moves derive from belly dance and burlesque and are influenced by the vernacular (African American), jazz, Broadway theater, music video and hip-hop dance, cheerleading, and gymnastics. In turn, exotic dance influences social and theater dance forms. Thongs, the skimpy covering of buttocks and genitals seen on public beaches, were first worn by strippers, as were high-heeled platform shoes. Specific moves associated with exotic dance have become *de rigueur* on MTV (Music Television), in social booty dancing, and in strip aerobics or pole dancing in gyms.

Table 1 shows a palette of exotic dance moves that I have observed, not all performed by any particular dancer or in any specific club. Dancers create movement sequences drawing upon *some* of the dance vocabulary and accoutrements listed below depending upon their creative skill, club, and government jurisdiction.

Just as toe shoes identify the ballerina, five-to-eight-inch heels, often stiletto platform shoes, are the exotic dancer's signature. Placing the dancer above the ordinary, the heels provide a semblance of elegance. Yet, they also constrain motor freedom by making it necessary for the dancer to take short "submissive" steps and inhibiting her ability to run, thus making her appear vulnerable to a male approach. The heels modify the dancer's posture, arching her back and thrusting her breasts forward and her buttocks upward and outward, calling attention to the leg, breast, and derriere. In addition, the heels are phallic symbols elongating the female leg to its erotic pinnacle or pressing into the floor. The foot was an erogenous area of a woman's body in Victorian England and especially China.

Clubs usually have stripper poles, phallic symbols, that dancers drape themselves around or use for acrobatic tricks. In Kansas, some clubs have an automobile steering wheel in the stage ceiling that spins freely, and the dancers use it choreographically in a variety of creative ways.

## Components of Exotic Dance

Exotic dance usually has two components. First, we see a stage dance performed for the entire audience on a main stage and then also on ministages and runways in large clubs. Second, following a stage dance, a performer will dance for a particular patron who pays a fee for a table, couch, or lap dance.

## Table 1. Exotic Dance Moves

**Locomotion** (movement from place to place; four-inch heels are restraining):

strut (sexy mincing or stalking walk, leading with pelvis)

walk

turn

slide to floor

crawl, predator-like

from kneeling position, move knees outward and inward

on right knee, place left foot on floor, then step up on right

jump

leap

split

jump and land in split

cartwheel

somersault frontward or backward into a split

slide feet back from mirror with hands touching it

walk, brushing one foot in front of the other

pole work (at base):

twirl around own axis while circling the pole

place back to pole and extend right leg

hands go up side of torso

handstand with legs touching pole and slide to floor in split

squat with back against pole

sit straddling pole, arch backward, unfasten hair tie to let hair flow with movement

hold onto the pole with one hand and twirl around it

bend backward, one leg bent at knee

thrust buttocks outward, slap one buttock

walk to pole, hook leg and twirl around pole, toss head back, shake hair

pole work (on pole):

lean against pole, swing up with hands, fling body outward, and then legs grab pole

shimmy up pole

turn upside down, holding on with thighs, bounce buttocks sliding down

shimmy up pole, split legs outward, extend arms outward as thighs grip pole turn around pole, grab it and shimmy up, right leg extended outward

lean back, straighten up

lean back with legs outward horizontally, bring them up to chest

turn upside down, holding with one leg hooked around pole, the other in bent shape

spin, holding with legs, backbend, brush hair

hold with hands, split upside down, legs vertical and together grasp pole, arms extend

move body toward and away from pole

lean back, holding with one or both hands

flip one leg up in arc, followed by the other

bicycle legs

extend legs in split perpendicular to floor, holding pole with one or both hands

hang upside down by one leg, the other leg and arms out to sides

hook right leg around pole as support to twirl around pole

hold pole with right hand as support to twirl around pole, right thigh lifted

turn body upside down, open legs straight or bent

turn upside down and slide down in split

lower self onto both knees, descend into split

slide down pole to one shoulder

**Gesture**

self-touch:

move hands over body, creating curvilinear designs

run hand up extended leg

move hands from between the breasts, up the neck, and over the face

brush stomach, breasts, inner and outer thighs, genitals, buttocks

press breasts together

toss hair back with hand

toss hair by rotating head

pull hair on head

spank buttocks

spin on buttocks

spread buttocks apart

lick fingers

flash (lower G-string to expose pubic area)

open legs to reveal vagina ("spread show," "go pink," "pink blossom shot," "spread eagle," "the big bird," "bloomin," "pink bouquet," "money spread shot"

pose, preen

rotate head with loose hair

facial choreography:

> make eye contact

> move eyes (glance sideways, half close eyes, wink, bat eyelashes) to engage a customer with expectation of tip or sale of dance

> raise eyebrows

> smile

> pout

> stick out tongue

> lick lips

gyrate hips and torso

thrust hips back and forward and rotate hips ("bump and grind")

rotate hips into a squat (like a screw)

undulate body or body parts

shimmy breasts

bend torso parallel to ground

bend torso to peek through one's legs

on knees, bend back over rail

on patron's lap, bend back and up (wheelbarrow)

shake buttocks

thrust buttocks toward spectator

thrust pelvis toward spectator

quiver and tremble the body

snake arms upward

arms circle body

pull strings of G-string

palms (move hands on) the mirror

raise arms overhead and push breasts into mirror

rotate knees toward and away from each other ("butterfly")

kneeling, hinge torso backward

standing or prone, bend leg back from knee

> bend backward with hands and toes on floor (backbend) or from knees

resting body on back of shoulders, extend legs up wall

hold foot and extend leg full length

swing leg over patron's head

circle leg

hold foot and extend leg full length

extend leg out to patron's shoulder to make garter accessible for the patron to place tips

stand and arch torso backward

stand with torso bent over perpendicular to floor and extend one leg and both arms out to side

sit with torso bent over parallel to floor, extend one leg out to side, bend the other leg with knee on ground to the other side and foot toward center of body

breathe heavily

lie prone on floor, spread and close extended legs

lie prone on floor, raise buttocks up and down

on hands and knees, vibrate the buttocks

on all fours, undulate the torso

pretend to be caged

supine on floor, arch torso

supine on shoulders, extend leg and wiggle and rotate foot

supine on floor, open and close extended legs

supine on floor, hook legs behind head

squat with knees turned outward

contract genital muscles ("wink vulva")

bend back over tip rail from a kneeling position

hump rail

stand on rail

stand on hands with legs in a split

stand on head with legs in a split

remove heels and dance

collect tips with breasts

mouth song

touch patron:

    swish hair over patron's head

    brush patron's hair with hand

    balance with hands on patron's shoulders, thighs, or knees while arching backward or otherwise moving precariously kiss patron's cheek or forehead

hold patron's hand

"pecker check" rub of dancer's head on patron's crotch

place buttocks in patron's lap

straddle patron

grind or friction body against patron's body

place legs around patron's neck

**Level:**

stand in pose

kneel

hang on a pole near ceiling

"floor work" (moving on hands and knees or back or stomach) refers to childlike
    behavior, sexuality, transgressive female sex role

**Place:**

stage

runway

table ("table dancing" for a fee; on floor near the patron's table, dancer's legs often
    between the legs of the seated customer; on a pedestal near the table, on the
    table)

lap ("lap dancing" for a fee; patron sits on chair and dancer gyrates, flips head,
    arches back)

couch (same as lap dance but patron sits on couch)

shower

**Costume and make-up:**

creates stage identity

color is significant (red suggests passion; white suggests purity and virginity;
    black suggests nighttime and sultry female)

**Exposure:**

striptease (taking off one's clothes in a suggestive and seductive manner;
    commonly worn are a short dress, gown, robe, strip pants with front and back
    panels, gauntlets [elbow-3/4-length gloves], beaded bra with optional tassels,
    pasties, G-string or T-bar, underpants, jewelry, hose, very high heels)

go topless

flash (lower G-string to expose pubic area)

go bottomless

spread show (open legs to reveal vagina, "go pink")

spread buttocks to reveal vagina and anus

**Props and Acts:**

fan dance (used to circumvent New York's nudity laws: it was illegal to be nude while moving, but not standing; ballerina Sally Rand used a fan because she could not afford a costume)

tassels (fastened to pasties [areola breast covering] and twirled, sometimes in opposite directions)

boa (several feet-long scarf of feathers, fur, or delicate fabric; dancer or patron use tip to stroke the other's body)

"Eve" act with boa constrictor

imaginary lover

audience member brought on stage to dress in sultan turban and taught the "belly dance"

trained bird removes clothes from stripper and carries them away

whipped cream and chocolate put on and taken off body

pole (silent dance and sex partner, prop for performance to display different parts of the body)

gloves (play invokes penis, fellatio)

patron takes off dancer's t-shirt with his teeth

## Showcase

The dance showcases (auditions) the performer for tips and for "personal" dances, an ego and economic boost for the entertainer. A stage dance usually has one to three songs, during which time the dancer, moving in intentionally rhythmical patterns, appears clothed as some character/persona, becomes topless, and then, in some clubs, also becomes bottomless.

The revelation of nudity in a striptease, usually during the third song, is the "climax" of the erotic fantasy. Nudity is to exotic dance what a punch line is to a joke. Indeed, nudity distinguishes adult entertainment from other forms of dance, such as old-fashioned burlesque and two new transformations of exotic dance that focus on the participant rather than on the patron, namely, striptease aerobics and striptease therapy. Embedded in the culture of its time, exotic dance by definition must be "naughty" by revealing more of the body than is seen in public and by evoking fantasy. Otherwise, it is not adult entertainment. A dancer's perspective is that if you don't look down or in the mirror, you don't know you are performing naked. Moreover, the dancer is a whole person, and if the patron only sees holes, he looks like the ass.

In exotic dance, nudity communicates a range of meanings that appear in mainstream arts, as discussed in Chapter 4, which provides a historical and contemporary context for exotic dance. In exotic dance, the performer is an art form in motion, a living sculpture, and idealized beauty. A dancer has a body to experience, to master aesthetically, and to communicate various messages. Some circular stages in exotic dance theaters allow the audience to move around to see various angles and perspectives of the dancer's presentation, much like museum-goers move to observe a statue. Through nudity, dancers communicate the message of the beauty of their moving shapes with finely molded planes and rippling curvaceous surfaces. The beauty of the moving body includes texture, defined musculature, flickering shadows and highlights, hints of the skeletal frame and vertebrae, and the product of hard work in creating and maintaining a buff, sensual body.

From beauty contests, plastic surgery, cosmetics, and pin-ups, we see that American culture has long worshiped pulchritude, and exotic dance is part of the culture. Nudity in exotic dance may communicate a message of high status when the body is made beautiful at substantial financial expense or personal self-discipline. Moreover, nudity in exotic dance projects preciousness because of its relative scarcity outside of the arts. The unclothed body may poke fun at the pretense of clothing (expensive, military, or judicial, for example) and the obsession with self, mocking the typical person's self-presentation and social class. The dancer may remove attire that reflects conspicuous consumption and a person's inner self or aspirations. Some nudity conveys modesty through the dancer's slow and coy style of moving.

Given the tradition of nudity in mainstream theater, contemporary exotic dance is, therefore, an outgrowth of important twentieth-century artistic developments. The contemporary aesthetics of Western arts are to probe what has been deemed off-limits and find new objects to look at, or new ways to look at familiar ones. By stripping the body, the exotic dancer in an adult club confronts the artistic challenge.

Some entertainers give highly skilled performances. Here is a typical dance sequence showing creative skill that I observed:

> First Song. Dancer walks onstage. Wipes mirror with cloth to best reflect her image. Twirls on her own axis while circling around the pole. Holds pole with right hand as support to twirl around pole, right thigh lifted. Places back to pole and extends right leg. Turns around, grabs pole, and shimmies up, right leg extended outward, leans back, straightens up,

leans back with legs outward horizontally, brings them up to chest. Flips body upside down on pole, extends legs in a split, slides to floor. Hooks right leg around pole as support to twirl around pole. Sits down, arches backward, unfastens hair tie to let hair flow with movement. Twirls around pole, shimmies up pole with both legs, hangs upside down by legs. Slides to knees, extends torso forward, legs bent outward. Stands with back to pole, arches head back. Swings up pole with one foot on stage rail, one hand on ceiling hook. Descends to floor, knees swivel toward and away from each other. Leans back against the mirror, extends hands upward, turns around, moves hands down body, faces mirror, twirls, creating self-images twirling along mirror to right and then reversing direction. Sits down, flips head back. Walks to pole, twirls around it with right foot up. Lifts body onto pole with hands, flipping legs back and out. Hangs by one leg, the other extended outward, splits legs, descends to floor, head first. Places hand modestly over pubic area. Shimmies up pole, turns upside down, holding on with thighs, bounces buttocks sliding down. Twirls about pole, bends backward, one leg bent at knee. Shimmies up pole, moves body toward and away from pole, splits legs. Descends and twirls around pole; music accelerates as does movement. Slides back against pole, hands go up side of torso. Moves to edge of stage for patron to reward her performance by putting bill in her garter.

Second Song. Wipes mirror. Walks to pole, twirls about it, leg hooked. Shimmies up pole, turns upside down holding with one leg hooked around pole, the other in bent shape extends outward. Stands with back to pole and removes her top. Shimmies up pole, spins in backbend, brushes her hair, upside down, splits legs, extends them vertically and together, grasps pole. Descends to floor, flips hair back and forth, on hands and knees bounces buttocks, kneels, stands. Twirls about pole.

Third Song. Takes thong off. Backs up to mirror, creates S shape, slides to seated position, opens and closes legs. Walks to pole, hooks leg and twirls around pole, tosses head back, shakes hair. Descends pole into split, then rises with legs vertical to floor, buttocks first with torso bent forward, stands upright, tosses hair. Leans against pole, swings up with hands, body flung outward, and then legs grab pole. Vibrates legs in descent to floor. Circles pole. As foot pushes off from stage rail and one hand grasps a ceiling hook, swings up pole. Descends to floor with one, then the other leg. Leans against pole, twirls, head arched backward. Shimmies up pole, splits legs outward, extends arms outward as thighs grip pole. Descends, receives tips, walks offstage.

### Private Dance

In the private dance, the dancer focuses on the patron's responses in order to act out a personal message and create a sense of intimacy and spontaneity not manifestly intended for the entire audience as in a stage dance. Creatively and imaginatively, dancers converse and connect with the patron, whose purchased "commodity" is a license to dream.[16] The dancer "says"—through body and facial movement, proximity and touch—"I am for you and you alone," inspiring a fantasy that might stimulate patron thoughts about assignation with the dancer, including possession, foreplay, and intercourse. The fantasized relationship may be romantic or loving with commitment beyond the financial transaction. In a patron-focused dance, a patron may get the personal attention of an attractive female who would not otherwise "give him the time of day." Or he may be reminded of what it is to be desired. Moreover, the patron often becomes part of the improvisational performance, that is, entertainment for other audience members in the club who may identify with the patron.

A romantic relationship commonly includes a dinner or nightclub date with the pair seated proximate and touching as a sign of interest. Consequently, in individual patron-focused exotic dances, the performer is similarly close to the patron, prompting a fantasy of romance and creating a multisensory and emotional communication not found in a stage dance. If the dancer was only to perform on stage, remaining distant from the patron, this would, by contrast with individual patron-focused dances, denote coldness and impersonality toward him. Onstage, the dancer is viewed as if on a pedestal and inaccessible. The impersonal Bugaku, an erotic dance performed by the New York City Ballet in a three thousand-seat opera house at distances of several hundred feet from the general audience, provides an illustrative contrast with individual patron-focused dances. Bugaku is communication between a man and woman onstage as they simulate the consummation of a marriage for an entire audience. An individual patron-focused dance, however, is a communication between one dancer and one patron.

Private dances may be in the general seating area, a set-apart space, or a private booth or room. VIP rooms provide privacy and prestige, for which, of course, the patron pays. VIP rooms, according to John Gray, founder and CEO of the Spearmint Rhino chain founded in 1989, help alleviate embarrassment and offer value in a one-to-one experience. In 2011, the chain had fifteen clubs in the United States, six in the United Kingdom, one in Australia, and one in Canada.

*Bugaku*, photographer Costas.

Table dances are performed by clothed (or initially clothed and then partially or fully unclothed) performers who dance close (one to six inches) to an individual customer at his table, sometimes on a small portable platform ("box") or in special places in a club. A couch dance is similar to a table dance, except the customer sits on a couch, and the dancer stands on the floor or couch and straddles or performs between the customer's legs, usually in a less public area of the club. Couch dances are similar to those in three-sided booths in which a customer sits on a bench and the dancer stands on the floor, or on the bench with a foot on either side of the customer. In lap dancing, or "friction dancing," a performer sits on a customer's lap (upon which she may place a towel) and then dances for a fee and tips. She may straddle his lap and brush or grind against him or stand between his legs and slide up and down his body. Shower dances feature performers on stage under a shower in a Plexiglas booth.

New York's Melody Theater (it later became the Harmony Theater) is said to have pioneered the idea of strip shows with audience participation, both onstage and off, during the 1970s. Writer David Steinberg reports that lap dancing became part of the San Francisco scene when, in 1980, Jim and Artie Mitchell had in-the-buff dancers at their extravagant sex show at O'Farrell Theatre sit on the laps of patrons for tips. Danielle Egan described a lap dance as holding the keys to her patron's pleasure:

I was in control. It was my movements, my seduction, and my actions that drove the situation while he laid back in submission. He could not touch my vagina, butt, and/or breast with his hands, nor could he get up off the couch to move during the dance. It seemed to move straight eroticism away from the . . . equation of penis + penetration = real sex. . . . It's a highly erotic act moved by the force of fantasy and light touching as opposed to the thrust of intercourse.[17]

There are private dance variations. In Washington, DC, clubs Good Guys, JP's, and Joanna's, patrons walk up to the stage one at a time and stand at the front edge where a nude dancer performs a personal dance and receives tips.

Onstage at Crazy Girls, 7th Veil, Nude City, Jumbos, or Cheetah's, all Los Angeles clubs, a dancer will move close to a particular patron seated at the stage rail and give him a "private" dance. At Omar's in Lansing Michigan, a topless dancer crawls over a patron lying onstage with his feet on the floor, and performers at Little Darlings in Las Vegas give a private dance on the patron's bench seat in a booth.

Science got sexy about meaning. Psychologists investigated how patrons in a Las Vegas exotic dance club viewed the meaning of nudity and the distance between performer and patron. In their 2000 study, researchers found that nudity and performer-patron proximity do convey distinct meanings, and restrictions diminish the erotic expression and emotional impact on the patron. Legal cases cite this study.[18]

## The Art of It

Women who perform exotic dance determine their self-representation and can earn six-digit incomes through tips and fees to dance for individual patrons. Exotic dance is dance. But, an art? Yes, according to a general definition and possibly according to court decisions. The answer is controversial but important because artistic expression is protected under the First Amendment. *Webster's Ninth New Collegiate Dictionary* defines art as: "skill acquired by experience, study, or observation" and "the conscious use of skill and creative imagination." Some performers graduated from performing arts schools, as did Samantha (Chapter 5). Entertainers have danced in prestigious ballet and modern dance companies or competed in gymnastics. Others lacking formal training draw on social dance and learn on the job. Vanna Lace graduated from the Canada's National Ballet School, but as her body became voluptuous, going from a B-cup to a D-cup

A Dancer Prepares, photographer Chris Dame.

bra, it also became non-balletic in today's market for very thin ballerinas. So she became a feature dancer. Janet Feindel described her own situation this way:

> I realized I had a choice. I could stay at the National Ballet and earn a hundred and sixty dollars a week in the corps de ballets or I could be a star at Marvin's. Naturally I picked being a star! A lot of my friends at the National were shocked. But stripping, ballet, it's all the same. Dancing is an addiction.[19]

What most fascinates men drives creativity as exotic dancers compete for market share. Patrons may tire of sameness and seek novelty. If one dancer offers more innovation, then others may try to attract patrons

DC-style "Private Dance," photographer Chris Dame.

Janelle On Stage, photographer Chris Dame.

Floor Moves, photographer Chris Dame.

through being yet more distinct. The physical workout, the narcissistic and exhibitionist thrill of being admired and desired, the fantasy about being the most beautiful woman in the world, and the power to control patrons also stimulate creativity.

In the course of observing many exotic dance performances, I could see that there is often more going on than evoking sexual fantasy. For example, I saw creative parody—a dancer making fun of the pretext of clothing, such as wearing and stripping a police uniform or a cowboy outfit, and poking fun at gender identity or femininity by exaggerating their attributes. Adult club competitions for the best innovation push the imagination. The desire for risk and adventure also seed the new. If a dancer does not develop the requisite skills for the unique, she is likely to earn little and leave the business.

Although a dancer may imaginatively interpret choreography created by another person, her performance bears her own stamp. She'll improvise in response to her own mood, the music, and, most importantly, her patrons' responses. Sometimes called "free-style dance," in contrast with performing choreography or a script determined beforehand, improvisation is the essence of American jazz—freedom within limits. Dancers select their own stage names and identity, outfit to shed, and high heels to keep on. They decide on their grooming, the tease, body disclosure, dance theme and movements, and dancer-patron connections. To keep looking good, they figure out what they need to do to maintain weight and muscle

Pole Dancing, photographer Trace Grundstrom, courtesy Déjà Vu Consulting.

tone. Performers draw on creative acting skills to make any patron feel he's the greatest guy in the world and, therefore, willing to buy individual patron-focused dances. Dancers discover their own way to induce a patron to relax, and they learn how to "talk up" a man with stories and flattery ("You are my favorite customer," "I've missed you," "I love to hear about your work"). Dancers often create fantasies about themselves, feign attraction to the patron, and pretend to be embarrassed about bodily exposure.

In gentlemen's clubs, exotic dance is an art form that takes place in a theater. An entrance fee provides access to a place where professionals perform on a raised stage with special lighting, a commercial music system, and a master of ceremonies and/or disc jockey. Similar to mainstream dinner theaters, tables and chairs for audience members are arranged in areas where exotic dancers also perform. "Ushers" (floor managers or doormen) seat patrons, answer questions, and ensure proper audience behavior. As has traditionally been a feature of many major opera houses, clubs often have a special "VIP" room for audience members who pay for special ambience, alcoholic beverages, and attention. Backstage, there is a dressing area for performers.

## Pecking Order and Social Class

In mainstream US culture, the aesthetic pecking order in dance places classical ballet at the apex. Exotic dance is more "lowbrow" (with its own criteria of serious artistic value) than "highbrow" art. Exotic dance is not one of the forms of dance privileged by both the dance community and the general public, notwithstanding public perception of ballet as disreputable in the mid-nineteenth century when dancers were part of the demimonde. Sociologist Gary Alan Fine pointed out in 1991:

> Classical ballet . . . has established critics, expansive venues, and charitable events to support it, well-funded companies, international links, textbooks and theories, schools, professional organizations, and so on. Through its historical development, it has been certified as part of elite culture.

By contrast, Fine adds, "Exotic dance has no such infrastructure. . . . Those who work in vineyards of exotic dance are typically seen as lower class, and worse, they lack the pretensions that come with Art."[20]

However, since Fine's article was published, exotic dance has had best dancer competitions at local, regional, and national levels with substantial prizes. Po'lympics, a pole dance spectacular, is a high-flying nationwide finals competition. (Pole dancing is the most physically demanding expression of a dancer's skill—a false move can turn a stunning routine into a bruising disaster.) Charitable events featuring exotic dance are held, international links are active, and exotic dance schools and professional organizations for dancers and for club owners are growing. Dancers take classes during the day and practice in the clubs at night. There has been an annual Association of Club Executives' exposition for more than fifteen years. Doctoral dissertations focusing on exotic dance in anthropology, social work, theater arts, and women's studies continue to be churned out. Analyzed at scholarly conferences, exotic dance has its place in dance and theater arts history books, dictionaries, and encyclopedias.

Note that dance, as both art and entertainment, often provocatively challenges the status quo. Exotic dance in American culture has an evolving style with historical roots of deviance. Behavior disapproved of by mainstream society is an integral part of the art, entertainment, and lure for performers and patrons alike. Exotic dance transgresses through risqué excitement: it's "sinful" or "naughty" to dance nude, to look at nude performers, and to engage in a dancer-patron monetary transaction. The social body responds with constraints (including laws, club rules, morality, and economics), depending on the time and place and the way the physical body is perceived.

Social class and elitist bias emerge. In 1994, Melanie Wells wrote in *Penthouse*:

> People go to strip clubs to see beauty, and it's fucking elitist for people who go to museums to look at paintings and statues of beautiful bodies to denigrate strip clubs. These museum-goers are staring at beautiful nude bodies for pleasure, and it's supposedly high art.[21]

Sociologist Pierre Bourdieu called attention to aesthetic expressions reflecting and affirming status and becoming sites of symbolic conflict between classes.[22] Beer-drinking pretzel eaters versus wine-drinking quiche eaters! But today the wealthy are also exotic dance patrons.

## Artistic Value

The serious artistic value of exotic dance is borne out in the writing of mainstream dance critics and scholars, presentations at dance conferences, and exotic dance competitions. As early as the 1930s, dance/theater critics were reviewing exotic dance. They discuss a dancer's style, quality, depth, subtlety, complexity, sophistication, and sexual poetry. Moreover, the impact exotic dance has on other forms of dance is further evidence of its artistic value. Different dance forms influence each other, and patrons of one dance form often are inspired to explore others.

Choreographers need resources for their work. Dance forms on the margins often contribute to the Western aesthetic for innovation. World-renowned choreographer and founder of the New York City Ballet, George Balanchine featured a sexy burlesque striptease queen in his 1936 ballet, Slaughter on Tenth Avenue. His penchant for visiting the Crazy Horse Saloon in Paris for the midnight striptease show inspired his work on this ballet. Former New York City Ballet dancer Toni Bentley recognized the stripper as a Balanchine dancer sans leotard. She writes in Sisters of Salome:

> Partial, simulated, decorated, and disguised nudity is part of the appeal of a ballerina. . . . Stilettos are toe shoes with a stabilizing training heel; both elongate the female leg to its erotic pinnacle. . . . The figure-forming beauty inherent in ballet costumes and footwear is erotically related to the bondage element of classic strip lingerie. The turnout in ballet is its sexual core.[23]

Bentley tried dancing in a strip cabaret and experienced its power, freedom, creativity, and adulation. She was surprised by how gentlemanly the patrons were.

Broadway plays such as Pal Joey (1940), Star and Garter (1942), and The Naked Genius (1943) spotlight strippers as characters. In 1959, Jerome Robbins directed and choreographed the Broadway show Gypsy, based on the life of stripper Gypsy Rose Lee, and revivals of the show have been staged as recently as 2003. Other exotic dance-inspired works include Striptease, choreographed by modern dancer Mark Morris. Broadway star Bob Fosse's work in nightclubs and burlesque joints had a lasting influence on his choreography. He produced renditions of exotic dance in musicals—for example, to the comic show tunes, "Hernando's Hideaway" from The Pajama Game and "Whatever Lola Wants" from Damn Yankees—and in suggestive ballet in the film All that Jazz. Jawole Willa Jo Zollar, a modern dancer based in New York City and founder of the Urban Bush Women dance company, has spoken of the influence on her dances of the strippers she saw in her childhood. Her stage is peopled by lusty, forthright women. The Pepatian troupe presented the work Como Desnudarse (How to Undress), featuring the dance "El Striptís," at the 92nd Street Y in New York City in 1997. Eliot Feld's Ballet Tech performed his Pianola: Indigo with its burlesque bump and grind. Madonna and her backup singers do stripper moves, including crotch grabbing and floorboard grinding. Touching the crotch, as Michael

Jackson did in his "Thriller" routine and as Christina Aguilera does in concert, is as much a power move as a sexual gesture. Working as a stripper while attending the San Francisco Art Institute influenced Karen Finley's performance art.

Professional exotic dancers have appeared in videos since the 1980s because the pretty models the producers wanted didn't always know how to dance in a sexy way. Fatima, a choreographer whose clients included Michael Jackson, frequents strip clubs to learn moves to help female artists express their sexuality. At the 2006 MTV Video Music Awards, the Pussycat Dolls, who got their start as neo-burlesque dancers, won the Best Dance Video with choreography that included stripper moves.

Artistic value was an issue in *Lora Harrell v. Diamond A. Entertainment Inc.* (US District Court, Fort Myers, Florida). Judge Susan C. Bucklew ruled in favor of the dancer's lawsuit for back employee wages and fees and to be allowed to perform in the club. For a woman to dance in the club, several club staffers told the judge, all she has to do is "look good and be moving." The judge said these two criteria did not qualify dancers as "professionals" and therefore exempt from certain labor laws. Other staffers said, "All they do is walk around and swivel their hips." Yet, in 1954, Eugene Loring's modern dance, *All Alone*, consisted mostly of walking and posturing. Postmodern dancers Trish Brown and Lucinda Childs often strip their postmodern choreography down almost to just the act of walking.

"Looks and moving" are actually verbal shorthand criteria for what most people evaluating dancers recognize but cannot put into words. Indeed, many ballet critics cannot verbalize qualities of movement. Marcia Siegel chose to study movement analysis (labanotation and effort/shape) to describe better for her readers what happens in a dance, that is, to "replay" the performance. Club staff members who audition women have most likely developed what is called "connoisseurship." This is an acquired ability to judge quality on the basis of past experience, training, and observation of many exotic dancers. Dancers and patrons also develop this ability.

When exotic dance club auditioners say prospective performers have to be "moving," they mean performing in the style of exotic dance—sexy, flexible, seductive—using a variety of steps, maintaining eye contact with patrons, and exhibiting physical balance, musicality, and personality. Ballet choreographer Val Caniparoli, casting for his *Gran Partita* for Pacific Northwest Ballet, noticed a particular dancer and said, "I want her. She just struck me—the way she moved . . . and the way she handled herself in class. I liked her immediately." Similarly, modern dance choreographer

Mark Dendy said, "I was like, 'I want her—no, you don't understand, I want her.' Right away I knew I wanted to work with her, because her spirit is there."[24]

Most exotic dancers are more interested in making money than making art. However, aesthetics and economics are not mutually exclusive and can be combined. Indeed, principal dancers in ballet companies often earn extra income as guest artists at galas and in other companies.

The CR would be surprised to find that "the girl next door" is the adult entertainment "devil." I am always taken aback to see unassuming young women without make-up and dressed in jeans, sweatshirts, and sneakers enter the club and then, wow! From out of the dressing room, they move onto the stage, transformed into sensuous theatrical presences, dancers at ease in their costumes and skin.

In their efforts to stand out, dancers manicure their nails with shapes, colors, and patterns and make up their faces with eye shadow, eyeliner, eyebrow pencil definition, paint, powder, and rouge. Blush appears between the breasts. Dancers may vary their contact lens color. They cut, braid, color, or disguise their hair with attached hairpieces, wigs, or head coverings. They depilate their underarms and legs and shave or wax the pubic area to create designs, appear virginal, and allow viewable genitals. I listened to Scarlet, at one hundred and twenty pounds and five feet five inches, say with dismay, "I'm too fat. You're constantly worried about your appearance. I take diet pills and water pills. It's a real competitive business." Many dancers use tanning machines and work out for body definition and weight control. Some clubs require a certain weight.

Most dancers are young. So an older dancer tries to appear young by mimicking what is nonexistent in reality. She makes her lips appear full, skin smooth, eyes clear, hair lustrous, teeth white, gait bouncy, and body tanned, oiled, and buff. She rouges her cheeks to trigger attention. Maturing dancers who want to keep on dancing try plastic surgery.

The twenty-first century witnessed a boom in tattooing anywhere on the body, and piercings of the ears, nose, eyebrow, armpits, navel, lip, tongue, nipple, clitoris, and labia are seen as acts of fashion, eroticism, self-love, and identity. Performers may enhance or parody the "ideal" body with surgically enhanced breasts and flesh reduction.

Suggestive costumes include special undergarments, cocktail décolletage, or scanty dress and sequins. Feathers and fur are linked to slang: bird, chick, pussy, bitch—animals associated with low intelligence and thus subject to the fantasy of a man's right to make the wearer captive and domesticated at his will. Props such as a phallic snake or a swan neck may arouse. Dancers play with symbols of femininity: costume color, high heels, garter belts, gloves, cleavage, hair, and lips.

Why do some performers appear vulgar and others appear artistic on stage? Vulgarity is usually due to a lack of dance experience or natural grace, so movements are awkward and exaggerated. When a dancer lacks skill or beauty, she may substitute "lewd" movements to attract patrons' interest. Certainly, a dancer may deliberately attempt to be vulgar.

## Dance "Class"

Admittedly, for an attractive female without prior experience as an exotic dancer to flunk an exotic dance audition is rare, except in the upper-end clubs, which are highly selective. However, transferable skills from experience in other dance (e.g., ballet, modern, jazz, tap, disco, salsa) or in gymnastics, modeling, cheerleading, and music help a novice somewhat to approximate an exotic dance. Ceci had a swing dancing background. Prior to her audition, she watched the exotic dancers for a couple of hours. Then she copied what she saw them do. After a few months, she became an accomplished exotic dancer.

Most learning in life is informal and experiential. Within ballet—and in exotic dance—the transmission of knowledge and skill to the novice occurs in several ways: through an informal teacher's direction or example (modeling a dance routine), or through supervised practice and coaching from dancers and club staff. At Old Higgins Heavenly Bodies in Cook County, Illinois, Yvette gives an auditioning dancer a two-hour training, shows her a how-to film, and explains the dos and don'ts. An instructor may create situations in which the student manipulates movement in response to a problem, such as how many ways a person can turn. A club in New Orleans has a doorman who assures patrons that there are "no chicks with dicks." However, some of the best dancer coaches are transvestites.

Dancers also learn on their own by watching other dancers in person or on TV—especially on programs such as *Dance Hall, Dancing with the Stars*, and *So You Think You Can Dance*—in music videos, movies, and social dance places. Students can go to www.how-to-strip.com. Amy, a third-generation dancer, watched *Solid Gold, Soul Train*, and *American Bandstand* on television. Dancers learn from rough trial and error, using mirrors to see how they look or experimenting at home, in the club dressing room, and onstage. Some clubs require new dancers to watch the "old-timers" dance for a specified number of hours before performing. Eventually, they develop their own style. For many dancers, getting up from a floor position in platform heels proves difficult and looking good doing it, almost impossible. It may take a while for a dancer to develop the upper body strength to lift herself up the pole and then move her body horizontally and vertically around the pole. There are schools for exotic dance feature performers. Weasel's Sportsman Rendezvous has offered, since 1982, a small, informally structured, year-round program in Eagle River, Wisconsin; others include Naked Assets and Pure Talent Agency. Smaller programs have been Steele Mill's Nova Training Program, STDM Productions; Skyline Services; Diamond Dance Academy; and Carolina School of Feature Entertainment.

Exotic dance can itself be a classroom for creativity in other arts. Skills learned or enhanced in exotic dancing include memory of movement vocabulary and discipline in preparing to perform—scheduling, grooming, attire, make-up, and choreography. Exotic dancers learn to adapt to the unpredictable, and they sharpen their sensitivity to human behavior—getting along with coworkers (other dancers, DJs, managers, bartenders, doormen) and diverse patrons. Successful dancers become acute observers of verbal and nonverbal communication in order to sell a fantasy of themselves and to create the patron's fantasy. Dancers commonly gain self-esteem and self-confidence appearing nude before strangers. Listening skills capture patron dialog, stories, and interests. Diablo Cody, formerly known as Brook Busey-Hunt, went from stage to page. She wrote about her experience in *Candy Girl: A Year in the Life of an Unlikely Stripper* and later went on to win the coveted Oscar for the Best Original Screenplay with her *Juno*.

## Adult Play for Pay

The make-believe between dancer and patron is playful, although the pay is serious business. Why do men play in exotic dance clubs? An exotic dance patron's vulnerability to seduction depends on why he goes to a club and generally who and what excite him. Age, income, profession, ethnicity, and religion may affect his susceptibility to a dancer's wiles. The reasons for frequenting a club are amazingly multiple.

Patrons may seek a refuge, a place to hang out, relax, and be entertained. People pay to play for the attention. Bachelor parties celebrate a forthcoming marriage and "educate" the groom by focusing on female sexuality. Athletes and sports enthusiasts come to exotic dance clubs to celebrate or mourn game outcomes. Businessmen at conventions seek an adventure and change of pace. Men and women who frequent the clubs often seek aesthetic pleasure in the beauty and gracefulness of the nude female body. Being ravished by female pulchritude is a magnet for some patrons.

Patrons may frequent an upscale club because the pleasant ambience facilitates business transactions or because their business network meets there. Aspiring rap stars flock to "Magic Monday" at the Magic City strip club in Atlanta, the "Motown of the South." They hope to create a buzz for their music and network with disc jockeys, music producers, and stars who conduct their business while about fifty dancers move to hip-hop soundtracks. Everyone parties and listens for trends bubbling up from the streets. Big-timers "make it rain" by flinging dollar bills toward the ceiling that billow down and shower the dancers. Competitive rap stars in a club lead to thousands of dollars for the dancers. Since at least 2003, strip clubs in Atlanta have been launching pads for new hip-hop records planned for radio. Producers believe that if strippers can dance to it, the song has potential to be a hit—in other words, the butts don't lie. Dancers give songs a try so the record label representatives will make it rain heavily.[25]

Many patrons go to the clubs for some companionship. Connection with a live dancer in a one-on-one experience can partially compensate for our very impersonal society. Many of the patrons just want to talk to the girls, to unload what's on their chests. I have heard about numerous patrons, often married or with significant others, who were seeking "understanding" listeners. Some men feel safer with exotic dancers, who are perceived as "vulnerable" in their nudity and not competitors or judges. An accountant who was dancing in Seattle had a regular patron who worked at Boeing. He paid for "dances" wherein dancer and patron sat and talked. When patrons develop an interest in and loyalty to one dancer and come to see her frequently, as if she were his real girlfriend, the patrons become "regulars." The dancer feigns reciprocal interest. Many men face live metaphors in motion. In her experience, Katherine Frank found that gifts to and learning about a dancer made the encounter appear more genuine, countering the exchange of money that undermines real relationships. A patron may purchase a dancer's costumes or cosmetic surgery and thereby engage in reshaping a woman's body to more closely resemble his fantasy image. Dancers reported patrons giving dancers cars—and for no more than a dance or her time in the club, but I did not meet such recipients. Other patrons hope to have a real relationship with a dancer, sexual or otherwise. There are patrons who become dancers' true friends and some marry them. Of course, assured of not being rejected, a patron, however, may leave when he chooses.

Men commonly seek a sexual thrill—fantasy or reality. But their expeditions to exotic dance clubs may be nothing more than quests toward the unknown. Some men visit clubs as if they were tourists, expecting to see the revelation of woman's sexual self. Curiosity is often a draw; for some men, lovemaking occurs in the missionary position in the dark and with clothing on, so they have never seen the nude female body. I was at Good Guys in Washington, DC, when a Middle Eastern man from a culture of great modesty went up to the stage to tip a nude dancer. All of a sudden, overcome by embarrassment, he darted out of the club to the laughter of the other male patrons. Nude dancers say that, in their interactions with patrons, the men look at their faces, as Rupp and Wallen found in their research experiments. Some patrons told me they prefer dancers to be only topless, as that "leaves more to the imagination." There are patrons who just like to view and fantasize about a variety of women and still remain faithful to one. A dancer, Velvet, observed: "Patrons see something they don't see at home. Men want something other than the norm. Guys want what they can't have."

The clubs attract men who like to show off to dancers and other patrons—a macho man is a big spender and a magnet for women. These men are often drawn to clubs because gender roles are not blurred here as they are increasingly in society. A man who suffers impotency or performance anxiety can feel manly and dominant when he pays for a dance without having to work to cultivate a real relationship with a woman and risk failure. Male identity and bonding may be bolstered through the fantasy of phallic man with money. Although a patron may find pleasure in playing the dominant role by dispensing tips and fees to dancers, he may find the inversion of the male dominant stereotype by female seduction also appealing. Katherine Liepe-Levinson describes performing spectators who find pleasure in "mimetic jeopardy," scripted transgression. Going onstage at the dancer's invitation, a patron becomes a "star performer." Lying on his back as a nude dancer plucks a dollar bill from his forehead with her butt cheeks, the patron purchases the thrill of voluntarily exposing himself to a kind of danger, including being in front of a scrutinizing audience.

Some patrons are unhappy, shy, lonely, or lacking relationship skills. The "naughty" and pretending aspects of the clubs entice. Lust and degeneracy attract some men: "perverts" and "suckers" the dancers call them. A patron receiving medical attention went to clubs to see dancers with physical and psychological qualities the polar opposite of what he tended to see in treatment facilities. A man who has been brought up in a fundamentalist family and is ashamed of his body and sexuality may be drawn to the dancer's comfort with her body and sexuality. A woman stripping for a man appears shamelessly proud of her sexuality and her body, powerfully counteracting his everyday image of women who are ashamed of and inhibited about their sexuality, women toward whom he might tend to feel guilty and responsible.

Watching and fantasizing about exotic dancers sometimes even saves a marriage. Older married men want to feel young and sexy again. Gabrial said, "I'm your spark when your wife fizzles. Men like to go home in a frisky mood." Being aroused by gazing at a dancer may encourage a man to go home and have sex with his beautiful or not-so-attractive wife. A male friend of mine, who was in a car accident and healed physically, was unable to make love with his lovely wife—that is, until he started going to exotic dance clubs.

Most people engage in sexual fantasy occasionally, and fantasies are generally recognized as part of healthy sexuality.[26] The fantasies expressed through exotic dance may whet the appetite for reality or be fulfilling in themselves. However, sexual desire and action upon desire are independent. Desire is integral to exotic dance theater. Interestingly, and counter to CR charges that exotic dance ruins marriages, researchers found that sexual fantasies about others, rather than about one's partners, do not interfere with the ability to maintain a relationship over time.[27] Clubs are akin to men's erotic dreams: men tend to visualize themselves making love to multiple partners in public or unknown settings. In their fantasy worlds, the men almost never have to put their ego on the line and come on to a woman; instead, the woman makes the first move in a great sexcapade. Men like experiencing erotic abundance. Studies of male sexual fantasies found the most frequent fantasies are memories of past sexual experience as well as experiences that have not occurred but are exciting to imagine. A man's power to drive a woman wild is a typical theme, and common images include nude or semi-nude females, intimacy, seduction scenes, sex with a new female partner, sex with two or more women, different sexual settings, positions and practices, questionable partners, things one would never act on in real life, orgies, and submission and dominance.

In the past, clubs did not permit a woman unescorted by a man to enter. I heard stories about prostitutes coming to pick off dancers' patrons. Another story involved an irate wife entering a club and breaking a beer bottle over her husband's head. But club manager Stephen McWilliams asked, "Whores, lesbians, and pissed-off wives? I mean, really, what other kind of women would want to enter a topless club? That was the misconception of female customers twenty years ago." Increasingly, women are becoming a regular fixture in the clubs. Why are women paying or having their male companion pay to play in adult clubs? Some are curious, thinking about dancing onstage or learning how to seduce a man. Many women have the habit of competing with each other for male attention. A female patron remarked, "It could be that we simply want to keep a watchful eye on our boyfriends/husbands. Or maybe that we want to learn a thing or two to keep him happy."

## "Satan's" Ploys

The dancer's remunerative game is to inflame a patron's fantasy, turning the table on male control. I found that dancers and patrons often can't tell you what they think is seductive because they haven't thought about it or they don't have the vocabulary. Thoughts may be visual, as Gerald Zaltman, marketing professor at the Harvard Business School, has found through his work at the Mind/Brain/Behavior Interfaculty Initiative. People could not explain their views about products they use but images captured their feelings. So it is not surprising that a dancer can rarely explain how she is a high-income earner or a patron can explain how he is seduced. Much is intuitive, absorbed instantly. When I visited clubs in order to describe in court whether the dancer's performance had artistic merit, I drew upon my movement analysis training to observe the performer-patron connection. Performers engage in a cornucopia of ploys, both onstage and off-stage, to get tips and sell private dances.

Dancers (or, to the CR-Activist, Satan incarnate) artfully lure men (and women) through a kaleidoscopic bombardment of expectations and kinetic and other sensory signals. The dancer creates a sexual fantasy that draws upon the sexual scripts in both everyday life and the media—namely, courtship and common understandings of space, nudity, self-touch, and interpersonal touch—so she and the patron can enact a play together.[28] Excitement is heightened when the fantasy's outcome is uncertain and includes an element of risk or transgression.[29] Although the dancer draws upon personal experience, there appear to be some evolutionary universals in female seduction, such as the focus on displaying breasts, hips, and bodily proportions that mark sexual identity and youthfulness, that is, the capacity for reproduction.

Dancers take aim at the bodily and mental powers of patron perception. A dancer's ability to read a patron and creatively respond to his fantasy is essential. Grooming, costume, humor, music, and club ambience, as well as patron vulnerability and willingness to participate in fantasy, contribute to the power of seduction.

Dance and seduction go together like hand in glove. The Latin origin of the word "seduction" means to lead or attempt to lead astray, enchant, or entice into a wrong or foolish course, especially a sexual act. The association of dance and seduction reaches beyond recorded time. Salome's dance of the seven veils so intoxicated the king that he gladly ordered a beheading in return for her freely given charms. In our modern era, we remember Mata Hari as a dancer first and a spy second; the attraction of her dance seduced powerful men, who then told her their secrets in bed. A very powerful US congressman, Wilbur Mills, had to resign because of his relationship with a stripper named Fanne Fox. However, in French "seduce" has a broader meaning, namely, "charm" or "attract" or "engage" or "entertain." The French meaning, applicable to exotic dance, is tightly bound with *plaisir*, the art of creating and relishing pleasure of all kinds.[30]

The art of seduction through dance, more than a physical courtship duet, embodies the thought of the seducer and seduced. After all, the brain is a full-fledged "sex organ." The mind-body cocktail has led governments and religious groups worldwide to ban or impose controls on dancing for fear of its power to sexually arouse. I have seen dancers allure, bewitch, tantalize, beguile, coax, flatter, and exploit men in a fantasy seduction. The women's salesmanship/marketing may be subtle or brazen or a mix of styles.

## Turning On

> There's language in her eye, her cheek, her lip;
> Nay, her foot speaks. Her wanton spirits look out
> At every joint and motive of her body.
> Shakespeare, *Troilus and Cressida*, Act IV, Scene 5, Line 55

Contrary to CR assumptions, exotic dance is a theatrical performance—all about pretend. Like an actor, the dancer needs to induce feelings in herself to sustain an outward appearance of friendliness that evokes a patron's feeling that she cares about him. She needs to exhibit common courtesy despite negative treatment by patrons. Negative (ticks and twitches) nonverbal body language may interfere with seduction efforts.

Dancers get ready to play the fantasy game with scent, dabbing themselves with the perfume they think will seduce patrons. Fragrance calls out, "Notice and like me," "love me," and "I am sophisticated." In fact, psychologist Piet Vroon refers to personal smell as "the secret seducer." The human body broadcasts its own olfactory aphrodisiacs, especially in the groin and armpits. Apocrine glands in the skin, mouth, feet, and vagina secrete pheromones that produce physiological and behavioral changes in another person. Scent, essential in the mating rituals of many animals, is a powerful trigger of mood, memory, and emotion and has a long-standing association with sensuality and alluring femmes fatales. In the Bible's Song of Songs, olfactory imagery bespeaks of sexual intimacies. The interpretation of smell occurs in parts of the brain connected with emotion and feeling. Smell influences our behavior often without our being aware of it.

A dancer remarked, "I think that if a girl doesn't look like she is enjoying herself and having a good time, a customer can pick up on that . . . you always need to leave your problems at the door." A dancer's smile must be convincing, eye contact burning, and energy vibrant. In addition to dance movements, the tease, nudity, sexuality, personality, story-telling, artistic expression, creativity, confidence, and musicality, physical appearance, and perfume contribute to seduction. A dancer may begin her performance with dollar bills (the common tip) in her garter belt, and other dancers may tip her to encourage similar patron behavior—in other words, to get the men "to loosen up."

"Talking the talk" also leads to success. Using the patron's name, complimenting him, and speaking about his interests oils the seduction. Talk often puts a patron at ease. Dancers may remark on a patron's likeable traits over and over to convince him that he's special. Successful performers usually do not directly ask a patron if he/she wants a private dance but instead says something like, "You seemed to be interested in my stage dance, would you like a little personal attention?" When a patron asks a dancer to sit and talk and then doesn't buy her a drink or a table dance, she excuses herself with a warm smile and says something like, "A pleasure to meet you, but if you're not up for a private dance now, I hope you won't mind if I come back later."

A dancer's subservient and welcoming signals give patrons permission to initiate interaction. Patrons may ask for a dance or may want dancers to approach them and ask if they want one. Approaching a patron from a side angle and slowly moving around to face him is more seductive than a full face, front torso approach that can be potentially challenging and threatening. Open body postures can also be perceived as welcoming. The dancer tries to establish boundaries around her and a patron to create a private safe haven, not a claustrophobic box.

## Reading for the Connection

A dancer's ability to read a patron is essential as she decides to whom to send erotic messages to solicit an individual patron-focused dance, and maybe another dance, and perhaps to develop a regular patron. Listening to a patron helps a dancer to discover his fantasies and tastes. She can assume a persona in an attempt to create and maintain his belief that his desired sexual or other experience is possible. The integration of mind and body, or what psychologist Howard Gardner calls "interpersonal intelligence," is critical to a dancer's economic reward and a patron's pleasure.

Dancers scope a club for signals—such as multiple drink orders and large groups of men—from patrons who want to play. Clothing and jewelry divulge something about a patron: his beliefs, his sentiments, his status, his occupation or religion, and especially his income. A dancer observes the way the patron sits, his facial expressions and especially his eyes—the "mirror of the soul." Terrence Burnham and Brian Hare found that people are more generous when they are watched. Are patrons' eyes direct and expressing interest or are they roving, checking out other dancers? An unblinking gaze is clinical, whereas an indirect gaze suggests self-consciousness and a need for the dancer to offer reassurance. Darting eyes convey nervousness and suspiciousness; a furtive glance reflects an intimidated but interested patron. A wink is teasing. A wide-eyed patron is engaged in what is going on; perhaps he is surprised or naïve. Knitted eyebrows are the trademark of a man weighted down with responsibility. A male come-on can be detected in raised eyebrows, a smile, and a tilted head.

A knack for reading faces can save a dancer time and effort. The face is telling, be it playful tongue licking or flicking, feigned disinterest, signs of nervousness, or feigned sexual gratification. A patron's spontaneous smile indicates friendliness, perhaps a beacon of desire. A grudging or smirking mouth or poker face is usually a brush-off by a conceited man who harbors a sense of false superiority. An ear-to-ear grin shows an upbeat person. A frozen mouth signals a person who shields feelings. A patron who bites his lower lip is nervous. Lips parted show an openness and interest. Upturned corners are positive, but a tight-lipped or trembling-lipped expression is cold. Licking one's lips or tongue flicking is a sexual come-on. A chin thrust forward suggests pugnacious determination. Flowing nostrils attend excitement. A man with crossed legs is guarding his most sensitive organs. Sitting hunched over characterizes a man bent by burdens who would welcome light entertainment.

Dancers encourage the connection with patrons by displaying the readiness cues of courtship behavior.[31] A performer may preen, self-grooming, stroking her hair, fixing her makeup. Her eyebrows flash and she holds the patron's gaze, smiles. She orients her body toward a patron, closing off other individuals.

Piquing a man's interest and keeping him wanting more is seductive. Dancers feed off a man's excited reaction—he likes to feel a woman is inflamed because of him. Dancers may perform an illusion that is an extension of the viewer's desire, such as little girl, biker chick, schoolgirl, farmer's daughter, coquette or seductress, independent woman, innocent little Lolita or siren, cowgirl, nurse, cheeky flirt, or dominatrix. Mary, for example, plays Santa at Christmas and is tipped well for her effort. Dancers tell fictional stories about themselves to complement patrons' fantasies. In the course of a performance shift, dancers may play many roles. Patrons observe a man getting a table dance, which creates interest and expectation for their own possible interactions. Of course, some patrons know the dancer's nonverbal and verbal "come-on" is part of a fantasy game—indeed, an extension of child's play. Yet, still undercover police occasionally try to ensnare dancers by eliciting their fanciful sexy talk and movement and then charging them with solicitation for illegal prostitution.

A club owner in Chicago showed me a videotape that he had directed and that all new dancers are required to watch. It showed what a dancer should look for in a patron, how to approach him, and how to stand to block distractions while she talked to him. When Sarah Katherine Lewis went for drinks for her patron, she worried about getting back

> to strong-arm him into a private show before some other girl sidled up to him and stole the session that I'd earned by laying all the groundwork. He was at a crucial, unprotected point: drunk, but not too drunk, and horny, thinking about panties or crotches or whatever it was he liked when he stared between a dancer's legs.

Lew reflected that it was up to her to sell him an expensive show and that if she wasn't careful,

> he could feel pressured—and a pressured customer would bolt. I had to be light and flirtatious, as if the money were merely an awkward formality between him and management. I needed to give the impression that I was so into him I'd do a VIP for free if they didn't make me charge.

She said she ultimately made the "kill."[32]

I was surprised to learn that Sapphire, whom most people would call physically unattractive and a poor dancer, earned far more money than the dancers who attract and dazzle with their looks and performance. As it turned out, however, Sapphire knew how to read and relate to a man, to talk with him, and make him feel at ease.

## Parody

The CR does not recognize the richness of theater arts, including parody and humor, which are part of a dancer's seduction toolkit. Of course, withholding and coyness in stripping to nudity have an element of seductive tease. But by flaunting sexuality, the dancer makes fun of it. Stripping from, for example, a businessman's suit to nudity pokes fun not only at the pretense of clothing but also at conspicuous consumption, and perhaps white collar capitalism, as well as staid religious beliefs about modesty. The derriere packs a double whammy. It symbolizes eroticism and also derision and abuse. Because clothing signifies an individual's place in culture, when it is cast off, social boundaries are less clear. A patron unaccustomed to nudity can be put at ease with humor.

## Moving It

Movement attracts attention. Slow motion permits the patron to see how the dancer moves over the stage or on the pole as she fuels his fantasy. Some clubs have a nightly "uptime" lineup in which the DJ calls every dancer, by name, to the stage, one at a time. Such a moving spectacle may seductively introduce a dancer or refresh a patron's memory.

"I make eye contact. You got to go eyeball to eyeball," explained Angel. Eyes, the organ of vision, are also the organ of communication. They beckon, "come hither." Looking intensely into a patron's eyes, a dancer captivates him and shows him her interest. She may close her eyes in self-absorption and pleasure or intersperse eye contact with downward glances in counterfeit modesty. She may look furtively, blink slowly, roll her eyes, glance flirtatiously, and even play peek-a-boo. The gaze indicates degrees of attentiveness and arousal and welcomes a patron into her line of sight. Eyebrows rising and falling acknowledge a patron's presence.

Smiles, grins with exposed teeth, and pouts are evocative. A smile shows recognition, friendliness, warmth, unalloyed delight, coyness, and joie de vivre in contrast to a grimace and frown. A dancer may blow kisses and pucker her lips. Star bites her lower lip, slips her finger into her mouth, or licks her lips, suggesting something delicious, maybe the pleasure of fellatio or cunnilingus. Sarah Katherine Lewis recalled, "I made sure to keep my lips wet and parted—a cocksucker's mouth, glossed with frosty pink. 'Cum lips.' . . . Customers loved cum lips."[33] Tilting the head beckons coyly. Loose hair suggests lack of constraint. A dominatrix visage marked by frowns, grimaces, angry lip biting, or tongue flicking may bewitch some patrons.

Making waves of motion flow from head to toe—weaving serpentine shapes, pausing suggestively, and resuming movement—is seductive. A dancer invitingly tilts her relaxed head to reveal the neck and throat more openly. Hair preening usually accompanies sexual arousal in every-day courtship, so this too is in the seduction arsenal. Curvilinear, fluid, or percussive movements make female attributes noticeable. Breasts are shimmied and buttocks are shaken, thrust, and rotated (hence the phrase "bump and grind") in stylistically mimed sex acts. Aspasia recalls, "I did not have to be a strong hustler to get my tips. I truly moved and grooved across the stage. I rocked and was very focused. I truly made my body sing. The crowds loved it." Squatting in front of a patron seated at the edge of the stage and opening her garter for him to place tips is both enticing for the patron and financially rewarding for the dancer. Dancers develop their own high-heeled strut. Dancing on a pole, a phallic symbol, allows gym-nastic moves that show off both skill and the body from unusual perspec-tives. Pole dancing lets patrons see "bottom scenery." Mirrored walls are both backdrops and, sometimes, the dancer's "partner" as she moves her hands or other body parts along the surface, reinforcing her image. To show empathy, a dancer may "mirror" a patron's posture, energy, or move-ment to make him feel affirmed and desirable.

## Close Up and Touching

Self-touch is a marker of sexual allure in American courtship. So self-touch serves to capture a patron's focus and direct his gaze during an overload of stimuli in the club. By touching her own body, costumed or nude, es-pecially parts usually covered on an American public beach, a performer points to her best sexual assets. Dancers may cup their breasts together, grab themselves as in autoerotic ecstasy, and stroke or slap their buttocks. As they caress themselves, dancers luxuriate in their own essence. A danc-er's self-touch may show the patron where she would like him to touch her in fantasy. He can identify with her self-touch, and fantasizing his hands as hers, he is thus possessing a beautiful woman.

In 1928, the burlesque dancer Hinda Wassau, trained in modern dance, may have been the first to run her hands over her body while stripping, setting a precedent for exotic dance. Through self-touch, an exotic dancer delineates her identity as an independent, beautiful, sexual, and empow-ered female, who cares for herself and creates a boundary between herself and the audience. By touching her own nude body in a public setting—in keeping with the historical tradition of adult entertainment—a performer transgresses social mores of mainstream society. Self-touch is also artistic, ephemeral body decoration appealing to a patron's aesthetic sensibility: the dancer creates designs, sculpting lines and curves over the body and through her hair and into space, using her fingers like a paintbrush. Since women tend to stroke their necks more than men and may touch their mouths and lips with their fingertips when aroused, the dancer does this to captivate a patron. Touching herself, the dancer may also convey modesty, a protective shield and covering as a tease.

A multiple club owner said his stages were fourteen inches high because the higher the stage, the less money a dancer will make. By moving close to a patron, a dancer creates a romantic ambience and illuminates her grooming and scent. Proximity permits the dancer and patron to get feedback from each other. They can detect signs of interest, including pupil dilation and eye widening. Thus, it becomes possible to communicate effectively as both participate in the performance.

A dancer touching a patron has seductive merit in creating a "conversation," a mutual electric aura. Because there is a massive involvement of skin in sexual congress, any brief touch, such as a dancer shaking a patron's hand, can be symbolic. John, manager of clubs in Columbia, South Carolina, tells dancers to put their hand between the patron's elbow and hand. Why? On many mantle pieces sit wedding pictures that show the woman's hand on the arms, a sign of closeness. Artists and poets refer to the power and grace of touch to envelope human feeling. Of course, powerful cultural norms and religious strictures surround touch and physical contact because they relate most particularly to sex, aggression, dominance, and power.

Touch can be titillating. Exotic dancers stir emotions as they swish their hair over a patron's head, chuck under his chin, brush a hand over his hair, or run their fingers through it. A dancer also makes a patron feel good when she puts an arm around his neck, puts her hands on his shoulder or thigh for balance while arching backward or otherwise moving in a precarious way, and kisses his cheek, forehead, or hand. Neck massages may lure a patron. A dancer may blow in his ear. When patron and dancer are seated proximate, the dancer may play footsie and cross or uncross her legs. The power of touch in seduction is suggested by a study that found servers who briefly touched their patrons in eating establishments received larger gratuities than those who did not use touch.[34] Elected and electable leaders also tend to touch voters.[35]

Closeness between dancer and patron is essential in overcoming "noise" to convey seductive dance messages through sight, sound, smell, and touch. Ultra-rapid facial actions, some lasting as little as one-twentieth of a second, lay bare feelings that cross our faces spontaneously and involuntarily. The music is often loud as part of the aesthetic ambience of contemporary adult cabarets, so proximity is necessary for dancer and patron to hear each other speak, complimenting and flattering in a soft voice. Dancer-patron proximity prevents smells from cigarettes and beverages from overwhelming the scents of perfume and pheromones.

Because patrons vary in their physical abilities to see, hear, and smell, proximity is also important for effective communication. For the most part, men are not allowed to touch the women, and most men sit wonderfully passive in their seats as the women slither and gyrate on their bodies. However, blind patrons want to touch the dancers, with the women's consent, to get an "image" of the dancer. Visually challenged patrons have even petitioned a local council to permit nonsexual touching. Some clubs allow patrons' nonsexual touching of the outer legs (in a kind of a gentle holding motion), or, putting their arms around the back of the dancer as she puts her weight on the men chest-to-chest.

Exotic dancers may perform tip tricks to seduce patrons to joyfully give them generous gratuities. I saw these tricks at Sirens in a hamlet near Ithaca, New York:

- A dancer places a patron's dollar bill in his mouth and then removes it between her cupped breasts.

- A dancer places a patron's dollar bill underneath his shirt collar near his ear, blows in his ear, and then takes the bill between her cupped breasts or her teeth.

- A dancer places a patron's dollar bill in his mouth while he is seated in a chair next to the stage. Then she does a headstand between his legs and snatches the bill by squeezing it between her buttocks cheeks.

- A dancer places a seated patron's dollar bill in his mouth and, from onstage, she places her feet on his shoulders and lifts her body so she can pick up the bill with her buttocks cheeks.

In another tip trick, a dancer invites a patron to lie back on the stage with his feet on the floor. She takes his dollar bill, moistens it with her mouth on a vertical fold to make it "stickable," and places it tent-like over his forehead and nose. Then, facing away from him, she bends over and backs up over the bill, and, watching between her legs, quickly picks it up with her buttocks cheeks. She might grab it with her hand if she starts to lose her grip.

## Music and Setting

With its ineffable quality, music may generate amorous interest that sweeps through the dancer's and patron's bodies. Dancers select music that moves them, makes them feel comfortable and sexy, and hopefully puts patrons in a good mood and thereby vulnerable to seduction. Essie said, "Sometimes I don't take anything off. I can't look out at the crowd. I just have to get into the music. I don't think about what I do. Creativity comes. It's what turns you on." The age and socioeconomic status of a club's clientele guides musical selections. Sustained external rhythms can change internal rhythms, heart rate, and breathing in addition to releasing rushes of emotion. Song texts often convey seductive messages. Music associated with special events and from films or musicals can evoke the memory of specific characters and their actions. Instruments sometimes have symbolic sexual associations.

A club's atmosphere complements the dancer's seductive strategy. Comfortable chairs and couches help a patron relax. Low, soft lighting creates a romantic environment. Twenty watts of flickering black light ensure that the dancers will look awesome, hiding their cellulite and other imperfections. The low light and fog machines enhance the mystery of a woman's eroticism. A dancer may stand over a machine placed in the stage floor as fog rises up between her legs. Poles allow for gymnastic moves. DJ and bartender comments to patrons about tipping the pretty lady or getting a private dance oil the seductive engagement. Some clubs have as many as a dozen large TV screens that show images of women and sports games that provide a basis for conversation.

## Socially Redeeming Values

Exotic dance offers socially, psychologically, and economically redeeming values for dancers, patrons, a workforce, and the general public. Yet, it is uncommon for the CR to recognize anything positive about strip clubs. A Bakersfield, California, TV weatherman refused to work on the day the station broadcast a positive strip club story. As a Christian, he said he did not want to appear to be endorsing it and was let go because he violated his contract.[36]

Performers gain a feeling of empowerment and self-esteem through earning a livelihood, having a flexible schedule to attend college or take care of their children, and using the opportunity for exercise. Clubs employ dancers and other nightclub staff and economically support a workforce of service providers, from beverages to furniture. The state gains tax revenue, tourism, and conventions.

Patrons find a change of pace in adult cabarets. Their tips to a dancer onstage and requests for individual dances for a fee and also tips (at the patron's table, couch, on his lap, or in a shower) represent a jackpot for dancers. Extended counterfeit intimacy is manifest in continuous tipping and repeatedly buying a dance and becoming a regular. Yet, patrons willingly risk exploitation of their seductive vulnerability when they enter a club to play the fantasy game. Dancers talking to patrons can put them at ease and make them feel good about themselves. Exotic dancers say they help some men perform their conjugal role by providing fantasy or giving suggestions on how to please a woman and rekindle a sexual flame in their marriage that has since dissipated. Thus, the performer-patron connection provides mutual pleasure. On occasion, one hears of a patron "addicted" to a club. What this means is unclear, especially since "striptease addiction" is not spelled out in the psychological literature.

The body's entire motor system is activated almost instantly by exposure to sexual images and the more intensely sexual the visuals, the stronger the electric signals emitted by the participants' spinal tendinous reflexes. However, the sensations of sexual arousal, desire, and excitement are governed by two basic and distinctively operating pathways in the brain—one that promotes sexual enthusiasm and another that inhibits it. Having sexual brakes not only dampens the urge to commit rape or sexual abuse, but also the desire, giving the lie to notions that "all men are the same" and would be likely to rape their way through the local maiden population if they thought they could get away with it.[37]

Some exotic dancers provide a kind of "therapy" for those patrons who want a sympathetic ear for their woes. In a study that compared patients treated by trained psychotherapists and another group treated by humanities professors with no psychological expertise, both groups reported improvement at the same rates. Jonathan Engel, a professor of health care policy at Baruch College, concludes that effective psychotherapy seems to require a willing patient and an intelligent and understanding counselor who meet and speak regularly in confidence.

Working with his patients, psychoanalyst Michael Bader gleaned insights into possible patron motivation to fantasize in exotic dance clubs. He argues that pathogenic beliefs in childhood account for sexual fantasies, which are an attempt to solve problems without compromise or accommodation in what is required in a real relationship. The function of sexual fantasy is to undo the beliefs and feelings interfering with sexual excitement, to ensure both our safety and our pleasure. Our fantasies convince us that we're not going to harm or betray anyone and that if we feel fully aroused, no one will suffer.

Moreover, with the ever-present risk of deadly sexually transmitted diseases, sexual fantasy is safe "sex." Peter S. Statts, Division of Pain Medicine, Johns Hopkins University, reported at the American Pain Society October 1999 meeting that envisioning pleasurable sexual fantasies increased pain tolerance, improved mood, reduced worry and tension, and enhanced participants' feelings of self-worth.

The fantasy and dancer-patron touch of exotic dance have additional health benefits. Researchers found that touch releases the hormone oxytocin, which is associated with emotional safety.[38] Touch promotes enhanced health and well-being and mitigates the destructive effects of negative environmental events, injury, infection, and social isolation, now considered a major health risk. The release of oxytocin creates a psychological bond that appears to ward off some of the physical, as well as psychological, ill effects of stress. It also lowers blood pressure, heart rate, and cortisol levels for up to several weeks. VCG Holding Corp., which operates adult entertainment clubs in ten states, hired Empire Research, based in New York City, to find out why guys go to adult clubs, why they stay there, and why they come back. According to VCG president Michael Ocello, the report suggests that going to adult entertainment clubs can reduce stress by decreasing cortisol, elevating testosterone, and releasing oxytocin, which creates a sense of well-being. In addition, visiting an adult club stimulates the same parts of a couple's brains that were stimulated when they first started going out. Ocello recalled, "Women have been telling me for years that if you want to spice up what happens when you get behind the bedroom doors, you have to spice up what happens before you get there."[39]

Trying out exotic dance is a way for the everyday woman to become comfortable with her body and get physically fit. Wives, girlfriends, and wannabes are purchasing videos that will help them use the art to heat up their relationships. These women are also flocking to classes where pros teach them how to stage striptease. The Learning Center in Malvern, Pennsylvania, offered a class in "The Art of Exotic Dancing for Everyday Women," and in a companion eighty-six-minute instructional video, an exotic dancer with twenty-three years of experience teaches students, from different backgrounds and ages (twenties to fifties) how to get in touch with their femininity and denied sexuality through striptease dance. There is even pole dancing for Jesus. Crystal Deans, a former exotic dancer, offers free monthly classes to women who bring church programs to her Best Shape of Your Life studio in Spring, Texas.[40]

Thus far in sharing my odyssey toward understanding the adult entertainment exotic dance, I have explored reasons for CR hostility toward this popular entertainment and CR-Activists' battle tactics against it. We have considered the reality of exotic dance, what's going on between dancer and patron inside the club, why they are there, and the benefits they get. And with patronage that sustains an industry and many everyday women legitimizing stripper moves and poles as mainstream exercise and fun, why is it that some lawmakers and judges are still clucking their tongues and supporting the suppression of exotic dance and the violation of our civil liberties? Putting the matter of nudity and touch in historical and contemporary context makes the CR-Activist specific attack on them in exotic dance appear unseemly.

# Nudity, Touch, and Sex

## Marginal or Mainstream?

Nakedness reveals itself. Nudity is placed on display. The nude is condemned to never being naked. Nudity is a form of dress.

JOHN BERGER

If all you see is the hole . . . you look like the ass.

ANONYMOUS DANCER

## "Sinful Nudity" Is American

The exposure of flesh, bodily touch, and sexuality—what CR-Activists assail as sinful in exotic dance clubs—has a long history in mainstream society. However, the concept of modesty has changed over time for most people. For example, the amount of flesh that could be displayed has increased from the feet upward until bathing suits in public reveal all but the genitalia, buttocks cleft, and areola. In the media, underwear went public, then bodies, with frontal nudity, the flaunting of body parts, and simulated sex.

Of course, the meaning of nudity has a historical context. In the 1820s, public debates over nudity focused on the length of ballet dancers' costumes. At that time, a leg was called a "limb," and it was covered, even for sunbathing and swimming. In 1827, citizens reviled a French ballet dancer, Madame Francisque Hutin, for the "public exposure of a naked female." She wore a long silk skirt covering loose trousers fastened at the ankle. A glimpse of a loose trouser-clad thigh when the dancer pirouetted and her skirt flew up was conflated with total nudity—yet not an inch of flesh beneath the waist showed; nor was the costume translucent.[1]

Public nudity appeared in the 1840s theatrical *tableaux vivants*: female performers posed as "classical nudes" on revolving turntable stages to allow "more revealing" views. The "living statues" only slightly changed positions. The twentieth century saw the fully nude moving body in all kinds of performing arts. The emphasis on physical fitness contributed to a body culture orientation.

Moving nude dancers in popular art appeared from 1912–1929 in Florenz Ziegfeld's revues in New York City. Flirting with naughtiness, the revues at first presented feminine nudity veiled. In 1923, Carrie Finnell, a vaudeville tap dancer, took off articles of clothing to keep the audience's attention. Unembellished nudity was still taboo at this time, so dancers used gimmicks to give the illusion of nudity, such as anal cleft-concealing G-strings with glued pubic hair. Dancers also wore wraps that enabled them to flash nudity, delivering quick intimate glimpses.

In the 1930s, Sally Rand covered and fleetingly exposed her nudity with two huge ostrich fans. A consequence of her influence was the transformation of burlesque in the late 1940s from a focus on slapstick and satiric comedy to a preoccupation with bare female flesh and the strip club, which evolved into the exotic dance gentlemen's club. Famous strippers from that time included Lili St. Cyr, who had studied ballet; Tempest Storm (I saw her still dancing at the 2002 Miss Exotic World Pageant); and Gypsy Rose Lee, the first star performer at Minsky's Republic Theater in 1931. Since the latter half of the nineteenth century, burlesque dancers—forerunners of exotic dancers—were pacesetters in bodily disclosure in mainstream society, and they challenged the preservation of the bourgeois, patriarchal social order. Indeed, the credit for some of women's gains in sexual freedom over the past hundred years must go to entertainers, for it is impossible to make this kind of gain without women who are willing to work on the marginal cutting edge of society.

Topless dancing, showing the full bare breast, evolved from burlesque and was prevalent by 1932. This semi-nudity has persisted as a precursor to the contemporary full nude dancing that became popular after World War II and has come to define adult entertainment exotic dance for more than fifty years.

To place exotic dance in context, nudity is now an embedded tradition in theater (plays and musicals), opera, and theater dance (for example, ballet, modern, jazz). A form of costume, nudity communicates a variety of messages that comes from people's traditional and changing ideas, behavior, and tolerance in mainstream everyday and theatrical life, as well as an individual's experience and perception.

Many non–Christian Right and other religious and non-religious groups do not consider nudity on any stage to be sinful or degrading. After all, nude bodies are part and parcel of nudist camps, many beaches, and some college antics. The amicus briefs in support of free expression in the Supreme Court case, City of Erie v. Pap's A.M., by the Erie Civic Theatre Association, Roadhouse Theatre for Contemporary Art, Center for Protection of

Free Expression, Alley Theatre, Association of Performing Arts Present-ers, actress Kathleen Chalfant, Dance/USA, playwright Tony Kushner, the Looking Glass Theatre Co., playwright Terrence McNally, Oregon Shake-speare Company, dancer/choreographer Yvonne Rainer, performance art-ist Rachel Rosenthal, Theater Artaud, Theatre Communications Group, and the Walker Art Center provided innumerable examples of the meaning of nudity.

Conventional wisdom is that the purpose of nudity in exotic dance is to erotically excite and to convey messages of sexuality, temptation and al-lurement, pretense of sexual availability, and longing. But nudity on stage may convey messages of humiliation, moral decay, shame, oppression of women, and crime. Among some Africans—for example, the Igbo, Ibibio, and Yoruba in Nigeria; Kikuyu in Kenya; and Kom in Cameroon—women showing themselves nude is an act of shaming, a great curse, and a refusal to recognize male authority.[2]

Nudity may refer to divine manifestation, affirmation of life, and sexu-ality intertwined with spirituality. Religious importance attaches to body image, for the body is embodied religion.[3] Nudity may be the perfect dress because no cloth is worthy of some performers. Genesis recognizes that God created Adam and Eve in his own image, naked: "And God saw ev-erything that he had made, and, behold, it was very good" (Genesis 1:31). Some people claim it was not Adam's nakedness that was his sin, but, rath-er, his disobedience to God by eating the fruit that God forbade (Genesis 3:10–11). A preacher says that not once are we told that God disapproved of David dancing naked in the street after a battle victory, Isaiah walking naked from town to town prophesying, St. Francis of Assisi wandering the land naked, or Jesus being baptized naked.[4] Christianity has demonstrat-ed respect for the nude human body as evidenced by the Vatican's thou-sands of sculptures and paintings of the naked human form.

The CR does not appear to be aware of or appreciate American culture's use of nudity as a metaphor in theater to convey a variety of messages. Indeed, nudity may be the very medium to criticize aspects of American society that the CR also abhors. Performing artists often choose nudity to communicate messages of freedom, independence, acceptance of the body, modernity, and relief from artificial and arbitrary social conven-tions. Nudity reflects the historical tension between how the body was revealed in the past and is revealed now and represents a challenge to conservatives. Through nudity, performers may communicate messages of self-love and esteem, glamour, and youth. Nudity can also signal being unashamed and understanding what it is to be human.

Performing artists may communicate yet other messages about, for example, nature, nurturance, birth, harmony, honesty, lack of disguise, simplicity, innocence, and the satisfying of curiosity. There is an awesomeness about the woman's body—the source of all human life. The absence of pubic hair—which, at one time, was illegal to show—signals prepubescence and virginal innocence; it's like sanitized classical statues. After early humans lost most of their body hair and were naked for some time, they made clothes that attracted the dirty human body louse (evolved from the human head louse) that lives only in clothing; thus, nudity can convey cleanliness, health, and wholesomeness. Nudity may be selected for artistic purposes to convey the fragility, vulnerability, ugliness, disease, and mortality common to all humans.

Nudity may be an integral part of creative work in plays and musicals. The following are but a few such productions given in large and small localities across the United States. *Fräulein Else*, a production of the McCarter Theatre, Princeton, New Jersey, focuses on a nineteen-year-old placed in a morally repugnant situation by her father, who needs money within forty-eight hours to avoid financial ruin and imprisonment. Her parents suggest she use her feminine charm to obtain money from a former elderly client. In return for his money, Else must stand naked before him for fifteen minutes. Standing naked on stage, she finds her complete physical submission to be inherent in his demand.

Stagings of Shakespeare's *Romeo and Juliet*, *Measure for Measure*, *Othello*, and *Macbeth* have included nudity. Indeed, the Washington Shakespeare Company in the Washington, DC, metropolitan area played *Macbeth* in the "full Monty." A critic called the all-nude production "eerie, intelligent and visually arresting." But "we become inured to the nudity."[5] Nudity is seen in many theatrical works, including the New York Shakespeare Festival's *Hair*, Peter Shaffer's *Equus*, Peter Cattaneo's *The Full Monty*, Paul Foster's *Tom Paine*, Michael McClure's *The Beard*, Tom Eyen's *The Dirtiest Show in Town*, Tom Stoppard's *Travesties*, Terrence McNally's *Love! Valour! Compassion!* and *Lisbon Traviata*, David Edgar's *Pentecost*, Sam Shepard's *Curse of the Starving Class*, Norman Allen's *Nijinsky's Last Dance*, Ovid's *Metamorphoses*, Mary Zimmerman's *S/M*, David Kershar's *The Naked King*, Bruce Norris's *The Vanishing Twin*, David Rabe's *Hurly Burly* and *In the Boom Boom Room*, David Hare's *The Blue Room* and *The Judas Kiss*, Tracy Letts's *Killer Joe*, David Dillon's *Party*, Bill Corbett's *The Big Slam*, Anita Gabrosek's *Disengaged*, Heiner Müller's *Hamletmachine*, Charles L. Mee's *Big Love*, Martha Clarke's *The Garden of Earthly Delights* and *Vers la Flamme*, Caryl Churchill's *Mad Forest* and *Cloud Nine*, Elizabeth Egloff's *The Swan*, John Guare's *Six Degrees of Separa-*

tion, Doug Wright's *Quills*, Craig Lucas's *Missing Persons*, Christopher Kyle's *The Monogamist*, Jules Feiffer's *Carnal Knowledge*, Lorraine Hansberry's *Les Blancs*, David Storey's *The Changing Room*, Richard Adler and Jerry Ross's *Damn Yankees*, Fred Ebb and John Kander's *Cabaret*, Tennessee Williams's *A Streetcar Named Desire* and *Orpheus Descending*, Simon Morley's *Puppetry of the Penis*, and Duncan Sheik and Steven Sater's *Spring Awakening*. And there are many more examples.

Non-erotic nudity symbolizes the ravages of disease and the characters' physical and emotional vulnerability in Tony Kushner's *Angels in America, Parts 1 and 2*. In Margaret Edson's play, *Wit*, the lead succumbs to cancer, shedding her clothes as physical deterioration and fragility are put aside and the spirit is released in freedom.

Musicals such as *Hair*—a rock musical by Gerome Ragni, James Rado, and Galt MacDermot, which opened October 29, 1967—brought nudity, including a glance at pubic hair, to a New York City Broadway theater. The 1969 musical *Oh! Calcutta!* by Kenneth Tynan and Jacques Levy, showed female and male frontal nudity, extremely close couples, and group body contact. The musical questions the standards of morality, sexuality, individualism, racism, violence, drug use, loyalty, and social acceptance in America. Robert Schrock's *Naked Boys Singing*, a 1999 musical revue presented at the Actor's Playhouse in New York's Greenwich Village pokes fun at customary mores. Stephen Sondheim and James Lapine's *Passion*; John Kander, Fred Ebb, and Terrence McNally's *Kiss of the Spiderwoman*; and A. R. Gurney's *Sweet Sue* feature scenes with nudity.

Examples of nudity in opera include Richard Strauss's *Salomé*, Sergey Prokofiev's *The Fiery Angel*, Camille Erlanger's *Aphrodite*, Carlisle Floyd's *Susannah*, Hugo Weisgall's *Esther*, Giuseppe Verdi's *Rigoletto*, Richard Wagner's *Die Walküre*, Arrigo Boito's *Mefistofele*, Jules Massenet's *Hérodiade*, and Henry Purcell's *The Indian Queen*.

Nudity is part of theater dance (including musicals that feature a lot of dance). In the first three decades of the twentieth century, the famous American modern dancer Isadora Duncan established nudity or near-nudity as an important element of her art. Her work projected modern, liberated, natural humanity in an age of factory mechanical production, when women's clothing took a turn toward the unnatural with corsets and heels. Later landmarks in mainstream dance theater included California-based Anna Halprin's *Parades and Changes*, which premiered in New York City in April 1965. Dancers undressed and dressed three times to convey the idea of finding your identity and place in space. The performance led to a warrant for Halprin's arrest. She did not stage the piece again until

1995, as part of her seventy-fifth birthday retrospective show. Subsequent milestones did not occasion police interference. Yvonne Rainer's *Trio A*, performed in 1966 in New York City, showed nude dancers with American flags hanging from their necks in protest against repression and censorship. The 1970 classical ballet *Mutations*, by Glen Tetley and Hans van Manen, revealed a nude man dancing a slow solo, a nude couple performing an entwining duet, and three nude henchmen. *Mutations* is a contemporary danced ritual for the transformation of the human body and a celebration of movement.

American choreographer Mark Morris's *Striptease*, with its "down to the buff" commentary on the anti-eroticism and loneliness of burlesque, created an uproar in Belgium in 1988. Director of dance at the Théâtre Royale

*Mutations,* © photographer Antony Crickmay/V&A Theatre/Victoria and Albert Museum, London.

de la Monnaie, where the queen sometimes occupies a box, Morris performed nude. "Artified" is what Morris disparagingly calls forms of dance that traffic in sexual teasing disguised as beautiful, virtuosic dancing. He is interested in exposing the buttocks, that is, the innocent, hardworking motor of action, soft and round, seat of humility, and vulnerable target that gets kicked. He also focuses on the crotch, giving birth, disclosing something private inside being forced out. Bill T. Jones's much-acclaimed modern dance *Last Supper at Uncle Tom's Cabin/The Promised Land*, first performed in 1990 and in several cities, featured nudity among an assemblage of up to fifty company and community members. Performers were tall and short, fat and thin, black and white, old and young—all devoid of disguise, vulnerable, and unashamed, pulling together against the disparate strains of conflict over race, sexual orientation, gender, poverty, and age. Jones conveys our common humanity. The nudity of the all-male modern Creach/Koester Dance Company in its 1998 *Study for a Resurrection*, performed in St. Mark's Church in New York City, affirmed the body's beauty and vulnerability. For years, choreographers/dancers Eiko and Komo have appeared nude on stages across the United States. "Naked: A Living Installation" was performed in March 2011. A naked man and woman move with glacial slowness, intimate scale, and audience proximity. "We can see their stomachs and chests moving as they breathe, almost feel the tiny shifts of a finger or a foot." [6]

Although nudity in mainstream dance is not usually targeted, as are the nudity "sins" attributed to exotic dance, Concerned Christians for Good Government in Durham, North Carolina, angrily complained about male and female nudity during the 1979–1981 American Dance Festival (ADF) performances. Housed at Duke University, ADF is a revered summer dance program that offers college credit and presents new and established modern dance works. The festival's director recalled that Reverend Jerry Hooper asked, "'How many of you are going to be righteous or wicked?' . . . We got city funds to support the Emerging Generation series, but there were repercussions and other money dried up."

In 2003, *Dance Magazine* remarked on the recent increase in performers appearing nude onstage. "It is about dancers doing what artists do—making meaning." Nudity, the magazine noted, has gone beyond the 1970s streaking, which was for shock effect. The meaning may be "a paean to the grace and beauty of the arrangement of the human body itself," "tribute or insult to contemporary standards of beauty," "movement possibilities that arise when the body is unimpeded by clothing," or "a subtext for the conveyance of straightforward honesty—the naked truth."[7]

134

Nudity is common in performance art. Examples include the works of Rachel Rosenthal, Karen Finley, and Tim Miller. Nudity, semi-nudity, and sexual activities are common in film and may in fact be shown in motion picture theaters to minors with parental consent. Examples of such films include *All that Jazz, American Pie, Troy, Swimming Pool, Something's Gotta Give, Monster,* and *In America.*

The CR considers topless dancing and even the old-fashioned pasties, which cover the nipple and areola, as nude and sinful. What the breast means to the bearers and beholders has cultural and personal resonance. The exotic dancer's uncovered breast may communicate many of the messages conveyed through nudity. Many American "tit" men have an almost hypnotic obsession with female orbs and get an erotic charge from them. Breasts dominate in men's magazines such as *Juggs, Voluptuous,* and *Busty Beauties.*

Yet, a review of 190 different societies[8] revealed that few insisted upon the concealment of women's breasts. Furthermore, there was no relationship between covering breasts and the importance of breast stimulation as a form of erotic play. People need scripts to define a situation as being potentially sexual.

Topless sunbathing in public venues is common in Europe. In many societies, men are sexually indifferent to the exposed fat-encased mammary gland. The nude female breast seen in public merely symbolizes fecundity and is regarded as a utilitarian appendage for suckling the young.

## Simulated Nudity

Simulated nudity—whatever that is—is often restricted in CR-Activist-initiated ordinances against exotic dance. In addition to nudity, what might be considered "simulated" nudity has been widespread in "high art" ballet and modern dance. The faux nudity of skintight leotards and body suits reveals nipples, genitals, and anal clefts. New York City Ballet choreographer George Balanchine's use of close-fitting sheaths approximated the flesh. Modern dance choreographer Mark Morris thinks that a dancer in a milliskin unitard or simulated sex pas de deux in ballet and modern dance is a great deal more "pornographic" than the nudity in his *Striptease.* Faux nudity appears in dance performances in high schools, colleges, and community centers. The John F. Kennedy Center for the Performing Arts, Washington, DC, gave public school students a cue sheet designed to help them understand and enjoy American Ballet Theatre's *Without Words.* The sheet states, "The women wear flesh-colored leotards and the men wear flesh-colored shorts. The simple costumes emphasize the shapes created by the dancers' bodies."

## Self-Touch

The City Attorney in Seattle focused on the female genitalia because people don't like to speak about "down there." He hoped to get the jury to associate the dancer with wanton lewdness and obscenity as well as inciting men to criminal acts by continually mentioning her "unmentionable." He failed, and the jury acquitted the dancer after viewing the video and hearing my explanation of the artistic, communicative meaning of a dancer creating artistic patterns on her body through self-touch.

Self-touch is part of artistic expression in many forms of dance and other performing arts. I touch myself in jazz, flamenco, salsa, hip-hop, and Middle Eastern dance. I slap my buttocks and sensuously run my hands down the sides of my breasts and hips and across the front of my torso. In the nineteenth century romantic ballet, La Sylphide, self-touch is both provocative and protective when a man approaches. The incessant, preening self-touch of The Firebird, an early twentieth century classic ballet, is a marker of her sexual allure. US pioneer modern dancer Ruth St. Denis choreographed Radha with a section called the "Dance of Touch." Her palms stroke her arms, the back of her hands caress her face, and she traces the outlines of her breasts and hips.[9]

Sensual self-touch in public is exemplified by many pop stars. Michael Jackson clutched his crotch in concert and on television, and Madonna touched her buttocks and breasts. Tai chi, a Chinese martial art described as slow-motion kung fu, in essence a dance, uses self-touch: moving both hands down one's backside over the buttocks.

## Dancer-Patron Touch

You can do it at the airport, on the beach, and in mainstream theater. Performers paw patrons in the Broadway musical Cats. Many mainstream dances have performer-audience touch.[10] But no touching in an adult entertainment exotic dance club? Some governments claim any pressing of the flesh in that setting, even a handshake, to be obscene, clearly diminishing an erotic message. Yet, heterosexual body contact in dance has a long history. In a 1799 account of the waltz at its loosest, the man grasped the long dress of his partner, so that it would not drag and be trodden upon, and lifted it high, covering both bodies closely as they whirled on the dance floor. His supporting hand lay firmly on her breasts, at each movement pressing lustfully.[11]

In *City of Anaheim v. Janini* (1999), a California state judge, in his ruling on lap dancing, referred to the "dime-a-dance"—that is, taxi dancing—as an established tradition in America dating from the 1920s and continuing today. For a fee, men could dance with a woman in a taxi dance hall or palace. Taxi dancers were so named because, like taxis, their services were hired by customers for short periods and metered by a time clock. Grinding bodies tightly together without moving from a spot was "to dance on a dime." To urge the taxi dancer to keep the customer moving, the floor manager would say, "Git off dat dime!"

More than half a century ago, taxi dances caused public outcries about touching, privacy, prostitution, morality, and government regulation—issues still on the table today concerning the ten to twenty dollars or more lap dance. A social reform movement sought to wipe out taxi dancing, considering it prostitution. But patrons reported it was hard "to make these girls." And police can't arrest a man for what occurs in the privacy of his own pants. Between 1920 and 1940, taxi dancing primarily attracted European immigrants. A taxi dance hall in Chicago had at one time six hundred men and sixty-eight girls. In 1930, New York City had thirty-seven dime-a-dance palaces, thirty-five thousand to fifty thousand male customers per week, and twenty-five hundred to three thousand employed female dancers. Women initially danced in same-sex pairs, some performing a twisting of the hips to showcase their attributes in order to sell dances to the men. When dancing with customers, the women rubbed their bodies against them and wriggled. Some dancers allowed men to dance behind them and fondle their breasts. Women eager to dance more sensually moved to the center of the hall, where they could not be clearly observed by the other patrons who were on the sidelines. If a cop arrived unannounced, common on Saturday nights, the orchestra started playing the waltz "Margie" to alert the dancers.[12] Females almost always captured more denunciation than their male partners because the middle-class reformers were obsessed with instilling in the dancers the virtues of "true womanhood."

Taxi dancing has existed in clubs in Latino barrios for more than thirty years. In California, the dancers attract mainly undocumented immigrants from Mexico, who enjoy the music, the female companionship, and the courtesy denied at other places where women treat them "like dirt." In New York City, Dominican American women from Manhattan go to Queens on the weekends to dance the *bachata* and *cumbia* in bars and nightclubs frequented by lonely Ecuadorian and Mexican men. The taxi dancers earn from fifty to one hundred and fifty dollars a night. The large two dollar-a-dance halls attract young men and women. The smaller clubs and bars draw workers after their restaurant work shifts end about midnight; the dancers there tend to be slightly older, friendlier, and maternal.

Today lap dance moves are similar to young adult and junior and high school student male-female social dance partnering in "da butt," "freaking," "booty dancing," "doggy dancing," "front piggy-backing," or "dirty dancing."[13] Lap dancing differs from taxi dancing and social dancing in several ways: the female exotic dancer has little or no clothing, the men usually keep their hands off the women, the dance takes place in a licensed adult entertainment club, and the dancers can earn one hundred and fifty to one thousand or more dollars a night.

Booty Dancing, photographer Angela Cluchey.

## Simulated Sex

Whatever simulated sex is—for example, a metaphor for broader human communication—CR-Activists fight what they fantasize. The meaning is in the eyes of the beholder. Randall Bezanson gives many examples of how a viewer ascribes meaning. The eye and brain perceive what is then neurologically filtered and reconstructed in light of the person's culture and experience.

People dramatically can differ in their perceptions of the same dance, as I found in my study, *The Performer-Audience Connection: Emotion to Metaphor in Dance and Society*. In an audience with members of ordinary intelligence, 45 percent of the survey respondents saw no emotion in a duet involving a male and female dancer, whereas 55 percent observed simulated sex, "x-rated." A male engineer's perception made him feel "horny." A male lawyer saw ecstasy as the dancers were "lying as if spent," and he felt "excited." By contrast, some people described the same duet as mechanical, stilted, robot-like, and computerized. "It made me feel like I was watching androids or mechanical mannequins," said a respondent. The audience will create all sorts of narratives to account for the movements of dancers onstage—regardless of the choreographer's or performer's intention.

In *The Relativity of Icarus* (1974), two male dancers represent the mythic airborne figures of Daedalus and Icarus. They touch each other in a cantilevered duet. Some spectators viewed the dancers as father and son, which they are in the story, while others saw an implicit simulation of homosexual love.

"Simulated sex" could be interpreted to encompass the pelvic action that is integral to the dances of Latinos seen onstage and off. These dances include the rumba, cha-cha, and mambo from Cuba; bolero from Puerto Rico; samba from Brazil; and merengue from Haiti and the Dominican Republic. Mexicans dance to *banda* music with the *quebradita*, a little break in which the man straddles his partner and leans her back parallel to the ground. Forward and backward hugging bodies and intertwined legs characterize the hot *lambada* dance of Brazil.

Types of dance that could run afoul of indecent, lewd, and obscene regulations also include the social and theatrical flamenco dance, which expresses personal emotions of longing, love, passion, and pride. The concept of *duende* refers to a spirit or energy that induces a dancer into a kind of ecstatic state, exhibited by the flamenco's passionate body tension and release, facial concentration, hard-hitting foot stamping and staccato striking of heels on the floor, curvaceous fast movement, and knife-sharp pivots, in addition to the accompanying music and song. Respectable people in Argentina and the United States rejected the tango, born in Argentina, as "simulating sex." The public display of a couple in tight embrace, performing intricate footwork, has the effect of sexually arousing some observers.

Renowned early modern dancer Martha Graham, focusing on the beauty of the body, choreographed pelvic movements symbolic of the thrust of intercourse in her dances.[14] Choreographer Christopher Wheeldon considers dance sexy, ballet being about the sensuality of young bodies moving, some ballets being explicit about simulating intercourse. To wit, a man and woman consummate a marriage in George Balanchine's *Bugaku*. Robert Joffrey Ballet's *Astarte* has a male dancer strip his way to the stage from the audience seating area until he is in nothing but briefs; he engages in sexual gyrations with his partner, the goddess Astarte, until each one separately reaches a simulated climax. The Washington Ballet presented a cabaret called 7 x 7 in its school rehearsal hall: seven commissioned works in seven minutes, all on the theme of love. This kind of production, too, could run afoul of ordinances banning simulated sex.

CR-Activists single out the marginal adult cabaret nudity, simulated nudity, self-touch, touch of another, and simulated sex for opprobrium at the same time mainstream theater examples abound in past and contemporary history. I spotlight two kinds of litigation that stem from CR views and CR-Activist action. The first case involves bench trials in Maryland in which I was involved for nearly a decade. The second case illustrates jury trials in Minnesota in which I also played a role. These cases have similarities as well as substantive, contextual, and legal differences.

# "Rottweilers" Lock Their Jaws

Bench Trials

Going after nude dancers is easier than catching murderers.

CLUB OWNER

In 1996, Councilman Walter Maloney of Prince George's County, Maryland, contacted a Christian Right organization, the National Law Center for Children and Families, known for being an adult business killer. Maloney wanted assistance in developing a proposed adult use zoning bill. The County overlooked what Judge Herbert F. Murray had said in federal court about a Maryland case, *Hughes v. Cristofane* (1980). In that case, the judge ruled that it is not a substantial government interest for the Town Council of Bladensburg in Prince George's County to regulate adult entertainment.

## Arrests in a Family Business

Morality in Prince George's County led to an uncivil, expensive police raid on the small, unassuming Showcase Theater. It had no citations for violating the law. Yet on March 22, 1999, at eleven o'clock on a Saturday night, ten dancers at the small one-stage private club seating up to seventy-five customers were arrested for public indecency by a thirty-person riot squad! The raid is all the more shocking because the establishment is a family-owned business, located in an industrial area, not visible from a main street, difficult to find, and the only business open at night in that area.

Larry Bledsoe, a former thirty-year US government employee, is a member of the six-person corporation that owns Showcase Theater. In 1996, his daughter told him she was a nude dancer. He was devastated: "I didn't think I brought up my daughter that way." "Samantha" explained to her parents that dancing was a legitimate business, and that they should see for themselves. Dancers needed costumes, so she suggested that they could visit clubs to sell costumes. Bledsoe and his wife, Fran, decided to do just that.

Eventually, on November 13, 1998, Bledsoe, Fran, "Samantha," her husband, and a doctor and his wife opened Showcase Theater in the Beltsville area of Prince George's County. Modeled after Tampa's Mons Venus, it is a no-alcohol private nude club with stage and lap dancing. Dancing since age three and a graduate of Suitland Performing Arts High School, "Samantha," who is also a paralegal, danced at Showcase until she became pregnant.

Showcase Theater patrons pay an annual eight-dollar membership, or a three-dollar-per-visit, plus a twelve-dollar entrance fee. Independent contractors, the dancers fill out an application form, audition, and are selected on the basis of appearance, ability to dance, experience, and agreement to random drug testing. The six to twenty dancers scheduled each night have included a former FBI agent, teachers, single moms, secretaries, and college students. In a lap dance area, topless dances cost thirty dollars; with bikinis, twenty dollars. The dancers pay the club five dollars per lap dance up to twelve dances, after which they keep the full fee.

According to club officials, dancers, police, and press reports, the riot squad entered the club with weapons in full combat readiness: laser guns

Showcase Theater.

pointing at dancers, twenty customers, a manager, a bartender, and two owners. The police forced the customers and dancers to lie spread-eagle on the floor with hands behind their heads and the others to kneel as they were handcuffed. The police threatened, "Don't move or talk or we will use physical force and fuck you up." An officer wearing combat boots kicked a dancer in the ribs and bruised her. Customers were searched and their identification checked against a computer listing. Joining the Prince George's County police officers in the raid were Sheriff Department deputies and officials of the State's Attorney's Office, which had obtained a warrant for arrests. The warrant triggered C-MAST—County Multi-Agency Services Team—action (about twenty agencies including fire, health, building, and public works) to find any kind of code violation.

The police forced the first dancer processed to go outside in pouring rain. Barefoot, in her bikini, hands cuffed by a plastic strip behind her back, she was ordered to get into the rear of a seat-less old van/paddy wagon that had broken glass covering the floor. The dancers had to brush it aside so they could sit. Other dancers asked for a female officer to be in attendance while they changed from dance attire into street clothes.

Showcase Theater advertisement.

"Samantha."

Although two female officers were on the premises, three male officers watched the dancers. This violated the rules of the theater: onstage is public, but offstage is private! The police asked the dancers to sign a paper stating that they were forced by the club to dance nude. They refused. The police informed the dancers, who were held for five hours, why they were arrested only upon release, when they were given citations. The dancers were not finger-printed, presented before a magistrate or judge, or read their Miranda rights. Moreover, the police released their names to the press.

During the raid, the police damaged the Showcase Theater door frame to the ladies' bathroom, the laser light system, the locks to the dancers' personal lockers, and two plastic containers. The police seized property that included six thousand dollars in cash, a checkbook, a camera, files, computer memory, a handwritten log of club needs, the membership list, contracts, a lease, and bills.

Showcase Theater owners Larry Bledsoe and George Kopp and manager Joseph Johnson were charged with ten counts of "conspiracy to violate public indecency laws" for nude dancing, a misdemeanor carrying a penalty not to exceed a fine of one thousand dollars or six months in jail or both. Ten dancers were each charged with conspiracy. The County

Code defines nudity as "a state of undress so as to expose the post-pubertal human male or female genitals, pubic area or buttocks with less than a full opaque covering, or the showing of the female breast with less than a fully opaque covering or any portion thereof below the top of the areola, or the depiction of covered or uncovered male genitals in a discernibly turgid state." Moreover, the club was cited for not having a dance hall license permitting dancing—lap dances—between entertainers and patrons. The club also received a zoning violation for lacking a valid use and occupancy permit—which it had.

## Why Raid Showcase Theater?

A law on the county books had not been enforced. "We refuse to act . . . if they don't prosecute," Captain Gary Corso said. On- and off-duty police officers had visited Showcase Theater since its opening. The club was actually tipped off by an officer the night before and the night of the raid. Apparently, State's Attorney Jack Johnson enacted the complaint in response to church member agitation. "It was the state's attorney's gig," said a police officer.

In addition, the neighborhood Vansville Heights Civic Association doesn't like adult businesses. Its members fear the proliferation of adult businesses will spoil their town's image. Showcase Theater was the fourth adult-oriented business that located in the Beltsville Route 1 corridor. The others are Warwick Books, Adult Lingerie Center, and Diablos, a small exotic dance biker bar that evoked community complaints about noise and rowdiness. The night of the Showcase raid, Diablos received a police knock on the door and citations for liquor and flashing (dancers showing nudity).

Swales Aerospace objected to the opening of Showcase Theater because it is in the path of Swales's employees, customers, and potential customers traveling by foot and vehicle to its thirteen buildings in the Paulen Industrial Center. Elmer W. Travis, president of Swales, complained that Showcase Theater appeared to be a disreputable establishment that would attract undesirable individuals to the area and make those conducting business at Swales uncomfortable. Showcase Theater opened weekdays at 3 p.m., starting December 14, 1998. Later, it changed its hours to open at 6 p.m.

Prince George's County Councilman Maloney and State Senator Arthur Dorman had told Captain Corso that they were *personally offended by the clubs*. Of course, no one was forcing them to attend these businesses. Dorman then led an effort to prompt the State's Attorney's Office to conduct the raid. On December 23, 1998, Maloney requested that the Prince

George's Office of Business and Regulatory Affairs conduct an investigation of Showcase Theater and that the Director of Public Safety more actively enforce the county ordinance limiting nude performances. Maloney sent copies of these requests to Captain Corso, Corporal Frank Tremper, Gloria Robinson of the Vansville Heights Civic Association, and Karen Coakley of the Beltsville Civic Association. On February 2, 1999, Maloney wrote to the president of the Economic Development Corporation: "It would be of great mutual benefit if you could support my efforts to enhance the business and quality of life climate in the Vansville area by removing and limiting the spread of sexually oriented businesses."

Senator Dorman's anti-obscenity bill, introduced on December 18, 1998, had gone nowhere. Rumor was that he threatened to withhold funding for the State's Attorney's Office unless there was a raid. Jack Johnson's office obtained an arrest warrant for the raid, estimated to cost twenty to thirty thousand dollars. The state is trying "to kill a fly with a sledgehammer," said one observer. Maloney asserted, "We'll keep putting pressure on them until they leave." Dorman echoed the sentiment: "My hope is that we keep harassing the clubs until they get the hell out of here."

## Club Fights and Wins First Round

Showcase Theater fought back in court, invoking the US Constitution's free speech protection. Dance is language-like artistic expression. It is not mute. At the initial court hearing, the Showcase Theater lawyer, Richard I. Kovelant, told the judge that an anthropologist with expertise in dance as nonverbal communication (me) would be testifying.

Jabeen Bhatti, a reporter for the *Washington Times* who had interviewed my husband about his research in the Langley Park area of Prince George's County, called him to find out my views. He told her to interview me directly. She assured me that the conservative viewpoint of her paper—as well as her close association with Assistant State's Attorney Michael Herman, who was present at the first court hearing and wanted to know what my position was—would not affect her professionalism. Bhatti said she wanted to see a balanced article and was helping another reporter write the story. She had accurately reported my husband's views, and she had trained at Columbia University's Graduate School of Journalism (Columbia is one of my alma maters), so I took her at her word. I spent time with her, explaining what exotic dance is, its history, how it communicates, the myth of adverse secondary effects, and the laws related to freedom of expression, especially in Maryland.

Contrary to what Bhatti had told me, her own byline appeared in a *Washington Times* article—*minus* nearly all the information I gave her. Instead, she reported the adverse secondary effects myth about exotic dance. Then a *Washington Times* editorial (January 16, 2000) indignantly spotlighted Bhatti's statement as reported on its metropolitan page (December 23, 1999):

> Exotic dance adult entertainment with its nudity, and occasionally a performance sitting on a patron's lap, is a form of dance, art and fantasy that conveys various messages, says Professor of Dance at University of Maryland, Judith Lynne Hanna. . . . There are actually lots of acts that might fall under Mrs. Hanna's description which yet bear no relationship to the First Amendment—and which don't belong in a family newspaper either.

TV Channels 5 and 8 and the American Radio Urban Networks (with 115 affiliates) captured this news and asked me to elaborate about exotic dance and the court case, which I did. Several dancers and I exchanged perspectives.

On December 16, 1999, defense lawyer Kovelant submitted a motion to dismiss the criminal charges stemming from the Showcase Theater raid on several grounds. He argued that Showcase Theater was not a "public place" as defined in the County Code: "any park, lake, stream, stadium, athletic field, playground, school yard, street, avenue, plaza, square, bus, train, or rail depot, station terminal, cemetery, open space adjacent thereto, or any other place commonly open to the public." Unlike these places, Showcase Theater is a private club located in a private building in an industrial area. Advertised as an adult club with nude dancing, it charges admission and membership. The lawyer pointed out that the legislature sought to protect an unsuspecting public against exposure to nudity as contrasted with people intentionally choosing to view nudity in a theater cloistered from public view. The defense argued that Prince George's County exempted public nudity in certain performance areas associated with a production. Showcase Theater dancers performed in a theater with lighting, stage, costumes, props, and musical accompaniment. Kovelant cited my explanation of exotic dance. Most importantly, the defense argued that the Prince George's statute was unconstitutional for being overbroad by sweeping within its prohibitions what may not be punished under the First and Fourteenth Amendments, in addition to having a chilling effect on free expression.

In court on December 17, 1999, the attorney for the state, Jay Madden, surprisingly acted like a spoiled little boy. He actually rubbed his genitals in the courtroom. He objected to my presence as an expert court witness and claimed nude dancing for sexual gratification was not art and not protected. It was his responsibility to produce the record for the case, but he only had part of it. He took the partial file and ran away. Kovelant reported to the judge, "He disappeared and won't come back." So the judge sent the sheriff to bring Madden back to the courtroom and then reprimanded him, "Don't you ever take my files again."

After court, Kovelant bemoaned, "This is a cabbage patch city. I'm from New Jersey [meaning a more sophisticated place without lawyers like Madden]. The state's attorneys have no talent. . . . They knew the case was a loser and they needed a fall guy; that's why Madden was assigned and not dismissed."

On Valentine's Day, 2000, Princes George's County District Court Judge Thurman Rhodes, in *State of Maryland v. Bledsoe et al.*, dismissed criminal charges for nude dancing, ruling that it is protected under the US Constitution. He agreed that the County Code's definition of public place did not apply to Showcase Theater. Significantly, Judge Rhodes said the code:

> imposes a chilling effect on the constitutionally protected expression of nude dancing. Moreover, the legislative history and purpose of the County ordinance did not show how it furthers an important or substantial governmental interest. The specific regulation is clearly directly related to the suppression of free expression.

Two days later, I was on the Bev Smith Show of the American Urban Network for a two-hour radio interview about the decision.

Angered by the "Valentine's Day massacre," State's Attorney Jack Johnson and his assistant Jay Madden appealed the decision to the Circuit Court, which sent it back to the District Court for trial. Attorney Jonathan Katz argued that this was double jeopardy and the appeal went nowhere.

But Johnson was determined to continue to work with legislators against nude dancing. The game plan was to work against the clubs through the Alcoholic Beverage Control Board, County and State. Tactics apparently included harassment, including entrapment and set-ups. Although Showcase Theater and its attorneys have appeared before two different judges, the club has yet to recover requested property that had been seized in the raid. In an inspection, the Showcase Theater landlord was subjected to charges stemming from a "leaking roof" and "loose railing," which were fantasies.

Three weeks after Judge Rhodes's decision, a firebomb closed Showcase Theater for seven weeks. A gas can was found near where the arsonist went to work. When Bledsoe told me this, my first thought was "the government strikes again." But rumor has it that a disaffected dancer and a jealous club owner in nearby Baltimore, whose dancers had left to work at Showcase Theater, were involved. A week prior to the fire, Showcase Theater reprimanded and fined a dancer for letting a patron lick her. She cleared out her locker a few days before the fire and went back to a Baltimore club where she had danced and had an affair with the owner. With a relentless war against the clubs, internecine sabotage doesn't help.

## Round Two: The 2003 Attack

True to his word to continue the pressure against exotic dance clubs, Johnson, elected Prince George's County Executive, sent a draft of a new ordinance to the County Council in fall 2003. Former Assistant State's Attorney Herman was now Johnson's chief of staff. Ralph E. Grutzmacher, the legislative officer who drafted the bill to ban full nudity in public places, impose buffers between dancers and patrons, and require strip clubs and their managers to be licensed, told me it was in response to high demand for public safety services from adult entertainment-type activities, meaning homicides and brawls, that drained police resources. When I asked what the evidence was, he answered that he did not know of any. The police had said so, but he could not name one member of the police department. When I asked who would know, he referred me to the police chief; he was just a "pen," he noted.

When the Prince George's County Council introduced the new CB-86-2003 ordinance, the Office of Audits and Investigations determined that there should not be a negative fiscal impact on the county as a result of enacting the ordinance: "Additional revenue would be generated through the issuance of licenses and the penalties levied on violators. There will also be additional costs to the County for enforcement and background checks and related expenses." However, left out of the calculation was the fact that the ordinance would hurt the club businesses and cost the county lost taxes from these establishments, the services they purchased, and unemployed workers.

### Public Hearing on Proposed Exotic Dance Regulations

The court reporter's transcript of the Prince George's County Council public hearing on November 25, 2003, does not begin to capture the tenor of unprofessional behavior, the rudeness and ridicule of speakers by several of the councilpersons. One councilman sat up front picking his nose. Addressing the Council without evidence, Johnson contended that the clubs cause a burden on the County and that the ordinance was meant to prevent crime and eliminate the exploitation of young people. The mayor of Landover Hills, Neil Lee Walker, expressed this view: "These clubs are a blight on the community. Adult entertainment clubs . . . present a negative image on communities."

A local resident, Voltaire Ronquillo, mentioned that he did not want to have to answer his child's questions about the club. Kate Tsubata, president of the West Lanham Hills Citizens Association, linked an increase of rape and attempted rape in her neighborhood to "a highly criminally stimulating environment" due to clubs combining alcohol with highly sexually charged entertainment. Three men from her neighborhood were shot in the parking lot of Club Amazon. But the detective handling the case told me that those murders could have happened anywhere. Clubs were blamed for the lack of new quality development, an increase in vacancies, and a loss of the tax revenue base in the billions of dollars.

Local counsel for Showcase Theater, Jonathan Katz, offered, for the legislative record, a file box containing published studies and other research material on exotic dance clubs and their impact on communities. The material had been assembled by Luke Lirot, a First Amendment attorney in Florida. "Study after study, scientific study after scientific study, shows no significant negative secondary effects from adult entertainment," Katz told the County Council. My mini-study of police calls for service in Prince George's County supports this statement.

Lirot's letter to Katz on November 21, 2003, stated:

Quite candidly, . . . the characteristics of any individual business are the direct result of the responsibility and attention used by the owners and operators of any business, rather than the general nature or content of the expressive activities taking place therein. . . . The misunderstanding of adult businesses usually results in the adverse effect of precipitating unconstitutional, censorial, and divisive legislation, more so than anything else.

Councilwoman Marilynn Bland expressed the common sentiment in Prince George's County that those who live outside the county should stay there. She asked Katz, "What part of Prince George's County did you say you lived in?" He replied, "I do not live in Prince George's County. My client, Showcase Theater, is a business citizen of Prince George's County." Bland continued, "And where do you live?" Katz answered, "I live in Montgomery County." Bland asked, "So do you have strip clubs there and nude dancing that's allowed there?" Katz replied, "Montgomery doesn't have that and they should. They've got problems there, too. I've lived in DC for many years and only two or three miles down the street from me on Wisconsin Avenue are Good Guys and JP's, two adult entertainment establishments located next to many upscale establishments, including the new Russian Embassy. You will not see any negative secondary effects there." Annoyed, Bland retorted:

> I was just looking for a yes or no, really, where you live, because I would just hope you would recognize that *we're here, we recognize what's going on in Prince George's County* and maybe the effect . . . we have information for this jurisdiction, and we're here to make the decision. And I just find it appalling when . . . people can be on the outside and come and offer that type of testimony . . . . I can respect your right to speak . . . . I heard you say the box is there, but . . . you know, that's not important to me.

Katz responded:

> I spent a lot of time in Prince George's County. I was a public defender lawyer here for two years. You're going to be hearing from a Prince George's County corporate citizen, Larry Bledsoe, in a few moments. I am very familiar with what goes on in Prince George's County, and what I suggest is the way to attack crime and perceived blight is to attack it for that, not to send the First Amendment down the river in the process.

Of course, where a person lives has nothing to do with defending the First Amendment. Besides, many Prince George's residents and businesspeople support the clubs or they would go out of business in our capitalist society.

When Bledsoe got up to speak, Councilpersons David Harrington, Camille Exum, and Samuel Dean laughed during his presentation, perhaps out of embarrassment. Bledsoe explained:

> I became involved in operating Showcase Theater about five years ago after a thirty-year career with the federal government. I worked and served in such organizations as the US Customs Service, the Bureau of Alcohol, Tobacco and Firearms, the USDA's Office of Inspector General, and the Peace Corps. For over twenty of those thirty years, I was a supervisor and manager of both people and programs.
>
> I am opposed to CB-86-2003. It will cause Showcase Theater to close its doors as it will not be profitable. With the restrictions imposed in this ordinance, a dancer will not be able to express herself and to create an exotic fantasy for customers. Customers will go elsewhere, to other Counties, the District, or to underground operations. The bill will only stop legitimate adult businesses in Prince George's County; it will not stop the underground activities that thrive and tend to go beyond legal dancing.

The void will only create a greater demand for underground activities.

I assure you that Showcase Theater is operated strictly and with comprehensive policies and procedures in place to prohibit and to guard against illegal activities. We have a closed-circuit television system both inside and outside to protect both the customer and the dancer. These cameras are monitored and activities recorded to assist against any and all undesirable activities. We employ managers and bouncers as a means to head off any potential problems before they occur. All of these employees, as well as thirty-plus dancers, are tax-paying citizens. Many of them are single mothers, college students, or career-minded individuals who make extra money as a part-time dancer. All of these people will be out of work and some may go on your welfare rolls.

As a small family business, we pay our taxes, including federal, state and local taxes, along with personal property and real estate tax on the building housing Showcase Theater. This past year our real estate tax increased significantly as did the property value.

I urge you to withdraw CB-86-2003. In this day and age with increased crime, problems with education, health care, and with underpaid officers, teachers, and other government employees, our valuable monetary resources can be more effectively spent. It just doesn't make sense that Prince George's County is setting up an additional government structure and spending valuable resources to oversee and control a nude dancer. No evidence has been presented that shows that such dancing contributes to any adverse conditions.

I was stunned when Harrington furiously asked Bledsoe where he lived. Bledsoe said he had lived in Prince George's County for twenty-some years—until he was raided and a gun put to his head. The councilman mouthed "fuck" and barked, "I'm deeply offended by your remark, your testimony. . . . Sir, I find *your testimony to be offensive.* You suggest that because . . . you're going out of business . . . now we're going to increase the welfare rolls?" Bledsoe responded, "Where else are these single mothers going to get employed unless you're going to give them a job? Some of them type and some of them are managers." With disdain, Harrington continued:

Let me suggest something to you, sir, that I think we have enough jobs in Prince George's County where I would welcome the fact that they would resign and leave your establishment. And if your testimony—I found it humorous at first—but if your testimony . . . here, is that your business is needed to help fund schools and police officers, let me say that I will—I will personally recommend to the County Executive to use our reserves to

help fund those and wouldn't mind one minute . . . passing this legislation. I, in fact, think that this legislation doesn't go far enough, and if it
were not for the Office of Law who advised us, and let me say ably advised
us . . . I don't think Thomas Jefferson wrote the Constitution to allow public display such as what you've established, sir, I really don't.

Bledsoe then spoke up: "Can I ask you if you've been to a strip club?"
Harrington retorted, "And you expect me to say that publicly?" Bledsoe: "I
think I saw you one day over at . . . ." Harrington: "You think . . . ." Presid-
ing over the incredibly tense, heated, unruly hearing, Councilman Tony
Knotts urged:

> Wait, wait, wait, wait, wait, wait. There is [yelling]—*shut up*. There is a
> concern here. You cannot, I will not allow you to say what you said to my
> colleague. It's absolutely unfair, inappropriate, and it is not going to hap-
> pen here. It may happen in Montgomery County, it's not going to happen
> here. Do you understand that?

The exchange that followed went as thus:

> Bledsoe: "I apologize to you."
> Knotts: "Mr. Harrington?"
> Harrington: "Mr. Chairman, I thank you for your leadership, sir, because
> I was deeply offended by that . . . remark and I'm offended by the testi-
> mony. I am offended that someone would come—do you live in Prince
> George's County, sir?"
> Bledsoe: "I did, sir, for 27 . . ."
> Harrington: "No. Do you *live right now in Prince George's County?*"
> Bledsoe: "May I answer?"
> Harrington: "Go ahead."
> Bledsoe: "I do not live in Prince George's County right now. I lived for 27
> years in Prince George's County until this County raided my business and
> threw me on the floor, and handcuffed me over nude dancing."
> Harrington: "Mr. Chairman, I will try to act in the decorum way, but I
> find—and the lawyer here, you might as well take your box home, okay,
> but I find, I find your testimonies here . . ."

Colonel Jeff Cox, Prince George's County Police Department, also addressed the Council at the 2003 public hearing. *He did not single out licensed
exotic dance clubs as having problems.* Rather, he referred to places

> that advertise themselves as cafes, photo studios, event halls, or some
> other vague descriptor, but in fact they are hosting go-gos, live entertain-
> ment with alcohol consumption and various forms of adult entertain-

ment. . . . Many establishments have absentee owners that rent the space to anyone who is willing to pay. These often result in the property being used for large-scale events, drugs and alcohol, prostitution, dangerous levels of overcrowding and live adult entertainment. Frequently little or no notice is given to the police department prior to these events and we are often inadequately prepared to deal with the explosive violence that follows them. . . . In summary, these establishments that allow these types of entertainment and atmosphere that we are discussing today create a climate of lawlessness and violence. When you mix in the drugs, alcohol, and weapons that are often part of this overall experience, the recipe for tragedy is certainly present.

Seemingly, it did not matter to the Council that Cox's testimony did not apply to licensed exotic dance clubs.

LaVerne Williams, of Hyattsville, identified herself as president of the Lewisville Citizens Association and also as the chairperson of the Civil Association Group of Northern Prince George's County, which consists of eight communities in that general area. According to her testimony, it was a "terrible thing" for a nude club to place a poster on telephone poles in the community, "not at high, but down low where the little children going to school would see them. It's insulting to me that somebody would do this, and I'm a 78-year-old great-grandmother. . . . Also, we've had the problem of crime at these clubs."

A CR-Activist, Arthur McKnew, representing the Maryland Coalition against Pornography, which opposes any nudity whatsoever, provided testimony from "an exotic dancer who's one of our members. She's forty-five years old, has some lasting effects from her two years as an exotic dancer." Of course, many people have lasting effects from their workplace experience, whatever it is.

Samuel Karkenny, a businessman, testified about commercial concerns. He said the government wanted to drive the clubs out and take their land for development. The Council first took over car lots to repurpose them for development. He told the Council:

You know we have to address this gang problem particularly with our growing Hispanic community, in addition to our other situations. . . . I just want to see a cohesive plan of where we're going and this is what really bothers me. . . . I'd hate to get bogged down in courts with it.

I happened to speak with him after the hearing. He said he was single, goes to clubs, is a civil rights activist, and wanted to help the clubs.

Councilman Thomas Hendershot commented on exotic dance clubs—

obviously as a matter of faith because not a scintilla of evidence was offered during the hearing:

> In my view, they do exploit women in the worst kind of way and many
> believe that public safety concerns, including rape and prostitution and
> other sex-related crimes in neighboring communities, directly result from
> the presence of these establishments. That means we got to get a handle
> on this. . . and maybe even we need to get rid of them. For the benefit of
> those in the business that we've heard from, I am led to believe that there
> is a shortage of such establishments in Potomac, in Columbia, in An-
> napolis, in Bethesda, in many other upscale communities in Montgomery
> County, Fairfax County, Howard County, and others throughout our state
> and throughout this region. And I would encourage you to seek to pursue
> your commerce and pursue your businesses in those communities. And if
> you can't succeed there, why in the world would you think it's okay to pur-
> sue that commerce in . . . working-class communities like Prince George's
> County?

County officials said that because strip clubs in Prince George's have not
been regulated or licensed, they did not know how many were operating
in the county.

## Regulations (CB-86-2003) Passed

The Council certainly did not consider the opponents' voices and materials submitted at the hearing. It did not open "the box" nor did any of
the Council members read my submission on how exotic dance communicates. At the end of the public hearing, the Council voted unanimously
to ban full nudity in public places, impose buffers between dancers and
patrons, and require strip clubs and their managers to be licensed. Violations of the bill were subject to criminal penalties. The County Executive
signed the bill on December 3, 2003.

## Legal Challenge

On January 16, 2004, Luke Lirot and Jonathan Katz—on behalf of Showcase Theater and the clubs that joined the suit, Stardust Inn, Club Exstasy,
and Bazz & Crue—filed a complaint and asked for a preliminary injunction to prevent county threats to the First, Fifth, and Fourteenth Amendments to the US Constitution. The county agreed to abate enforcement of
the new ordinance pending a trial on the merits of the case. Federal Judge
Roger Titus consolidated this agreement with the request for a preliminary injunction. Backing away from a legal challenge, the County Council

passed Resolution No. CR-12-2004, repealing Chapter 81, 2003 Laws, the exotic dance club regulations, of Prince George's County. The US District Court for Maryland order on February 26, 2004, administratively closed the case. New legislation on the same subject was proposed for adoption at a later date.

It's par for the course that opponents in litigation try to discredit the opposition's proposed expert court witnesses. My experience has been that this usually occurs in court. But on December 22, 2005, I received a call from the University of Maryland Office of Legal Affairs that Maria Agres of Citizens against Exploitation of Women had submitted a Maryland Freedom of Information Act request for access to and a copy of the following:

1) Any and all documents, files, reports, correspondence and other records that concern, relate to, or evidence grants, grant application, grant receipts, research funding, and research-related financial records for or on behalf of Judith Lynne Hanna, currently a Senior Research Scholar at the University of Maryland–College Park. Pertinent records will also include those available from other University of Maryland campuses or divisions in addition to College Park; 2) Any and all financial and/or ethics disclosure records, forms, reports, and other materials that concern, relate to, or evidence Judith Lynne Hanna; 3) any and all administrative and other inquiries that concern, relate to, or evidence Judith Lynne Hanna including, but not limited to, conflicts of interest and research integrity.

Agres wrote that she agreed to pay copying and postage fees of not more than one hundred dollars and that she was "prepared to pursue whatever legal remedy necessary to obtain access to the requested records." She noted that "willful violation of the open records law can result in a fine of up to $1,000 and the award of actual damages, punitive damages, reasonable counsel fees and other litigation costs." The letter was copied to attorney Robert Andrew Manzi, who obviously wrote the letter. He has practiced law in Prince George's County for about thirty-five years and is City Attorney for the towns of Greenbelt, Laurel, and New Carrollton, which are located in the county.

The university had none of the material requested.

## The Battle Continues: Round Three

In 2005, the Prince George's Council was at it again. So, too, was Jack Johnson. Up for reelection for a second term as County Executive, he needed to show some accomplishment. Prince George's County still had a high rate of well-documented crimes involving personal injury or death and a decline in the broad public perception of the quality of life. As reported in the January 22, 2006, edition of the *Washington Post*, hundreds of citizens attended a forum to complain about increasing levels of crime (in 2005: 173 homicides, 3 percent increase in sexual assaults, 24 percent in robberies, 45 percent in carjacking). Yet, Prince George's County appeared to be using undocumented problems to divert attention from its seeming inability to cope with real problems.

## Commissioned Report

Desperate to find problems with exotic dance clubs, the County Council commissioned a twenty thousand-dollar study from Pennsylvania-based consultants Gentile-Meinert & Associates. Interestingly, a *Washington Post* editorial, August 8, 2006, noted: "Guided by the profligate spending habits and unchecked power of County Executive Jack B. Johnson, Prince George's has devoted a few million dollars to commissioning reports" that are "slender, overpriced and generally unread . . . a joke, their contents unavailable to county taxpayers, who paid for them."

The study was not publicly released, but a newspaper reporter obtained a copy and sent it to me for comment. I shared some problems with this adult entertainment impact "study" with the reporter and Prince George's elected government representatives, along with my guide for policy makers in *Journal of Planning Literature* (JPL) and my shorter "Legislative Talking Points."

Once again the County disregarded all valid and reliable social science reports, except for the "studies" that had been submitted to the Council. The County proceeded to harass the clubs with more business-disrupting raids and inspections, plus another "new" ordinance, CB-61-2006.

## Raids on Club Exstasy

Under Maryland law and the Court of Appeals of Maryland Rules of Procedure, any issue relative to the use of the Club Exstasy property should be resolved by civil litigation under the exclusive jurisdiction of the District Court of Maryland for Prince George's County. Nevertheless, the police told the club management to ask all patrons to leave immediately and to close the business and not reopen; otherwise, the manager would be arrested. No trial on the merits!

On May 13, 2006, at 2:45 a.m., the county police raided Club Exstasy without a warrant yet another time and closed the club. Owner Eric Roozen was fined three hundred dollars for not being cooperative. Club Exstasy was cited for not having fire retardant paint on the wall and lockers in the bathroom. In still another raid, twenty cops remained in the club for four hours. Club Exstasy had not corrected one of the violations. Further, the police harassed patrons, citing them for jaywalking and for not parking between the lines in the parking lot.

## Harassment of Showcase Theater Continues

The County subjected Showcase Theater to further action—a set of multiple inspections and citations for minor things—by the County Multi-Agency Services Team. Larry Bledsoe had the infractions corrected and made numerous calls for inspection of the corrections—calls that went unreturned. Then he was fined for not having had an inspection! The county cited Showcase Theater for not getting a final inspection from a fire more than five years ago. Yet, the fire marshal had inspected the club twice in two months at the request of high-level county officials. Showcase Theater received a property maintenance citation for open dumpster lids left by the trash pickup company, for cracked siding shingles, and for minor trash that had blown onto the property on a windy day.

Showcase Theater was cited for fire hazard violations, even though the club had recently been approved by the fire department: the upstairs, only used by the dancers as a dressing room, had misleading pointing arrows on the exit sign. The fire escape door lacked a hydraulic mechanism. Showcase Theater was cited for obstruction of egress for storing water on the side of otherwise unused stairs. The DJ speaker wires were cited for being encapsulated in plastic. One county official videotaped the girls—without permission; a female county employee was taking notes. In turn, Showcase Theater captured the raid on film. Business went on. Indeed, seventy-seven patrons came in during the approximately half-hour that the county employees were there. They had nine other places to inspect.

On Saturday, February 25, 2006, Bledsoe thought that the Liquor Board tried to set the club up for a violation even though Showcase Theater does not have a liquor license. About 10:30 p.m., four or five men were standing and talking outside the entrance. Frequently, patrons will mill about outside, talking among themselves or looking for their membership cards prior to entering. One man approached Robert Rash, who worked at the cashier office, window, flashed a badge, and stated, "liquor inspector." Rash asked him to wait and went to find the manager. Before he could be found, a customer exited the electronic door and the "liquor inspector" entered the club.

Immediately, two additional men approached the cashier and attempted to enter Showcase with what appeared to be two six-packs of beer. Rash explained that, by law, patrons are not allowed to bring any liquor into the club on Saturday nights when the exotic dancers performed nude. The three men appeared not to understand and continued in their attempt to enter Showcase. Finally, they left the entrance and returned several minutes later without the beer. Meanwhile, the manager explained to the "inspector" that Showcase did not allow alcohol when it featured nude dancers. A Showcase security employee observed two of the men in a corner pouring something into a cup. As he approached them with a flashlight to ask what they were drinking, he spotted a liquor bottle on the floor. So, he ushered the men out of the club and observed them get in a van with the "inspector."

More serious for the residents of Prince George's County, on July 2, 2006, the weekend of seven homicides in the county, Lieutenant Henry White was assigned to marshal county resources to conduct a raid on Showcase Theater. At 12:20 a.m., thirteen county representatives, eight police officers, and five officials from health, fire, environmental resources, building, and zoning descended upon the club from a huge van plastered with the County Executive's name. Was Johnson trying to give the appearance that he was protecting the county?

## More Laws

County Bill 31, introduced June 11, 2003, was a proposed zoning law concerning closing a business or withdrawing a Use and Occupancy Permit (UNO). Attorney Luke Lirot said it had no due process or consistency. It would permit the county to exercise expedited enforcement to close businesses that, in an official's view, are unlawful and have activities that pose an imminent danger to the health, safety, and welfare of the public. This was contested in court.

Even though the county justifiably wanted to eliminate the approximately thirty to fifty unlicensed "clubs" that had opened up in garages, warehouses, and event halls and offer alcohol, go-gos, and adult entertainment, a bill such as County Bill 31 could also be used to harass the licensed, law-abiding exotic dance clubs. Once again, the Council ignored Colonel Jeff Cox's testimony that it was not the licensed clubs that caused problems.

Another attack on the clubs came from the Maryland State Legislature through Prince George's County representatives. House Bill 922, the "Bottle Club" bill, pertaining only to Prince George's County, became law in 2005. It enabled the county's licensing board to revoke liquor licenses issued to establishments that have exotic dancing. A club may not know-ingly allow patrons to bring alcoholic beverages for consumption into the establishment nor can the club dispense setups. But do setups mean selling colas, juices, or bottled water? Violation is a misdemeanor, and, on conviction, the violator is subject to imprisonment not exceeding two years and a fine not exceeding ten thousand dollars or both. There were other harmful restrictions that would affect Showcase Theater, which does not hold a liquor license—for example, nudity and specified sexual displays are prohibited at bottle clubs.

Bledsoe wrote a letter to the bill's sponsors, Senators John A. Giannetti Jr. and Leo E. Green and twenty-three other senators and delegates. He included thirty-three signed and dated letters from county citizens who opposed the bill. Bledsoe noted that the bill was introduced as a result of citizen concern in Laurel about Club Amazon's intention to open as an ex-otic dance club near a church. Although he also opposed this, he saw the bill as overkill and illegitimate. I also wrote to the senate sponsors and to half a dozen legislators whom I had met at social occasions. I attached copies of my JPL article, my critique of the county's commissioned reports, "Legislative Talking Points," a *Washington Post* Q&A, and my mini-study of calls for police. I also had discussions with Senator Green and several legislative assistants. Nonetheless, the law passed. Bledsoe did not mount a legal challenge.

However, the venerable Legend Night Club and its co-plaintiff, the Clas-sics Nightclub, joined together to challenge the state statute meant to ban strip clubs. In April 2009, Judge Marvin J. Garbis of the US District Court for the District of Maryland, Baltimore Division, struck down the statute, finding it would place unconstitutional limits on free speech while vio-lating the Fourteenth Amendment's guarantee of equal protection. As it turns out, legislators had carved a very particular grandfather clause into the bill, allowing any nightclub that had received an adult entertainment license before August 15, 1981, to remain in business. Not so coincidental-ly, Tommie Broadwater, a former Maryland state senator who relinquished his seat after a federal fraud conviction in 1983, owns a gentlemen's club, Ebony Inn, that received a license on August 14, 1981. "The Court finds Plaintiffs to have established beyond any reasonable doubt, that the Leg-islation's 'grandfather clause' was deliberately crafted to favor the poten-tially connected former Senator," Garbis wrote. One more reason, he said, to scrap the law. Moreover, the law was overly broad. The owners of Fed Ex Field, for example, could be punished for allowing a Redskins player or coach to give a team member a congratulatory pat on the bottom during a game. And the government certainly did not demonstrate that the restrictions serve a "substantial government interest."

## "New" Regulations (CB-61-2006)

Considering the 2003 bill too hastily passed, government officials in Prince George's County held a public hearing on July 16, 2006, for yet another bill regulating adult entertainment. At the hearing for CB-61-2006, I felt like I was in church. Councilman Harrington was giving awards to young people affiliated with a church. Prayers began the meeting. The Council passed the bill on July 28.

Like rottweilers, Prince George's County officials and religious conservatives had locked their jaws in defiance of our civil liberties. CB-61-2006 severely infringes upon the First Amendment (as did CB-86-2003). In sum, the ordinance restricts where dancers can appear nude; prohibits tipping until the end of the performance; requires a six-foot distance between dancer and patron; bans dancer self-touch, simulated sex, and simulated nudity; and mandates the type of theater stage lighting. CB-61-2006 suppresses expression and chills creativity through vagueness. In addition, it discriminates by requiring only exotic dancers to get licenses and only exotic dance clubs to close at a certain hour. The bill overlooks how dance, nudity, and space communicate. The fantasy of romantic interest between dancer and patron is suppressed with a separation distance of six feet. Patron touch of the dancer's hand or garter belt to provide a tip during a performance communicates interest and awards meritorious performance. Patrons in DC exotic dance clubs serving alcohol regularly approach nude dancers on stage to give them tips. Self-touch is an integral part of many dances such as jazz, flamenco, and modern. Because the instrument of dance and sex is the body, any movement can be interpreted as simulated sex. Erotic dance is erotic because it "simulates" sex. Theater is, by definition, simulation, make-believe. "Simulated nudity" is a vague term. Dancers in ballet, modern, and other kinds of dances wear body suits that give the appearance of nudity. Lighting conveys meaning.

Prince George's County Council's stigmatizing treatment of dancers (implying that most are dirty, diseased, inferior, or are prostitutes) is reminiscent of other stigmatizing actions throughout history based upon occupation, religion, and race, including white treatment of blacks during slavery and segregation. How a few scraps of cloth or stillness on stage or a specified dancer-patron distance will eliminate the supposed negative effects of the clubs is a mystery.

## Another Lawsuit against Prince George's County

Showcase Theater, Club Exstasy, and Bazz & Crue filed suit against CB-61-2006, which was, at minimum, the county's third try to eliminate exotic dance clubs. Judge Marvin J. Garbis heard the case in Baltimore, Maryland, November 20–21, 2006. The judge combined this case with a somewhat similar case brought by a club in Baltimore. Not surprisingly, CR-Activist Scott Bergthold's office was in court, trying to help Prince George's County.

Although every case is unique, the attorney for the Baltimore club, Jimmy Bell, was startling in appearance and behavior. Lacking professional ethics and etiquette and the usual court decorum, he directed his associate to talk to me for some time before the trial about working as an expert court witness on his case. Bell used my services, prolonged the case a second day, but did not remunerate me. He strutted into the courtroom, giving a flashy fashion show with dress from an earlier century. Day 1: red and white saddle shoes and tie to match. Day two: pink shoes and tie to match. Usually attorneys let their experts know when they will be on the stand and the kinds of questions they will be asked. But Bell put me on the expert court witness stand for his client's case without forewarning. He exited the courtroom and returned with a large bag. He withdrew underwear and other props, held up an item, and asked me the meaning each conveyed to me, from a grandma's pair of panties to a thong to a sports bra to a see-through bikini top. After he held up a jar of honey and a bar of chocolate, I was worried that he'd show me something kinky I didn't know about. Following my testimony about what exotic dance is and my fielding of Bell's stunt, the male dancers in the gallery stood up and applauded (not allowed in court). They loved my presentation—it made them feel that what they were doing was respectable. The judge was patient and showed a sense of humor.

On April 12, 2007, Judge Garbis handed down his decision. He wrote:

The Gentile study was seriously flawed and was inadequate to support the County's secondary effects conclusion with regard to the conduct restrictions in CB-61. For example, Gentile acknowledged that "you can't categorize what I've done as meeting a statistics methodology, rigorous scientific requirements. You would categorize it as a survey that has gone through a process." Moreover, Gentile conceded that some of the businesses in his study do not even provide adult entertainment. Gentile also stated that he had no empirical evidence to support the claim that there was a secondary effect or an increase in crime. His conclusion was supported "exclusively" by previous studies done by others, remote in place and time from the County of today. Gentile testified that his conclusion that adult businesses cause a decrease in property values was based on "interviews with some people within relative close proximity" and the "whole reasonableness" of the issue.

And Prince George's County paid Gentile-Meinert & Associates twenty thousand dollars for this. Judge Garbis continued:

> The County has not produced any credible evidence that the conduct restrictions it seeks to impose on adult entertainment businesses such as Plaintiffs' would reduce the alleged secondary effects it sought to alleviate, such as drug dealing, the spread of STDs, and an "atmosphere of deviance." . . . Indeed, there is nothing of any substance to support a conclusion that the secondary effects alleged by the County (such as rape, robbery, assault, theft from automobiles, etc.) would be reduced at all by requiring dancers to perform on an elevated stage, keeping patrons six feet away from performers, prohibiting tips during performances, banning any physical contact between patrons and entertainers, etc. Accordingly, absent the Savings Clause, the conduct restrictions in CB-61 would not pass constitutional muster. . . . However, the Savings Clause restricts the applicability of the conduct restrictions to obscene conduct. Such conduct is not afforded First Amendment protection. Accordingly, by virtue of the Savings Clause, the conduct restrictions in CB-61 are valid and enforceable, but, of course, only with regard to conduct that is obscene under the Miller standards.

In response to the plaintiff's request for attorneys' fees, the County not only challenged this but the entire decision. But the judge let the decision stay.

Will the county protract the chase game? Appeal? More harassment? Further legislative muggings of the clubs as a red herring for the county's inattention to serious crimes with victims? Ironically, Prince George's County aspires to be a convention site with full hotels. The presence of adult entertainment attracts conventioneers and tourists, as well as tax income for the local government. The six largest centers for exotic dance clubs also happen to be the largest convention markets in the United States: Dallas, Houston, Atlanta, Miami–Fort Lauderdale–Orlando, Las Vegas, and Los Angeles. Angelina Spencer, executive director of the Association of Club Executives, has explored "The Exotic Economy." She estimates that the Atlanta metro area boasts about forty clubs with an economic impact of a whopping $240 million per year. This is more income than all three of the city's major sports teams generate. This extra income for the government translates into better roads, more police and fire services, and improved school systems.

When Prince George's County Executive Jack B. Johnson negotiated a deal with the developer Peterson Companies for the massive National Harbor project in 2004, agreeing that the county would pay for road and sewer improvements in exchange for the developer's donation of $3.5 million over ten years to local charities, $700,000 for community groups in 2005 and 2006 was forthcoming. Johnson and the Council set up a committee that included pastors Kerry Hill and Delman Coates. This committee gave $54,000 to nineteen of the county's most powerful churches in the months before the 2006 competitive Democratic primary between Johnson and former state delegate Rushern L. Baker III. Johnson won. Thus, it is not surprising that the county government responds to a constituency that seeks broadly to impose its morality.

## Denouement

But Johnson's gig was finally up. Rushern L. Baker III was the new County Executive. Bledsoe joyfully called me on November 12, 2010, with the news. Showcase Theater owners reveled in the disclosure that the FBI arrested Johnson, Prince George's County Executive for eight years. He was charged with political corruption and overheard on a wiretap telling his wife, Leslie, to get rid of potentially incriminating evidence—to tear up a $100,000 check from a developer and flush it down the toilet and to stash a wad of $79,000 cash in her bra. Witness tampering and destruction of evidence charges were added to his "pay-for-play" in accepting bribes in exchange for awarding county contracts. Others in Prince George's County were charged with conspiracy and smuggling people into the United States. Forty-six police officers were suspended for misconduct. On May 17, 2011, Johnson pleaded guilty to two felony charges; he admitted in court that he took more than four hundred thousand dollars in bribes during his eight years as county executive.

In the Prince George's legislation and bench trials, a protracted CR-Activist attack, we witness a combination of CR-Activists seeking to impose their views on a community concerned with improving its image. Over the years, the rottweilers kept their jaws locked despite the fact that exotic dance is a popular form of theater art fantasy that does not cause the alleged problems. The court repeatedly ruled that the county's legislation violated the First and Fourteenth Amendments. The costs to the taxpayer for the attempts to drive the clubs out of business could have paid for the many deficient services in the county. Alas, the absurdity seen in this saga is not atypical of other cases, and judges do not always make decisions based on evidence. Now we turn to charges against exotic dance in Minnesota that illustrate how jury trials can play out.

# Shooting Nude Crotches

## Jury Trials

Contemporary art challenges us. It broadens our horizons.
It asks us to think beyond the limits of conventional wisdom.
ELI BROAD

"Public indecency" criminal charges (up to ninety days and/or a fine of seven hundred dollars) could be filed for dancing nude in the City of Cannon Falls, Goodhue County, Minnesota. This 1998 ordinance was established on the basis of Cannon Falls's findings: "to deter criminal activity, to promote societal order and public health, and to protect children."

Cannon Falls is located thirty-four miles from St. Paul. The population, 98 percent white, is about 4,000 with a median resident age of 36.9 years. Average household income is $40,721; house value, $124,400. Twenty-three Baptist, Catholic, Evangelical, Lutheran, and Methodist churches serve the small population. Aided by CR-Activists, ecumenical opposition to exotic dance clubs influences the town.

The ordinance prohibits knowingly and intentionally appearing in a public place in a "state of nudity." While the definition of "public place" includes "any location frequented by the public, or where the public is present or likely to be present, or where a person may reasonably be expected to be observed by members of the public," it specifically exempts from the definition "enclosed single sex public restrooms, enclosed single sex motel rooms and hotel rooms designed and intended for sleeping accommodations, doctor's offices, portions of hospitals and similar places in which nudity and exposure is necessary and expected outside of a home." The ordinance also provides that the nudity ban "shall not apply to any theatrical production performed in a theater by a professional or amateur theatrical or musical company which has serious artistic merit."

However, the courts have not enunciated a legal test with criteria for determining "serious artistic value," meant as protection for what appears in mainstream theater. The exemption may keep some ordinances from being overly broad and thus unconstitutional. Defining serious artistic merit for many people is like defining pornography. Justice Potter Stewart could

165

not define it, but nonetheless famously said in his opinion in *Jacobellis v. Ohio* (1964), "I know it when I see it." Vagueness of the law of obscenity "invites arbitrary and erratic enforcement of the law."

As pointed out earlier, CR-Activists directly or indirectly keep alive the assault on exotic dance. Reinforcing old stereotypes, instigating attacks, and providing support strategically, financially, and legally, they weave independent church groups and organizations in a web of alliance. Cannon Falls had enacted an anti-nudity ordinance that was challenged by a local club. Class Act supported the trials of four of its dancers charged with violations. The dancers received either "not guilty" judgments or dismissals. The law, which could not withstand the jury verdicts, remains on the books but is ignored by local law enforcement.

Yet, Benton County, Minnesota, on July 3, 2001, enacted and immediately enforced the very same ordinance. Part of the St. Cloud Metropolitan Statistical Area, one hour north of the Twin Cities, and one hour south of lake and resort areas, Benton County has a population of 30,000 and is more diverse and less affluent than Cannon Falls. The attorney, Randall Tigue, who defended the dancers criminally charged in the Cannon Falls anti-nudity cases, also served as the defense attorney in the subsequent two Benton County trials for dancers criminally charged with violating its ordinance (liable for up to one thousand dollars and three months in jail). Let's look at these cases within the CR-Activist climate.

## Class Act in Cannon Falls

Tigue filed a motion to dismiss a criminal complaint against "Destiny," one of four dancers similarly charged with nude dancing, noting the "necessarily and customarily expected" exemption stated in the ordinance and the insufficient detail of the complaint. Tigue also noted that the establishment plainly was not a public place where nudity is forced upon unwilling observers or participants. Other than the fact that nudity occurred during the course of the performance, no fact was alleged that would enable a neutral and detached magistrate to find probable cause to believe that the defendant's performance lacked "serious artistic merit." Judge Thomas W. Bibus denied the motion, but allowed: "If Defendant puts forth substantial evidence that the alleged conduct in the Class Act Gentleman's Club is a qualifying theatrical production," then the burden is on the state. The judge also referred to the ordinance's purpose of combating "negative secondary effects."

Tigue then asked me to serve as an expert court witness. On Monday evening, October 27, 2000, I saw a special performance by "Buena," one of the dancers charged with public indecency, staged especially for me because Class Act is closed on Sunday and Monday. I examined the premises to see if it met the criteria of a theater and evaluated the performance, using the criteria many judges use in exotic dance competitions and many clubs use in auditioning dancers.

## Destiny's Case

The next day, the first police officer prosecutor Elliot Knetsch called to testify said he saw Destiny dance for about thirty seconds, but had no recollection of her performance, except that she was nude. Another officer testified that he arrived after Destiny had completed her dance and witnessed none of it. Rather, he testified he only observed Destiny walking off the stage. The prosecutor claimed the dancer was posing and that wasn't dance. But stillness is certainly an aesthetic choice, often as a contrast to movement and a way of accentuating it. In fact, a December 22, 2000, *New York Times* modern dance review is titled: "Pose. Stop. Hit Another. Don't Forget to Thrust" and refers to the "impolite thrust" and "climactic."

Club manager Rick Hermann testified that the dance I saw was of the style and quality of the dancers at Class Act. The prosecutor retorted that what I saw wasn't a real performance because there was only one audience member. Hermann explained that when a club first opens there is often just a single patron. In response to Tigue's general question about Class Act, Hermann described the club, which meets the criteria of what constitutes theater. He told the jury he auditioned dancers, looking for talent, the ability to relate to customers, and personality. He also looked for performers who have a dance routine and interesting costumes.

Tigue argued that the Cannon Falls anti-nudity ordinance exempted "nudity that was necessarily and customarily expected." Class Act had been a nude club since at least 1986. In 1998, the City of Cannon Falls annexed the area where Class Act sits. Before the jury, I explained how exotic dance was exempted from the ordinance as a "theatrical production performed in a theater by a professional . . . theatrical . . . company which has serious artistic merit" and where nudity is expected. I discussed how exotic dance is a form of dance, art, theatrical performance, and adult entertainment. I noted the diversity of dance and differences in theatrical performance, from traditional to contemporary. For example, some dance companies are short-term, composed of dancers on contract, similar to what is the case at Class Act. At that club, contract dancers work together for a theatrical production under the direction of the manager and DJ.

Knetsch skeptically asked if Class Act had a list of performers, a program, a cast listing, titles of the performances, a director, a script, and a written dance training manual. He asserted the dancers were "posing rather than dancing" and "Class Act had only mere props of theater." One police officer said there was no listing of dancers in the entryway. But on the wall adjacent to the table where patrons pay an entry fee, a marquee does list the names of dancers.

The prosecutor asked what artistic merit there was in a dancer spreading her legs. And then he incessantly fixated on vaginas. So I addressed the beauty of the body and curiosity about it, and the variety of patrons with different motives for attending an exotic dance club. I talked about Eve Ensler's The Vagina Monologues, a tribute to the female genitalia. (Donna Hanover, New York City Mayor Rudy Giuliani's wife at the time, was to star in the play.) And I referred to Judy Chicago's art show and book, The Dinner Table. On each of thirty-nine place settings in the art installation was a vagina appropriately decorated to symbolize a famous woman in Western civilization.

The dearth of prosecution evidence on the issue of whether the performance lacked serious artistic value led Tigue, in his closing argument to the jury, to retell attorney Clyde DeWitt's now legendary story about his first day on the job as an Assistant District Attorney in Houston, Texas. DeWitt was hired right out of law school, and the district attorney in Houston was a veteran of many a courtroom battle. DeWitt was called in by his boss and told, "Son, I want to show you how the Texas Court of Criminal Appeals has eulogized my skills as an attorney." The veteran DA showed DeWitt a published decision of the Court of Appeals that had reversed a conviction in a case the DA had tried. According to the opinion: "Not only was there insufficient evidence to support this conviction, there was no evidence to support the conviction." Upon reading this opinion, the veteran DA turned to the young rookie and said, "Son, do you realize how good of a lawyer you have to be to get a conviction with no evidence at all?"

After telling DeWitt's story, Tigue told the jury, "If you find Destiny guilty based upon the evidence submitted to you in this trial, then Mr. Knetsch will have undoubtedly earned the right to make that same boast to every young attorney in his office. On the issue of lack of serious artistic value, Mr. Knetsch not only has failed to produce proof beyond a reasonable doubt, to produce proof by preponderance of the evidence, he has produced no evidence at all."

The prosecutor's theatrical credentials and knowledge didn't convince the jury. On the basis of Tigue's skill and with my two-hour testimony, the jury acquitted Destiny of public indecency for dancing nude. Usually with an acquittal of one of four dancers all similarly charged, the cases against the remaining three defendants would be dropped. But not in the City of Cannon Falls! Consequently, Tigue went to the city council meeting and argued for the dismissal of the three other cases. Elliot Knetsch had claimed that the defendant was merely lucky with a favorably disposed jury. An agitated councilman said he didn't care about court costs and wanted each of the other women prosecuted. Moreover, he asked, "Why weren't there more arrests?"

For the second case, a charge against a dancer who performs under the name "Paris," I went to Cannon Falls to see a regular Class Act performance. Tigue wanted to take away any arrows in Knetsch's quiver. I observed dances and interviewed dancers and patrons for seven hours.

## Paris's Case

Tigue assumed Monday, December 11, 2000, would be jury selection. But Prosecutor Knetsch had submitted a *motion in limine* and supporting memorandum requesting the court prohibit the defendant from presenting evidence to the jury that Paris's "stripping actions constituted a theatrical production performed in a theater by a professional or amateur theatrical or musical company, which has serious artistic merit." This was Knetsch's preemptive strike to keep me from testifying before the jury as I had in the first acquittal case. Knetsch said the motion was based upon the record established in the prior case and argued:

> Common sense must be employed by the court to distinguish legitimate "theater" productions from the sexually titillating activities of dancing nude. The Defendant's position that her activities, combined with a disc jockey playing records and a bouncer keeping the peace, constitute a "theatrical company" is insulting to all legitimate and serious theater companies. The stripping "productions" have no legitimate actors, no scenes, no playbills, no acts and no dialogue. The clear intent of the stripping is to sexually excite and titillate the men who frequent the establishments. Legitimate theater on the other hand, appeals to the social, political, economic and even scientific facets of a culture with the purpose of informing, persuading or entertaining an audience. The court must apply logic and determine the stripping activities are not performed by a theatrical company. Courts have had no difficulty distinguishing between movie theaters and "adult" movie theaters. In the case before the court today, the State seeks to prohibit public nudity where the reason for the nudity is the nudity itself, rather than where it is incidental to a serious artistic expres-

sion. More to the point, the nudity undertaken by the Defendant was the entire purpose, focus and intent of the "production."

Without ever establishing his performing arts expertise, the prosecutor made numerous fanciful assertions. He exhibited no knowledge of the range of theatrical companies, no survey of what would be considered "insulting," no definition of "legitimate," no awareness that dancers sometimes talk with patrons during their performances, and no understanding that stripping productions not only entertain but also inform people about the female anatomy and provide opportunities, for example, to relax and to talk with someone about problems. Knetsch showed no awareness that much entertainment in all manner of theatrical production succeeds because it sexually excites and titillates its audience. The prosecutor seemed ignorant about nudity being the climax of the striptease, a part of the performance, not the full content. He appeared naïve about dance company operation and about dance being primarily nonverbal and not scripted but choreographed or improvised. There is even a type of dance called "contact improvisation." Dance has a visual and aural tradition of transmitting routines from one person to another.

Knetsch quoted my description from the first case of every dance movement I mentioned seeing at the special performance for me at Class Act and then asked me, "Were the genitalia exposed? Could you see the vagina?" I replied that it depended where the dancer was on the stage relative to where I was sitting. I then proceeded to discuss the awe and beauty of the vagina—everyone's passageway into this world—and *The Vagina Monologues* and *The Dinner Table*.

After I was on the stand for forty-five minutes, Judge Thomas Bibus ruled against the prosecutor as he had in the first case when Knetsch also tried to prevent me from testifying. The judge said I was a compelling expert witness and the prosecutor had five days within which to appeal. On the fifth day, Knetsch notified Tigue that he would not appeal the judge's opinion.

I started packing to go to Cannon Falls again for Paris's trial. A couple of hours later, the prosecutor said he was dropping the charges against Paris. On December 22, 2000, Knetsch filed with the District Court Administrator dismissals of citations against the remaining two dancers who perform under the names "Michelle" and "Buena." The sudden dismissal of remaining charges, however, may not have been entirely due to Knetsch's prospect of another imminent legal defeat.

After the first acquittal, the normally conservative *Cannon Falls Beacon* printed a signed editorial discussing first, Al Gore's concession speech when the 2000 election was finally decided and second, an opinion about the local case against the club. The editorial writer remarked, "I think it's time for another concession speech, this time from the Cannon Falls City Council. It's time to give up the fight to close down Class Act." The editorial continued: "The City was expending thousands of dollars on jury trials for nude dancing, at a time when the city was going to have to give up its own emergency police dispatch service, for lack of money to fund it." The writer concluded:

> So what we're being told is, the City would rather fight battles it has maybe a 50/50 chance, probably less, of winning, than to keep a valuable city service that tax payers have, and en masse said they'd be willing to pay to keep. Now lest you think I'm just some flunky for Class Act or its ownership, think again. I've never been to the place, nor do I ever plan on going. I'm also not the world's biggest fan of [the club owner]. I am, however, a big fan of our dispatch and our dispatchers. Council members have challenged the public to find money to keep dispatch; conceding the issue of Class Act is a good first step.
>
> I expect a little flack for taking the stance I have; I know there are some in the community who are adamantly opposed to having a strip joint in our midst. For me, the choice is easy: use the money spent to prosecute Class Act cases to save dispatch.[1]

Thus, it appears that when forced to choose between morality and fiscal conservatism, on occasion, fiscal conservatism prevails.

## Sugar Daddy's in Benton County

During the summer of 2001, Benton County police cited four dancers for violating the public indecency ordinance as a result of undercover videotape evidence. Deputy Sheriff Scott Steinberg shot video in Sugar Daddy's Club, on US Highway 10 in Sauk Rapids. One dancer pleaded guilty because she was getting married and leaving St. Cloud. The other three dancers, however, were left to face trial.

### Amy's Case

In *State of Minnesota v. Amy* (2002) a four-woman, three-man jury found the first dancer to go to trial "not guilty" after seventy-five minutes of deliberation in a two-day trial. Randall Tigue, again the attorney for the defense, argued that nudity is customarily expected in exotic dance clubs and is markedly different than nudity thrust upon an unsuspecting, unwilling public at large. On the courtroom stand, the police officers in the undercover operation agreed!

The state's evidence was secretly shot videotape of dancers on stage for about an hour. However, the videotape showed clearly only two forty-second segments of a ten-minute dance that twenty-one-year-old Amy performed. The prosecutor showed the jury only eighty seconds of overt sexual imagery, while the five hundred other seconds in the dance could not be seen! An anonymous respondent to a *St. Cloud Times* article on the case put it this way: "How easy it is to only show PARTS of a video. The only part she had clothes off. What a joke." Nonetheless, Kathleen Reuter, assistant Benton County attorney, in her closing argument echoed the police officers' claims that "only acts that were representative of the whole were shown." Yet, recall that nudity is the climax of the dance, usually occurring during a third song of a three-song dance in which the dancer appears on stage clothed for the first song and partially removes her clothes for the second.

For its witness, the state called a former modern dancer, Colleen Callahan-Russell, who had never even been to Sugar Daddy's. Callahan-Russell claimed a master's degree in dance (meaning modern dance, a rebellion against ballet, rejecting its formal five positions, codified movements, toe shoes, and primarily male-dominated companies in favor of creative movement, bare feet, and primarily female-dominated companies). She said she had movement analysis training, and was currently a high school dance teacher who has developed standards to evaluate student work in modern dance. She has been affiliated with panels of the Minnesota Dance Alliance and Minnesota Arts Alliance that evaluate candidates for grants to choreograph new work (certainly not exotic dance). Callahan-Russell admitted she had been to an exotic dance club once. But she knew about exotic dance from television. Television? The media continually presents mere snippets of actual exotic dance and sensationalizes it in a moralizing tone. Moreover, television—for example, in shows such as *Jerry Springer*—perpetuates the myth that exotic dance clubs cause negative effects. Callahan-Russell said her colleagues thought it was a joke that exotic dance, by any stretch of the imagination, could have any artistic merit.

For the defense witness, Tigue called on me, whose area of expertise dramatically contrasted with that of the state's witness. He asked me various questions about my background. I said that I have a PhD (my dissertation in anthropology at Columbia University was on dance as nonverbal communication), and I have had movement analysis training. I served as an evaluator for the National Endowment for the Arts and the Washington

DC Commission on the Arts and have been a dance critic for the venerable *Dance Magazine*. And, most important, I have been studying exotic dance since 1995. This includes visits to nearly one hundred and fifty clubs to observe what actually goes on and to interview the stakeholders (dancers, managers, patrons, club personnel, and community members). I have presented this research in peer-reviewed scholarly meetings, periodicals, and books. In 2002, I served as one of four judges at the national Exotic World Pageant held at the site of the Movers and Shakers Burlesque Museum and Striptease Hall of Fame in Helendale, California. In 2005, I served as a judge at the Exotic Dancer Expo.

On the basis of the videotape only showing graphic body parts from the latter portion of Amy's dance, the state's witness said the dancer's performance had no artistic merit and ridiculed the notion. Callahan-Russell said a dance had to have something bigger than the self to have serious artistic merit. It could not be entertainment in a commercial venue. Yet, her requirement for serious artistic merit would eliminate professional dance. People do not buy tickets to the ballet to be bored. Indeed, Balanchine said he aimed to entertain audiences. Furthermore, professional dancers appear in venues that are part of the economy.

On the stand, I used visual overhead transparencies to reinforce my verbal explanation to the jury about how exotic dance is a form of dance and art performed by an informal company in a theater. I described the exotic dance aesthetic standards for serious artistic merit. Tigue asked, "Did Amy's dance on the videotape have artistic merit?" I demurred, replying, "I cannot make a judgment on artistic merit based on two forty-second segments of a ten-minute dance."

The state has the burden of proof in criminal cases and could not prove its case beyond a reasonable doubt on the basis of its evidence and testimony. The jury deliberated an hour and fifteen minutes and ruled in favor of the dancer—not guilty. Jury forewoman Pam Benoit told St. Cloud Times reporter David Unze, "The conclusion we came up with was that there wasn't enough on the video to make the judgment (about artistic merit). One of the experts couldn't judge that clip, so how could we?" Jurors agreed with the county, however, that Sugar Daddy's is a public place that is not exempt from the ordinance because it was a place where people could reasonably expect to see nudity.

Unze's articles, "Jury Acquits Dancer of Nudity Charge" (July 24, 2002) and "2nd Nude Dancer to Be Tried" (August 13, 2002), appeared in the St. Cloud Times. A respondent on the newspaper's online chat remarked, "Jurors would have liked to have seen Amy's entire performance to judge its artistic value. Yeah, I kinda wanted to see that too."

*Community Positive Feedback on Exotic Dance*

Of the nineteen Benton County jurors summoned to serve, fifteen told the attorneys they wouldn't close the clubs down if they had the ultimate power to do so. The news media had reported that the economic recession, rising cost of living (8–10 percent), and declining state and federal aid were painting a grim picture for counties. So it was not surprising that in the online chat feedback, respondents criticized Benton County's wastefulness in going after a business that brought income to the county.

ABOUT THE ECONOMY

Wooo hooo! WTG! I'm so glad the prudes in Benton County will have to eat this one. Vote them out.

The BIG question now will be what will the County commissioners and the County attorney do next?

Basketball Jones: Only a few PRUDES are behind this ordinance. Most NORMAL people don't spend their time trying to force others to conform to their sense of morality through the use of, or should I say the misuse of law. How much more of your county taxpayer funds r u going to waste before u realize u look dumb? . . . If u don't like these clubs, just stay away.

As of last December the County had spent $25,299 on the nudity ban. However, that amount isn't the total cost.

SECONDARY EFFECTS

Other responses on the chat line related to the claim that clubs caused negative secondary effects; to ridicule of the county attorney, Robert Raupp; to restricting freedom; to misplaced morality; to respect for women; and to artistic value.

Eye Candy: Scientific research shows NO 'SECONDARY EFFECTS' as Benton County asserts, and yet they passed the ordinance.

I guess a woman's body is totally indecent and should never be out of bed clothes.

Yeah, women should just be at home in the kitchen, barefoot and pregnant, right?

Raupp=Idiot: I heard that Raupp had to watch that whole 10-minute tape for hours and hours on end in his office in order to decide which 30 seconds to use.

Maybe Raupp can get a job dancing at the male club. He will be looking for work.

MMMmm, I don't think I would tip him.

Whispering from Wind: I wouldn't tip him either; maybe we could let him wait tables.

I was thinking, there was a tape of one of the women dancing. Is that legal? Do you think they were informed they were being taped?

The people who managed to persuade the commissioners to vote for this thought it would get rid of these strip clubs, but you can't eliminate them. (Only 1 commissioner had the courage to vote against it!) . . . . I'm sure the commissioners won't have the guts to repeal it either since that would make them lose face with the public who persuaded them to enact it in the first place.

TRAMPLING RIGHTS

Basketball Jones: This ordinance was pursued by a few people who got together, probably in church, and decided they want everyone to live by their morality.

The morality police. We should all do what they say, because they know what is right for us and them.

Voice of Reason from the present: The true issue is whether it should be legal. It may be trashy, but trashiness (like beauty) is in the eye of the beholder.

It's not like they're dancing nude in the parking lot!

Seig heil eh?

I know of 80+year-olds who think this is a stupid ordinance.

MISPLACED MORALITY

Why do they not prosecute priests "dancing" with kids?

I don't think you'll find too many priests in the strip club, but then again maybe that's part of the problem.

We should not be legislating morality. Leave that to the Islamic governments. This is what happens when we mix religion and government.

If the women don't CARE if they're viewed as sexual objects, who are we to stop them?

My view as a woman, if you got it shake it. It's honest money and it pays the bills!!

Aw c'mon Benton County. Let these gals bounce their jugs if they want to!

Pragmatist: The man who would go to a strip club to gawk at women will just go to the beach or the mall to gawk at women. Are they less of a sex object in a bikini than nothing at all? . . . You are disrespecting her by telling her she can't make her mind up, that she is immoral and "subservient," that she needs you to step in and protect her. . . . . . I'm not endorsing going to strip clubs . . . but eliminating them will not build us that elusive city on a hill. The puritans tried it hundreds of years ago, the Muslims are trying it now, the Catholics are continually trying it along with a host of other denominations. It won't work. Go ahead and raise your family in God, share your views and why you think they are correct, then let others decide for themselves.

I think we should just level the playing field and open up a couple of male strip clubs so that we women can view the men as sex objects.

Here's your artistic value: Dancer better looking than wife.

## Community Negative Feedback on Exotic Dance

Adversaries of nude dancing had already expressed themselves in the process of getting the ordinance enacted and key reasons for their hostility were addressed in Chapter 1. Nonetheless, here are illustrations of the few comments Benton County opponents sent the chat line. Their discussion centered on morality, sin, adverse secondary effects, the protection of children, the promotion of women as sex objects, and NIMBY.

And we are supposed to believe that people come to Sugar Daddy's for the artistic value? What a crock.

Nude dancers this week, ho's next. Where do we stop?

I'm guessing most really don't care about the actual dancing, it's more "I don't want it in my backyard" kinda thing, right?

## Serious Artistic Merit

I was pleased that Amy was acquitted but annoyed that Judge Thomas P. Knapp rejected Tigue's motion to have the state's witness dismissed as an expert court witness because she was ignorant about exotic dance. So after the trial, in preparation for the next cases, I interviewed Douglas Sontag, the dance program director for the National Endowment for the Arts (NEA). Surely a national agency's procedure for evaluating artistic merit should take precedence over that of a local high school teacher. The NEA process for judging the serious artistic merit of a dance performance would not accept any detective's undercover recording as the basis for such.

NEA panelists/evaluators/critics use filmed or videotaped material solely as supplementary to evaluating live performances of dances for serious artistic merit. Recordings are two-dimensional, whereas live performances are three-dimensional. *NEA evaluators rely primarily on site visit reports of actual theatrical performances prepared by connoisseurs in the specific kind of dance they are evaluating.* Only the videotaped performances the dancers themselves submitted and cued to where they want the panel to start watching are appropriate. A videotape made and/or edited by others would be the other's point of view rather than that of the dancer. Sontag said that in a legal case with serious consequences, it behooves the court to have evaluators who know the genre and only to use films or videotapes that meet the above criteria. The videotape the state submitted does not meet NEA criteria to begin to consider serious artistic merit. Even if the prosecution had a professional full-view videotape of the entire performance, it would fall short.

## Brandy's Case

Despite Amy's acquittal of criminal charges in the first trial, the community feedback, and the earlier Cannon Falls jury acquittal of a dancer charged with indecency, Raupp would not dismiss the same misdemeanor charges against the two other dancers. Nor would the judge dismiss the cases. Raupp said, "We have one guilty and one not so far, and I'd be interested to see what another jury thinks." The "guilty" case was not from a trial but the dancer's decision to end the issue expeditiously because she was getting married and leaving town. Raupp's pursuit of another trial further jettisoned any credibility and respect he may have had among some community members.

For the second Benton County trial, I prepared additional visuals that emphasize how nudity is integral to exotic dance and is expected by patrons. More importantly, other new visuals illustrated the concepts "serious" and "artistic merit" in addition to the criteria used by the NEA in assessing these qualities in dance.

Buoyed by the Cannon Falls and first Benton County case wins, Tigue eagerly selected the jury on November 25, 2002, for State of Minnesota v. Brandy. Tigue was pleased with the six jurors selected out of fifteen people called for jury duty. By court rule, Tigue could strike five; the prosecutor, three. Judge Knapp told the individuals called for jury duty that he would excuse those who have personal life problems or know the attorneys, witnesses, or police involved in the case. He explained that each of the lawyers would ask some questions.

To select jurors most likely to be favorable to his client, Tigue asked each potential juror about work; about affiliations with any social, religious, civic, or political organizations; about what the bumper stickers on his/her car said. He asked, "If there were picketing outside a 7/11 store to cause it to remove Hustler and Playboy, would you be sympathetic? Why?" Tigue asked if the potential juror rented DVDs and cared if the rental store had an adult section. He continued:

If you were to learn that Brandy earns her livelihood dancing at Sugar Daddy's, would that affect your view of her?

What is your attitude toward sex on a scale of 1 to 10, 10, the most liberal?

If you were queen/king for a day, what would you do about the justice system?

If you could do anything you want about Sugar Daddy's, what would you do?

What kinds of things do you read?

Who is the person you most admire?

Can nude performance ever have serious artistic value?

Prosecutor Kathleen Reuter also questioned each juror:
Would seeing the video cause you issues?

Would you object to the officer's use of secret surveillance evidence?

Concerning whether nudity itself involved artistic merit, could you follow the law and put your biases aside?

During the trial, the prosecutor called Officer Neil Jacobsen. The officer said the movement that was videotaped was the same as the movement off-camera, and that the video was a fair representation of the entire performance, namely, "the dancer only going from man to man and showing herself." Tigue asked Jacobsen if he could think of any place where nudity is more normally and customarily expected than a strip club. "No," the officer answered. Deputy Sheriff Scott Steinberg also testified that he saw no kind of movement other than what was on the tape. He, too, testified that he could think of no place where nudity is more normally and customarily expected than in a strip club.

The video was a fair representation of Brandy's entire performance? It included three songs that were 9 1/2 minutes long total, and there were only 3 minutes and 59 seconds during which the dancer on the videotape could be identified as most likely to be Brandy. And for this identification, some assumptions had to be made. One could see half her body on the pole and then the next image was two legs with toes extended upward in a V shape. There were zero full-body shots. Nor could one see the breadth of the stage, the costume worn prior to the striptease, the colors of the costume, the stage entrance and exit, or the interaction with the patron. The longest image, 11 seconds, was a crotch shot.

Once again, the state called Callahan-Russell. This time she, too, had prepared visuals. One defined her notion of serious artistic merit: "a product of earnest (care and thought) work that employs a creative process at a high level of quality that conforms to the standards of that art form and has merit, a claim to commendation for excellence and deserving high esteem." The second visual showed the rating categories of exemplary, proficient, novice, and emerging for the criteria of the dancer's use of body skill, spatial acuity, energy, time, and interpretation. But these are the basic elements of any dance and do not distinguish the characteristics, for example, of ballet from hip-hop or exotic dance.

Although Callahan-Russell's "serious artistic merit" concept referred to "quality that conforms to the standards of that art form," she proffered no specific criteria for exotic dance. At this trial, she said she had been to three exotic dance clubs (as opposed to one the last time she testified) and knew about exotic dance from movies, television documentaries, and the Internet. Tigue asked her to name a movie, television documentary, or Internet source. But she couldn't identify any. Moreover, by the "standard of that art form," she apparently meant dance as opposed to visual art, not ballet as opposed to exotic dance. Callahan-Russell asserted that she had judged all sorts of dance by the same criteria, a clear violation of any serious judge's procedure to evaluate each dance form according to its own criteria of appropriateness and competency. And on the basis of seeing about four minutes of body parts—no full-body shot—Callahan-Russell asserted that Brandy's performance had no serious artistic merit.

Once again, I testified as I had at the first Benton County trial. However, I added visuals on serious artistic merit and the NEA's criteria for evaluating dance. I told the jury that I could not even consider the question of serious artistic merit on the basis of the state's evidence.

In closing argument, Tigue reminded the jurors that in our judicial system the defendant is presumed innocent until proven guilty beyond a reasonable doubt. He also reminded them that, in response to his question about what they would change about the judicial system, they had all replied that they would not change anything. He asked the jurors to remember the person they most respected and admired. Then Tigue continued, "If the person most respected and admired was accused of having committed The Texas Chainsaw Massacre, you wouldn't believe it and you would presume innocence and demand proof beyond a reasonable doubt. So, consider the facts of proof in this case as seriously as you would if the person you admired were accused of The Texas Chainsaw Massacre." Tigue restated the facts. First, Brandy was nude. Second, the exception to the anti-nudity ban was a place where nudity was expected, and the officers said nudity was expected in exotic dance clubs. Third, "any theatrical production performed in a theater by a professional or amateur theatrical or musical company that has serious artistic merit" was exempt from the anti-nudity ban.

Then the judge read the Benton County ordinance and deliberation instructions to the jury. A lightbulb went off in my brain as I listened—the state, its witness, Tigue, and I had been focusing on Brandy's performance, but the focus could also have included the theatrical company. In this case, the undercover videotape would also be irrelevant because it did not show the informal theatrical company at Sugar Daddy's—that is, a full evening's performance. After the trial, when I spoke with the jury forewoman on December 8, 2002, she expressed surprise about this omission.

The jury went to work at 11:30 a.m. Tigue's rule of thumb is that if a jury deliberates more than an hour and a half, it is likely to give a guilty verdict. As the hours passed, anxiety ran high among the members of the defense team. Tigue thought the best-case scenario would be a hung jury. However, eight hours later, the jury arrived at a "not guilty" verdict. Needless to say, Brandy was overjoyed. The owner of Sugar Daddy's not only paid the legal fees of the dancers who were charged with violations, but he also offered each dancer and a friend all-expense paid vacations to wherever they wanted to go.

Curious about the lengthy deliberations, I phoned the jury forewoman, a white, thirty-nine-year-old married female package handler. She said the jury was divided. "Being the jury leader, it was hard. Can I do this fairly? When you come in as a potential juror you start judging. Oh, a stripper. I shed a few tears." At the beginning of the deliberations, three jury members—a single thirty-year-old male furniture delivery driver; a forty-three-year-old male married plumber; and a twenty-eight-year-old female married parts manager—decided right away that the state didn't prove Brandy guilty beyond a reasonable doubt. The jury forewoman soon agreed with them. She said they were impressed by Tigue's argument and style in protecting people's rights and by my testimony. The forewoman thought, "The State should have given them a better video and paid its witness to get experience in exotic dance."

The battle was with two other women, a white, single fifty-year-old female (who reads Cosmopolitan, which often features material some people would consider risqué) and a white, married forty-two-year-old female farmer. The issue was about "keeping the personal out of it. We didn't like what we saw," said the forewoman. The last four hours were spent going over and over the argument that it was the state's job to prove its case and the state only showed portions of the dance. "For example, the dancer had pants on and then she didn't—but they did not see how it happened," noted the forewoman. Concerning the issue of public place, she thought the ordinance examples of exceptions were so different from an exotic dance club that the county didn't mean exotic dance clubs to be exempted. But one woman was adamant that there was no artistic merit, so the other jurors convinced her that nudity was customarily expected in exotic dance clubs.

On the basis of the two jury acquittals, Raupp reluctantly dismissed the pending charge against the one remaining dancer. The forewoman was unhappy with a newspaper report that quoted Raupp saying twice that the jurors found exotic dancers' performances had serious artistic merit and for this reason he was dismissing charges against the one remaining dancer. The fact was that the state had not proven the performances lacked serious artistic merit.

Tigue told the St. Cloud Times that, similar to the first case, of the sixteen potential jurors questioned, only one—if given absolute legal power—would have closed the club. The other fifteen would leave it alone. This, combined with the community talk-back, suggests that the Benton County board was catering to a minority of CR-Activists and some misinformed citizens.

### Community Talk-Back

The St. Cloud Times online feedback to the state loss was similar to its poll results after the first Benton case for criminal violation of the public indecency ordinance.

> Basketball Jones: This is the USA for cripes sake. It's a slap in the face of all the people of Benton County to have had this law passed in the first place.

> JustaGuy from Royalton: This verdict should send a very clear message not only to the County Board, but also to the County Attorney's Office, that this ordinance is not only ridiculous, but borders on illegal and should be reversed.

> Being a free citizen requires one to be smart enough to realize that you need to allow freedoms you don't like.

> . . . the next thing to be made illegal will be something you enjoy or make a living at.

> Time for a new Board of Supervisors.

> Message to Benton County Attorney: Basketball Jones: "Awwww Rick,. . . I'm sorry ur side lost as I know how important oppression and control of others is for u and ur religion. . . . Now let's vote the boneheads out of office who catered to this little special interest group and cost the taxpayers a fortune. What we really need r laws that deal with the negative secondary effects of a government like that in Benton County."

Opponents spoke of protection of children and morality:

> Benton County Board, thanks for doing the right, moral thing by trying to protect the public. Perverts get cable.

## Coda

The Minnesota cases illustrate how CR-Activist-influenced government marshals "evidence" to squelch exotic dance. The cases comprise a series of performance events and different community and government responses that are based on religion, culture, politics, and jurisprudence. First, the dancers created what they considered artistic work, but what the detectives labeled illegal acts. Then there were videotaped performances that the state presented as evidence but the defense dismissed as a perverted distortion. A third performance took place in court: the judge, prosecutor, defense attorney, jurors, and witnesses were the actors. The attorneys probed the jurors' experiences and views to select those they anticipated would be most favorable to their arguments. Fourth was the closed jury performance. The debate concerned the merit of the state's evidence and the jurors' lack of bias versus personal likes. It's possible that unspoken underlying presumptions may have had an impact. For example, views that female dancers were transgressive or exploited as objects of the male gaze or that the clubs caused harm to the community.

The attacks against exotic dance in Maryland, directly against the clubs, and in Minnesota, against the clubs through assaults on the dancers, raise the issue of treatment of dancers. Prince George's County Councilman Thomas Hendershot, among many others, has claimed exotic dance clubs exploit women in the worst kind of way.

# 7 Exotic Dancers and Labor

## Need to be Saved?

To dance is to be out of yourself.
Larger, more beautiful,
  More powerful.
This is power, it is glory on earth
  And it is yours for the taking.

AGNES DE MILLE

The Christian Right asserts that women are tempted or forced through trafficking to work in adult cabarets, where they are abused by managers and patrons. At city or county council hearings, in courtrooms, on websites, or in publications, former dancers have testified to becoming born-again Christians, rescued from degradation and sin. A segment of the politically active Christian Right (CR-Activists) commonly spotlight women who tell only negative stories, some of which may be true, that caricature the entire adult entertainment industry. The testimonies suggest that the rights women have gained through the feminist movement and 1960s sexual revolution are causing their lives to fall apart. However, they don't mention that women may have problems that they don't leave at the club door and that there is no evidence that such problems occur more frequently or intensely here than in other businesses. In a sense, most workers are exploited, as CEOs rake in tens of millions of dollars annually at the same time their workers are paid minimally, overworked, or laid off.

CR-Activists use all the ammunition they can. For example, locking on to Kelly Holsopple's methodologically flawed, unpublished paper about lower-class, poorly managed clubs, ("Stripclubs According to Strippers: Exposing Workplace Sexual Violence"), CR-Activists include it in their court briefs, even though the author asked them not to use her work. Holsopple was program director of the Freedom and Justice Center for Prostitution Resources. Basing her study on a 1994 "collective voice" of forty-one women dancing in very different settings (bars, nightclubs, peep shows, and saunas), she described types of incidents that are reported to have occurred, especially in poorly managed "strip joints," "dives," and "carnival circuits." These venues were prevalent prior to the advent of the gentlemen's club with its business-style management. She also surveyed eighteen other non-randomly selected dancers in 1996 and offers descriptive statistics that say little because numerous clubs each have as many as one hundred and twenty dancers a week performing. Holsopple expressed dismay at the fact that her attempt to discuss workplace issues in strip clubs was taken as a reason to try to shut them down.

Also included in the CR-Activist case material against exotic dance is David Sherman's questionable testimony, "Sexually Oriented Businesses: An Insider's View," presented to the Michigan House Committee on Ethics and Constitutional Law, January 12, 2000. Sherman alleged, for example, that "rampant" drug use, as well as alcohol abuse, sexual abuse, tax evasion, and violence occur in clubs. But his credibility is suspect. He had worked as a Déjà Vu cabaret manager and, according to the club's attorney Brad Shafer, Sherman was paid to testify and was not under oath. Sherman said he never saw the problems he described occur. He stopped working at Déjà Vu because of an injury. Yet, while collecting workman's compensation, he was managing another club! A House member even asked him about his being investigated for fraud.

When *The Drama Review* requested photographs to illustrate my article, "Undressing the First Amendment and Corseting the Striptease Dancer," the owner of a nude club I had visited said I could photograph dancers at work with their permission. I spoke with dancers who were proud to have their pictures taken. I inquired about their career paths, past and present, and also asked, "What does your family think about your nude dancing?" Gabrial shared her unique background:

My father is a Pentecostal preacher. It's a sin to turn on a man. He said, "I'm praying for you and I hope you don't die." I'd go to hell. He'd wait for me outside the clubs with Bible verses. I was raised so strict. I had never seen a woman naked. I never wore shorts.

But she did not feel the need to be saved. After she married a former patron and had a family, she and her father reconciled.

Countering charges of harm to dancers are many dancers' views and facts about inside and outside exotic club life. A dancer said she was sexually harassed where she worked as an accountant, but never in the club.[1] She had regulars who came to see her time and again primarily to spend hours talking about their problems.

Dancers labor to entice, as described in Chapter 3. A dancer's income varies depending on how seductive she is, how hard she works. The type of club she works in, the local government regulations, season, shift, day of week, clientele, and, sometimes, the willingness to bend the rules make a difference. Researcher Geoffrey Miller and his colleagues found that women earn more during their peak period of fertility: they dress more provocatively and men find them prettier during their estrus.

## Kinds of Clubs

Although there remain small dives, and the "bad girl" reputation and "dangerous place" aura persist, exotic dance is an industry that has become increasingly upscale with a broad clientele. A former male bastion now includes women. Of the approximately four thousand clubs across the county, some are small businesses and others are owned by corporations. As the numbers of gentlemen clubs have exploded over the last thirty years, brand licensing has ensued as a logical model. For example, in 2010, Déjà Vu had eighty clubs. A brand-name club attracts a substantial customer base of travelers who know what to expect by the name.

Rick's Cabaret's common stock is traded on NASDAQ under the symbol RICK. Its clubs cater to males, twenty-five to fifty-five years old, with high disposable income—businessmen, business owners, corporate executives. About 30 percent of the weekend clientele is female. Rick's twenty-two owned, operated, or licensed upscale exotic dance clubs welcome seventy thousand patrons a month and earned about $21 million net income in 2010. The clubs, with decor and customer service similar to that of major steakhouses, are in New York City, Miami, Philadelphia, New Orleans, Charlotte, Dallas, Houston, Minneapolis, and other cities under the names "Rick's Cabaret," "XTC," "Club Onyx" and "Tootsie's Cabaret." Tootsie's has more than seventy thousand square feet of entertainment space and parking for fifteen hundred cars. It is open from noon until 6 a.m. and features up to four hundred entertainers daily. Rick's Cabaret also operates a media division, ED Publications, and owns the adult Internet membership website couplestouch.com, as well as a network of online adult auction sites under the flagship URL naughtybids.com. But note that the bulk of clubs are small, usually around six thousand square feet.

On the American Stock Exchange, VCG Holding Corp. owns sixteen PT's Show Clubs in eight states, and it was first traded here in 2004. Déjà Vu Consulting began in 1987 with a club in Seattle and now has many clubs worldwide, including Larry Flynt's Hustler Club. John Gray's Spearmint Rhino began in 1991 in Upland, California, and the corporation has grown to more than forty-two clubs in six countries abroad (United Kingdom, Russia, Austria, Czech Republic, Australia, and Japan) with about twenty-seven hundred employees and eight thousand contract dancers. Penthouse has about a dozen clubs in the United States, New Zealand, Russia, and Canada.

Larry Flynt's Hustler Club in Cleveland, photographer Trace Grundstrom, courtesy Déjà Vu Consulting.

188

Upscale clubs are well maintained, often with valet parking, grand entryways, plush chairs, mirrored walls, potted plants, rich natural wood, marble, many plasma televisions, four-star meals, humidors, shoe shine stations, posh restrooms with attendants, fountains and fireplaces, and comfortable dressing rooms for dancers—indeed a pleasant work setting. In 2010, Dennis DeGori, well-known operator of elegant entertainment establishments, brought the chef of an award-winning Italian restaurant in Chicago, eighty award-winning domestic and international wines and champagnes, and a fully equipped business center to his New York Strip Steakhouse & Cabaret in South Florida.

Some clubs are like grand old mansions with statues and antique decorations on the walls. Cabaret Royale is a pleasure dome resembling a European luxury hotel—sixteen-foot-high, hand-carved Spanish doors, imported crystal chandeliers, Italian marble floors, boutiques, and dancers performing atop baby grand pianos. The emporiums with sixty or more dancers per night, six stages, and private rooms seating half-a-dozen patrons have multiple levels, mezzanines overlooking the main floor, and different kinds of private lounges on successive levels. Champagne rooms run about two hundred dollars per half hour. Dancers frequently wear evening gowns and floor managers or hosts (bouncers) are in tuxedos. Stretch limousines can be seen outside the clubs. Special events include amateur night, dance competitions, feature performances, and mud, oil, or jello wrestling. Sapphire Club, in Las Vegas, is one of the largest: seventy-one thousand square feet, four hundred dancers at any moment, and five ATMs. It sold for $80 million in 2006. In 2010, a $30 million Hustler Club, designed to be an ultra-erotic event center to serve corporations that want to add a little spice to their events, opened in Las Vegas. The club has seventy thousand square feet spread over three floors and a basement, five bars topped by a year-round oasis, and a wedding chapel on the roof. It advertises itself with a million-dollar marquee and a fifty-foot torch flame.[2]

I visited opulent, glamorous, tastefully decorated clubs that provide dancers with spacious dressing rooms, lockers, toilet and shower facilities, and theater-style lighted mirrored dressing tables and chairs. Some clubs have in-house manicurists, hair stylists, tanning rooms, workout equipment, masseurs, make-up artists, sales shops for both dancers and patrons, food, and house moms who assist the dancers, often providing a shoulder to cry on. Club manager Mark Van Gelder in Benton County, Minnesota, designed Sugar Daddy's Club with a comfortable workspace for dancers and always has fresh flowers in the dressing room.

Clubs often have themes indicated by their titles, such as Circus, Circus.

In Dallas, the atmosphere at Baby Dolls resembles that of a post-athletic game party. Fare West, also in Dallas, catered to a biker crowd: seven motorcycles hung from the walls and ceilings. There was a bike video and a stationary bike for patrons. Paradise Found in Syracuse has a South Pacific design. Club Paradise Gentlemen's Club in Milwaukee requested the designation as a "Center for the Visual and Performing Arts" based on the club art collection consisting of a sculpture and two paintings. The designation would allow the club to admit underage customers, as long as they don't drink alcohol. The Milwaukee Common Council's Utilities and Licenses Committee voted 2–1 to grant Club Paradise the designation, but then the Common Council blocked it and the club withdrew its application.

Club variety is unlimited. Mary's Club in Portland, Oregon, features tattooed contortionist entertainers. In Eugene, the Silver Dollar Club offers an annual haunted house/strip club. The Palomino Club in Las Vegas plays host to a TV reality series, King of Clubs, on Playboy TV. The show follows the Gentile family who now operate the club, once a favorite hangout of Frank Sinatra and the Rat Pack. Complete nudity and full bar are permitted under a grandfather clause.

Clubs provide security because they want to attract moneyed clientele. Some establishments have a team of employees who have had background checks, are trained to deal with problems, and are armed with radios and flashlights. Clubs fasten cameras inside and outside the premises and hire off-duty police officers. A club may have a metal detector in the entrance.

Tonya Dee, a former dancer who wrote a manual for dancers, noted that a club owner may be involved in a police raid to clean house and get rid of whores and suspected drug queens/dealers. Large muscular male bouncers function by intimidation; female "bouncers," or floor managers, by charm. Michael J. Peter, credited with founding the gentlemen's club, says that when a big guy (bouncer) approaches or challenges patrons, they may become ready to fight in front of "their girl" (favorite dancer). By contrast, if a female hostess is sent to handle a problem and all male staff members disappear, the issue is handled amicably. Men won't fight with women.

As in any business, there are good, bad, and volatile bosses, male or female. Owners and managers may be "dirty old men" or "kindly fathers," collaborative or adversarial "moms." Primarily older male club owners and managers working with young female dancers evoke gender and generation divisions that can exacerbate disagreement over who gets what money and other working conditions.

It helps if a dancer in an adult cabaret can get along with people and has high self-esteem, which can armor her against being snubbed or the target

Club Security, photographer Judith Lynne Hanna.

of rudeness, such as someone saying "you're fat" or "you're unattractive." Some women who complain about their bosses have no comparable work experience, so they don't know if they are treated differently from workers in other businesses. Club owners have complained about dancers not showing up when they say they will, not following club rules, and not creating a friendly environment that attracts patrons. Dancers and patrons sometimes pay monitors to look the other way when protocol is violated.

## Good Bosses

Mike Rose, owner/operator of the Gold Club in Florida, wants aggressive, inviting managers, who welcome guests like it's a holiday dinner. Rose goes into the dressing room to tell the entertainers how great they look or how much he appreciates them for performing at his clubs. Angela worked in a club in New Orleans owned by a Greek who did his bookkeeping in Greek. Acting like a father to the dancers, he loaned them money when they needed it and saw that they got medical attention when warranted. He promoted business for the dancers with a doorman who lured customers into his club using rhymes or catchy phrases: "I've got something you've gotta see," he would yell. "No chicks with dicks, no weenies in the bikinis, no sluts with nuts!" This reassurance of the dancers' gender was a common theme, even in bars where as many as one-third of the dancers were, in fact, transvestites.[3]

Jeff Levy, who had worked for the MAL Entertainment chain of clubs before becoming Executive Director of the New Jersey Adult Cabaret Association, said MAL:

> goes to a great extent to be a good neighbor by keeping a safe and fun environment for entertainers, staff and patrons. And encouraging and rewarding the pursuit of educational goals of entertainers and staff. They can attend a GED program every Tuesday night. All books, tutors and testing are free; they even get a tip-out voucher. This is much like a major corporation giving tuition assistance and rewarding self-improvement. We also keep our staff and managers well informed on local, state and new federal legislation, any problems with our industry. . . . updated with . . . meetings, memos and email. MAL is also involved with several charities.

To recruit talent for his adult clubs in Detroit and Windsor, Michigan, Robert Katzman advertised on the back cover of The Lance, the student newspaper at the University of Windsor. Katzman's ad promised that his company would pay tuition for coeds who work as strippers—and keep up their grade point averages. Dancers would receive fifteen hundred to two thousand dollars in educational expenses per year for working three or four seven-hour shifts a week in his clubs. This money was on top of the dancers' ten dollars-an-hour wage, in addition to cash from tips and private dances. About twenty of the more than two hundred dancers were taking advantage of the tuition program, including women studying massage, nursing, and engineering.

Michael Ocello's VCG Holding Corporation trains dancers in current affairs, dress, and wine tasting to boost the women's earning potential, as well as his profit margins. Ocello was a mover and shaker in the eight-square-block Brooklyn village of about six hundred people in Missouri. He help set up the Brooklyn Adult Trust in 2002, funded by the village's adult businesses to provide awards for school achievement, scholarships, and money for other projects. Ocello estimates that in the past five years the adult industry, which sustains the village through the revenue it generates, has contributed about one hundred thousand dollars to the Trust.[4]

In Florida, evidence of mutual respect between dancers and a club owner became apparent in 1999 at two marathon Tampa City Council hearings, totaling about nineteen hours, on a proposed ordinance requiring six feet between nude dancer and patron. Testifying against the ordinance, and paying tribute to Mons Venus owner Joe Redner, dancers and their families and patrons turned out in force. Few people spoke in support of the ordinance.

Women also own and manage clubs. Dawn Rizos is owner and CEO of the award-wining club, The Lodge, which has been described as looking like it was airlifted to Dallas from a great national park of the American West. "The Lodge Way" is to treat dancers with respect, generosity, and appreciation. This policy attracts some of the best talent nationwide, engenders loyalty, and encourages dancers to strive to meet the high standards of The Lodge. In regular meetings, dancers can express ideas without fear of retribution. The Lodge solicits anonymous questionnaires for dancer suggestions and complaints. Dancers are welcome to stop by the boss's office to talk. The club also makes clear that dancers can move on to other jobs in the club, including management. There are periodic appreciation parties. Full-time students pay no house fees. When a dancer ran into financial trouble, The Lodge awarded her its annual scholarship covering tuition and books.[5]

Well-managed clubs protect dancers from inappropriate staff and patron behavior. Club owners, managers, or house moms mentor young dancers from broken homes or abusive relationships who are especially prone to poor work habits and lifestyle choices. Some clubs give dancers the opportunity to become part-owners and consequently increase their stake in the club's success. Clubs often mentor new dancers. Taya Parker, Entertainer of the Year and a *Penthouse* and *Playboy* model, who became a feature after being an in-house performer for more than eight years, was a mere eighteen years old when she went with a friend to a local gentlemen's club and got a job. Having no idea how to perform, she received training,

The Lodge, courtesy of The Lodge, photographer The Lodge staff.

along with a group of other new hires, for a month from the general manager, who welcomed questions. He supplied them with their first gowns and showed them how to manage their money and how to address the clientele. Dancers were rewarded with gifts for meeting the expectations in attire, dance and music, and scheduling.

Without exotic dancers, there is no exotic dance business. By helping dancers with their performance careers, lives, and transition plans, a club helps itself to refute the charge of exploiting women, to fight the persistent battle against the exotic dance industry, and to thrive economically.

## Bad Patrons and Bosses

Of course, CR-Activists focus exclusively on instances where men are abusive toward women. Club managers bear some responsibility for the behavior of patrons in their establishments. Bernadette Barton taped interviews with thirty-six dancers from nine clubs in San Francisco, Hawaii, and Kentucky and visited a total of thirty. She claims the strip bar is an environment that exposes women to the worst of men's behavior: rude-

*Above and facing page:* Lodge Dancers, courtesy of The Lodge, photographer The Lodge staff.

A Lodge Dancer, courtesy of The Lodge, photographer The Lodge staff.

ness, touch, and rejection that leaves them hurt psychologically. Yet, such behavior occurs in public places and a variety of workplaces. A man can verbally abuse any woman walking down the street or driving on the highway or grope her in a crowd. To say that the exotic dance workplace is negative without comparing it to other workplaces is meaningless. Moreover, if dancers go on to become, for example, a mayor, lawyer, PhD, professor, or business person, their experiences do not appear to be debilitating. The question is how often have dancers had negative incidents? Why? Considering the number of clubs, the number of reported problems is miniscule.

Strip bars and gentlemen's clubs may have their share of rude patrons because rude people are everywhere. The Men's Club in Dallas has three stages, two big TV screens, wingback chairs, a shoe shine station, and an upstairs with a pool table and fireplace. Huge plateglass windows draw in sunlight. The club has a patio with a pool open to dancers and patrons. On Friday nights, there is a band. The club serves gourmet meals. Membership, when I visited, was $650 a year, $2,250 for a corporation. However, dancers from another club told me they wouldn't like to work at the Men's Club for these reasons: expense account patrons talk down to the dancers; the entertainers have an attitude; some men paid several dancers to get on their hands and knees and crawl around them, barking like dogs. I had never heard of this. Of course, the dancers were not compelled to play animals.

Threats of being fired for noncompliance with managerial dictates have led dancers to leave clubs, dance elsewhere, or find other work—and to file lawsuits against the clubs. The underlying issue may be management showing disrespect toward dancers by, for example, sexually harassing dancers, calling them degrading names like "bitch" and "slut," pressuring them to go beyond the legal limits in dancer-patron exchanges, scheduling too many performers, failing to protect dancers against ill-behaved patrons, and pushing the women to purchase expensive costumes or have breast enhancement at their own expense (several thousand dollars).

A form of discrimination, sexual harassment[6] includes unwelcome sexual advances, requests for sexual favors, and other verbal or physical conduct of a sexual nature that affects the victim's work environment. Not long after starting her new job as a dancer in Boston, Jackie said she had to fend off relentless, unwanted kisses and pawing from her King Arthur's Motel and Lounge supervisor, who refused to give her desirable work schedules unless she slept with him. Jackie eventually complained to the owner and was fired. So she filed a sexual harassment complaint against the club with the Massachusetts Commission Against Discrimination and was awarded $27,000 in lost wages and $25,000 for emotional distress. Agents may book feature dancers in clubs where management tries to extort sex in exchange for paying the dancers' wages.

Club management and police, who are supposed to protect dancers, often assume that because women take their clothes off onstage (on the stage and in the area where patrons sit), they do not object to men seeing them nude offstage. Thirty-year-old Tracey brought a sexual harassment suit against PT's Show Club in Denver for refusing to restrict male club staff and patrons from entering, at will, the dressing room/personal hygiene room nearly every day and neglecting to replace the bathroom door. Some of these unwanted "guests" made unwelcome sexual jokes or contact. In such cases, I testify that American culture and mainstream theater entitle women to a private space for personal needs. Therefore, as in any performance space, the exotic dancers' dressing room, shower, and toilet are expected to be for them alone.

When a dancer enters the dressing room, she prepares herself to create a fantasy character different from her everyday person. Most dancers seek to keep their public and private selves separate. Dancers face the danger of being identified, stigmatized, stalked, and even assaulted because of old stereotypes perpetuated by the media and Christian Right. Being gaped at in a theater to earn money and being gaped at offstage is somewhat analogous to the difference between consensual sex and rape.

Dancers also object to sex discrimination in remuneration. Some clubs require independent contractor dancers to pay to work but not men who tend bar, the door, or the music. A manager may fine dancers for tardiness and absences but not men working for the club. Men may get benefits but not dancers. Dancers may be pressured to write/pose for club publications pro bono but not men.

## Pluses and Minuses

Frances had danced for fifteen years in Florida and Georgia. I asked her what she liked best about dancing. Her answer:

> You're your own boss. . . . It's good exercise, usually good money, it's fun, you get to listen to music, it's creative, you get to dress sexy, you meet lots of great guys, and make lots of close girlfriends.

I also asked her, if you could change one thing, what would that be?

> It's murder on your feet, if you're not just naturally beautiful, it's expensive to keep up your appearance, costumes are expensive. If you travel you're away from home . . . it's dangerous and lonely living out of a suitcase, you constantly are in danger of being ripped off for your clothes, CDs and money and other valuables. It's hard to decide which people you can trust; you're at the mercy of exorbitant house fees and DJ tips. There's no job security; you never know when a club will close or you could get busted for doing what you're told is okay to do at your job.

Frances said that she worries:

> What happens to the dancers after a court decision to close a club? I wonder if they are quickly able to find another place to work so they won't get behind in their bills. No one seems to really care about what happens to them. I only worked at one club that was shut down while I worked there. It cared enough to pay unemployment insurance for the employees.

As in any job, the first days can be anxiety-producing. Getting onstage, unclothed and dancing for the first time, usually evokes stage fright. Dancers compete for market share from patrons who tip and buy dances—and from managers who make schedules, assigning day or night shifts, weekdays, or the lucrative weekends. Dancers work in a volatile environment: good days, bad days. They engage in emotional labor, sometimes roller coaster-like, as do people in the entertainment, tourist, and hospitality industries. And as in these occupations, on good days, dancers are mostly affirmed, adored, and showered with money. On the bad days, they are ignored, rejected and insulted.

In some clubs, the dancers share camaraderie and bond with each other. "We're all sisters," says Tiffany. "We look out for each other and socialize outside the club." Dancers might team up for well-paying patrons who fantasize about girl-on-girl relations. A dancer might point out a patron who wants a dance when she is already engaged with another patron. Dancers do not interfere with each other's patrons. Yet, in other clubs, dancers may be dog-eat-dog competitive, wary of a dancer trying to "steal" a patron. Dancers form cliques that can be unfriendly to outside dancers who complain about being ostracized or having their costumes stolen or cut.

Racial segregation of dancers occurs, although the audience in white clubs is generally racially mixed. White clubs usually have a black dancer or two, but some club owners fear that black dancers will attract the young, hip-hop black guys who would scare away the white clientele. There are "black clubs," but there aren't a lot of them, meaning fewer opportunities for house dancers or features. Lady, a black house dancer in Detroit, Michigan, observed, "The black dancers themselves discourage a lot of other black dancers from working in the white clientele clubs. Being unique and different from all the white girls running around makes them good money." Novelty attracts patrons. This is the reason dancers choose to dance in different clubs.

The majority of dancers do not find exploitation to be a problem. However, stigma is a big labor problem, caused in part by CR-Activists who brand dancers unfairly with a "yellow band" or "scarlet letter" for "being immodest," "loose," and "sinners." Furthermore, people often subject dancers to social castigation for problems common to any place of public assembly. Some dancers may internalize society's negative views of them. Many often cannot tell their families about their work. Cheryl said that when her family found out she was dancing, she lost half of her trust fund. Dancers fear employers in their other jobs will find out about their dancing and fire them.

A dancer, who is also a licensed professional with two college degrees and a number of clinical skills, works at a hospital, which provides her with health care insurance and a long-time future. She reported that she almost vomited when her colleagues ridiculed a stripper featured in *Glamour* magazine. She was mortified that anyone could even jokingly suggest she become what, in fact, she already was.

For some women, exotic dance is an unconventional path to success that is paved with the pain of public misperception. Yet, performing in exotic dance clubs is far from a one-way trip to hell for most performers. And young people tend to be more accepting of stripping.

## Financial Disputes

A point of contention between exotic dancers and clubs, and among dancers themselves, is whether dancers are, or should be, independent contractors or employees. Independent contracting is a common corporate strategy practiced by CEOs from Bill Gates on down. From ballet to tap, many dance school owners and operators also wrestle with distinctions in dancer classification as they face the dilemma of classifying dancers as independent contractors or employees. Advice has appeared in *Dance Teacher Now*. In some exotic dance clubs, dancers may sign petitions and join unions and class-action lawsuits over their work status.

State law governs unemployment, work compensation, and disability. California law—29 Cal Jur 3d (Rev.)—defines the distinction between employee and independent contractor: "Employee: where a person performing work for another is subject to the orders, control, and direction of such other person (employer)." "Independent Contractor: if control may be exercised only as to the result of the work and not the means by which it is accomplished." The factor determining the status boils down to the common law of agency. The dancer is an employee if the employer sets up the means and details of the dancer's work in the club, such as: check-in time, schedules, requirements for drinks, stage dances, working the floor, incurring expenses for costly costumes, grooming, relationships with customers, fees for private dances, mandatory meetings, fines for violating club rules, or selling drinks to patrons or getting them to buy "ladies'" drinks. Employee status means a dancer receives wages, health benefits, workman's compensation, tax deductions, and the opportunity to unionize. As employees, dancers cannot reject men who wish a private dance. Employers report dancers' income. However, benefits are linked to an employee working full-time. Clubs may give dancers a salary (minimum wage) and permit them to keep tips but only a portion or none of the fees from private dances. Dancers lose the freedoms of independent contractors.

As independent contractors, dancers pay "rent," "house," "bar," "stage," or "tip out" fees to perform in the clubs in the same way an artist rents space in an exhibition hall or a haircutter rents a chair in a barber shop or salon, each in accord with specific rules. The dancers usually keep tips as well as fees or portions of fees for individual patron-focused dances. Independent contractors choose their schedules and when to take breaks; make artistic choices about their choreography, costumes, and music; and pay their own taxes and deduct business expenses. These dancers select the patrons for interaction and can exit from any fantasy, fleeting relationship they find unproductive or offensive.

Clubs usually prefer dancers with independent contractor status, and they may "fire" (refuse to rent club space) and blackball dissident dancers. Management may set take-it-or-leave-it house rules, pointing to a stream of young women ready to take a vacated place. Those dancers who bring individual and class-action suits against clubs for back wages and fees tend to be educated ex-dancers, aging or unattractive entertainers trying to bow out with additional income, dancers angry with a manager or owner, or performers persuaded to join a class-action suit. Many of these dancers do not care that the lawsuits may destroy the livelihoods of club personnel, dancers, and the business support industries.

Two exotic dancers in Seattle could not rally their peers to go to management about working conditions, let alone legal action, although the dancers all complained among themselves. However, in a comparatively small club in New Orleans, the dancers stuck together. Unified, the dancers didn't show up for work until a grievance was resolved. Without each night's earnings, the club suffered a big loss. Moreover, it takes time to recruit new dancers. So the dancers' complaints were quickly addressed.

Some exotic dancers have sued for violation of labor laws and settled out of court. Two San Diego women led a successful effort to organize topless dancers into a labor union in 1995. One of the dancers had been dancing at the popular Pacer's club for six years when she hurt her knees moving on four- to six-inch heels for eight-hour shifts. The club's management discouraged her from filing for worker's compensation. Surgery cost her more than $10,000. Subsequently, dancers rebelled when Pacer's management imposed "a house dance fee" of $5 for each hour they worked. Management considered a dancer's performance the club's product and therefore, the club was entitled to some of the dancer's earnings. However, the exotic dancers were earning minimum wage, $4.25 an hour, so the $5 an hour fee meant they were, in effect, paying to work and losing income. The Pacer's dancers affiliated with the Hotel and Restaurant Employees Union; in retaliation, the club fired the union organizer. A group of about six dancers kept the pressure on management, picketing outside the club between performances. Finally, management and the dancers agreed to a one-year contract and the controversy about the house dance fee went to court.

Two exotic dancers, Dawn Passar and Johanna Breyer, were fired and blackballed from performing in the San Francisco Bay area after they founded the Exotic Dancers Alliance (EDA) in 1993. The collective aimed to promote improved working conditions for dancers, free from sexual harassment and discrimination. The dancers asked club owners to put doors on bathroom stalls, get rid of roaches, fix exposed live wires, and improve crowded, small dressing rooms without ventilation. They also wanted to stop being sent home, suspended, or even fired, for what they deemed unjustifiable reasons. Club owners told me they could better control for drugs with open stalls. Passar and Breyer filed a wage grievance with the San Francisco Labor Commission against the Bijou Group, Inc. for treating performers as tenants/independent contractors and received monetary awards. Sexual harassment and discrimination against female dancers were also charged against the Bijou Group. The EDA argued that the dancers were employees and therefore entitled to hourly wages and the basic protections of California labor laws that prohibit employers from harassing workers, firing workers without cause, charging workers for the "right to work," or taking a share of workers' tips. The Labor Commission ruled in the dancers' favor and clubs were ordered to pay dancers wages and to stop charging stage fees. The corporation, which the dancers said exceeded $1.9 million a year in profit, declared bankruptcy in order to avoid paying the dancers' Commission-ruled back wages and refunding rent collected.

Being pro-union, and a former member of a teachers' union and of a federal employees' union, I wanted to support the dancer organizations.

Unions give dancers visibility as respected human beings striving toward improved working conditions. However, after much anguish, I realized clearly that being against the dancers who were claiming employee status was, in fact, being for dancers in general. The Federal Fair Labor Standards Act (Code of Federal Regulations, Title 29—Labor, chapter V, 541.3) exempts persons from employee regulations if they are engaged in creative work that requires the exercise of discretion and independent judgment: "Work that is original and creative in character in a recognized field of artistic endeavor (as opposed to work which can be produced by a person endowed with general manual or intellectual ability and training), and the result of which depends primarily on the invention, imagination, or talent of the employee." I testified to the dancers' work as artistic communication. If dancers aren't engaged in an artistic expression, then their work loses First Amendment protection!

A dancer in Las Vegas, Nevada, Brenda Lee—with the help of her husband, an Equal Employment Opportunity Commission lawyer, and yours truly—filed an *amicus curiae* brief in support of the clubs and independent dancers in a case in Las Vegas. The brief had some points I had not come across:

> By analogy to the copyright law, each dancer is analogous to an "author." As a general rule, the author is the party who actually creates the work, that is, the person who translates an idea into a fixed, tangible expression is entitled to copyright protection (17 U.S.C. section 102). Similarly, a dancer creates her own routines, expressions and manifestations uniquely those of its creator . . . if the defendants were to employ a dancer and exert full control over the performance, the author would then be vested to the defendant and would have a proprietor interest in any of the tangible expressions of each of the plaintiffs. Under this exception, if the work is for hire, "the employer" or other person for whom the work was prepared is considered the "author" and owns the copyright and possible derivative works, unless there is a written agreement to the contrary.

Lee noted that clubs use an audition process in selecting dancers for their clubs instead of the traditional hiring process.

I testified in four cases—including one in 1997 for the Mitchell Brothers O'Farrell Theatre in San Francisco (*Vickery, et al. vs. Cinema 7, Inc., et al.*) —that exotic dance was creative work. A bit of background: by 1988, the dancer's main income came from substantial fees and tips for lap dances. So San Francisco club owners stopped paying dancers wages. They began charging dancers "stage fees" for each shift they worked. At first, fees were

$10 or $15 for an eight-hour shift, and dancers tipped out the DJ, house mom, and doorman. In 1993, however, when some clubs hiked stage fees to $25 per shift, dancer resistance grew. Dancers who found themselves in a club with private booths, but who did not want to engage in any kind of non-fantasy sex with customers, were angry at having to pay huge new stage fees, such as the $125 fee at Mitchell Brothers. Many felt they had to choose: working at these clubs with such conditions or moving elsewhere or dropping out of the exotic dance scene entirely. Unique in the nation, San Francisco's mayor at the time only objected to street prostitution.

Inspired by the success of dancers in San Francisco, Anchorage, Minneapolis, San Diego, and Pittsburg for reclassification to employee status and back compensation, Ellen Vickery and Jennifer Bryce, two ex-dancers at Mitchell Brothers, pursued a class-action suit against the theater in the name of hundreds of former and current dancers. They eventually won a monumental $2.85 million judgment. Bryce, in her thirties, had been fired after being at the theater for six years. Jim Mitchell's view was that the theater has to make room for the eighteen-year-olds. (Note that mainstream theatrical shows change casts to freshen shows or when performers lose their looks or magnetism.) At the time, Vickery was still working at the club. A dancer had successfully sued O'Farrell Theatre eighteen months earlier because of two injuries from a fall at work and an assault by a customer.

Lily Burana, a former exotic dancer, decided in 1997, five years after leaving the world of stripping behind, to take one last jaunt around the country. She resumed stripping in order to understand what it means to do this work and then write about it. The first thing that had "pissed her off" about stripping in 1991 when she signed on at Mitchell Brothers was stage fees, although she acknowledged that the club offered the dancer a safe luxurious environment in which to work—stage, dressing room, lighting, music, and great earning potential. The dancers could select their schedules, but had to arrive at the theater an hour prior to the start of the show. At times, dancers had to do daisy chains (after performing, each dancer introduces the next to go onstage). Dancers had to sign out when leaving the building during their shift, presumably for safety reasons. Burana became the class-action representative for the dancers at that time.

Beth Ross, a labor rights attorney, took on the case and the dancers announced their lawsuit against Cinema 7, the Mitchell Brothers' parent company, in March 1994. The morning following the filing, the theater management held an emergency meeting and dancers were given the option of becoming independent contractors. They went for it, although the theater rules remained. The dancers signed a petition protesting the lawsuit. Burana said she was shunned by dancers. Preferring independent contractor status, a group of one hundred women working at Mitchell Brothers, led by dancer Stacy Crawford, formed the Independent Dancers Association (IDA) to promote their interests and raise funds to pay an attorney. Some people said that Mitchell and his staff had orchestrated this, but Crawford disagreed. She worried that employers could order dancers to do simulated sex acts and with whom and dictate many other work duties. The IDA newsletter stated that of the approximately one hundred and sixty women performing at the theater, one hundred and fifty-five were members of IDA. They elected a board of directors, which acted as a liaison among performers, club management, and attorneys. The pros and cons of employee status were spelled out. They noted that the touted employee benefit of worker's compensation would cover a very small percentage of those earning minimum wage and would preclude the right to sue the employer. Health benefits eligibility required working at least one hour more than part-time, an unlikely choice for management. Tax write-offs for expenses such as costumes, makeup, beauty services, and props would be reduced. Jobs would decrease. The faction of dancers who opposed the class-action was unsuccessful in their request to the judge to approve their independent contractor status and dismiss the class-action suit. They unsuccessfully filed several other lawsuits.

Two years later, after the dancers filed their suit against the club and unbeknownst to other dancers, Superior Court Judge William Cahill certified a class of about three hundred performers who appeared at the club between 1991 and 1995. Some dancers didn't think of themselves as employees or independent contractors. They were "joint venturers" in which each participant contributes something and takes something out. Their attorney, Joseph Wood, argued that the women contribute a certain amount of money and free work, whereas the club contributes a safe forum in which to dance nude in front of men. But the dancers spend seven-eighths of their time at the theater in earning tips and fees by doing their own work.

The club settled in summer 1998. Jeff Armstrong, the O'Farrell Theatre's manager believed that the class-action suit was being bankrolled by labor union organizers, who, in turn, were a front for organized crime, which hoped to break into the business. Mitchell's lawyer, Jeffrey Tanenbaum, thinks the underlying goal of Bryce and Vickery's suit was to unionize, and for such a campaign to succeed, the dancers must first win recognition as employees. Moreover, their attorney stood to collect big fees.

Dancers who bring suit for back wages and stage fees tend to win their cases, but few dancers take the clubs to court. The main reason for this, according to dancers, is the acute social stigma associated with stripping. Nancy Banks is the main organizer of a group of dancers alternately known as Success to Retire into Prosperity (STRIP) and the Strippers Society of San Francisco (SSSF)—a group that claims to be "the real voice of current active dancers in San Francisco."[7] The group provides a forum for dancers to discuss work issues. Speakers have addressed dancers about investment options, real estate, 401(k) retirement plans, group health insurance, child-care arrangements responsive to the dancer's schedule, and the social stigma attached to working as a stripper. Banks says that conditions have changed since 1996, that hostility between managers and dancers is "history." Managers now generally support and cooperate with dancers, settle disagreements between customers and dancers in a businesslike way, and are conscious of dancers' economic issues, scheduling limited numbers of dancers during slow daytime work shifts, for example. Clubs have video cameras for safety, security guards, and panic buttons that dancers can push if patrons step out of line.

It is her refusal to engage in prostitution, Banks insists, that keeps her high-end customers coming back—and paying big tips. She says she earns as much as four hundred thousand dollars a year—and owns a Bay Area home, three cars, and two horses. She likens the one hundred and twenty dollar fee she pays to the New Century Theater, one target of recent police raids, to a barbershop's charge for the freelance use of a chair. Eliminating the private rooms, Banks said, would smother the financial promise of stripping in San Francisco.

Employee lawsuits alleging dancers are misclassified as independent contractors are gaining traction in federal and state courts in California, District of Columbia, Florida, Massachusetts, Montana, and Texas. Attorney Brad Shafer said dancers and their attorneys who specialize in dancer class-action lawsuits extort huge financial settlements from clubs and owners: "a shakedown pure and simple." "We have seen not only the same attorney filing lawsuits against competitor clubs, but actually 'professional plaintiff' dancers who file case after case."[8]

Two issues that remain unaddressed by both San Francisco police and the district attorney's office are the continued collection of illegal stage fees by virtually all strip and lap-dancing clubs in the city, and the failure of the clubs to pay dancers wages, despite repeated rulings by the San Francisco Labor Commission, San Francisco Superior Court, and the US Equal Employment Opportunity Commission requiring such pay.

The Exotic Dancers Alliance became a nonprofit organization and published a manual called No Justice, No Piece! A Working Girl's Guide to Labor Organizing in the Sex Industry in 1998. EDA members occasionally travel to other places to teach groups how to unionize. Notwithstanding the dancers' challenge to clubs, for the most part, collective effort is minimal as dancer Teresa Dulce put it: "Dancers are unique creatures, they're independent." Monique said, "You can't get them to agree to buy a birthday gift. They try to exert power and control. They won't show up for work just to show their power." Dancing is also a short-term job, so the women don't feel it's worth investing time and attracting attention outside the club, especially when they could get fired for "agitation." Moreover, the top girls follow the action, so the same dancers who work the Indianapolis 500 head to sites for the Olympics and conventions. Teresa started Danzine, which served as an information exchange about health care, employment issues, personal finances, taxes, and voting. She also published a journal by that name—with the tagline: "created by and for angry fems in the biz"—and put up a website. She received a fellowship and grants and went on to set up a thrift store and a nonprofit organization on behalf of dancers.

There are also tax issues involved in exotic dancer labor relations. State and federal Departments of Labor and the Internal Revenue Service weigh in on dancer-employee arrangements or special accounting by club owners who use independent contractors. The IRS has the authority to assess employer Federal Insurance Contributions Act (FICA) and Federal Unemployment Tax Act (FUTA) taxes on tip income that employees fail to report both to their employers and to the IRS. A dancer who performed at a Déjà Vu club in the Midwest filed a request (known as an "SS-8 investigation") with the IRS to determine her employment status. She had signed four separate Dancer Performance Leases specifying that she pay a fee for the right to use the club premises. For the SS-8 investigation, the IRS sends a questionnaire about three areas to the presumptive employer—behavioral control, financial control, and relationship of the parties. Shafer challenged the IRS's jurisdiction to invoke their three-part test in a dancer context. In 2008, he said the IRS issued a concise and definitive ruling stating that when clubs are using his type of legal independent contractor structure, entertainers, as a matter of law, cannot be found to be employees of the club and the IRS does not even have jurisdiction to rule on dancer claims. Labor law standards may not be governed by IRS determinations.

## Truth Be Told

Although dancers may care about their patrons, they also see them as "ATMs." The women don't think they are the ones being exploited: more than one dancer said, "The men are the real suckers." Independent contractor or employee, exotic dancers want fair grievance procedures and respect. Everyone benefits from positive human relations.

A dancer in Las Vegas promised:

> I will still visit strip clubs after I quit. It's an industry that will never die, an industry that's based on man's most primal instincts. Dancing has transformed me from a wide-eyed little girl into a mature and sometimes very skeptical young woman. I'll take the skills I learned as a dancer with me for the rest of my life.

When exotic dancers testify positively in print, on talk shows, and in courts about their work, they help to de-stigmatize the clubs and dancers among open-minded people by dispelling stereotypes and thereby ameliorating efforts to eliminate the industry. On the other hand, disaffected dancers often create dissension within a club, make scheduling and general management difficult, and provide ammunition to CR-Activists. These dancers litigate for back wages and fees and justifiably against sexual harassment, discrimination, personal injury, and a threatening work environment. Mutual respect between exotic dancer and club owners/management create partners instead of combatants. A good reputation spreads by word of mouth and responsible performers will want to work in a club where they are treated well. Dancers sharing good ideas about business and community relations, and also good contacts among their patrons, can help defend a club against CR-Activist-propelled attacks and improve the dancers' and clubs' bottom line.

Evidence challenges the CR fantasy that exotic dancers are forced, exploited, and degraded club labor. Of course, working conditions vary among the clubs, as they do in any workplace. There are bad bosses and risks of inferior workplaces everywhere. One only has to go to a bookstore and see shelf after shelf filled with tomes on how to get along with your boss and make it in the workplace.

CR-Activist-instigated government regulations for the so-called protection of exotic dancers is questionable. Each locality has its own restrictions, and dancers who perform in different jurisdictions have to learn the regulations particular to that area. Requirements that exotic dancers wear pasties, invisible or opaque, cause health concerns, such as discoloring of the nipple. Latex pasties burn and a mother could not continue nursing her baby because of the soreness. The fact that regulations single out exotic dancers stigmatizes and discriminates against them. I wonder what income, loans, educational tuition and college expenses, daily fresh flowers, financial counseling, and training in work habits the CR-Activist organizations provide.

As noted, CR-Activists find performers who have had negative experience in the exotic dance workplace and who need support and convince them that they can overcome their difficulties by becoming born-again Christians and saved. CR-Activists then bring these disaffected performers into public venues to testify about the harmful effects of the exotic dance workplace. However, labor conditions are beneficial for most dancers. Furthermore, CR-Activists argue that the turpitude of exotic dance invites sexual assault and other crime. Let's look at some of the evidence of aggression, attacks on property, prostitution, drugs, bribery, and abuse of authority related to exotic dance.

# Christian Right Claims Club Crime

## Where Are the Bodies?

"No, no. No crime," said Sherlock Holmes, laughing. "Only one of those whimsical little incidents which will happen when you have four million human beings all jostling each other within the space of a few square miles."

SIR ARTHUR CONAN DOYLE, "The Adventure of the Blue Carbuncle"

Humankind cannot bear very much reality.

T. S. ELIOT, *The Four Quartets*

Within a segment of the politically active Christian Right nationwide, Phil Burress, leader of Citizens for Community Values (CCV) in Ohio, declaims exotic dance as a "blight plaguing the community with increased crime." He pushed through the state's Draconian exotic dance regulations. Clubs are an incitement to sexual assault, murder, other violence, prostitution, bribery, drugs, and property damage. True? If so, the main point is, are these problems disproportionately represented in exotic dance establishments compared to other businesses or institutions? Who is doing what to whom?

CCV worries about the sinful clubs causing men to brutalize women. But perhaps they should be more concerned about a place like their state university. In 2006, Ohio State, with an enrollment of nearly fifty-two thousand students had fifty-three incidents of forcible sex, the highest number among universities in the United States.[1] As a volunteer for the Victim Assistance Sexual Assault program of Montgomery County, Maryland, for a decade, I can attest to university males creating havoc.

A phone call from a stranger at about 5 p.m. on Friday, November 22, 2002, certainly moved me to continue to dig into the downside of exotic dance. Joe said he was in Philadelphia and had read my article "If This Is Stripping, What Is Adult Entertainment?" in *Exotic Dancer Bulletin*. Saying he was an unemployed editor in his late forties, Joe told me he had been to clubs over the years, and he accused me of doing a whitewash on exotic dance clubs, that the clubs exploit and degrade women who permit men to touch them and give blow jobs in back rooms for money and drugs. Joe was surprised I had not heard about the stripper who went to a motel with a man who threw her out the window and then over a bridge. He read about it in the *National Enquirer* and heard about it on TV.

The cabarets I visited had few, if any, convictions for crime. When I travel to a place to testify, club owners driving me through the area might point out a club that "gives us a bad rap." But criminology studies show that, overall, exotic dance businesses have no more, or often fewer, problems than other places of public assembly. I read news and National Criminal Justice reports to broaden my knowledge, and I have found far more reports—and convictions—of clergy sexually abusing children and adults than of exotic dance clubs causing the harm alleged by church people and misinformed others. Exotic dance is not more dangerous than other forms of dancing, and dancing is usually a safe profession or recreation.

Here are illustrative incidents from my research into the downside of the exotic dance industry. The incidents of murder, other violence, prostitution, drugs, and bribery are the exception, not the rule.

## Murder: Boyfriends, Husbands, Police, Mafia, and Others

A different kind of case for me as an expert court witness occurred after a quadruple shooting took place near the Déjà Vu SeaTac club in Seattle. An exotic dancer had dumped an alcohol- and drug-addicted boyfriend. He had done construction work at Déjà Vu but lost his job and she had been financially supporting him. The dancer moved into a duplex behind the club with her new boyfriend, the club manager who had just been fired because of drugs. Dejected, the ex was hanging out in a parking lot shared by the club and duplex. One evening the dancer left work at 9 p.m. and returned to her apartment. Her ex went there about 2 a.m. and shot her and her current boyfriend, killed an innocent bystander, and then committed suicide. The dancer lost an eye; her boyfriend got palsy.

The bystander's estate and the living victims sued Déjà Vu SeaTac. The legal theory behind the suit: the shooting was foreseeable because women who work as nude dancers have a higher expectation of violence against them. Here's where I came in. I was asked to testify as to whether the exotic dance club environment was conducive to violence. I had been to the club, as well as to many other adult theaters. Was I ever fearful in exotic dance establishments? Never. And I had gone to some clubs by myself. Indeed, had I been able to wear high heels and a bit younger, I would have felt comfortable dancing in many of the cabarets.

Founder and director of the Council of Abused Women in Portland,

Oregon, Susan Hunter filed an affidavit on behalf of the estate. She had provided counseling to women in the sex industry and had tried to direct women out. Hunter is part of the fringe of women who believe exotic dancers are harmed whether or not they know it. She believes these dancers are coerced and consequently their civil rights are violated. In the affidavit, Hunter offered anecdotal evidence about club violence. Hunter went so far as to say that women who perform in exotic dance clubs have the same experience as those in concentration camps.

In another case, an actor and yoga teacher, Paul Cortez, twenty-six years old, was convicted of the 2005 murder of twenty-one-year-old Catherine Woods. She apparently rejected him and his self-appointed role as a white knight who would stop her from working as an exotic dancer. A classically trained ballerina from Columbus, Ohio, Woods had come to New York City determined to make it as a Broadway dancer. When Cortez told Woods's father that she was dancing at a Times Square strip club, she severed the relationship with Cortez.

Other cases include the 1996 shooting death of Nicole Cox. Her husband, Cameron Cox, went to the Stir Crazy club in Miami where she was working and shot her. She had recently moved out of the apartment that she shared with him. In 2006, at the Foxy Lady in New Bedford, Massachusetts, three people died and two were seriously injured. Scott Medeiros, thirty-five years old, suited with body armor, a black SWAT uniform, mask, and boxes of bullets, entered the club through an unlocked back door and sprayed about one hundred rounds from a military-issued M-16 and a semiautomatic pistol. Club manager Tory Marandos and floor host Bobby Carreira, who had repeatedly told him to stay away from the club in the past, were killed. Medeiros was angry that Carreira had fathered a child with his ex-girlfriend, one of Foxy Lady's female bartenders. When Police Special Forces arrived on the scene, a firefight ensued and then Medeiros shot himself.

But a rejected lover assaulting his beloved is certainly not a club-specific phenomenon. Annually, there are about 1.7 million incidents of workplace violence, 18,700 related to domestic situations. Domestic problems—usually involving spouses or significant others who are thought to be cheating or terminating a relationship—often spill over into the workplace. According to the US Justice Department, in 2004, 1,139 women were killed by current or former intimate partners. Violence and aggravated assault in the exotic dance business are mostly related to failed relationships with a dancer or an aggressive athlete or anti-club agitator. But the source of such crimes is unrelated to the characteristics of the exotic dance hospitality industry. The Smith Brothers's song heard on *A Prairie Home Companion* radio show is too commonly apt.

I love her very much
If she hurts me, I will kill her
If I can't have her, I'd rather she be dead.

Although workplace violence accounted for 18 percent of all violent crime in the last seven years of the 1990s, the exotic dance workplace was not identified by the National Crime Victimization Survey, from the Bureau of Justice Statistics in 2001, as at-risk for violence. Police officers experienced the highest rate of violent crime, 261 incidents per 1,000 officers. Retail workers were attacked at a rate slightly higher than those in other fields. Cabbies ranked third, with 128 incidents per 1,000 drivers. There were shootings at post offices, schools, and colleges—most famously, twelve students and one teacher gunned down by two classmates at Columbine High School in 1999 and thirty-two people killed by a student at Virginia Tech in 2007. In 2009, a psychiatrist, Major Nidal M. Hasan shot and killed twelve soldiers and one civilian at Ft. Hood in Texas. An Amish schoolhouse in rural Pennsylvania and missionary training center in Colorado also had such violent crime.

The Mafia is believed to be involved in strip clubs. This may have been common in the 1950s and 1960s in Las Vegas. But today criminal elements have waned in the industry and clubs are owned by businesspeople, professionals, and corporations on the stock exchanges. Nonetheless, the past pokes into the present. In 1998, federal prosecutors accused John Gotti Jr., son of the imprisoned Gambino crime family boss, and his lieutenants of engaging in an extortion scheme to seize control of Scores, a strip club on Manhattan's Upper East Side. They supposedly controlled the parking and coat check services and got kickbacks from the dancers. A bouncer and a waiter at Scores were killed in June 1996. In 2001, in Miami, Florida, a federal jury convicted two members of the Gambino crime family with the slaying at The Dollhouse in Sunny Isles of a dancer, Jeanette Smith, wrongly thought to be an FBI informant. Frederick J. "Fat Freddie" Massaro, a restaurant owner who oversaw the Gambino family's South Florida operations, had ordered her killing.

Club competition for market share got rough in Nevada. Four people pleaded not guilty to charges that they conspired to kill Timothy Hadland for criticizing the North Las Vegas Palomino Club and its owner to cabdrivers. When cabdrivers don't suggest a particular club to customers, it costs the club thousands of dollars in revenue from potential clientele. Those charged in the murder included a Palomino Club worker. Hadland was found near Lake Mead with Palomino flyers scattered around his body. In 2000, Jack Perry, son of the Palomino's owner at the time, shot and killed an employee he thought was trying to buy the club. Perry pleaded guilty and was sentenced to fourteen years to life in prison.

In New York City, a twenty-four-year-old dancer's throat was slashed with a kitchen knife and her boyfriend's hands were nailed to a two-by-four during an early morning invasion in 2000. This was seemingly motivated by two bandits' search for thousands of dollars that the exotic dancer kept stashed in a floor safe. She earned her living performing at an upscale East Side Manhattan club called Tens. The murder was related to robbery, not the exotic dance industry.

## Different Violence

Celebrity athletes and rappers can be combustible. This is especially likely when they come to the clubs with their bodyguards and "posses," or crews, sometimes in an entourage of twenty or more people. In February 2007, a tragic shooting at the Minxx Gentlemen's Club in Las Vegas left one of the club's security team members paralyzed and two others injured. Apparently, Adam "Pacman" Jones, a defensive back for the Tennessee Titans, got upset with a dancer in the midst of his "making it rain" (she picked up cash he had tossed into the air before she was given the okay). He grabbed her by the hair, rammed her head into the stage, and punched her in the face. A security member was trying to restrain him when one of Pacman's entourage smashed a bottle of champagne over the club employee's head. More security arrived and as Pacman was being subdued, he said, "You're going to die tonight. I'm going to smoke you." The club managers asked all patrons to leave. But one returned and opened fire with a semiautomatic weapon.

Four National Basketball Association players were present during a shooting outside an Indianapolis adult club. On December 6, 2006, former Indiana Pacers star Stephen Jackson, notorious for coldcocking a fan in 2004, was charged with criminal felony for recklessness, misdemeanor battery, and disorderly conduct. A fight broke out between Jackson and another club patron, Quentin Willford, inside Club Rio. Outside the club, another man, Deon Willford, hit Jackson with his vehicle. Jackson pulled a gun and shot five bullets into the sky.

Abductions of and assaults on women may occur anywhere, including outside exotic dance clubs. In 1997, a dancer waiting for her boyfriend to pick her up after her shift at the Bottoms Up dance club in Pittsburgh was kidnapped, raped, and beaten by two men. Two years later, a house dancer in Tucson was abducted by a patron, Michael Harvey, who had a lengthy criminal record. He had been asked to leave the club for inappropriate behavior and later returned. As the dancer was trying to jump-start her vehicle in the parking lot with the help of the club's doorman and a patron, Harvey offered his help. Then he pulled a gun and forced the dancer into his car. When the police caught Harvey, they found cocaine on him. In Virginia Beach, a Navy man abducted a dancer after following her home from J. B.'s Gallery of Girls club. Most clubs now have someone walk a dancer to her car in lit parking lots equipped with cameras.

## Dancer Aggression

It's usually ex-boyfriends and husbands who cause problems in the adult entertainment business. But dancers can harass, threaten, assault and abuse patrons, and fight with each other. A former Las Vegas exotic dancer, Robin Kelly, of Simi Valley, pleaded guilty to stalking and extortion. She began harassing *Las Vegas Review-Journal* cartoonist Jim Day on the Internet after he ended their seven-year affair in April 2000. She made annoying phone calls and sent threatening letters and e-mails before setting up a website that featured intimate photographs of herself and the married Day. She was sentenced to seven months in jail and placed on five years' probation.

In 2003, David Buhler and a buddy visited The Schoolhouse, a southern Michigan topless club. Kasey Ann Colvin, a twenty-year-old dancer hovered over Buhler and asked, "Do you want some of this?" Colvin, who had recently given birth, shot milk from her breast into his face. He angrily contacted the club manager, who apologized and offered him free soft drinks and lap dances. But Buhler contacted the police and filed an aggravated assault complaint. In another case, a patron claimed a dancer had hit him with her breast.

A former exotic dancer in Panama City, Florida, received a five-year suspended sentence for flying into a rage when management asked her to leave the Show 'N Tail lounge for breaking a club rule. She threw a drink on the bartender, damaged the dressing room, kicked out one dancer's tooth, and loosened another with her six-inch stiletto heels.

Koleen Brooks, a former stripper for fifteen years at Shotgun Willie's in Denver and the mayor of Georgetown, a small mountain town, faced a recall election for supposedly baring her breasts in public and intimidating city workers. Local residents speculated that she made up a story about being threatened in order to get sympathy. She was charged in 2002 with falsely reporting an assault.

## Attacks on Property

In a rare case, an Atlanta gentlemen's club owner Michael Childs admitted he ordered a competitor's club burned down. As noted earlier, in Gary, Indiana, vandals attacked the Delilah's Gone Platinum building on the exterior and interior, causing substantial damage to the walls and windows, interior décor, sound system, and the dance stage floor.[2] Vandalized twice, the club, which did not have a liquor license, had been the target of protests by nearby residents who didn't want more adult entertainment businesses in their neighborhood. At Tom Kats' Gentlemen's Club in San Juan County, Washington, Jerome Charley refused to pay for a number of lap dances and scuffled with a bouncer. Charley left and then rammed his minivan a good three feet inside the club. Three men were escorted out of a gentlemen's club in Winchendon, Massachusetts, when one of the group touched a dancer. Angered, the men vandalized cars, attempted to run over the manager in the parking lot, and returned later to set the club on fire.

## Prostitution

The nonviolent crime of prostitution? Of the approximately four thousand clubs, only a few (such as the well-publicized case of the Gold Club in Atlanta) have had charges—and convictions—against dancers for prostitution and against club owners for pimping.

NBA stars Patrick Ewing and Dennis Rodman were among the prominent athletes subpoenaed to testify about sexual favors allegedly given to sports stars at Atlanta's nude Gold Club. NFL players Jamal Anderson and Terrell Davis, as well as former Atlanta Hawk Dikembe Mutom, were also called to testify at the 2001 trial. Owner Steve Kaplan was charged, along with sixteen others, in a racketeering conspiracy including prostitution, money laundering, loan sharking, and ties to organized crime. Kaplan's attorney Steve Sadow acknowledged that professional athletes were entertained free of charge at the club, known in the trade as "comping." However, Kaplan denied federal prosecutors' claims that he arranged for Gold Club dancers to have sex with celebrities to raise the club's profile and lure more customers. He pleaded guilty to one federal charge of racketeering.

Several dancers told me they knew women who would be prostitutes if they did not have the opportunity to dance. Indeed, in a small club in

New Orleans, when the dance business was really slow, some performers were said to hook. Dancers have reported that they knew of instances of "dirty mixing," turning a trick, but the dancers were discreet. To try to get a particular dancer to engage in prostitution, some patrons claim other dancers do so. Frances said that some clubs create situations that lead to prostitution. Some girls had hundreds of dollars in accumulated fines and they turned to prostitution to work them off; customers paid the clubs to let the girls get off to turn tricks.

On the other hand, Gabrial said, "girls beat a girl because she did prostitution in the club." Moreover, many clubs have both strict rules and video camera oversight everywhere. Magdalene reported that most dancers she knew wouldn't have risked their jobs over prostitution.

For Scarlet, "the real clincher was once I had sex for free with a guy just a couple of weeks after he offered me $1,000 for sex. I realized I was just being stupid . . . the next guy I could get to give me money for sex I would have had for free was going to give me the money."

A dancer working prostitution out of a club may get it closed and put all the other girls out of work, so dancers and club managers often try to prevent prostitution on the premises. However, in jurisdictions such as the "Block" in Baltimore, and the streets of San Francisco, California, government looks the other way. Mitchell Brothers O'Farrell Theatre is the most notorious emporium in California, with multiple ongoing shows: New York Live! was a strip show/lap dance palace; the Cine Stage presented adult films; in the dark Copenhagen Lounge, decorated in red velvet, patrons with long red flashlights sat along the wall and examined the dancers up close; the Ultra Room featured two women in a glass booth with sex toys; and the Green Door offered live lesbian sex shows and a shower show. A glass-walled room with an outside ramp made it possible for busloads of tourists to stay together as a group as they peered into the room. Inside were booths where a dancer and patron could have privacy above the knees. I saw four, then three, and finally only two legs. At the O'Farrell Theatre, dancers could rent small bed-dance rooms to interact with a patron.

It was not clear why, after years of turning a blind eye to long-standing sexual activity in the San Francisco clubs, the vice squad decided to raid the theaters in May 2004. Three undercover officers walked into the nearly empty New Century club and were, they said, all openly and unapologetically solicited for sex almost before their eyes had adjusted to the darkness. An identical scenario unfolded at the Market Street Cinema. Nine dancers and three club managers were arrested during the two raids. The

218

dancers were charged with prostitution; the managers, with "keeping a house of ill repute." However, District Attorney Kamala Harris dismissed the charges: her primary concern about adult theaters was the safety of the women who work there, not the sexual nature of their work, and she intended to prioritize murders, rapes, and narcotics crimes.

Although I only saw a few Eastern European women, who were known to be free agents, in the clubs, there were claims of Russian "sex slaves." Foreign women are said to be enticed with promises of earning money in dance clubs but then forced to engage in "side work" to pay off debts. The woman's passport is taken from her, and she is told she owes the price of her plane ticket, the costs of drivers to take her to and from the clubs where she works, club booking fees, room and board for the duration of her "contract," and bogus visa registration fees. Women are considered a commodity with unlimited financial returns. Victor Virchenko, a dance instructor from the Krasnodar region of Russia, and Pavel Agafonov, a Russian national who lived in suburban Atlanta, pleaded guilty to various counts of immigration fraud and illegal transport of minors across borders. They were sentenced to prison in 2001. The men collaborated in bringing six Russian dancers to Anchorage for a nonexistent event they called "Russian Winter in Alaska," as well as other fictional folk events. The dancers were ordered to perform in a strip club and to turn over their earnings to a third man, Tony Kennard of Chugiak, Alaska. In 2005, Veniam Gonikman was indicted in Detroit on twenty-two counts for operating Beauty Search, a corporate cover for smuggling fifteen Eastern European women to the United States. Gonikman forced the women to work in Detroit strip clubs, allegedly for twelve hours a day, and give their earnings of more than $1.5 million to Gonikman and his nine associates. Living lavishly, he had been hiding out in the Ukraine when he was arrested and sent to Detroit to face charges.[3]

However, the Academy for Educational Development organizational unit on human trafficking, directed by Andrea Bertone, did not identify exotic dance clubs as a site for trafficking abuses. Yet, Focus on the Family and other CR-Activist groups have collectively received about $80 million dollars in grant money to combat human trafficking, claiming strip clubs as a key culprit.

Prostitution has a variety of definitions that can be differently interpreted. In Pasco County, Florida, the police charged eighteen dancers with prostitution. But then the district attorney changed the charges to indecency, lewdness, and obscenity. The dancers I testified on behalf of were acquitted. Occasionally, the term "prostitution" is broadly defined, as in New York, to include acts other than intercourse, oral sex, or sodomy. Prostitution in California law is sexual intercourse or any lewd act between persons for money or other consideration. In *City of Anaheim v. Janini* (1999), a California state judge ruled lap dancing is not prostitution. The Old Higgins Heavenly Bodies club in Cook County, Illinois, was charged as a house of prostitution because the state definition includes any touching of the sex organs of one person by another person for money. Undercover vice officers had lap dances. No grinding upon the covered or uncovered genitals of the officers occurred, and there was neither touching nor independent acts of sex. Once again, a judge ruled lap dancing was not prostitution.

Does a dancer creatively taking tips constitute prostitution? In September 1997, when area residents learned that Sirens had opened as a nude club in MacLean Hamlet in New York, they picketed the club. Rumors of prostitution flourished, so an undercover investigation ensued. The district attorney charged the club co-owner with two counts of "promoting prostitution in the third degree," alleging she "knowingly advanced or profited from prostitution by managing, supervising, controlling or owning . . . a prostitution business . . . involving . . . activity by two or more prostitutes." The third count was for "permitting prostitution." One dancer had two charges for prostitution, and another dancer had one.

I was asked to testify about the expressive meaning of the charges against the dancers. The club had closed, so in freezing weather, the owners brought in special heaters and asked several dancers to demonstrate the tip tricks for me (described in Chapter 3). They brought their boyfriends to act as patrons. The women also demonstrated their other dancing. Later, in court, after hearing my testimony about how exotic dance is a genre of dance, art, theater, and nude play, the twelve-member jury unanimously ruled the dancers not guilty of prostitution. But the adversaries had accomplished their mission: the young married owners lost their club. They also lost their marriage, which collapsed under all the stress, including death threats to their young daughter.

## Drugs

Clubs often have drug checks, including drug-sniffing dogs. One man went from being a vice president of First Virginia Bank and visiting the club after hours to doing drugs and delivering pizza for a living. Subsequently, he lost the pizza delivery job and was showing up at dancers' homes. The dancers called his boss to ask him to give the man work. Although drugs are widespread in the United States, there is no evidence that illegal drugs and alcohol pose more of a serious problem for dancers than for any other occupational group. Illegal drugs can be easily obtained in schools and universities. In Bellevue, Washington, where people wanted exotic clubs closed because of drug problems, the place with the highest incidence of drug use was the high school!

## Bribery

In 2003, the FBI raided the San Diego City Hall offices of Councilmen Ralph Inzunza, Charles Lewis, and Michael Zucchet and three clubs owned by forty-five-year-old Michael Galardi in San Diego and Las Vegas. The federal inquiry focused on whether public officials had been bribed with tens of thousands of dollars, including campaign contributions, in attempts to change laws regulating strip clubs. Galardi pleaded guilty and was sentenced to two-and-a-half years in federal prison for bankrolling the political scandal that became known as "Operation G." His testimony led to the convictions of four former Clark County commissioners and two San Diego City Council members (the conviction of one has been overturned). Galardi complied with requirements to pay most of a half-million dollars in fines and restitution, forfeit $3.85 million to the federal government, and divest himself of his clubs in Las Vegas.

Sometimes government officials demand clubs pay bribes. For example, Sam Riddle, former aide to Detroit City Councilwoman Monica Conyers, allegedly asked for twenty-five thousand dollars to get approval for a strip club license transfer from the former Zoo Bar to Déjà Vu Consulting. Riddle said that Conyers would not only vote against the transfer but also would work against the strip club. A seven-count indictment charged Riddle with conspiracy, extortion, and making false statements to the FBI. Prosecutors agreed to drop this case when he pleaded guilty in another similar one.[4]

## Violations of Laws Specifically Regulating Clubs

Dancers who perform in clubs in different places often unwittingly violate local ordinances on exposure of skin and proximity to patrons or dancer-patron touch. Many clubs are very controlling. I saw a dancer, who had been previously warned about breaking the law, fired on the spot. Here is probably the first full description of what should not show.

The area at the rear of the human body (sometimes referred to as the gluteus maximus) which lies between two imaginary straight lines running parallel to the ground when a person is standing, the first or top such line being 1/2 inch below the top of the vertical cleavage of the nates (i.e., the prominence formed by the muscles running from the back of the hip to the back of the leg) and the second or bottom such line being 1/2 inch above the lowest point of the curvature of the fleshy protuberance (sometimes referred to as the gluteal fold), and between two imaginary straight lines, one on each side of the body (the "outside lines"), which outside lines are perpendicular to the ground and to the horizontal lines described above and which perpendicular outside lines pass through the outermost point(s) at which each nate meets the other side of each leg. Notwithstanding the above, buttocks shall not include the leg, the hamstring muscle below the gluteal fold, the tensor fasciae latae muscle or any of the above-described portion of the human body that is between either: (i) the left inside perpendicular line and the left outside perpendicular line, or (ii) the right inside perpendicular line and the right outside perpendicular line. For the purpose of the previous sentence the left inside perpendicular line shall be an imaginary straight line on the left side of the anus: (i) that is perpendicular to the ground and to the horizontal lines described above, (ii) that is 1/3 of the distance from the anus to the left outside line, and the right inside perpendicular line shall be an imaginary straight line on the right side of the anus, (i) this is perpendicular to the ground and to the horizontal lines described above, and (ii) that is 1/3 of the distance from the anus to the right outside line. (The above description can generally be described as covering 1/3 of the buttocks centered over the cleavage for the length of the cleavage.)[5]

The owners of Larry Flynt's Hustler Club were fined $525 in 2004 by the city liquor board for violating the prohibition on sexual touching. In describing the transgression involving a dancer and an off-duty cocktail waitress, the club attorney said: "If I were to familiarly hug Mr. Mohney [Flynt's partner], our breasts have touched." This comment generated mild irritation and impatience among board members. "If I hug my mother, that's technically breast-to-breast touching. . . . My question is how do you interpret these rules?"

A Rolling Meadows sports bar owner in Chicago was hit with a fine for serving alcohol before 11 a.m. to customers headed to a Bears game. In 2002, Edward Law, a quadriplegic, sued the Wildside Adult Sports Cabaret in West Palm Beach, claiming that the exotic dance club violates the Americans with Disabilities Act because the lap dance room does not have wheelchair access. The lawsuit also asserted that the counter around the stage where dancers perform is too high, making it difficult for Law to see the stage and set down his drinks.

There are laws related to obtaining licenses. Gentlemen's club impresario Michael J. Peter pleaded guilty in May 1996 in US District court to conspiracy to commit mail fraud. He said he had lied on a liquor license application when he did not mention that members of the New York Gambino crime family owned part of his business. He was fined twenty-five thousand dollars and sentenced to prison. In 2002, his felony conviction was overturned, but he had already served two years and sold the club chains he owned, as ordered by the court. Not permitted to hold a liquor license or be a principal in an adult club operation prior to his exoneration, he had engaged in club consulting services, including developing innovative Internet product offerings. He has since regained his civil liberties and once again owns clubs.

Laws restricting proximity between dancer and patron lead to litigation. Tampa has twenty-five exotic dance clubs. Lap dancing had been a popular and robust form of expression in the city for more than twenty years. In 1982, Joe Redner opened Mons Venus, renowned for its lap dances. The club is one room filled with nude women dancing, touching, and massaging patrons. Grabbing is permitted, but no penetration. Mons Venus typically earns $2.5 million annually. Redner has been arrested about 140 times for his operation of the business. Interested in changing things, Redner in 1999 pumped $67,000 into a challenge to Bob Buckhorn for his city council seat. Buckhorn raised more than $150,000 but was clearly unhappy that he had to defend what he thought was an uncontested seat. Redner won 25 percent of the votes!

Buckhorn retained his seat and he and Mayor Dick Greco—who, interestingly, once frequented the clubs—came up with the "Adult Entertainer Separation Ordinance," which bans lap dances by making it illegal for a dancer to perform within six feet of a patron, with a $1,000 fine or six months for each violation. Mayor Greco signed and dated the ordinance before the public hearing was even concluded—indeed, a back-handed way to close down nude clubs. For the public hearing, Redner and his staff organized an incredible "grassroots movement" of dancers, patrons, vendors, suppliers, concerned citizens, cabdrivers, a cancer patient in a wheelchair, a quadriplegic on a gurney, women with children (some of whom addressed the council), veterans, and a female network engineer who goes to Mons Venus with her husband. Redner had arranged for a truck to dispense pizza to his supporters. In a room filled with five hundred people, the first hearing lasted sixteen hours, from 7 p.m. to 1:30 a.m. and continued the next day. More than one hundred people testified against the ordinance. Merely a handful spoke in favor.

Commentators paid tribute to Redner: "Redner is a local folk hero because he helps us fight statism." "If you do anything, build a statue to Redner and thank him." They also spoke against the ordinance: "Buckhorn should focus on housing and education and have a six-foot rule for football games." "Moral arbiters? The regulations open a Pandora's box." One citizen asked, "Why is the sky falling now? The clubs have been operating for twenty years without problems. Why should the city create new crimes when it can't deal with ones already on the books?" Some other arguments: "When a churchman commits a crime, you don't take away the church. When athletes do drugs, do we ban the sport?" One man said that after going to a club and seeing a professional dancer, he became a devotee of all kinds of dance and opera. Another person said, "I'm reminded of the Middle East treatment of women." One man admitted, "I'm religious, but I have faith in free choice. God is the judge." Another man agreed, saying "The Bible says not to judge." And yet another offered this testimony:

> As a born-again Christian, I find it quite shameful the totalitarian tactics that are quite often used by people who call themselves Christian when the only Christ that I have record of, in the Bible, was a friend to publicans and sinners, and that he always said it was your faith that saves you. I firmly believe that there has been an orchestrated effort in this city and in this county to run out all adult-oriented businesses, and that it has been pushed forward gradually by silent encroachment, as are all attempts to reduce people under despotism. . . . Please do not seek to create a whole new class of criminals to further your political careers. And, for God's sake, don't do it in the name of Christ, because far too many of you will be told he never knew you.

A minister said, "The drug addicts and the prostitutes that I have worked with have never been in the adult entertainment business." A citizen added:

> I feel it is grandstanding in order to win votes on the basis of an arbitrary morality issue . . . and it strikes me as pitifully trivial and petty. The only thing it will achieve is making Tampa look like a laughingstock in the eyes of the world. Some people who claim to speak on behalf of God have got the needle stuck in the moral and ethical groove of that old broken record.

Many people talked about how they were helped by the dancer's income. The paraplegic brother of a dancer testified that because of his sister's ability to earn a decent income, he was "able to stay with her and enjoy the benefits of family life, rather than be warehoused in some despicable facility." A soldier in uniform said he wasn't fighting to see Americans' inalienable rights taken away. A former soldier recalled:

> I am a veteran of the United States Army. I sat in that desert for six months wondering when the next chemical ray was going to come, if I was going to get my chemical mask on in time, or if I was going to make it home, all the bombs, the firing that's going on. That really wasn't a concern to me because maybe I would die for my country and for freedom. You dishonor me with some of the decisions you're proposing. You dishonor anybody who ever swarmed at the beach, fought in the jungle, or said a prayer for this country. Why don't you take a look to your right and look at that flag, if you would, please? It's an American flag, not a Chinese flag, doesn't look like a Cuban flag.

Those supporting the ordinance cited religious morals and the fiction of adverse secondary effects. A woman said, "The laws are founded on the word of God—lap dancing is morally wrong." Another said, "I'm a mom. I have to explain to my kids. I appreciate what the council is doing." Of the two cabdrivers who spoke in favor of the ordinance, one clearly articulated religious arguments. The other mentioned one customer's report:

> I picked up a seaman down at the port and took him to the Mons Venus, and gave him my cell phone number. . . . When he called me back to take him to his ship, he told me about the bad experience he had inside the Mons Venus, that he had $800 in his pocket, and that three girls were with him at one time, one sitting on each leg, one dancing very close to him—he gave them some money as he went along. But when he left the club, the whole $800 was gone out of his pocket, so the girls had lifted $800 off of him obviously.

But it is also possible that he wantonly spent the money he had or he didn't have as much money with him as he thought. The cabdriver reported that another customer said his wife left him because she found out he was hanging out at the club. The cabdriver also commented that dancers told him that performers do turn to drugs because of the lifestyle at the Mons Venus.

Public hearings rarely stop ordinances, but the hearings often help clubs in challenging ordinances in court. Clubs can document that they made known their opposition before bringing suit. The 1999 Tampa ordinance caused dancers to go from being private contractors and capitalists to being criminals. At first, trials involving some three hundred people, who were arrested for violating the new city law mandating a six-foot distance between dancer and patron, resulted in multiple county judges reaching opposite decisions: convictions, pleas, and a ruling that the ordinance was unconstitutional. The combative logjam choked the courts—and the trials just stopped. But Tampa is in Hillsborough County and its decency warriors then pushed through the big lie of adverse secondary effects, prompting new legislation regarding distance between dancer and patron. By eliminating lap dances, this legislation makes it difficult for exotic dance stakeholders to make a living.

The actions of one delinquent adult nightclub in Dallas have led to drastic changes in that city's regulations. In March 2008, it was discovered that a twelve-year-old girl had worked for two weeks at the Diamond Cabaret. So now, for all employee records, clubs must include a person's age, an original photo, valid driver's license copy, fingerprints, and a Texas criminal history report. This information would become public record, a scenario intimidating to dancers and likely to deter some women from dancing in Dallas. Moreover, in its effort to destroy clubs, Dallas also prohibited clubs from having anything—for example, doors, walls, drapes—that blocks visibility in the club, hampering private dances.

## Questionable Police Tactics

Although the purpose of law enforcement is to prevent crime and catch criminals, sometimes police officers themselves are the problem. In a sting operation at Rick's in Seattle, the police arrested twelve dancers on charges of obscenity, violation of no self-touch, and they stationed an opposite-sex officer in the dressing room while the dancers changed clothes. When Elaine, who did not go nude onstage, asked if the male officer could leave, a female officer laughed, "Look what you do for a living. Think of him as your brother." This dancer's brother had raped her as child! At the jail, officers asked, "Aren't you all prostitutes?" Elaine was so traumatized, she could not continue as a dancer. "They treated me as less than human." Rick's and the dancers filed a lawsuit against the City of Seattle. On the witness stand, a senior police officer, under oath and with a straight face, presented counterfeit evidence to discredit Elaine's assertion that she was so distraught that she quit dancing the day after she'd been forced to undress in front of male officers, arrested, and strip-searched. He held up a dancer sign-in sheet dated a month after Elaine's arrest that showed her signature. But the officer was forced to admit that he had put a new date on an old sign-in sheet when Elaine noticed the pen writing on the top and bottom of the sheet differed. "The same color pen was always used for the date of sign-in and the signatures," she testified.

I've seen vice- and riot-squad members assert problems that don't exist so that they can hang out in the clubs with beautiful nude or semi-nude women. Unfair, dubious practices are multiple. A club owner in rural Maryland finally closed his club after much police harassment. He said the police hired a prostitute to solicit an undercover officer in his club, and then the police arrested her and charged him for permitting illegal acts on the premises. In Winter Park, Florida, police agents spearheaded an undercover investigation of Club Harem because an officer at police headquarters said the city wanted to get rid of the club. The police raided Club Harem and painted it as a den of drug dealers. This convinced the Florida Division of Alcoholic Beverages and Tobacco to revoke the club's license to serve alcohol. However, the club's attorney Steve Mason discovered a tape showing that the police had an operative who sought to steer drug dealers to the club. Not only that, the police operative had outstanding felony warrants, so the proposed sanctions against the club were dropped. The upshot was that Club Harem sued the city on September 10, 2010, for six years of unlawful harassment that injured the club financially and hurt its reputation and patronage. The City of Winter Park paid two hundred and fifty thousand dollars to Club Harem and Mason with a proviso in the settlement agreement that proscribed discussion of any liability or disparagement of any party.[6]

Police have discretion, but when told to make arrests, they do so, even if they know the charges won't hold up to challenge. This has a chilling effect on dancers and patrons. Moreover, some jurisdictions can close a club on the basis of charges of illegal acts. Police raids and arrests may occur in a club when a new police contract is going to be reviewed and the chief wants to show his department is on top of things. During an election, an incumbent politician, in response to some constituents' opposition to adult entertainment, may trigger surprise police operations against the clubs as a campaign tactic. A club owner attributed some police raids to a vendetta against one of his dancers, who had dropped her police officer boyfriend. In fact, the Roanoke case mentioned in Chapter 2 was instigated by a policeman who had been rejected by his dancer girlfriend. And CR-Activists persistently demand police predatory incursions into the clubs in order to harass them out of business.

"Operation Overexposed" was the 2005 Metropolitan Bureau of Investigation (MBI) "vice" sting at Cleo's, one of the largest adult venues in

Central Florida.[7] MBI agents arrested fifty-two Cleo employees and patrons on charges ranging from drug dealing to public nudity to soliciting an alcoholic beverage. To date, more than twenty of those people have been convicted, according to MBI director Bill Lutz, though most of the convictions resulted in probation and small fines in exchange for pleas of guilty or no contest. Pleas are often easier than going to court with the legal expense required. But there are lingering questions about how agents conducted the investigation and how they handled evidence. The MBI had bungled two previous stings in an effort to shut the clubs down. The Bureau claimed that the dancers exposed their "labia majoras" every time the officers entered the establishment. The dancers said that the police were patronizing the club weekly, acting as high rollers, often dropping four hundred dollars or more in a couple of hours. Officers groped the dancers, pulling aside their G-strings, and got the dancers drunk, even the eighteen- and nineteen-year-olds. An agent assured a dancer who had expressed suspicion of his being a cop by showing her his penis. Another charge was selling drugs to patrons at the bar or to friends of the dancers. Instead of taking notes while they were inside the club, the agents said that, whenever a dancer asked them for drinks or bared more than the law allowed, they left themselves voice mail notes on their cell phones. But in light of Cleo's loud thumping bass and rattling walls, it was questionable whether the agents could talk loudly enough into their cell phones to be heard over the din. And—the agents unlawfully erased their voice mails.

In Palm Bay, Florida, fifteen police agents raided Club Goddess in October 2003 and threatened dancers with arrest if they continued to dance in the club. The dancers fled, and the nightclub was effectively closed without any specific authorization or court order. Harassment of businesses protected by the First Amendment constitutes a de facto prior restraint. Threats were more effective than actual arrests. With an arrest, a dancer could contest charges, and if acquitted she could file suit for false arrest.

For sixteen years, Roxanne's in Fort Lauderdale never had a problem with prostitution or drugs. But then, twenty police officers and the chief visited the club. The owner and his dancers were arrested, although they had stayed within the law written by the Commission of Fort Lauderdale. Six police officers per night, in combat outfits and carrying guns, came into the bar, harassing the customers. The police officers said that they were going to close the club down, whatever it took.

For many years, clubs in the Salt Lake City area featured totally nude dancing and no alcohol. Then in 2001, the city council outlawed nude dancing. Shortly thereafter, the city decided to aggressively enforce the ordinance without notice, even though a lawsuit contesting its validity was underway. The city wanted to intimidate the clubs. Police officers forced their way into areas of the club where customers aren't allowed, a violation of the Fourth Amendment's "unreasonable searches and seizures." The same officers went back to the same club with a repeat performance. A dancer deemed not properly respectful was taken to jail and booked on charges of interfering with a police officer. When the clubs involved in the raids filed a federal action for damages arising from unlawful searches and seizures, the city responded with an administrative action to revoke the business licenses of the clubs. After some negotiation, the city reneged, and the clubs dropped their Fourth Amendment lawsuit. But the city refused to drop criminal charges against the dancer, so she went to court. The ordinance was specific in granting the police inspection power only over areas of the club in which customers were permitted. The court ruled against the city and the dancer accepted a settlement of about ten thousand dollars.

In the Old Higgins Heavenly Bodies case, after the undercover police officers left the club, within about ten minutes a dozen non-uniformed and another seven uniformed officers returned to the club and shut it down. Male officers barged into the dancers' dressing room while they were naked. A total of fifty-five dancers and two managers were transported in paddy wagons and squad cars to jail. Police personnel called the women expletives all night and into the morning. At no point were the dancers given their Miranda rights. When one dancer asked for an attorney, she was shoved. When a dancer could not raise her hands, as the police asked, due to recent breast augmentation surgery, her arms were forced up. She took umbrage to this and was shoved into a cell. When she called her husband on her cell phone to call an ambulance, the sergeant cancelled the ambulance. Most of the dancers were released at 5 a.m. The dancer who needed medical attention wasn't released until the next afternoon.

I first learned about the Autauga County, Alabama, police harassment of Michael Mims, when an article about me in the St. Petersburg Times led to an invitation to debate County Commissioner (and Holiness preacher) Michael Morgan on the Alan Colmes Fox News Radio Show on February 16, 2007. The local news and TV reported that the County Sheriff's Office and Alabama Beverage Control Board (ABC) had cited Mims for allowing a patron to have physical contact with a dancer in an all-male revue in his 31-65 Club.

I called Mims for his side of the story. He said he's a forty-one-year-old retired Air Force disabled vet. He returned to Alabama in 2003 and bought an established nightclub. Twice Morgan tried to block Mims's request for a license. So, along with the sheriff, his mom, and a lawyer, Mims met Morgan, who gave in, with restrictions: the club must close at midnight on weekdays and at 2 a.m. on weekends and be free of known drug dealers. Mims agreed, got his license, and was open for almost four years without any problems.

To attract female customers, he hired some male dancers out of Nashville, Tennessee, to perform on February 6, 2007. According to Mims:

> Everything was going great except for my computer sound problems caused by an undercover cop unplugging and plugging the speaker she was sitting near. The law and Morgan had sent in three undercover agents to try and bust me. . . . One undercover agent started fondling a dancer's butt and smacking it, but as I was computer-distracted I didn't put a stop to it. Nor did my bouncer who was also distracted by arguing with an undercover about not checking her driver's license even though she looked about fifty. The cops came pouring in along with the Alabama Beverage Control Board . . . they brought in drug dogs and DEA agents. No arrests were made. I got a $200 fine for allowing a patron to touch a dancer.

On the Colmes show, I reported what Mims told me. Morgan spouted the myth of adverse secondary effects. I challenged this, as did Colmes.

Mims's problems continued, starting around June 2007:

> Morgan was in the news again because someone told him I was going to change my nightclub into a strip club. . . . Yes, I have joked about changing mine into one, but made no plans . . . . I am thirteen miles from Maxwell Air Force Base and secluded enough that I'm sitting on a gold mine right at the top of the exit. The hotel and couple of gas stations and food joints across the freeway bridge beg me to change my club to increase their sales. If I knew I could legally, and could get the financial backing, I would.
>
> The police harassed my patrons by setting up roadblocks on both sides of our highway to entrap people. They got like thirty-eight DUIs [driving under the influence of alcohol citations] in one day. The press printed a zero tolerance article on the front page of the news, but . . . almost thirty-two of the DUIs made were from people coming back from Montgomery clubs or home parties; only about two or three were from my club. I am on a freeway exit, so a lot of people go to Montgomery to party if they don't like the band I have playing or the entertainment that night. Sometimes a state trooper was within fifty feet of my building which makes people not stop . . . . They have even pulled me over leaving my club and gave me

a warning because one of my two tag lights burned out. . . . It tears them up when I give them a hair sample any time they come snooping around for drugs. All the local sheriffs and undercovers tell folks they have been given orders to step up the heat and close me down.

When Mims told me that the Autauga county commissioners were considering legislation against adult entertainment, I sent them a copy of my 2005 *Journal of Planning Literature* article, which summarizes the key issues, and gave Mims the name of a First Amendment lawyer. (Mims thanked me and joked, "I think I'm falling in love with you. Are you married?") But a police car parked for two months across the road in plain sight of the nightclub's front door deterred patrons, and Mims filed for bankruptcy. However, he did rally local Masons and patrons to vote Morgan out of office by a landslide!

Another example of police misconduct comes from Indianapolis where a police officer, Francis Ingram, pleaded guilty to bribery, sexual battery, and criminal confinement. He admitted that he arrested exotic dancers on minor charges, then offered to release them in exchange for sexual favors. A former dancer had provided a taped conversation with Ingram to the police.[8]

## Stigmatization of Exotic Dance

Beyond questionable police tactics, one could reasonably argue that the real "crime" related to the exotic dance industry is that government, religious groups, and the general public stigmatize exotic dancers, as well as club owners, patrons, and the industry as a whole. The City of Arlington, Texas, requires clubs to have an eighteen-inch stage and a six-foot buffer zone or, alternatively, a solid, clear unbreakable glass and/or Plexiglas wall prohibiting physical contact between the entertainer and her audience. Restrictions impede the dancer's use of space—a key element of any kind of dance communication. Because erotic messages require proximity, the ordinance mutes or suppresses the dancer's artistic choice. The wall dehumanizes the dancer and forces upon patrons the message that she is like an infectious patient or leper in a hospital isolation ward or a prisoner or caged animal in a zoo. Because the patron cannot directly tip the dancer to thank her for the performance and let her know she has achieved artistic merit, his expression is suppressed. The impact of the ordinance is like a salesperson not being able to hand a customer a receipt.

The stigmatization of dancers causes them to be considered as instigators of crime, such as rape, and to be mistreated, for example, in renting and child custody. Groups trying to "save" dancers from the "harms" of the exotic dance industry, such as the church group in Dallas helping dancers leave exotic dancing, are also stigmatizing them, assassinating the dancers' characters, denying their authority as independent decision-making women, and re-sowing false myths. Women who have danced in exotic dance clubs have lost their positions in the mainstream world.

Because of the stigma, a dancer was rebuffed in her efforts to rent an apartment. The Nebraska Equal Opportunity Commission filed a lawsuit in 2004 against an Omaha real estate company, the Richdale Group, owners of the Vanderbilt Apartments, because it refused to rent an apartment to a woman after she listed her occupation as a "dancer" at the Bottoms Up Lounge in Council Bluffs.

Stigmatized women are judged more harshly than others. Below are a few more stories of women who suffered the consequences of the stigma attached to being an exotic dancer.

Michele Clark, a slightly built twenty-year-old topless dancer from Erie, Pennsylvania, was convicted of aggravated assault for using excessive force against a man who attempted to rape her in an alley. A simple "no" usually sufficed to ward off men. But one night, Ronald Daniel, 27, a drunk, married father of two from Melbourne, Florida, followed Clark to the ladies' room where she said he grabbed her buttocks. Later, as she tried to avoid him by leaving through a back door, he followed her into an alley. He pinned her against a wall putting his hands up her shirt and fondling her breasts. She kneed him in the groin and crossed the street. He then followed Clark for two blocks and grabbed her hair. She didn't remember how she defended herself, but he had fallen to the sidewalk, and she fought to get away. She kept kicking Daniel because he grabbed the waist of her shorts trying to pull her to the ground. Clark shattered his jaw.

Clark's conviction stirred up a firestorm of anger among *Washington Post* readers of the "Dear Ann Landers" column. One said, "A slap in the kisser does not fend off a rapist. . . . The jury is punishing the woman for being a topless dancer, an occupation that is perfectly legal." Another reader wrote, "No woman deserves to be raped, whether she's a streetwalker or a soprano in the church choir." From Fairmont, West Virginia, came this: "We tell our women to say no, defend themselves, do their best to get away—and when they do, they are held responsible for the assailant's injuries. I would like to know the collective IQ of that jury. They sound like a bunch of idiots." Another West Virginia respondent said, "If this had happened in our town, the guy would have lost the family jewels to the girl's dad and brothers. He wouldn't be moaning about his jaw."

While on duty in Irvine, California, police officer David Alex Park pulled a dancer over in the early morning hours. Her shift at the Captain Creams Club had just ended. He cited her for weaving and speeding her BMW and gave her a sobriety test, which she passed. Then he told her that if she didn't fondle him, she'd go to jail for driving with a suspended license. She complied out of fear. Park then sexually assaulted her, eventually ejaculating on her clothes. She filed a $10 million complaint against the city and Officer Park. After a nine-day trial, a middle-aged jury of eleven men and one woman acquitted the officer of all three felony charges of sexual battery. The officer's attorney stated that "Lucy got what she wanted. She's an overtly sexual person." The prosecutor said, "Park didn't pick a housewife or a 17-year-old girl. He picked a stripper. He picked a perfect victim."

John Elders, Leilani Rios's track coach at California State University, Fullerton, gave her the choice between staying on the Titan team or continuing to work as an exotic dancer at a local night club: "To remain an exotic dancer would detract from the image and accomplishments of her teammates, the athletic department and the university." But "stripping paid the bills," allowing her to be the first member of her family to go to college, and "cross-country running for Cal State Fullerton is just exercise." Rios said the problem started when the college baseball team dropped into the Flamingo Theater where she was performing and ultimately reported her to the coach. After she threatened legal action, the coach allowed her to practice with the team. Her poor grades, most likely the result of the stress of being dismissed from it, prevented her from competing.

In Sacramento, the Capital Christian Center School, part of one of the largest Assemblies of God churches in the country, expelled a kindergartner because her mother, Christina Silvas, twenty-four years old and single, worked as a nude dancer. "If you choose to do the wrong thing willfully, then God's word instructs me as to what my responsibility is," said Rick Cole, head pastor. Silvas took the job at Gold Club Centerfolds in part to afford the four-hundred-dollar monthly tuition at the church-run school.

The stigma of exotic dance is so great that needy charities sometimes refuse "stripper-tainted" funds. Deloris Dickson had run Club 55 in Washington, DC, for more than forty years. Several of her one hundred employees, like Dickson herself, have struggled through the trauma of breast cancer with their mothers, sisters, and daughters. So when Dickson asked her employees if they would join her in donating their time and energy to a benefit for the National Breast Cancer Coalition, the women enthusiastically agreed to give the receipts from an entire day's work to the charity. But the Coalition refused the money. So the exotic dancers promptly donated the more than five thousand dollars they had raised to Children's Hospital for cancer research—except for a one thousand-dollar gift to the Mautner Project, which supports lesbians suffering from cancer. The receptive organizations care more about a cure than an unfair stereotype.

The involvement of a "stripper" in purported misdemeanors or felonies makes the news, as do incidents when exotic dancers are the victims of crime. In an unusual situation when a dancer heroically acted when no one else did, her picture and story plastered the front page of the St. Petersburg Times. The stigma of being an exotic dancer was overlooked, and she was even invited to attend Sunday services at Mount Pleasant Baptist Church. In 2007, Angel Perez, a twenty-five-year-old, five-foot-tall dancer who worked at Envy Gentleman's Club, rescued nine-year-old Dontae Lopez from pit bulls. She and her forty-year-old boyfriend, Donell Howard, were driving on Florida Avenue when they heard Dontae's screams as he was running through traffic to escape the pit bulls chasing him. Angel leaped out of the car, armed only with Mace and her fists. She helped fight off the dogs, and her boyfriend carried Dontae out of harm's way. Dontae suffered several bite wounds. Perez had severe bites, including an arm wound that required twenty stitches. Having met many dancers, I wasn't surprised about Angel's heroism. Dancers need chutzpah and strength to counter social norms.

Stigmatization of the exotic dance industry also affects club owners. An upscale club owner in Philadelphia was very sensitive about being in the adult entertainment business. He gave me his background: he came from the restaurant business by way of private school and an Ivy League education. So concerned about potential problems, he had a metal detector placed in the club entryway and eighteen cameras throughout the facility.

This is not to say a club owner cannot overcome stigma. Michael Ocello, a fortyish former exotic dancer who performed for women and later became president of the national VCG/PT's Showclub chain, won election to the Mehlville School Board in south St. Louis County, Missouri. Voters overlooked his being the butt of jokes and the target of scorn from the "holier than thou" crowd. In July 2009, Ocello presided over the closing bell for NASDAQ, one of the world's largest financial exchange companies. His personal image and company logo loomed thirty-five-feet high on the NASDAQ building in Times Square. Ocello proudly proclaimed, "It was TRULY a great day for VCG and everyone in our industry because we are being recognized as legitimate business in the corporate world."

Exotic dance club patrons may be subject to stigmatization. In 2003,

FBI agents searched Cheetah's strip club in Las Vegas for records of payments or gifts made to several current and former elected officials. During their search, the agents seized a videotape that depicts City Councilman Michael Mack receiving a lap dance. He was not one of the officials under investigation. However, Mack acknowledged having a lap dance and said he was embarrassed by news of the tape and regretted the impact it would have on his family. He was engaged to be married for the third time.

In several cases, men have lost their jobs due to incidents involving exotic dancers. Bob Dell, the longtime coach of the Mineola, New York, Massapequa High School baseball team, was suspended in 2003 because fifteen of his players made a clandestine visit to a Cocoa Beach, Florida, exotic dance club during spring training. He announced that he would sue the school district for unfairly blaming him. A Columbus, Ohio, high school baseball team committed an "error" off the field during a road trip in 2001. The team hired exotic dancers through a service advertised in the telephone book to perform in their hotel room, the Columbus Dispatch reported. The school authorities suspended fourteen players from school for a week, kicked them off the team, and suspended head coach Tim Graham. He resigned his coaching and teaching position at the school. Mike Price was fired by the University of Alabama in 2003 without coaching a single game because of behavior, including spending hundreds of dollars at a topless bar, an embarrassment for a once-proud football team. Price had agreed to a seven-year contract, worth $10 million, that had a clause saying he could be fired for any behavior "that brings (the) employee into public disrepute, contempt, scandal, or ridicule or that reflects unfavorably upon the reputation or the high moral or ethical standards of the University."

Chuck Kalogianis, a successful attorney in New Port Richey, Florida, a family man, and an unopposed candidate for the Democratic nomination to the US House of Representatives in 2002, had to deal with his past as an exotic dancer in Massachusetts. He had a two-year stint with "Men in Motion" when he was a law student in Boston. He wore a bird costume that masked his face but exposed his legs. At the end of the performance, Kalogianis would do a chicken dance and tear off the bright yellow costume to reveal his French bikini thong to crowds of women throwing money. The dancer label kept popping up, and he ultimately lost, for whatever reason.

The stigma of exotic dance even extends into the realm of video games. Pro BMX bike rider Dave Mirra filed suit against video game publisher Acclaim Entertainment Inc., seeking more than $20 million in damages. He claimed that a "pornographic" game featuring strippers on bikes hurt his image.

Three students at Jacksonville University were punished for installing a stripper pole in an on-campus apartment and taking pictures as fully clothed women performed on it at a party. A school spokesman said the party's hosts violated the university's alcohol policy, broke rules against indecent behavior, and made unapproved changes to university property. A female residential adviser said the party degraded women. A female student who won a dance contest also was disciplined.

In addition to the stigma factor, there is also the threat of sex bias lawsuits against men for conducting business in exotic dance clubs. Although people conduct business in informal settings like golf courses and church socials, when men routinely entertain business associates at exotic dance clubs to win contracts or otherwise further their business, some women coworkers are uncomfortable in such establishments. They complain of feeling discriminated against. Such complaints have led some businesses to prohibit company activity in the clubs.

Under the burden of stigma, exotic dance clubs may be prohibited from advertising in mainstream newspapers and magazines or they are required to pay higher ad rates than other businesses. In 1997, an ad in the *City Paper* in Washington, DC, was $14.60 for 25 words or fewer. But lumped together with, for example, escorts, in-call places, and dominatrixes, exotic dance fell under the heading "Adult Services." And an ad in that section cost $150 for 25 words or fewer.

Government and other attorneys work hard, as is their job, to discredit and shake up witnesses. But they have been especially nasty to court witnesses who are "tainted by the exotic dance stigma." In the Department of Consumer Regulatory Affairs Alcohol Beverage Control Board hearing in Washington, DC, an attorney cross-examining me was so rude and out of line that the chair admonished him no fewer than a dozen times.

## Hypocrisy

Asked why Dallas with its forty clubs was a mecca for strip clubs, Dawn Rizos, owner of the award-winning The Lodge, answered:

> Because we're in the Bible Belt. There's a church on every block, and men just like to sneak around . . . . They get a little bored with their wives, they can come in here and get some flirtation . . . then they go home and feel so guilty about it that they treat their wives nicely. It's very Baptist. If you're going to give up sin, you got to sin.[9]

CR-Activists constantly lecture the country on the need for family values and morals. As some wear the breastplate of righteousness, their own impulses and behavior are what their co-religionists damn, including illegal activities. A dancer at Show 'N Tail had a client who was a minister; he admitted to being able to spend hundreds of dollars on her because he had been pilfering from the offertory plate. In 2010, Republicans with a family values brand held a fundraiser at Voyeur in Hollywood, California, spending $1,946 at the club.[10]

Marty Klein points out:

> Hypocrites like Ted Haggard, David Vitter, Randall Tobias, Mark Foley, Bill O'Reilly, and Newt Gingrich [and Larry Craig, Mark Souder, George A. Rekers] are not, it turns out, anomalous. Rather, they represent something very American about sexual discomfort with who they are, an apparent refusal to admit and accept their sexuality, and a desire to limit others' sexual expression while struggling with their own.[11]

For example, Rev. Ted Haggard, who founded the evangelical New Life megachurch in Colorado Springs, had a three-year relationship with a male prostitute.[12] Some people propelled into becoming CR-Activists, such as the anti-porn advocate Phil Burress, seek forgiveness for their sinful living and to escape the dark impulses that beset them. They believe they get a pass from God that covers their transgressions, and they strike back at a culture they blame for the debacle of their lives. Christian evangelical activist and writer Jim Wallis says the scandals do not show that Christians are hypocrites but that "we are all sinners and utterly dependent on the grace of God."

Using the logic that CR-Activists, planners, and legislatures apply to exotic dance for monitoring misbehavior, there should be raised platforms and bars to separate children from priests and pastors in church or teachers at school because the adults just might sexually molest the children. In fact, innumerable adults have actually been convicted of such crimes, although churches often settle with victims so that the crimes are not made public. Church silence abets and shows tolerance for abusers.[13]

In 2009, the Kinsey Institute at Indiana University in Bloomington acquired the Freedom From Religion Foundation's (FFRF) "black collar crime blotter" files, dating back to 1985.[14] This archive, filling fourteen large shipping boxes, contains clippings, organized by state, that detail criminal and civil cases involving clergy, with a focus on crimes of sex abuse. FFRF estimates that in the last decade, as many as four thousand clergy were covered in the national, regional, and local print media.

Psychologists Piercarlo Valdesolo and David DeSteno found that moral hypocrisy is merely the convenience of acting virtuously even when doing something the person would condemn in others. Moreover, according to DeSteno, anyone on the "team is excused for moral transgressions. Group cohesion . . . extends our moral radius of lenience." Most active in condemning others and trying to eliminate clubs for adults who choose to frequent them, CR-Activists have failed to root out sexual molesters among their own clergy. Indeed, instead of helping victims, the church hides the abuse by clergy and aids and abets abuse by insisting on silence to avoid scandal and to protect church finances, assets, and public image. For example, Robert Gray, the former thirty-year pastor of Trinity Baptist Church in Jacksonville, Florida, was arrested in 2006. Twenty-two people, including one man, came forward to accuse Gray of sexually abusing them. The abuse dated back to 1949, and some of the victims were as young as six. Key leaders knew and kept silent for years, and the church is still supporting him. In a keynote address, Reverend Jerry Falwell offered a response to this abuse:

> When you hit a bump in the road . . . forget the bump in the road. That's all it is. You've got to move on . . . nothing nor anyone can hurt any of us as we keep our eyes on Him. If I get disloyal to this Book, or to the Lord or to my wife and family, I can hurt myself. But as long as I stay focused on Him, there's no way anyone, anywhere, from the *Washington Post* to the *New York Times* to all the television networks, and etcetera, etcetera, who can hurt me or you, or any of us, because we are kept by the power of God through faith unto salvation.[15]

Falwell said not a word about protecting the flock's innocent children. Christa Brown, founder of Voice to Stop Baptist Predators and coordinator of SNAP-Baptist (Survivors Network of those Abused by Priests), criticized Falwell's dismissive choice of words: "What Falwell should be sermonizing on is, 'Why did no one in the church put up a roadblock and stop this man?'"[16]

A sense of entitlement to sex outside of marriage "can come from the minister's self-assessment of the burdens of ministerial work," says Traci C. West. At the beginning of his tenure as pastor of a small African-American church in a small town in New England, Alton Pollard was invited to lunch to meet some of the local ministers, who offered him this counsel:

> Almost to a man, they proceeded to ply me with their opinions and pointers on sexual protocol. Clearly, care and precaution in the pursuit of one's "extra-curricular" plans and not right character and conduct, was key.

Fraternal counsel was even provided in terms of when and where I could
hold local liaisons . . . not the first time I had been exposed to the under-
side of what in select circles is known as "preacher culture."

Yet, laws prohibit strip clubs from being located within five hundred to
fifteen hundred feet of a church or school. The assumption is that churches are "good" places and strip clubs are "bad" ones. However, the evidence
shows no such clear-cut reality. There is no evidence that buffer zones do
anything other than protect the sensibilities of churchgoers. I mention
the sexual abuse by church leaders not to disparage the good works of the
churches. Rather, it is to suggest that believers' energies directed against
establishments outside the church—such as exotic dance clubs, which objectively have a "good bill of health"—could better be turned inward to
their own churches to protect children from clearly illegal behavior that is
covered up.

## So, Where Are the Bodies? Evidence?

I have described criminal cases related to the exotic dance industry. Yes, on
occasion, violence, prostitution, and drugs appear in exotic dance clubs,
but not disproportionately compared to other occupations, as attested
to by studies of police records across the country and US Department of
Justice reports on crime. As do some college students, homemakers, and
women in various professions, some dancers engage in prostitution. Sure,
pimps prospect in clubs, just as they do on the beach or at bus stations, and
some clubs exclude unescorted single women on the grounds they may be
prostitutes seeking customers. But most of the violence associated with
exotic dance clubs has nothing to do with the clubs but with domestic conflict—that is, violence inflicted on women by men they know—that occurs
everywhere.

Furthermore, I have presented a litany of the more common unconstitutional incidents of governments acting on "moral" or naïve grounds to
single out a particular group/industry for not only disapproval but also
punitive regulation and ultimate destruction. Entrapment, incompetence,
hypocrisy, and absurdity abound.

On the basis of spurious "studies" conducted over the years, CR-
Activists and others trumpet the secondary effects doctrine. As discussed
earlier, the doctrine justifies regulations of exotic dance clubs to prevent
their causing harm to the public good. However, as noted earlier, when
scholars, planners, and lawyers applied rules of the social sciences, they

found that clubs do not negatively impact their surroundings. In fact, some exotic dance clubs have positive effects. Methodologically rigorous studies of exotic dance conducted by researchers in the fields of anthropology, biology, criminology, law, planning, psychology, real estate, social work, theater, and women's studies, as well as archival data, show the clubs caused no more problems than any other business.

Gentlemen's clubs are big business and owners seek to protect their investment and bottom line. Consequently, it certainly is to their benefit to create a safe, comfortable environment that attracts moneyed clientele and dancers who do not traffic in drugs or prostitution in the club. Clubs commonly engage in prevention to avoid police involvement. Monitoring takes place, including using detectives, drug-sniffing dogs, and cameras in public and "private" areas. Large elite strip clubs, or chains of small clubs, sometimes have random spot checks to assure ethical behavior. They may hire companies to conduct background searches on employees. Management personnel intervene when someone steps out of line and regularly walk dancers to their cars when the club closes. One club had had a murder in its parking lot, and when I visited the club a year later, my male colleague was patted down at the door. I was surprised to be carded. It had been a while. A senior citizen, I asked, "Do I look underage?" The doorman replied, "You're a woman"; only men were patted down for security reasons.

Exotic dancers overwhelmingly say they feel safe, not fearful, and desire to work within the law. A dancer who has been a feature for many years and has nursing training said she did not see abused dancers. Rather, dancers are less likely to be in abusive relationships because they receive adoration and gifts from many men.

Dancers often help to keep each other in line and to fight crime. For example, a twenty-year-old dancer tripped up a counterfeit ring. When a patron paid her four one-hundred dollar bills after his three-hour lap dance, with eleven more stashed in his right sock, she thought the bills looked genuine, but told club management they smelled like vinegar. The police were called. Secret Service agents said they believed the counterfeit bills were doused in vinegar to fool dogs used to sniff out contraband at the border.

CR-Activists fear the consequences of men's volcanic sexual eruption upon seeing nude dancers. Yet, I did not see uncontrollable patrons or find reports of club patrons convicted of sexual assault after visiting an adult club. However, I did learn about innumerable cases of clergy convicted of pedophilia and other heterosexual and homosexual sexual assault. The

clubs are about adult fantasy for consenting adults, not harmful duplici-
tous seduction of children by clergy who conflate sex and fantasy.

So it seems unreal to hear CR-Activists scream about instances of crime
associated with exotic dance clubs that are not representative of the industry. CR-Activists may truly believe that people involved with exotic dance
clubs are injured in God's eyes. However, it also appears that the secondary
effects doctrine cloaks the true motive for trying to eviscerate exotic dance
clubs—the Christian Right's definition of morality and Dominionism.

CR beliefs inspire CR-Activists to attack sexuality through various battle tactics. Exotic dance adult entertainment—a theater art of fantasy and
tease—is a target. The Maryland and Minnesota cases described in Chapters 5 and 6 illustrate litigation before a judge and before a jury in response
to false charges. To rebut accusations of exotic dance exploiting women, I
described their working conditions. An overview of crime related to exotic
dance undercuts CR-Activists' claims to the contrary. Aggression and indecency at times comes from those who abuse their positions in religion,
government, and law enforcement. So how does the exotic dance industry
defend itself?

# 9

## Stripping Your First Amendment and More

> You stupid idiots, you can classify anything as sexual if you really want to, so buggr off and leave the strip clubs alone!
> IRISH READER on regulating US exotic dance clubs

The month I was asked to work on my first exotic dance free speech case in Seattle, the US Supreme Court ruled against the federal government's honorarium ban that violated my First Amendment rights (US v. National Treasury Employees Union et al., 1995). As a US Department of Education employee, I had initiated the lawsuit against the prohibition of government workers from receiving payment for articles or speeches created during their own time and that had nothing to do with their government jobs. Flush with this success, I thought challenges to state and local government assaults against the First Amendment would be a cinch.

Little did I know that the First Amendment conflict at the local and state levels was so entrenched: years deep, geographically wide, and fueled with lots of gas for a segment of the politically active Christian Right to drive onward. Propelled by deeply emotional convictions and fear of temptation, CR-Activists feel justified in wiping out any enticement. The battle has led to street-type harassment and to government efforts that infringe on exotic dancers' and patrons' free expression, micromanage adult business, and threaten the existence of exotic dance clubs and our civil liberties.

## The Defense of Exotic Dance

Without patrons defending and supporting the clubs, they would go out of business. Benefits abound for patrons who may find eroticism, art in motion, and much more: entertainment, companionship, acceptance, and enhanced feelings of self-esteem. Clubs provide a pleasant environment in which to hang out or seal a business deal, for male bonding through a shared experience, and to meet sympathetic women who are nonjudgmental listeners. Patrons gain the health advantage of stress relief. Research led by Peter S. Statts, Division of Pain Medicine, Johns Hopkins University (reported at the American Pain Society, October 1999 meeting) found that envisioning pleasurable sexual fantasies increased pain tolerance, improved mood, reduced worry and tension, and enhanced participants' feelings of self-worth. These rational and passionate defenders challenge the highly charged, acrimonious religious, feminist, and governmental attempts to squelch exotic dance.

## Duel in the Desert and Moral Scold

A duel in the desert occurred in Scottsdale, Arizona, in 2005. The city's only two clubs, Babe's and Skin Cabaret, operated for years without any problems. But in December of that year, in response to the high-profile purchase of Babe's by adult film star Jenna Jameson with her partners, the Scottsdale city council approved amendments to their sexually oriented business ordinance of 1993. The new law required dancers to stay at least four feet away from customers, thus effectively banning lap dancing. So Jameson announced plans to file a lawsuit and launch a referendum drive to overturn the ordinance. At a well-attended, highly contentious city council meeting, it soon became apparent that the clubs had a lot of community support. However, despite testimony and the threat of litigation, the council chose to follow the advice of their highly paid and infamous CR-Activist attorney Scott Bergthold. The clubs raised almost $250,000 in political contributions and outspent their opponents almost 25-to-1. By a margin of 53–47 percent, voters defeated the city-backed ordinance (Proposition 401) that would have placed drastic restrictions on the city's only exotic dance clubs.

In 2006, by a margin of 63–37 percent, voters in Seattle overturned strict new rules on the city's exotic dance clubs requiring dancers to stay four feet from patrons, banning direct tipping, outlawing private dances in VIP rooms, and mandating bright lighting in the clubs. Voters did not want their city to be known as "a moral scold." The clubs raised $866,000 for a petition drive for the referendum and later paid for numerous TV ads portraying supporters of the measure as sanctimonious. Supporters of the dance club ordinance raised no money.

At times, non-adult businesses and conventioneers help defend exotic dance. In Atlanta, smack in the Bible Belt, business trumped the Bible, religion, and morality. When the city wanted to get rid of the "sinful" clubs, the International Poultry Exposition (known affectionately as "Chicken Pluckers of America") came to the rescue. The organization holds the largest annual convention in Atlanta. The Chicken Pluckers told the city that if its government interfered with exotic dance clubs, they would move their convention to another city that had adult entertainment. So Atlanta has one of the most liberal adult entertainment laws in the country. Complete nudity, full contact, and liquor are legally part of the landscape of the nearly forty strip clubs in Atlanta.

## Reactive and Proactive Club Resources

Turnabout may be fair play and a club defense. Every weekend for four years, Pastor Bill Dunfee and members of his New Beginnings Ministries in central Ohio protested Tommy George's Foxhole, an exotic dance club in a nearby town. In the club's parking lot, with signs, video cameras, and bullhorns in hand, the church folks videotape customers' license plates and post them online, and they try to save the souls of anyone who comes and goes. Finally, in 2010, fed up with these antics, George and the dancers finally accepted Pastor Dunfee's constant invitation to attend his church. In a counterprotest, they parked themselves outside the church, wearing see-through shorts or bikinis and belly rings and toting Super Soakers (water guns); many danced to music blaring from George's bright orange Dodge Challenger. An evangelizer to strippers in California flew to Ohio after reading news reports about the confrontation. She and a stripper-turned-Christian from Michigan, as guest preachers at the church, urged the congregation to rethink their protests. "It's not our job to tell these women that it's time to get out of the clubs. Just love them. Let the Holy Spirit draw them out." Strippers protesting outside the church turned down seats at the service offered to them by members of the congregation. But then women from the church began filing into the street, hugging the strippers and apologizing to them, leaving both sides brimming with emotion. But a stripper explained, "Our hearts are with Jesus, but our bodies are at the Foxhole." Although both sides agreed to sit down together, neither leader seemed willing to declare the end of the war. As long as church members try to curb business at the club, George said he'll keep going to the church on Sundays with carloads of friends and strippers.[1]

Although individual exotic dance clubs have fought with each other and alone in the culture wars, many now realize the strength in unity. An annual exotic dance club exposition; magazine, website, and list-serv publications; state, regional, and local associations; and a nationwide Association of Club Executives (ACE), founded in 1999, are allying many of the clubs against their common enemy. The ACE trade association of America's adult nightclubs has as its mission "to provide and share information concerning the political and legal status of the industry and to further provide a platform for the strategic planning of initiatives to combat negative challenges." ACE helps member clubs and affiliate state club owners' associations by providing resources and referrals. In addition, ACE has been instrumental in starting nearly thirty affiliate state associations that have their own leadership.

ACE state chapters help adult nightclub owners stay in business and thrive, instead of just surviving—or worse, going out of business. By sharing knowledge and networking, the organizations strive to build a formidable defense capable of heading off challenges created by CR-Activists. ACE state chapters conduct secondary effects studies and anthropological and epidemiological studies, and they find lobbyists, First Amendment attorneys, and expert court witnesses to help them. The chapters track progression of bills through the state legislatures, raise funds, offer political education, conduct nonpartisan voter registration, and join forces with groups that share similar goals in protecting small business, freedom of speech and expression, due process, and equal rights.

In countering attacks on their businesses, exotic dance clubs take offensive and defensive action in the courts of public opinion and law. Cabarets make preemptive efforts to halt the passage of restrictive ordinances by lobbying and giving presentations to local councils and state committees, as well as supporting open-minded political candidates. Some club owners and exotic dancers even run for political office. Proactive measures increase the likelihood of preventing harmful bills from being introduced or, if introduced, keep them from being passed. Clubs, individually and through ACE affiliates, develop good neighbor policies to show that clubs are productive parts of their communities. For example, they change their exteriors to fit in with other businesses and participate in community charitable events. In 2011, led by its president, Michael Ocello, ACE launched Club Owners Against Sex Trafficking (COAST), a program to help Americans recognize illegal activity. Clubs have been falsely accused of purveying trafficking. As Assistant Attorney General Thomas Perez of the Department of Justice Civil Rights Division has pointed out, the influx of immigrants has increased the potential for sex trafficking and involuntary servitude.

At the helm of ACE, Angelina Spencer sent out eight hundred voter registration kits to adult nightclubs, lingerie stores, and adult bookstores across the country. Approximately one hundred and sixty thousand customers filled out voter registration cards on the spot and others took the cards home to mail in. This effort was more successful than ACE ever anticipated and it got much publicity. Patrons with voter registration cards got free admittance to some clubs.

## Indirect Support

Club protestors can inadvertently support exotic dance. In 2007, in the tiny town of Thorp, Wisconsin, some residents picketed Chubby's North Gentleman's Club when it moved into town. But most of the *Chippewa Herald* readers who left anonymous comments on the paper's website said they didn't have a problem with the adult nightclub. One respondent enthused, "Thanks Guys, was happy for the protesters and the *Herald's* coverage: I had no idea there was a strip club in Thorp until you people stood out there with your signs! If not for you I may have just drove by but now I know to stop to get a beer and a show! Chubby's should be paying you and the *Herald* for all of the free advertisement!"

Inadvertently, overreaching CR-Activists' fervor and ruthless tactics may also benefit the exotic dance industry. Rev. Barry Lynn says these activists have hijacked Christianity and claim to speak for all people of faith. Such groups as Americans United for the Separation of Church and State (AU), Interfaith Alliance, and Freedom from Religion Foundation (FFRF) help the exotic dance industry by fighting CR-Activists' efforts to impose a theocracy. Leaders of Christian mainline denominations and other religions advocating pluralism have been working to diminish CR-Activists' activities.[2] Some Christians and Jews filed complaints against the Fairfield Christian and World Harvest churches, the separate affiliates of which run Ohio politics from the pulpit. After years of turning the other cheek, the United Church of Christ, a liberal Protestant denomination, signaled a manifest impatience with CR-Activists and an increasing willingness to weaken them. This church has sharply criticized the Institute for Religion and Democracy, a watchdog and advocacy organization, for supporting groups within mainline denominations that would further a conservative theological and political perspective. Raising their profile, progressive churches have undertaken advertising and e-mail campaigns to combat CR-Activists' misuse of the media; intolerance of, for example, single mothers and gays; and calls to withhold donations from non-conservative Christian groups. Rev. Michael Livingston said, "Mainline Protestant and Orthodox churches have been pounded into irrelevancy by the media machine of a false religion; a political philosophy masquerading as gospel; an economic principle wrapped in religious rhetoric and painted red, white and blue."[3]

More than a thousand clergy from thirty-nine states met in May 2006, "to wrest the mantle of moral authority from Conservative Christians."

Clergy for Fairness (including the Interfaith Alliance, Anti-Defamation League, Union for Reform Judaism, National Council of Jewish Women, Unitarian Universalist Association of Congregations, and evangelicals) petitioned against a proposed constitutional amendment to ban same-sex marriage.[4]

The Campaign to Defend the Constitution placed a full-page ad in the *New York Times*, denigrating Rev. Pat Robertson, Rev. Jerry Falwell, and Dr. James Dobson. "We're DefCon, protecting the Constitution from people like these. We believe our elected leaders put their hand on a Bible and swear to uphold the Constitution. Not the other way around."[5] However, long overshadowed, liberals of various faiths have yet to match the fervor and success of CR-Activists.

Organizations also oppose the White House Office of Faith-Based and Community Initiatives, a fancy term for mandatory taxpayer-supported religion. FFRF and AU help taxpayers who object to government financial support to churches and religious organizations to hold conferences to advise groups on how to apply for federal grants as part of the effort to bolster social service programs.

Some individual pastors defend exotic dance. Rev. Mike Kaminski has witnessed the transformation of the industry since the 1970s when he was a police detective living on the "block" in Baltimore, a rough area with strip joints. More than thirty years later, with the advent of gentlemen's clubs, he is calling attention through his writing to the bad rap the industry gets. As a chaplain for Wild J's Gentlemen's Club in Harrisburg for five years, Pastor Mike has gained firsthand knowledge of club life.

## The Constitution

The exotic dance legal defense relies on the Free Speech clause of the First Amendment as interpreted by the US Supreme Court. By law, exotic dance is expressive communication ("speech" rather than "conduct" in the legal sense) and therefore constitutionally protected. Ordinances singling out one kind of dance or nightclub evoke the anti-discrimination protection of the Fourteenth Amendment. And the absence of due process calls forth the Fifth Amendment guarantee. The adult cabaret defense also relies on its challenges to government arguments for the need to regulate the business through social science critiques of what governments offer as evidence and through conducting new studies.

## The Courts Speak and Misspeak

The Supreme Court's decisions related to exotic dance have been rooted primarily in the governmental interest to protect the populace, alcoholic beverage regulations, zoning ordinances, and morality. Courts have upheld "reasonable time, place and manner" regulations that they perceive as content neutral. However, contrary to what some in jurisprudence assert, dance consists of *content-filled* elements of expressive communication. Many courts and legislatures have been hampered in their deliberations by not having before them knowledge (drawn from the social and behavioral sciences, as well as the arts and humanities) about dance, nonverbal communication, and exotic dance that would clarify what exotic dance is and how it communicates (Chapter 3). Some judges have been unaware of or have overlooked the facts that dance educators explain to their students at the pre-collegiate level: dance communicates all kinds of ideas and feeling through body movement and stillness using space, touch, proximity to an observer, and costume. There appears to be a lack of comprehension of research methods that allow the distinction between fantasy and fact. Legislators' and judges' "common sense," "reasonableness," "morality," or adherence to overruled case law leads them to embrace what is unconstitutional, limiting civil rights.

## Evidence of Adverse Secondary Effects

Although the US Constitution and Supreme Court decisions would appear to protect the adult industry in its defense against CR-Activists, sometimes other courts and legislatures ignore them. CR-Activists and their allies argue for antiquated court precedents and deference to legislative bodies' unfounded rationales for exotic dance regulations. Below are important points of some key court decisions that are, of course, subject to different readings. The interpretations of lawyers I worked with on cases and the judges who decided them, pleadings and decisions, guide the summary points.

Sometimes federal courts aren't afraid to let the facts get in the way, and their decisions have changed the landscape for regulating adult businesses. Recent Supreme Court decisions ask for evidence for a government to justify its regulation of exotic dance. For example, in *City of Los Angeles v. Alameda Books* (2002), mentioned in Chapter 2, the court rejected shoddy data that CR-Activists rely upon.

*White River Amusement Pub Inc. v. Town of Hartford* (2nd Cir. 2007) held that, although the US Supreme Court has not "expressly decided the issue," its case law suggests that town officials must provide evidence of "negative secondary effects" before passing an ordinance to ban nude dancing. The R.V.S., L.L.C. v. City of Rockford (7th Cir. 2004) ruling means that a locality may not use its zoning power to regulate any type of dancing without offering sufficient evidence to support its rationale that the dancing causes adverse secondary effects. Parroting a canned preamble from another government's ordinance or open and explicit hostility toward and disapproval of the speech itself are not permissible purposes for a regulation. This point echoed the earlier Woodall v. City of El Paso (5th Cir. 1992) decision that it is illegal for cities to attempt to ban, regulate, or impose excessive location requirements just because they object to the dancers' sexually explicit messages. Peek-A-Boo Lounge of Bradenton, Inc. v. Manatee County (11th Cir. 2003) in Florida overturned regulations that dictated the physical layout of a club, permitted the sheriff to search the premises without a warrant, and banned nudity. The court reiterated that a city must now have evidence of the negative effects of the clubs prior to enacting an ordinance, and it must allow its evidence to be challenged. Flannigan's Enterprises Inc. v. Fulton County (11th Cir. 2001) also held that nude dancing in establishments licensed to sell liquor may not be banned without a factual basis to support the claim that nudity causes harm. A city cannot rely on foreign data that contradicts good local data.

Yet, some courts have turned a blind eye to conclusive proof that adult businesses have fewer or no more problems than any place of pubic assembly and side with governments in upholding baseless adult ordinances. For example, in Daytona Grand, Inc. v. City of Daytona Beach, Florida (2007), Eleventh Circuit judges Frank M. Hull, Stanley Marcus, and Judith H. Barzilay accepted shoddy data that the local government proffered as evidence for adverse secondary effects and the need to regulate clubs, not the plaintiff's challenge to the city's data and new solid social science research. The court referred to "reasonable and credible." Webster's Ninth New Collegiate defines "credible" as "offering reasonable grounds to be believed . . . of sufficient capability to be militarily effective." "Reasonable" is defined as "being in accordance with reason . . . not extreme or excessive . . . possessing sound judgment." The issue boils down to data. That is, what kind of data would the judges want as the basis for making decisions related to their financial well-being, family health, our military defense of the homeland, or counterterrorism? Governments have a high standard for making decisions about mundane matters like drainage and traffic, so why not have similar standards for adult businesses?

The US Supreme Court decided in *City of Erie v. Pap's A.M.* (2000) that governments may ban nude dance with time, place, and manner regulations as a way to combat negative secondary effects, but not with morality-based regulations, as in a prior case from Indiana, *Barnes v. Glen Theatre* (1991). However, a locality relying on secondary effects studies done by other cities or discussed in judicial opinions can be challenged as to their quality and relevance to the locality's own jurisdiction. Alas, Pap's went out of business and had not challenged the city council's findings or cast any specific doubt on their validity. The dissenting justices had written that "to believe that the mandatory addition of pasties and a G-string will have any kind of noticeable impact on adverse secondary effects [this was not questioned] requires nothing short of a titanic surrender to the implausible." They asserted that nude dancing is entitled to as much First Amendment protection as is any other form of expression. *Barnes* held that states may ban nude dancing in the interest of "protecting order and morality." However, Justice David Souter said it was the "secondary effects" of prostitution, sexual assault, and associated crimes of clubs like the Kitty Kat Lounge that justified Indiana's rule. The Fifth, Sixth, Seventh, Eighth, and Eleventh Circuit Courts treated Justice Souter's opinion as decisive.

The Supreme Court case, *City of Renton v. Playtime Theatres* (1986), has also been overridden. Renton held that government needed to rely on evidence to justify its decision that there is an important governmental interest in reasonable time, place, and manner restrictions on expressive conduct. Because Renton had no adult entertainment, it had no alternative but to look to outside studies. So the court held that where there are no local data, a city could rely on studies from other jurisdictions documenting "adverse secondary effects" of adult uses, if the local government reasonably believed the studies to be applicable to its own circumstances. Requiring a set distance of a club from the location of any residential area, school, park, or church also requires that there be alternative locations.

The Supreme Court in *Young v. American Mini Theatres Inc.* (1976) mandated that zoning to disperse entertainment and require separation from any residential area is permissible and in Detroit's "interest in attempting to preserve the quality of life in urban areas" and given the existence of alternative locations. Detroit had amended its anti–Skid Row ordinance to include regulation of the location of adult business on the grounds of preventing crime. This case gave rise to the secondary effects doctrine.

## Economic Impact

In *United States v. Playboy Entertainment Group, Inc.* (2000), as well as the district court opinion in that case, the Supreme Court decision held that when the government seeks to regulate speech and expression (and particularly in the adult entertainment arena) in such a way that there is a significant economic impact upon the entertainment business, the law is unconstitutional.

The Ninth Circuit Court in *Colacurcio v. City of Kent* (1998) upheld a ten-foot buffer zone between patron and performer, failing to recognize that stage dances and private table dances convey different messages. The court left open the issue of the buffer zone causing financial harm to businesses. However, pursuit of this issue became mute because the ordinance was apparently not being enforced.

## Time, Place, and Manner Considerations

In *Ward v. Rock Against Racism* (1989), the Supreme Court held that content-neutral time, place, and manner regulations are acceptable so long as they are designed to serve a substantial governmental interest and do not unreasonably limit alternative avenues of communication. We now know, according to current scholarly studies, that regulations to address mythical effects do not serve a legitimate governmental interest and suppress communication.

## Zoning and Alternative Locations

*Topanga Press, Inc. v. City of Los Angeles* (9th Cir. 1993) decided that sites that are legally available for adult cabarets must be reasonably accessible to the general public, have proper infrastructure (i.e., roads, lighting), and be generally suitable for commercial enterprise. Incredibly, some local governments include airports and oceans as the only possible locations for clubs!

## Governmental Interest

In *United States v. O'Brien* (1968), the Supreme Court determined that a government regulation is justified if it is narrowly tailored; not irrational, arbitrary, or capricious; and (1) it is within the constitutional power of the government, (2) it furthers an important or substantial governmental interest, (3) the governmental interest does not suppress free expression, and (4) the incidental restriction on First Amendment freedom is no greater than is essential to further that interest.

## Overbreadth

In *Spoons v. Kenneth Morckel* (2004), a US District Court in Ohio found that the ban on nudity, simulated sex, self-touch, and "improper conduct of any kind . . . that would offend the public's sense of decency" is unconstitutional under the First and Fourteen Amendments and overbroad. Lacking evidence of adverse secondary effects, the regulation served no governmental interest. Ohio's current ban is being challenged in court.

*Giovani Carandola v. George Bason* (4th Cir. 2002) ruled that the regulations on exotic dance had overbroad application. North Carolina's restrictions that banned simulated sex acts or the fondling of private parts, including the posterior, could prohibit the performance of ballet or flamenco dance or such productions as *Cabaret*, *Chicago*, and *The Full Monty*.

CR-Activists do not have a monopoly on disinformation. The Associated Press (AP) quoted Judge N. Carlton Tilley's statement about "unimpeachable" testimony in the *Carandola v. Beatty* (2005), ruling unconstitutional a ban on simulated sex. I had testified that because the instrument of sex and dance is one and the same, any movement can be seen as simulating sex, sexuality being in the eyes of the beholder: "Even the Irish *Step* Dance [a solo], which involves a rigid upper body and a leg pounding upon the ground, can be associated with the 'phallus pounding the female.'" But AP referred to "the novel idea that the rhythm of Irish *set* dancing [a group dance] would be banned under the law because it replicated the rhythm of sex."

This misinformation did not cause harm, but it did spark newspaper articles in Belfast, Northern Ireland ("Irish Dirty Dancing," *Belfast Telegraph*) and Dublin, Ireland ("U.S. Judge Rules that Irish Set-dancing Is Erotic," and "Dirty Dancing at the Ceili: So Irish Dancing Is all about Sex . . . That's the First We've Heard about It.") A multitude of readers responded in Belfast, and I participated in five radio interviews with hours of audience call-ins in Dublin (*Lunchtime Show*, *Gerry Ryan*, *TodayFM*, *Last Word Radio Show*, and BBC).

Some readers' responses: "That judge has it right. Hardly any of the Irish musicians I've met in London practise safe sets." "Now I'll never be able to look at Irish dancers the same way ever again." "So the poor maligned priests were right years ago when they closed down the *ceilidhs* [places for Irish dancing] . . . nothing but a hotbed of sex." "A step dancer told me that the motionless arms and torso were so the priest could walk by the window and not even know you were dancing." "What's wrong with SEX??? No accounting for taste (or reason) when it comes to human beings." "So the Taliban are active in North Carolina I see." "The judge's point was: 'You stupid idiots, you can classify anything as sexual if you really want to, so buggr off and leave the strip clubs alone!' It seems the judge is the only sane person in that crazy state."

The North Carolina legislature re-crafted the law and the new version has passed muster with US Fourth Circuit Court of Appeals (*Giovani Carandola v. Fox*, 2005). Now the prohibition on simulated sexual acts only applies to performances "that give the realistic impression or illusion that sexual intercourse [or masturbation, etc.] is being performed for the audience." The prohibition on "fondling" of buttocks, genitals, breasts, etc. only bars a performer from actually "manipulating specified erogenous zones." However, here again, "realistic impression or illusion" and "manipulating" are in the eyes of the beholder and any citation for violating the law is open to legal challenge.

In *Ways v. City of Lincoln* (8th Cir. 2001) the prohibition of "sexual contact" was deemed overbroad because it covered any business or commercial establishment. *Déjà Vu of Nashville, Inc. v. Metro Government* (6th Cir. 2001) was another case of overbreadth. *Triplett Grille v. City of Akron* (6th Cir. 1994) held that a ban on public nudity cannot sweep within its scope expressive conduct not generally associated with prostitution, sexual assault, or other crimes. The Supreme Court decision in *Schad v. Borough of Mount Ephraim* (1981) held that free expression is a right that cannot be banned and not a zoning use that is overbroad in proscribing all live entertainment, including nude dancing.

## Alcoholic Beverage Control

In *44 Liquormart v. Rhode Island* (1996), the Supreme Court ruled that liquor regulation permitted by the Twenty-First Amendment, which gave state and local governments authority to regulate establishments that serve alcohol, does not override the First Amendment. Earlier cases, such as *California v. LaRue* (1972), allowed the Alcohol Board of Control to ban nude dancing at premises it licensed, prohibition being nothing more than a time, place, or manner regulation of speech.

## Obscenity

One might reasonably ask why obscenity is one of the few categories of expression the First Amendment does not safeguard, In *Roth v. United States* (1957), the Supreme Court ruled that obscene material appealing to the prurient interest may be suppressed without proof that it will create a clear and present danger of antisocial conduct, recognizing that sex and obscenity are not synonymous. Sex is essential to human existence, violence is not, and yet the expression of any kind of violence is protected. The Supreme Court's decision in *Miller v. California* (1973) became the gold standard for determining whether a dance qualifies as legally obscene. It requires that all three prongs of the definition must be satisfied for a work to be constitutionally obscene: "(a) whether the average person, applying contemporary community standards *would* find that *the work, taken as a whole,* appeals to the prurient interest; (b) whether the work depicts or describes in a patently offensive way, sexual conduct specifically defined by the applicable state law; and (c) whether the work, *taken as a whole, lacks serious literary, artistic, political or scientific value.*" *Brockett v. Spokane Arcades, Inc.* (1985) said that the Supreme Court did not intend to characterize as obscene material that spoke to normal, healthy sexual desires. *Pope v. Illinois* (1987) is the legal gospel on artistic value. The Supreme Court ruled that a work need not obtain majority approval of a locality in order to be considered to have serious value, and the value of the work does not vary from community to community. Consequently, judges and juries in deciding whether sexually explicit material was largely obscene must assess the social values of the material from the standpoint of national standards.

## Prostitution

Prostitution has been variously interpreted. In *City of Anaheim v. Janini* (1999), the Supreme Court ruled that lap dancing is legal, not prostitution as the city asserted. The court referred to the 1920s' taxi dancing, the sale of a body-rubbing dance for a dime, that continues to this day, but at a higher price.

## Licensing

The federal court system has placed constraints on government use of licensing to regulate exotic dance. *Dream Palace v. County of Maricopa* (9th Cir. 2004) held that a county cannot publicly release sensitive information (dancers' names, addresses, and phone numbers) submitted by employees on their permit applications because this could expose them to harassment from "aggressive suitors" or people opposed to the industry. In *City of Littleton, Colorado v. Z. J. Gifts* (2004) the Supreme Court said that for an "adult business" licensing scheme to satisfy First Amendment requirements, the licensing scheme must provide assurance of speedy access to the courts for review of adverse licensing decisions and also provide assurance of a speedy court decision. The Supreme Court decided in *FW/PBS, Inc. v. City of Dallas* (1990) that licensing provisions may not constitute a prior restraint on freedom of expression by placing licensing at the discretion of any person unless that discretion is objectively limited. Moreover, government should make a licensing decision in a specific brief time period and provide the possibility of challenge to its decision through prompt judicial review and decision.

## Artistic Choice

The courts have restrained governments' restriction of artistic choice of dance movements and gestures. *Dream Palace v. County of Maricopa* (6th Cir. 2001) held that a regulation that bans simulated sex acts amounts to a ban on nude dancing, a constitutionally protected activity. "If Elvis's gyrating hips can fairly be understood to constitute a simulated sex act, one can fully appreciate the potential scope of the restrictions placed on erotic dancers in Maricopa County," Judge Diarmuid F. O'Scannlain wrote. *Schultz v. City of Cumberland* (7th Cir. 2000) determined that government cannot outlaw particular movements and gestures of exotic dance because such an action would deprive the dancers of a repertoire of expressive elements with which to communicate an erotic, sensual message. Protected expression cannot be unconstitutionally burdened.

## Dogma v. Pluralism

Irrespective of the US Constitution and Supreme, Appeals, and Circuit Court and state judicial decisions that restrict efforts to destroy exotic dance, some judges interpret case law their own way. CR-Activist judges seek to impose their vision of a Godly life upon the nation, obliterating modern civil and political pluralism. As the contest over adult entertainment exotic dance plays out in court, I hear omnipresent CR-Activist Scott Bergthold and his ilk argue in favor of restrictions on adult entertainment exotic dance as if legal constraints and scientific evidence do not exist. With consummate assurance, he convinces many people of his position, masking a pursuit of Dominionism. And despite the fact that the secondary effects doctrine no longer holds water in many courts, the exotic dance industry is increasingly accepted as legitimate, and young people think it's cool, we're in the midst of skullduggery manifest in the exotic dance controversy. CR-Activist leaders use the contestation much like politicians have used terrorism. They and their followers engage a variety of tactics to try to squelch the adult industry. Because exotic dance is stigmatized, the general public is unaware of or does not hold CR-Activists accountable for their adversarial behavior.

Recall that partly as a backlash to the 1960s sexual revolution and partly from fear of change, CR-Activists began flexing their political muscle in the 1970s and became emboldened, believing that they delivered the 2000 election to President George W. Bush. Rev. Richard Land of the Southern Baptist Convention put it this way: "As we say in Texas, [President Bush] is going to dance with the one who brung him. We haven't come to this place to go home and not push our values and our beliefs." He hailed "the welcoming of faith perspectives in public policy."[6]

I didn't ask to be an expert court witness. This mind-boggling adventure just fell into my lap. Amazed that, after the 1960s, there was such virulent animus toward exotic dance, I have tried to discover if CR-Activists' and others' negative evaluations of exotic dance clubs have any validity. I wondered why I kept learning that a clergyman or church group was behind the challenges to the existence of the exotic dance industry. Why was I repeatedly seeing CR-Activists who helped a government jurisdiction to draft and defend an anti-adult entertainment law in courtrooms?

It took a while for me to connect the dots and uncover evidence that runs counter to common knowledge. So I can understand a reader's surprise at first glance to read about what my son Aaron initially called my "seeing a conspiracy theory." But I hope the previous pages have disrobed a generally unknown truth that challenges the US democratic system based on the rule of law and diverse viewpoints. I appreciate the letter a stranger wrote to me:

> As a woman who loves the art of exotic dancing (both as a dancer and as an observer), I just wanted to thank you for not only writing such comprehensive articles about the industry but for taking the time to get them on the web for people to learn from. I wish you success in your attempts to educate people. It's a hard struggle, but the world changes one person at a time. One of the things I want to do in my life is make people more tolerant and understanding of the beauty of exotic dancing; to me, it's an incredible experience (again, both as performer and observer).

I have tried to show that CR-Activist aggression against exotic dance is based on belief in an infallible Bible that mandates distinct sex and gender roles. Deviations from patriarchy and female modesty are deemed abhorrent and sinful. CR-Activist political theocratic goals are articulated in the guise of advocating the quality of life for everyone. Latching onto a powerful and persuasive set of tropes, prejudices, and myths, CR-Activists' vociferous widespread public broadcast of the mantra that "exotic dance causes deleterious effects" has led to the perception, indeed hoodwinking, of many in the nation's mainstream. Denunciation resonates because of exotic dance history of some gangster-run strip joints in the past, media sensationalism, and spread of the myth of adverse secondary effects by segments of the feminist movement, the misinformed, "studies" commissioned by various governments, and even the professional American Planning Association.

Stigmatized, exotic dance is an easy scapegoat for perceived problems in America, and it's an easy target in the battle for CR-Activists to reclaim the public square for Christian political authority. They demonize those with other values. This has a chilling effect on exotic dance supporters, who are fearful of being hurt in their business and social or political life if they overtly defend this form of artistic expression. Exotic dance gets an unfair, bad rap despite the fact that there is no social or behavioral science evidence that exotic dance clubs cause problems disproportionate to any other public place of assembly. There is, however, evidence of positive effects—jobs with flexible hours, tax income, new and sustained proximate businesses, and patron welfare.

CR-Activists believe that men invariably lack self-control and will be tempted to assault women, that women will be drawn into the demimonde, and that family values (patriarchy) will be destroyed if clubs exist. Subsuming exotic dance within sinful pornography, activists point to dancers as the "diseased, polluting body" in society. Thus, the thorough hatred of exotic dancers, who are considered in some ways "feminists" and harbingers of Godless secular humanism and family breakdown. Rather than being submissive to a husband, women have the option, through adult entertainment, to take charge of their lives, explore their own potential, and use their feminine power to ensnare men en route to hell.

Yet, CR-Activists' "family values" are counter-indicated by hypocrisy. As has happened in the Catholic Church, an organization—namely, Voice to Stop Baptist Predators—was formed to assist children and adults sexually abused by pastors. Newt Gingrich admits that he was having an extramarital affair while he led Congress in impeaching President Bill Clinton for getting oral sex from a willing adult. Ted Haggard, Ralph Reed, Mark Foley, Lou Sheldon, Bill O'Reilly, Paul Crouch, Rush Limbaugh, Randall Terry, Robert Livingston, David Vitter, and Mark Sanford are on the list of the ever-growing "family values" leaders whose records include divorce, adultery, pedophilia, homosexuality, gambling, and embezzlement. Sarah Palin's teenage daughter had a child out of wedlock. The list is getting so long, its members could form their own political party. Oh, wait, they already have!

The crusade against exotic dance does not serve the larger public interest and is costly to the taxpayer, people's livelihoods, and, most importantly, civil liberties. Although "privates" (breasts, buttocks, and genitals) go public in an adult theater, you only see them if you are an adult who chooses to enter. Checking identification is adult entertainment establishment policy. And you can see the same and far more sexual expression in American mainstream performing arts.

Cultural conflict is fairly ubiquitous in American communities. The typical pathway for the majority of conflicts is that an offended citizen complains to an official. Then there is a legislative remedy proposed, a review by committee, discussions at a public hearing, and a vote by a public body, such as a city council. Resulting decisions are accepted without further ado. But strip clubs inflame the ardor of imaginary spectators and some who have actually been in a club, creating incendiary and litigious conflict. Real spectators inside clubs engage in fantasy with actual dancers while imaginary spectators outside clubs engage in fantasy about patrons and dancers.[7] Grievances about adult entertainment in nearly five hundred jurisdictions (Appendix 10) create sparks, brushfires, or firestorms, making exotic dance the crux of one of the most contentious law and public policy debates at the state and local levels in recent decades.

## Perils of Disregarding the Naked Truth

Much is at risk—and not just for the adult entertainment industry. In the effort "to promote the health and public welfare" of those it represents, government institutes regulations that hurt women's free artistic, moral, and economic choices; the performing arts; men's leisure opportunities; the market economy; and everyone's freedom.

Many exotic dance adversaries are the same people who have assailed the National Endowment for the Arts and tried to eliminate it. This assault creates a chilling effect on mainstream arts. Consequently, many artists apply for grants to support only "safe" "non-offensive," non-innovative work.[8] All kinds of dance self-censor. Yet, Western aesthetics require innovation.

An outcry flared anew in 2010 after a ten-year hiatus. Rob Boston writes: "Religious Right activists, feeling emboldened by their successes in the November [2010] elections, are on the prowl against 'obscene' or 'blasphemous' art, especially in tax-funded museums." Followed by some congressmen, William Donahue of the Catholic League (not officially or financially connected with the Catholic church) attacked David Wojnarowicz's "Fire in the Belly," a four-minute video in the *Hide/Seek: Difference and Desire in*

*American Portraiture* exhibit at the National Portrait Gallery, Smithsonian Institution. An eleven-second segment shows ants crawling on a crucifix, interpreted as ants being a microcosm of human society; frantic souls flee in panic in response to the AIDS epidemic as a seemingly impassive God looks on. The Smithsonian yanked Wojnarowicz's video, and this censorship elicited calls for the Smithsonian director to be replaced.

Some "shocking" dances that created public outrage in the past—but have since become our classics or influenced the art of dance—provide an aesthetic rationale for assuring free expression in all forms of art. Moreover, dance-makers in one dance form often draw upon other dance forms. The debate over exotic dance and performers bears similarity to earlier shock over "debauched" dances and ballet dancers who, until the early twentieth century, were considered part of the demimonde. Ballet, the waltz, jazz, flamenco, rebetika, and tango were considered immoral and stigmatized during their early histories. Isadora Duncan, often called the "mother of modern dance," challenged sexual mores and male-dictated constraints of ballet at the beginning of the twentieth century. Dancing to venerable music classics in bare feet, employing "natural" movement, and wearing body-revealing costumes—all signs of her anti-establishment lifestyle— she shocked audiences and was called a menace to the nation. Successful censorship might have removed her significant influence on the development of modern dance and ballet. Classics that initially came under attack include *Schéhérazade* (1910), showing the orgy of harem women dancing with black slaves, and *L'Après-midi d'un Faune* (1912), ending as a faun retrieves the scarf a nymph left behind and, after kissing it, falls upon it in symbolic sex. Both dances were served with indictments for indecency. Also, religious disfavor might have squelched George Balanchine's jarring *Prodigal Son* (1929). With rough-hewn imagery of depravity, the Siren, "goddess of whores," takes the youth's hand and puts it on her breast as he touches her crotch. The couple lies back and the boy's leg comes up and crosses over her in symbolic sexual penetration. Yet another dance that American censorship might have suppressed is Jerome Robbins's ballet *The Cage* (1951), a seemingly misogynist ballet that is contemptuous of procreation.

Choreographers need resources for their work, and society needs stimulation to develop. Dances on the margins challenge social norms, contribute to the aesthetic of innovation, and lay the groundwork for growth. Still, "nude erotic dancing" is an endangered species in much of the United States as hundreds of local and state governments have been attacking exotic dance, even multiple times over periods of years.

The Supreme Court, in *City of Erie v. Pap's A.M.*, said the requirement of

G-strings and pasties is a minimal restriction that does not diminish the erotic message, which is not true for contemporary exotic dance. Nonetheless, some jurisdictions, such as Jacksonville, Florida, required a form of bikini that covers more of the hip and buttock than is seen in swimming venues for families, as my camera documented. The question naturally arises why government should require more clothing for performers communicating a protected message before consenting adults in a controlled environment than it does for citizens walking around in front of children in public while intending to convey no message whatsoever. Ironically, nudity has been part of mainstream performing arts for more than one hundred and fifty years (Chapter 4).

CR-Activist-promoted imposition of such regulations as a separation between dancer and patron to prevent crime belies the criminal convictions and civil settlements related to priests and pastors sexually abusing children and adults under their care. Government efforts to "protect" exotic dancers and the community by regulating clubs more than other businesses actually endanger the women. Licensing and other regulations brand dancers as instigators of crime, or as lepers, and puts them at risk of losing their children. Moreover, licensing exposes dancers' identities and residences and makes them vulnerable to stalking. "Protection" regulations restrain dancers' economic and quality-of-life opportunities. Club closings not only harm the livelihoods of dancers, club staff, and all the club service providers (from furnishings to lighting), but the closings also push some women into welfare and encourage underground clubs and private performances to take place elsewhere. All females are harmed through the regulations of exotic dance by further entrenching in law the patriarchal regulatory power that feminists challenge.

Government is highly discriminatory against the exotic dance form of performing arts in restricting costume and creativity in dance movement and requiring special licensing and fees. Furthermore, government discriminates against exotic dance patrons and denies them its benefits. Government hurts its economic base—tax revenue and the employment of exotic dance service providers—and even urban development. Arthur Cotton Moore, an architect known for developing Washington Harbor and the Old Post Office Building in Washington, DC, asserts that exotic dance club use of old city buildings can help save the cities by contributing to the quality of life and making the city an exciting place to go. People want to be "where it's happening," tourists and conventioneers visit cities that have such excitement, and "empty nesters," mostly older and affluent, are drawn to a place that makes them feel young again.

CR-Activists oppose both exotic dance and what they allege it leads to. Civil rights activists are opposed to restrictions and fear what they might lead to.[9] Although evidence shows that the industry does not cause the alleged harms, numerous legislative, political, police, and judicial decisions corset the exotic dancer and wrap nudity in a cloak of law. These decisions have consequences that reach far beyond the adult entertainment industry and the arts community. You don't have to like exotic dance to still be concerned. Culture wars are actually wars in the sense that they inflict casualties. And when faith, ideology, or naiveté motivate controlling exotic dance for reasons that do not serve a democratic governmental interest, the door is opened to suppress other types of "free speech" on similar grounds. A government micromanaging any business threatens other investment. As professor and attorney Nadine Strossen puts it:

> Once we cede to the government the power to violate one right for one person, or group, then no right is safe for any person or group. So when we defend sexual expression, we are really making a stand not only against a specific kind of censorship . . . but for human rights in general.

## APPENDIX 1

## Exotic Dance

Exotic dance is (1) dance, (2) art, and (3) adult fantasy communicating various messages.

### 1. Dance

- is purposeful
- uses intentional rhythm
- has cultural influences
- uses **nonverbal body movement** in time, space, and with effort
- **communicates** through body movement, senses, music, costume, nudity, lighting/ambience
- employs own standards, as does every dance style

### 2. Art

- is a learned skill
- is creative and imaginative
- communicates within artistic style

### 3. Adult Fantasy

- is an **adult entertainment** style of dance and art performed in a theater setting
- contains risqué play in **high heels**
- derives **movements from popular forms**, Broadway theater, music video, jazz and hip-hop **dance**, cheerleading and gymnastics
- climaxes striptease by stripping to **nudity**
- has **self-touch** and **closeness and incidental touch** to patron to communicate special interest, comfort, immediacy, humanity, trust, and sensuality
- permits patron to **financially reward** dancer for effective communication

### Part 1. Stage Dance

- requires dancer to perform on theater stage **for entire audience**
- allows patron participation through gestures and tipping

### Part 2. Individual Patron-Focused Dance

- requires dancer to perform **for an individual patron** (for a fee) to communicate fantasy of special interest
- permits **patron participation** in dance through fee, gestures, and direct tipping

## APPENDIX 2

## Comparison

### Commonalities
**Verbal Language** and **Dance** (body language)
*both have*
Vocabulary
Meaning
Ambiguity
Emotion
Symbolism
Grammar
Content and Context

### Differences

| **Verbal Language** | **Dance (Body Language)** |
|---|---|
| Uses mostly prose, some poetry | Uses mostly poetry, some prose |
| Exists in time and volume | Exists in time, space, and effort |
| Communicates through words (sound and sight) | Communicates through movements (sight, sound, smell, proximity, and touch), costume, music, and lighting |
| Has written or spoken text | Has moving text |

# APPENDIX 3

## Exotic Dance Criteria for Serious Artistic Merit

### 1. Physical Appearance
- attractive body shape and tone
- hair, makeup, etc.

### 2. Costume
- 4- to 5-inch heels
- sexy attire

### 3. Movement
- graceful strut and posture
- standard bumps, grinds, shimmies, etc.
- smooth transitions between movements and positions: prone, kneel, stand, elevated on pole
- disrobes with attitude
- variety
- balanced use of stage
- interprets music
- proximity to patron

### 4. Personal Style
- creative uniqueness

### 5. Connection with Patron
- personality, proximity, smile, eye contact, touch, charisma

# APPENDIX 4

## Nudity in Exotic Dance

### Means

- this is adult entertainment—this is the climax of the striptease
- fantasy of a relationship
- eroticism
- nature
- health
- simplicity
- the body as an art form—nude sculpture in motion
- beauty of the body
- honesty
- the body as God's gift and worthy of the gaze
- innocence
- independence
- empowerment
- demystification of natural body
- status of well-maintained body
- parody of pretension clothing gives
- being human (without instigating crime or degrading women)
- trust

# APPENDIX 5

## Messages of Physical Distance

Distance in DANCE symbolizes distance zones in EVERYDAY LIFE*

Intimate Zone (0–1 1/2 feet)
    romance
    love-making
    mother-child bonding
    privacy
    comfort/protection
    wrestling
Personal Zone (1 1/2–4 feet)
    conversation among family and friends
Social Zone (4–12 feet)
    workplace activity
Public Zone (10–25 plus feet)
    formal lecture or music or dance concert

* From Edward Hall, *The Hidden Dimension*

### Analogies

Exotic Dance Individual Patron-Focused Intimate Zone *versus* Other Distance Zones in Everyday Life

- a parent teaching a child handwriting in the intimate zone *versus* a teacher demonstrating handwriting on the classroom blackboard in social zone
- a doctor examining a patient's body in the intimate zone versus a doctor reading a patient's medical report to the patient in the office social zone

### Characteristics of Individual Patron-Focused Exotic Dance

A dancer sends erotic messages by creating a fantasy of intimacy through bringing patron into her spatial sphere and screening out extraneous information.

Intimate spatial zone maximizes sensory reception:

- the sight of lip movement and eye contact (pupil dilation and expansion, brightness, winking and rolling, demure and bold glances, eyelash fluttering), facial color, and nose wiggle
- the sound of whispers and breathing
- the smell of perfume and breath
- the touch of shoulder, legs, or head.

## APPENDIX 6

### Expressive Contact in Exotic Dance

#### Conveys Meaning of Touch in Everyday Life

- Comfort/Support
- Friendliness
- Trust
- Inclusion
- Immediacy
- Humanity
- Play
- Affection
- Sensuality
- Desirability
- Love

#### Examples of Public Displays of Touch in Everyday Life

- Handshake
- Kiss on one or both cheeks or lips
- Hug
- Hand holding
- Arms entwined
- Arm around the shoulder
- Pat on the head

#### Absence of Touch Expresses

- Distance
- Coldness
- Disinterest
- Distrust
- Dislike
- Exclusion
- Rejection
- Alienation
- Violated expectations
- Rudeness
- Inhumanity

# APPENDIX 7

## Contact in Social Dance: Lap Dance Heritage

### Eighteenth to Nineteenth Century
WALTZ
- Man lifted partner's long dress to prevent its dragging and to hide his hand fondling her

### Twentieth to Twenty-first Century
TAXI DANCING (1920s to date) adults
- Man pays fee to dance with a woman in popular dance halls (e.g., a Chicago hall had 600 men and 68 girls. New York had 37 halls, 35,000 to 50,000 male customers per week and 2,500 to 3,000 dancers)
- "Dime a dance" was the fee; now it's $2 or more
- Like taxis, a dance is short and metered by a time clock
- "To dance on a dime" = tight body grinding

DIRTY DANCING (1960s to date; 1987 film) kids and adults
- Partners twine thighs, pelvises touch and grind.

DABUTT, BOOTY DANCING, FREAKING, DOGGY DANCING, WAXING, GRINDING, and FRONT PIGGY-BACKING, THE NASTY, BACKING IT UP (1970s to date; Spike Lee's 1988 *School Daze*) kids and adults
- Partners twine thighs, pelvises touch and grind.
- Female dances with buttocks rubbing partner's crotch.

## APPENDIX 8

## Exotic Dance Patrons

Dimensions of sexuality: psychology, culture, society, politics, and economics

Lonely or unhappy men
- Seek "understanding," nonjudgmental and emotionally supportive listener
- Seek attention from attractive woman desired as a spouse or lover or as spouse once was
- Seek refuge from real female involvement and pressure to perform sex
- Escape workplace political correctness about sexual harassment
- Hang out
- Escape work stress
- Avoid rejection and fantasize being liked and desired
- Seek excitement to perform marital sex role
- Recapture in imagination what's no longer in one's marriage

Hostile men (asked to leave club)
- Insult women verbally
- Grope women
- Hurl objects

Bachelor party group
- Celebrate
- Arouse and educate groom for new bride

Pleasure-seeking men (youth, workers, businessmen, and professionals)
- Seek entertainment
- Engage in adult play
- Seek aesthetic satisfaction (beauty of body and dance)
- Seek variety
- Seek excitement and adventure of "transgressive" and "foreign"
- Seek opportunity to relax
- Seek pressure-free female presence
- Observe what wife or girlfriend does not provide
- Fantasize and create own sexual script (safe sex)
- Have sensory experience
- Satisfy curiosity about the female body

- Support women's sexual liberation and empowerment
- Seek assignation
- Have safe sex (fantasy)

Macho men

- Seek male identity, bonding, and dominance through fantasy of phallic man
- Display social privilege by spending money ostentatiously
- Perform by spending money and dancing with entertainer
- Feel superior to women by being clothed
- Feel dominant by paying but without having to perform and risk failure
- Control of women by offering payment for dances

Victimized men

- Pay for being teased with an unrequited "date"

Female companions of men

- Seek to please companion
- Seek education
- Seek entertainment
- Seek aesthetic pleasure
- Seek excitement of "transgressive"

Bachelorette party group and young women

- Seek entertainment
- Arouse and educate bride for new groom
- Seek ideas to arouse lover or spouse
- Satisfy curiosity about the female body

Lesbians

- Seek attention from attractive women
- Hang out
- Seek entertainment
- Seek aesthetic pleasure
- Seek assignation

# APPENDIX 9

## Judith Lynne Hanna's Exotic Dance Expert Witness Court Testimony

Hanna also gave presentations at public hearings and regulatory boards and wrote reports for cases that did not require her testimony.

1. State of Washington Superior Court, King County.
   *Ino Ino, Inc. v. City of Bellevue*, 95-2-02025-9, 1995.
   *Ronda Remus v. City of Bellevue*, 94-2-27797-9, 1995.
2. Municipal Court of Seattle, Washington.
   *City of Seattle v. Darcy Poole*, 260398, 1996.
3. State of Washington Superior Court, King County.
   *Furfaro v. City of Seattle*, 96-2-02226-8, 1997.
4. US District Court, Clark County, Nevada.
   *Rojac Corporation v. Clark County*, A341884, Dept. xii, 1996.
5. US District Court, Southern District of Florida.
   *International Food and Beverage, Inc. v. City of Ft. Lauderdale*, 96-6577-Civ-Hurley, 1996.
6. Commonwealth of Virginia Circuit Court, City of Roanoke.
   *Commonwealth of Virginia v. Girls, Girls, Girls*, criminal action 97-957 and 971, 1997.
7. US District Court, Northern District of Ohio.
   *J. L. Spoons, Inc. v. City of Brunswick*, 1:97CV3269, 1998.
8. US District Court, Northern District of Texas, Dallas.
   *Baby Dolls Topless Saloons, Inc. v. City of Dallas*, 3-97-Cv-1331-r, 1998.
9. State of California Superior Court, San Bernardino County.
   *Pritchett v. Tom L. Theatres, Inc.*, SCV23015, 1998.
10. State of New York County Court, Tompkins.
    *New York State v. Langer*, 98-078A, 98-078B, 98-978C, and 98-079, 1998.
11. District of Columbia Department of Consumer and Regulatory Affairs Alcoholic Beverage Control Board.
    *Protest Hearing v. 1720 H Street Corp.*, 35901-98062P, 1999.
12. US District Court, Middle District of Tennessee.
    *Deja Vu of Nashville, Inc. v. Metropolitan Government of Nashville and Davidson County*, 3-97-1066, 1999.
13. State of Illinois Cook County Liquor Commission.
    *Cook County v. Licensee Loumar Corporation*, 1999.
14. State of Wisconsin Circuit Court, St. Croix.
    *East of the River Enterprises II, L.L.C. v. City of Hudson*, 99CV211, 1999.

15. State of Florida Eighteenth Circuit Court, Seminole County.
    *McKee v. City of Casselberry*, 99-CA1430-16E, 1999; *Koziara v. Seminole County*, 99-CA511-16P, 1999.
16. US District Court, District of Arizona.
    *Sunset Entertainment, Inc. v. Joe Albo*, 98-2099 PHY RGS, 1999.
17. US District Court, Northern District of Ohio.
    *J. L. Spoons, Inc. v. O'Connor*, 1:98CV2857, 1999.
18. State of Minnesota First Judicial District Court, Criminal Division, Goodhue County.
    *State of Minnesota, County of Goodhue, City of Cannon Falls v. Jessica Nicole Ann*, T6-00-5844, 2000.
19. State of Minnesota First Judicial District, Court Criminal Division, Goodhue County.
    *State of Minnesota, County of Goodhue, City of Cannon Falls v. Carla Shalon Lyons*, T6-00-0004631, 2000.
20. US District Court, Middle District of North Carolina.
    *Giovani Carandola, Ltd. v. George Bason*, 147 Supp.2d (M.D.N.C.) 2001.
21. US District Court, Eastern District, Pennsylvania.
    *Conchatta, Inc. t/d/b/a Club Risqué on the Delaware v. Col. Paul J. Evanko*, 01-1207, 2001.
22. State of Florida Thirteenth Judicial Circuit, Hillsborough County.
    *State of Florida v. Shawna Bohne*, 00-CM-024008, 2001.
23. State of Florida Sixth Judicial Circuit, Pinellas County.
    *State of Florida v. Laurie A. Anstine*, 00-20520MOANO, 2001.
24. State of Minnesota Seventh Judicial District Court, Criminal Division, Benton County.
    *State of Minnesota v. Amy Jo Draeger*, T2-01-2143, 2002.
25. US District Court, Northern District of Texas, Dallas.
    *Millennium Restaurants Group v. City of Dallas*, 3-01CV-0857-G, 2001.
26. State of Florida Eighteenth Judicial Circuit Court, Seminole County.
    *McKee v. City of Casselberry*, No. 99-ca1430-16e; *Koziara and Derienzo v. County of Seminole*, 99-ca511-16p, 2002.
27. State of Minnesota Seventh Judicial District Court, Criminal Division, Benton County.
    *State of Minnesota v. Brandy Lee Morcomb*, TX-01-2147, 2002.
28. US District Court, Northern District of Illinois, Western Division.
    *R.V.S., LLC. v. City of Rockford*, 03-C-50048, 2003.
29. US District Court, Northern District of Texas, Dallas.
    *Fantasy Ranch, Inc. v. City of Arlington*, 3:03-CV-0089-R, 2003.
30. US District Court, Southern District of Mississippi, Jackson.
    *A and C Entertainment et al. v. City of Jackson*, 3:01CV88WS, 2003.

31. State of Florida Sixth Judicial Circuit, Pinellas County.
     *State of Florida v. Shannon Malnick*, 03-12309MOANO, 2003.
32. State of Illinois, Civil Trial Division, Lake County.
     *XLP Corp. d/b/a Dancers, Baby Dolls, 41 News and Video Magic v. County of Lake*, No. 99-0788, 2003.
33. US District Court, Northern District of Ohio.
     *J. L. Spoons et al. v. Kenneth Morckel, et al.*, No. 1:04CV0314, 2004.
34. US District Court, Middle District of North Carolina.
     *Giovani Carandola, Ltd. v. Ann Scott Fulton*, No. 1:01CV115, 2001, 2004.
35. Superior Court of New Jersey, Bergen County.
     *Lighthouse Restaurant Services, Inc. v. Township of South Hackensack*, No. BER-L-5025-3, 2004.
36. State of Florida Sixth Judicial Circuit Pasco/Pinellas County
     *State of Florida v. Porcha Annie Hope*, 06-01316MMAWS-16, 2006.
37. State of Florida Sixth Judicial Circuit Pasco/Pinellas County
     *State of Florida v. Liberty Hacket*, 06-00857-MMAWS, 2006.
38. US District Court, Baltimore.
     *Wet Sands, Inc. et al. v. Prince George's County*, 8:06-cv-02243-DKC, 2006.
39. State of Florida Sixth Judicial Circuit Pasco County.
     *State of Florida v. Dawn Barr*, CTCO3-00798MMAWS-17, 2007.
40. State of Florida Sixth Judicial Circuit Pasco County.
     *State of Florida v. Alicia Julie Henry*, CTCOo600852MMAWS, 2007.
41. State of Florida Sixth Judicial Circuit, Pasco/Pinellas County
     *State of Florida v. Amy Melissa Gilbertson*, 06-6977-17, 2007.
42. US District Court, Western District of Pennsylvania
     *Bottoms Up Enterprises, Inc. and Island International Ventures, LLC v. The Borough of Homestead*, 2:07-CV-00344- TFM, 2007.
43. US District Court, Northern District of Ohio
     *84 Video/Newsstand et al. (12 plaintiffs) v. Sartini et al. (sixty-six prosecutors and law directors)*, 1:07-CV-03190-SO, 2007.
44. State of New York Division of Tax Appeals
     *Nite Moves v. NY State Department of Taxation and Finance*, X55076770202, 2008.
45. US District Court, Western District of Tennessee
     *Entertainment Productions, Inc., d/b/a Christie's Cabaret, et al. v. Shelby County, et al.*, 2:08-CV-2047, 2008, for the plaintiffs
46. State of New York Division of Tax Appeals
     *Greystoke v. NY State Department of Taxation and Finance*, 2009.

# APPENDIX 10

## Illustrative Jurisdictions that Attack Exotic Dance

Legislation and litigation (close to 500 noted in the press, newsletters, or observed by Judith Lynne Hanna, 1995 to 2011):

Adams City, MS
Adams Township, Butler County, PA
Aiken, AL
Alabaster, AL
Alamance County, NC
Albany, NY
Alexandria, LA
Allegheny County, PA
Amesbury, MA
Amarillo, TX
Anne Arundel, MD
Anaheim, CA,
Arizona
Ascension, Parish County,
    Donaldson, LA
Atlanta, GA
Arlington, TX
Augusta, GA
Austin, TX
Autauga County, AL
Baltimore, MD
Bangor, ME
Bates City, MO
Batvia, TX
Beaumont, FL
Beacon Wood, FL
Bedford Park, IL
Bellevue, WA
Beltsville, MD
Benton County, MN
Bettendors, TN
Billings, MT
Blountsville, TN
Bibb County, GA

Bluff City, IA
Boise, ID
Boone County, TN
Bosque Farms, NM
Boston, MA
Bothel, WA
Broadview, IL
Bridgeport, CN
Bridgeview, PA
Bristol, PA
Brook Park, IL
Brooklyn, NY
Brooksville, FL
Broward County, FL
Brunswick, CA
Burlington, NJ
Butler County, OH
Cajon, CA
California
Calumet City, IL
Camp Hill, PA
Campbell, CA
Campbell County, KY
Cambridge City, IA
Cannon Falls, MN
Canton, OH
Carlisle, IA
Carlstadt, NJ
Carmel, IN
Cass County, MO
Casselberry, FL
Center City, PA
Central City, KY
Charleston, WV

Chatham, NJ
Chatham, VA
Chattanooga, TN
Chesterton, IN
Chillico City, OH
Cicero, IL
Cincinnati, OH
City of North Charleston, SC
Chicago, IL
Clark County, NV
Clarke County, GA
Clarkstown, NY
Clarksville, IN
Clay County, MO
Chicago, IL
Claremont, CA
Clayton County, GA
Clermont County, MI
Clemmons, NC
Cleveland, OH
Cobb County, GA
Collierville, TN
Collinsville, IL
Colquitt County, GA
Columbus, OH
Cook County, IL
Corpus Christi, TX
Council Bluffs, IA
Covington, KY
Coweta County, GA
Cross Plains, WI
Cumberland, TN
Currituck County, NC
Dallas, TX
Dade County, FL
Dalworthington Gardens, TX
Davenport, IA
Dayton, OH
Daytona Beach, FL
Denver, CO
Derby, CT
Derry, PA
Destin, FL

Detroit, MI
Dickerson, TX
Dickenson County, KS
Doylestown, PA
Dubuque, IA
Duluth, MN
Eatonville, Easton, PA
Edwardsville, KS
Eliot, MA
Elkton, TN
Elkton, WI
Erie, PA
Erie Township, MI
Everett, WA
Fairfield, CT
Fall River, MA
Federal Way, WA
Ferndale, MI
Flagler, FL
Florence, TN
Fond du Lac, NY
Forrest County, MS
Fort Erie, NY
Fort Lauderdale, FL
Fort Pierce, FL
Fort Smith, AK
Fort Wayne, IN
Frisco, CO
Fulton, WI
Garland, TX
Gary, GA
Gary, IN
Glendale, CO
Gloucester City, NJ
Grafton, WI
Grants Pass, OR
Greenville County, SC
Gren Township, OH
Guadalupe, AZ
Hackensack, NJ
Hagar City, NJ
Halfmoon, NY
Hallandale Beach, FL

Hammond, IN
Hampton, VA
Hannibal, MO
Harrisburg, PA
Hartford, CT
Hartford, VT
Harvard, IL
Hattiesburg, MS
Henrico, VA
Henrietta, VA
Hickman County, TN
Higgins Township, MI
Hilliard, OH
Honolulu, HI
Hope, VA
Hopkins County, OH
Horry, AK
Hot Springs, AK
Houston, TX
Houston County, AL
Howell, MI
Hudson, WI
Huntsville, AL
Humphries County, TN
Indianapolis, ID
Indio City, CA
Islamorada, FL
Jackson, FL
Jackson, MI
Jackson County, MO
Jacksonville, FL
Janesville, WI
Jefferson, WV
Johns Creek, GA
Johnson County, KS
Johnston, RI
Juneau, WI
Kanawha County, WV
Kansas
Kappa, IL
Kennedale, TX
Kennewick, WA
Kent, WA

Kenton County, KY
Kitsap County, WA
Knox, IN (no club)
Knox County, TN
La Habra, CA
Lake County, FL
Lake County, IL
Lake Crystal, MN
Lakewood, WA
Lansing, IL
Las Vegas, NV
Latham, FL
Lavonia, FL
Lavonia, GA
Lawrenceville, LA
Layton, UT
Leavenworth, KS
Leon Valley, TX
Lexington, NE
Lickdale, PA
Lincoln, NE
Lincoln City, IL
Lincoln Park, OR
Litchfield, MN
Littleville, AL
Lodi, CA
Lodi, NJ
Los Angeles, CA
Louisville, KY
McCook County, SD
McHenry County, IL
Macomb County, MI
Macon, GA
Madison, ME
Madison Lake, WI
Manatee County, FL
Mankato, MN
Mapleton, IL
Marenisco Township, MI
Martinez, CA
Marysville, OH
Maumee, OH
Meadville, PA

Melbourne, FL
Memphis, TN
Menasha, WI
Metro Lake, IL
Metropolis, IL
Mendon, MA
Miami, FL
Miami Beach, FL
Miami Beach, MI
Midvale, UT
Milford Township, PA
Mifflin, OH
Milford, PA
Mills County, IA
Milwaukee, WI
Mineral County, WV
Mishawaka, IN
Missouri
Mobile, AL
Moline, MI
Monroe, MI
Monroe, OH
Monroe, WA
Montebello, CA
Morrisville, PA
Mt. Carmel, OH
Mt. Carmel, WI
Moreau, NY
Mt. Joy, NY
Mt. Joy, PA
Mt. Vernon, NY
Muldraugh, KY
Mundelein, IL
Nashville, TN
New Buffalo, MI
New Castle, NJ
New Harmony, IN
Newark, NJ
Newport, OH
Newport, KY
Newport News, VA
New Port Richey, FL
New York, NY

New York
Nicollet, MN
North Bay Village, FL
North Brunswick NJ
North Middleton, PA
North Webster, IN
Norwell, MA
Nye County, NV
Nyssa, OR
Oak Grove, KY
Oconee County, GA
Ogden, UT
Ohio
Oklahoma
Oldham County, KY
Olympia, WA
Orion Township, MI
Oroville, CA
Oswego, NY
Paducah, KY
Palm Bay, FL
Palm Beach, FL
Palm Shores, FL
Parker, CO
Pasadena, CA
Pasco County, FL
Pasquotank County, VA
Pembrooke Park, FL
Pennsylvania
Pensacola, FL
Peru, IN
Petoskey, MI
Phoenix, AZ
Pico Rivera, CA
Pierce County, WA
Pierce County, WI
Pills, PA
Pine Grove, LA
Pitt County, NC
Pittsburgh, PA
Platte County, MO
Plymouth County, MI
Pomona, CA

Port Angeles, WA
Port Canaveral, FL
Port Chester, NY
Port Treverton, PA
Poseyville, IN
Post Falls, ID
Prince George's County, MD
Princess Anne, MD
Providence, RI
Quakertown, PA
Rabun County, GA
Rack, NC
Raleigh, NC
Ramapo, NJ
Rancho Cordova, CA
Richmond, IN
Richmond, VA
Ridgeley, WV
Roanoke, VA
Rochester, NY
Rockford, IL
Rockville Township, PA
Romulus, MI
Rostraver, IL
Roy, UT
Runkley (Beltrami County), MN
Saginaw Township, MI
St. Augustine, FL
St. Charles, IL
St. Johns County, FL
St. Paul, MN
Salem, OR
Salem, SD
Salem, WI
Salem Township, PA
Saline County, KS
Salpan, CA
San Antonio, TX
San Bernardino, CA
San Diego, CA
Sandy Springs, GA
San Joaquin County, CA
Santa Fe, NM

Santa Fe Springs, CA
San Francisco, CA
Santa Rosa, CA
Sarasota, FL
Sayreville, NJ
Schenectady, NY
Schodack, NY
Scottsdale, AZ
Seattle, WA
Sedgwick, KS
Seminole County, FL
Shady Springs, GA
Shawnee County, KS
Shelby County, TN
Shoreline, WA
Simi Valley, CA
Sioux City, IA
Singer Island, FL
Snohomish County, WA
Snow Hill, MD
South Bend, IN
South Burlington, VT
South Hackensack, NJ
South Salt Lake, UT
Southgate, MI
Sparks, NV
Sparta, KY
Spencer, IN
Spotsylvania County, VA
Stamford, CT
Stark County, OH
State Line, ID
Stone County, MS
Stratford, CT
Stratford, WI
South Salt Lake, UT
Stephens County, SC
Strongville, OH
Sugar City, IA
Sullivan County, TN
Sunny Isles Beach, FL
Sunnyvale, CA
Sunny Valley, OR

Superior, WI
Smyrna, TN
Swansea, IL
Swatara, PA
Syracuse, NY
Tacoma, WA
Tampa, FL
Tarrant County, TX
Tarzana, CA
Taylorsville, UT (no club)
Tempe, AZ
Tennessee
Texas
Texarkana, AR
Tinley Park (Chicago), IL
Toledo, OH
Tompkins, NY
Tonawamda, NY
Torrance County, NM
Troy, MI
Troy, OH
Tualatin, OR
Tucson, AZ
Tukwila, WA
Tulare, CA
Tullytown, TN
Unalaska, AK
Union, NJ
Union Township, OH
Union Township, PA
Utah

Virginia Beach, VA
Waldo, FL
Warnernobbing, GA
Warren, GA
Warren, MI
Warrington, PA
Warwick, PA
Washington, DC
Washington
Wasilla, AK
Waterbury, CT
Wayne County, MI
Wellford, North Carolina
Wellford, South Carolina
West Alles, WI
West Jordan, UT
West Rockhill, PA
West Virginia
Westerbrook, ME
Westminster, CA
Westport, CN
Weymouth, MA
White River, VT
Winslow, NE
Winston-Salem, NC
Winter Park, FL
Wichita, KS
Wyandotte, MO
Yellowstone City, MT
Yucaipa, MT
Zumbro Falls, MN

More than one conflict may appear in a jurisdiction.

# APPENDIX 11

## Key Christian Right Political Activists and Revenue in the News, 1995–2010

### People

David Barton (WallBuilders, vice chairman of the Texas Republican Party)

Gary Bauer (Americans United to Preserve Marriage and American Values, formerly Family Research Council)

Scott D. Bergthold (law office devoted to regulating adult entertainment)

Phil Burress (Citizens for Community Values)

David Caton (Florida Family Association)

Ken Connor (Family Research Council)

James Dobson, Tom Minnery (Focus on the Family)

Jerry Falwell, Joel C. Hunter (Christian Coalition)

Thomas Fitton (Judicial Watch)

Ted Haggard, Richard Cizik (National Association of Evangelicals)

Deal Hudson (conservative Catholic, publisher of *Crisis*)

Bill Johnson (American Decency Association)

Charles Keating (Child Welfare Foundation)

D. James Kennedy (Coral Ridge Ministries, Center for Reclaiming America)

Peter LaBarbera (Concerned Women for America's Culture and Family Institute)

Tim (Council for National Policy) and Beverly (Concerned Women for America) LaHaye

Richard Land (Southern Baptist Convention)

Marvin Olasky (*World* magazine)

Rod Parsley (Center for Moral Clarity, World Harvest Church)

Tony Perkins, Jan LaRue (Family Research Council)

Ralph Reed (former Christian Coalition head)

Pat Robertson (founder, Christian Coalition and the Christian Broadcasting Network; his "electric church" is beamed to a daily audience of 1 million)

Phyllis Schlafly (Eagle Forum)

Alan Sears (Alliance Defense Fund)

Louis Sheldon, Andrea Lafferty, Phillip Cosby (Traditional Values Coalition)

Bruce Taylor (National Law Center for Children and Families)

Paul Weyrich (Free Congress Foundation, National Empowerment Television)

Donald E. Wildmon (American Family Association)

Wendy Wright (Concerned Women for America)

## Organizations

Figures on the top ten wealthiest religious right organizations are annual revenue figures obtained by Americans United for the Separation of Church and State from the most recently available official governmental filings from 2009 and 2010. Together, these groups raise more than $1 billion annually.

Agape Press (American Family Association)
Alliance Defense Fund, $30,127,514
American Decency Association
American Family Association, $21,408,342
Americans United
American Vision
Arlington Group (Alliance Defense Fund, American Family Association, American Values, Bott Radio Network, CatholicVote.Org, Raymond Flynn Center for Moral Clarity, Citizens for Community Values, Coalition of African American Pastors, ConservativeHQ.com, Coral Ridge Ministries and Center for Reclaiming America, Covenant Marriage Movement, Exodus International, Family Research Council and FRC Action, Fieldsted and Company, Focus on the Family and Focus on the Family Action, Free Congress Foundation, High Impact Leadership Coalition, Inspiration Television Network, Judeo-Christian Council for Constitutional Restoration and Vision America, Liberty Counsel, Liberty University, National Association of Evangelicals, Ohio Restoration Project, Salem Communications, Southern Baptist Convention, Susan B. Anthony List, Teen Mania Ministries, TeenPact, The Vanguard.org, Traditional Values Coalition, American Society for the Defense of Tradition, Family and Property)
Black Hills Neighborhood Citizens for a Better Community
Carolina Family Alliance
Center for Decency through Law
Center for Moral Clarity
Child Welfare Foundation
Christian Broadcasting Network/Regent University, $381,479,321
CitizenLink (from Focus on the Family)
Citizens for Community Values
Citizens for Community Virtue
Citizens for Strengthening Community Values
Chalcedon Foundation
Christian Coalition
Coalition on Revival
Concerned Women for America, $11,772,009
Coral Ridge Ministries, $17,263,536
Council for National Policy
Empower America

Family Research Council, $14,569,081
Florida Family Association
Focus on the Family, $130,258,480
Free Congress Foundation
Heritage Foundation, $64,765,247
Institute for Religion and Democracy
Jerry Falwell Empire
   Liberty University, $395,898,255
Jerry Falwell Ministries, $4,208,989
Liberty Counsel $1,371,795
Judicial Watch
Operation Rescue
Landmark Legal Foundation
Leadership Institute
Liberty Legal Institute
Liberty University
Morality in Media
National Association of Evangelicals
National Family Legal Foundation
Pat Robertson Empire
   Christian Broadcasting Network, $295,140,001
   Regent University, $102,741,261
   American Center for Law and Justice, $13,375,429
   Christian Advocates Serving Evangelism, $43,872,322
Simon Greenleaf School of Law in Orange County, now Trinity International
   University School of Law
Southern Baptist Convention Ethics and Religious Liberty Commission,
   $3,236,000
Traditional Values Coalition, $9,888,233
WallBuilders, $1,091,531

## Christian Networks

Christian Broadcasting Network
Trinity Broadcasting
Inspiration Network
Daystar
Three Angels Broadcasting
World Harvest Television
Praise TV
Worship Channel
Gospel Music Television
The Word Network
Family Net

# APPENDIX 12

## Arsenal of a Segment of the Politically Active Christian Right

- Use of electronic technology to communicate through church networks on how to attack clubs
- Promote a disinformation campaign about the impact of exotic dance clubs
- Lobby government to enact regulations of clubs to drive them out of business
- Have "prayer warriors" shadow legislators at public events as "lobbying" technique
- Change ordinances if clubs comply and survive
- Distribute voting guides
- Get elected to the legislature and judiciary
- Get appointed to government positions
- Create universities, law schools, and think tanks to educate students to actively support CR values
- Train lawyers and policy makers to craft and defend CR goals
- Provide legal services to draft and defend regulations
- Use police powers to raid clubs, make false arrests, intimidate club stakeholders
- Harass clubs with health, fire, etc. inspections
- Push for discriminatory licensing of exotic dancers
- Picket clubs
- Take license plate numbers of patrons and contact their families and employers
- Physically damage club property
- Threaten violence against club stakeholders and their family

# APPENDIX 13

## Reality and Myth: What Neighbors Say about Exotic Dance Clubs

### Summary of a Case Study in Charlotte, North Carolina, July 2001

The City of Charlotte, North Carolina, granted five M.A.L. Entertainment clubs eight-year zoning amortizations to relocate. M.A.L. Entertainment requested zoning variances for these establishments by presenting the results of several studies: neighborhood perceptions, crime analysis, and economic impact.

An anthropological, qualitative case study reported the perspectives of resident and business neighbors of three of the five exotic dance clubs—Twin Peaks, VIP Showgirls, and Temptations—chosen to reflect different kinds of economically developed neighborhoods. The research goal was to provide information on the extent and quality of residents' and business operators' perceptions of the impact of the exotic dance club on the neighborhood quality of life and what takes place at and around the club.

The City of Charlotte zoning regulations refer to a 1,000-foot radius as a measure of neighborhood, so structured interviews were conducted within this radius of each of three exotic dance clubs, eliciting respondents' firsthand knowledge of the club's positive, neutral, or negative effects on the neighborhood quality of life. Questions were both open-ended (permitting any kind of answer) and close-ended (fixed alternatives). Neighbors were asked the reasons for their opinions about the impact of the local club.

In addition, the investigator observed three exotic dance clubs during both daytime and nighttime hours of operation. Managers and six dancers in each business were interviewed about their perceptions of what takes place at and around the club and the neighbors' reactions to the club. Reports about exotic dance clubs in the *Charlotte Observer* newspaper were examined to obtain historical background for the case study.

Out of ninety-one interviews with three exotic dance club neighboring residents and business operators, eighteen dancers and three managers, there were no reports of adverse secondary effects—crime or property depreciation—as a result of the presence of these adult entertainment establishments.

Two male businessmen objected to the exotic dance clubs but offered no evidence that they harmed the neighborhood's quality of life. A car lot owner complained about "those places": a billiard hall behind his lot that had drunkenness, brawling, and murder, and an exotic dance club, a few doors down the street from his business. He claimed some people had parked in his lot, cluttered it with beer bottles, and collided with one of his cars. As a result, he was forced to put a railing around his lot. Another objector said that exotic dance clubs are sinful. Some residents and business operators were not, as a matter of cultural "taste," favorably disposed toward exotic dance clubs.

Several business operators in the exotic dance club neighborhoods commented on the positive benefits of being proximate to adult entertainment enterprises. The clubs attracted customers who became their clients, and the clubs' employees themselves were clients. Some businesses found a club advantageous as a landmark to find their establishments.

Many locals said the problems that exist in the neighborhoods of exotic dance clubs are over-development of the neighborhood area, congestion, noise, high employee turnover, and too many poor people in the vicinity.

## Interview Schedule for Neighbors of Exotic Dance Clubs

Introduction: I am Dr. Judith Lynne Hanna, a senior researcher from the University of Maryland. I am conducting research on people's views of the quality of life in their neighborhood. I have published books and articles on this subject. Here is my card.

I am interested in your opinions. What you say will be treated as anonymous in the research report unless you would like to be identified. I would be happy to let you know when a report of the study is available.

Name of club
Interviewee Name
Resident
Business
Address
Phone
e-mail
Date
Time
Gender
Ethnicity
Contextual Information
  Not available
  Refusal
  Other

Part 1.
1. How long have you lived [worked] in this neighborhood (area within walking distance)?
  Less than 1 year
  1–2 years
  more than 3 years
  other

2. In your opinion, in the period during which you've lived [been involved with a business] in this neighborhood, has the quality of life in the neighborhood changed?

    2a. In what way?

3. In your opinion, have businesses in this neighborhood impacted its quality of life in a positive or negative manner?

    3a. In what way?

    3b. What business?

    3c. When and how often does x happen?

    3d. Where else does it happen?

Part II. Additional Questions

4. If the respondent makes no mention of the exotic dance club in Part I, the following introduction will be made and questions will be asked: In the course of my research, I have studied some exotic dance clubs around the country. (The question addresses stigma of clubs so respondent may feel free to talk.) Has the ____ club had an impact on this neighborhood?

    4a. How?

    4b. When and how often does x happen?

    4c. How do you know x happens around the club?

    4d. Does it happen elsewhere? Where?

    4e. Have you ever been inside of the ____ exotic dance club?

        If yes: When did you go to the club?

        How often did you go?

        How long did you stay?

    [If relevant]

        Have you expressed your concerns to the exotic dance club management?

5. If relevant: In your opinion, is the ____ impact caused by the dancers, management or clientele?

6. Would you be willing to pay more for your house/apartment/business rent if the ____ exotic dance club were not in the neighborhood?

7. If the exotic dance club were located in another neighborhood, do you think the club would have the same impact? Please explain _____

8. I think that probably everyone knows something about exotic dance clubs. Where have you gotten information about the clubs?

    __ Film

    __ TV

    __ Radio

    __ Visit to the club

    __ Visit to a club elsewhere

    __ Discussion with person who visited

    __ Discussion with _____ (type of person who worked in a club)

___ Church/synagogue/mosque/temple, etc.

Other _____

9. Has a police officer or a local government official ever talked with you regarding ____ exotic dance club?

If yes, what about?

10. Ask:

Occupation _____

Age ____

Church/synagogue/mosque/temple, etc. activity _____

Thank you very much for your time.

# APPENDIX 14

## Protection under the Constitution of the United States of America

### Amendment I

Congress shall make no law respecting an establishment of religion, or prohibiting the free exercise thereof; or abridging the freedom of speech, or of the press, or the right of the people peaceably to assemble, and to petition the Government for a redress of grievances.

### Amendment V

No person shall be held to answer for a capital, or otherwise infamous crime, unless on a presentment or indictment of a Grand Jury, except in cases arising in the land or naval forces, or in the Militia, when in actual service in time of War or public danger; nor shall any person be subject for the same offense to be twice put in jeopardy of life or limb, nor shall be compelled in any criminal case to be a witness against himself, nor be deprived of life, liberty, or property, without due process of law; nor shall private property be taken for public use without just compensation.

### Amendment XIV

Section I. All persons born or naturalized in the United States, and subject to the jurisdiction thereof, are citizens of the United States and of the State wherein they reside. No state shall make or enforce any law which shall abridge the privileges or immunities of citizens of the United States; nor shall any State deprive any person of life, liberty, or property, without due process of law; nor deny to any person within its jurisdiction the equal protection of the laws.

# Notes

## Prelude

1. Among these are Balmer 2006, Hedges 2006, Brint and Schroedel 2009a, 2009b. This reference style is used: an author's name is mentioned in the text and the complete reference to the author's work is in the bibliography. Notes refer to specifics of an author's work and to relevant information. Where sources are not mentioned, the information comes from my fieldwork, e.g., Appendix 9 lists my expert witness court testimony for which I also conducted research.

2. Harding 2000.

3. Finan 2007, Gilgoff 2007.

4. Harding 2000.

5. Note: The surveys of sociologists Baker 2005 and Greeley and Hout 2006 found that Americans are not divided into two opposed camps based on incompatible views of moral authority and, in fact, they tend to share views. The researchers claim the culture war was a myth. But here's the problem. My work since 1995 relies on ethnographic data nationwide, set questions and open-ended ones, what is said and done, what I hear and see to investigate complex issues. I did find ongoing battles between religionists and constitutionalists. Greeley and Hout rely on sociodemographic data from the General Social Survey with predetermined questions conducted by the National Opinion Research Center since 1972. They focus on a sample of the total population over combined political eras from 1968 to 2004 (p. 42) to draw a big picture—more than thirty-six years that lack "the precision necessary for intricate investigations of complex issues" (p. 13). They do single out a two-year period for some analyses. Their discussion of sex is about premarital teen and extramarital sex, abortion, homosexuality, and pornography. My work discusses the communication of, for example, sexual fantasy, nudity, and proximity. They recognize that there are "zealous Conservative Christians who try to use their smoke and mirrors to enforce their convictions on the media, school districts, courts, and local governments" (p. 182). Similarly, Baker, using the World Values Surveys 1981–2000, which he asserts is "the most comprehensive test of the culture war thesis yet available," concludes that the culture war is largely a fiction. But readers can draw their own conclusions. See also Boston 2011b.

6. Boston 2011b: 8

7. Khan 2008.

8. Watson 2010.

9. Vitello 2008.

10. Personal communication, December 28, 2002.

11. Grossman 2003.

12. Crier 2005, Hamilton 2005, Hedges 2006.

13. Joyce 2009.

14. For example, Paul et al. 2001, Land et al. 2004, Hanna 2008a.

15. MacKinnon 1987.

16. Appendix 9 lists the cases for my expert court witness testimony.

17. Apostolidis 2000, Atkins and Mintcheva 2006, Balmer 2006, Brink and Mencher 1997, Cooey 1994, Crier 2005, Griffith 2004, Hamilton 2005, Harding 2000, Hedges 2006, Klein 2006, Kuo 2006, LaHaye 1963, Lienesch 1993, McGraw 2003, Malley 2004, Kroeger and Beck 1996, Miles 1989, Munsil 1988 and 1994, Rudin 2006, Sharp 2005, Weinstein and Seay 2006.

18. Allen 1991, Angier 1976, Jarrett 1997, Shteir 2004. Over the past six decades, numerous dancers have written about their lives as strippers: Lee 1957, Bruce 1976, Lewin 1984, Feindel 1988, Dragu and Harrison 1988, Futterman 1992, Snowden 1994, Mattson 1995, Tracey 1997, Burana 2001, Eaves 2002, Beasley 2003, Lane 2004, Howard 2004, Bartlett 2004, Diamond 2005, Cody 2005, Black 2005. How-to books are available: Dee 2002, Obourn 2003. Journalists' work includes "Misty" 1973, Meiselas 1975, Angier 1976, Scott 1996. Revised dissertations, some by former exotic dancers, include: Frank 2002, Liepe-Levinson 2002, Bruckert 2002, Egan 2006, Barton 2006. And scholars have been writing about exotic dance since at least the 1980s: Halperin 1981, Angioli 1982, Massey and Hope 2005, and Roach 2007.

## Chapter One

1. Wagner 1997.

2. Hedges 2006.

3. Leaming 2007.

4. Weinstein and Seay 2006, Banerjee 2008a and 2008b, MacFarquhar 2008. Hall (2008) went on his first tour as a religious Baptist. Then, when he wouldn't pray with his fellow soldiers, they ostracized him and threatened his life. Soldiers are pressured to attend state-led religious practices that some find offensive and false, humiliating and dehumanizing. They object to official military retreats at off-base churches, appearances of uniformed officers at religious events, displays of crucifixes at military chapels. The Military Religious Freedom Foundation has received more than five hundred complaints of religious bias a month, Lichtblau 2009. See also Rodda 2010.

5. Weinstein and Seay 2006: 173.

6. Eller 2007: 284.

7. Gilgoff 2007: 96.

8. Butler 2006.

9. *Church & State*, December 2008: 16.

10. Luo 2006.

11. Goodstein 2006; see also Warren 2002, Hendricks 2006.

12. Banerjee 2006c.

13. Cooperman and Eilperin 2006, Kirpatrick 2006.

14. Knust 2011: 17. See also Coogan 2010, who also suggests that those who rely on the Bible to support their position on sexuality are on shaky ground.

15. Adams and Apostolos-Cappadona 1990.

16. Arterburn and Stoeker 2000: 67, 137.

17. Ince 2005: 30–31.

18. Chandrasekaran 1995.

19. Davies 1984: 103.

20. Kolakowski 1971.

21. Hedges 2006.

22. Joyce 2009b.

23. Joyce 2009a. The group follows Piper and Grudem 2006.

24. Higgins and Browne 2008.

25. Leland and Adnan (2011) describe mannequins placed on a small stage outside a mosque in Baghdad. The mannequins are clothed in "Western dress" that shows the shape of the female body, but chaste by Western standards—long sleeves and hems, high necklines. The display sends the uncompromising message to Muslim women: "men who look at women in such dress become voracious monsters; women who wear it burn through eternity." Conservative Muslims believe the *abaya*, a loose garment that completely shrouds the body and head, showing only the face, does not inflame men's imaginations.

26. Pavela 2010.

27. Emerson 1963, Tiersma 1993, Hansen 2001, Robbins and Mason 2003, Zelezny 2007, Stone et al. 2008.

## Chapter Two

1. Kintz 1997.

2. *Church & State*, May 2010: 20.

3. Quoted in *ACE National Newsletter* 2006.

4. Ramsay 2011.

5. Kay 2008.

6. Gellman 2005.

7. Fuller and Miller 1997; Phifer 2001; Land et al. 2004; Linz et al. 2004; Fisher et al. 2004; Enriquez et al. 2006; Linz et al. 2007.

8. For example, Baron 1974, Donnerstein and Evans 1975, Linz et al. 2000, Chuku 2005, Morris 2005.

9. Moore 1998.

10. Amen 2007.

11. Ibid.

12. Schwarz et al. 2007, Vedantam 2007.

13. Echterhoff et al. 2008.

14. For example, see Lewin 1984, Frank 2002, Liepe-Levinson 2002, Egan 2006.

15. Albo 2008.

16. Leiby 1996.

17. MacDonald 2007.

18. www.ic2.utexas.edu/bbr/publications/other-bbr-publications/index.php.

19. Gilgoff 2007.

20. Agustin 2009.

21. *The Conservative Voice*, February 20, 2006.

22. Brown and Martin 2003.

23. *ACE National Newsletter*, January 28, 2009: 2.

24. Associated Press 2001.

25. See Gilgoff 2007: 173–183, 198–204.

26. Note that the CCV's sixteen thousand members led the 1990 assault against the Cincinnati Contemporary Art Center's *Robert Mapplethorpe: The Perfect Moment* photography exhibit. CCV placed ads in newspapers and carried out a massive letter-writing campaign. Although the police closed the exhibit on obscenity charges, a jury found the five photographs in question not to be obscene.

27. Finan 2007: 81.

28. *ACE National Newsletter*, May 15, 2010.


## Chapter Three

1. Paz 1995: 2.

2. *Miller v. South Bend*, 1990.

3. Shay and Sellers-Young 2005, Chapter 3.

4. Berger 1972.

5. Meiselas 1975.

6. Safire 2008.

7. Spivey 2003.

8. Feur 2010.

9. http://strip-tease.warnerbros.com/movie/production.html.

10. *ACE of California Newsletter* 2008: 11.

11. Letter to Jeff Levy in response to an article on adverse secondary effects, November 19, 2003.

12. Angier 1976: 76.

13. Levine 1994: 11.

14. Hanna 1983, 1987b ,1988b, 2006, 2008b.

15. Montagu 1971, Grammer et al. 1998. See Vedantam 2002.

16. Liepe-Levinson 2002, Frank 2002, Hanna 1998, 2005b, 2008a.
17. Egan 2006: 112.
18. Linz et al. 2000.
19. Feindel 1988: 24.
20. Fine 1991: 90.
21. Wells 1994.
22. Bourdieu 1984.
23. Bentley 2002: 4–6.
24. Ben-Itzak 1998: 7.
25. Blair 2010.
26. Abramson and Pinkerton 1995, Bader 2002, Kahr 2008.
27. Hicks and Leitenberg 2001: 48.
28. McRobbie 1984, Kimmel 2006.
29. Stoller 1985.
30. Sciolino 2011: 64.
31. Moore 2010.
32. Lewis 2006: 302.
33. Lewis 2006: 298.
34. Hubbard et al. 2003.
35. Smith 2008.
36. *ACE National Newsletter*, May 25, 2011: 11.
37. Both et al. 2004.
38. McEwen 2002, Insel et al. 2001, Coan et al. 2006.
39. Solomon 2010.
40. Oppenheimer 2011.

## Chapter Four

1. Allen 1991: 88.
2. Jones 1993, Chuku 2005: 208.
3. Allen and Winters 2003.
4. Bahr 2004.
5. Weldon 2007.
6. Sulcas 2011.
7. Patrick 2003.
8. Ford and Beach 1951.
9. Banes 1998.
10. Fisher 2007.
11. Katz 1973.
12. Cressey 1932, Hong and Duff 1976, Salazar 2008.
13. Chaplin 2000, Simmons 2002.
14. Bannerman 2010.

### Chapter Six

1. G. M. D. 2000.

### Chapter Seven

1. See Grimsley 1996 regarding sexual harassment in the automobile industry.

2. Mohney 2010.

3. Demovic 1993.

4. Leventis 2007.

5. Fountain 2011.

6. Section 703, Title VII of the 1964 Civil Rights Act as amended, Title IX of the Education Amendments Act of 1972, Civil Rights Act of 1991, and Executive Order 11246.

7. David Steinberg 2004b updated my familiarity with the San Francisco scene.

8. Shafer 2011: 18.

### Chapter Eight

1. *New York Times Education Life*, January 6, 2007.

2. Associated Press 2001.

3. Baldas 2011.

4. Egan 2010.

5. www.clk.co.st-johns.fl.us/minrec/ordinancebooks/1992/ORD1992-12.pdf; *Café 707 v. St. Johns County*, Eleventh Circuit Court, 1993.

6. Manes 2011.

7. Billman 2005.

8. O'Neal 2000.

9. Fountain 2011.

10. Feuer 2010.

11. Klein 2007.

12. McFadden 2007, de Moraes 2009.

13. Sexual scandals have rocked the Catholic Church from Boston to Berlin, Los Angeles to Ireland. Catholic priest John Geoghan abused at least one hundred and thirty children over a thirty-year period. In Boston, the church paid an $85 million settlement to five hundred and fifty plaintiffs in 2003. In 1997, a Texas jury awarded $119.6 million to nine former altar boys sexually abused by a Dallas priest. In 2005, the church in Oakland paid $56.3 million to settle fifty-six cases of sexual abuse of children by priests from 1962 to 1985. Msgr. Robert C. Trupia preyed on so many young boys from 1976 into the 1980s that his fellow priests nicknamed him "Chicken Hawk." The twenty-five-year stat-

ute of limitations precluded criminal charges, so victims pressed a civil lawsuit against the church in Tucson. That suit was settled for millions of dollars. In 2007, the Archdiocese of Los Angeles paid $660 million to settle with more than five hundred victims. Several religious orders—including Carmelites, Franciscans, and Jesuits—paid $144 million in separate agreements to settle eighty-six claims. More than fifty-seven lawsuits have cost the church more than $2 billion. The Diocese of San Diego alone paid a nearly $200 million settlement to 144 people.

The Survivors Network of those Abused by Priests (SNAP) drew attention to the sexual assaults committed by Catholic clergy. SNAP warned church leaders that the denomination's bottom-up ecclesiology is a haven for sexual predators who abuse church and congregational trust and, when discovered, move on to another state protected by the church's cloak of secrecy. By 2010, the pope confronted the public outrage but not to many people's satisfaction. See Balboni 2011.

    14. Dunn 2009.

    15. Allen 2006.

    16. Brown loved the church and was a "true believer." She was a naïve sixteen-year-old, who had never been on a single date or even held hands with anyone, when her minister, Tommy Gilmore, married and a parent, initiated counseling with her. He sexually violated her—all in the name of God. After months of abuse, Gilmore started telling her that she was the serpent and Satan's ally. He even made her apologize to his wife. After she told the music minister, Gilmore was moved to a new position at a bigger church. Three companies that insure a majority of Protestant churches told the Associated Press (French 2007) that they typically receive upwards of 260 reports a year of children younger than eighteen being sexually abused by members of the clergy, church staff members, volunteers or congregants.

## Chapter Nine

    1. Binkley 2010.

    2. Rudin 2006, Slevin 2006.

    3. Banerjee 2006a.

    4. Banerjee 2006b.

    5. *New York Times*, May 23, 2006, p. A15.

    6. Stamp 2004.

    7. Hanna 2012.

    8. See Hanna 2002a.

    9. Martin Niemöller, the German pastor who outspokenly opposed the Nazis and suffered internment at concentration camps, said, "First they came for the Jews, and I did not speak out because I was not a Jew. Then they came for the Communists, and I did not speak out because I was not a Communist.

Then they came for the trade unionists, and I did not speak out because I was not a trade unionist. Then they came for me, and there was no one left to speak out for me." Fritz Stern, a scholar of German history, said mixing religion and politics, Hitler saw himself as "the instrument of providence" as he fused his "racial dogma with a Germanic Christianity" that helped ensure his success.

# References

Abramson, Paul R., and Steven D. Pinkerton. 1995. *With Pleasure: Thoughts on the Nature of Human Sexuality*. New York: Oxford University Press.

ACE (Association of Club Executives) of California Newsletter. 2008. "AB 2914: Fighting the Proposed State Adult Business Tax." June 4(3).

ACE National Newsletter. 2006. "Tennessee." March 14: 2.

———. 2009. "Arkansas." January 28: 2.

———. 2010. "Missouri Legislature Passes Strictest Regulations in the U.S. Against Adult Clubs." May 15: 1.

———. 2011a. "From Baltimore Vice Cop to Full-Time Adult Club Chaplain: Meet Mike Kaminski." May 25: 5–6.

———. 2011b. "Opposition Research: CCV Claims Responsibility for Congressional Letter Urging US Attorney General to Prosecute Adult Entertainment." May 25: 2.

Acocella, Joan. 2004. *Mark Morris*. Middleton, CT: Wesleyan University Press.

Adams, Doug. 1980. *Congregational Dancing in Christian Worship*, rev. ed. Austin, TX: Sharing Company.

Adams, Doug, and Diane Apostolos-Cappadona, eds. 1990. *Dance as Religious Studies*. New York: Crossroad Publishing Company.

Adler, Amy. 2005. "Girls! Girls! Girls!: The Supreme Court Confronts the G-string." *New York University Law Review* 80: 1108–1155.

Agustin, Laura. 2009. "Jesus Loves Strippers: Christian Outreach." www .nodo50.org/Laura_Agustin/jesus-and-outreach-with-strippers.

Albo, Mike. 2008. "Kansas City Law Enforcement Seeks 'Eyes' to Combat Sex and Drugs." *Kansas City Star*, February 12.

Allen, Bob. 2006. "Falwell Terms Clergy Sex-Abuse Case 'Bump in the Road.'" *EthicsDaily.com*, October 31.

Allen, Cynthia Culp, and Charity Winters. 2003. *The Beautiful Balance for Body and Soul*. Grand Rapids, MI: Fleming H. Revell.

Allen, Robert Clyde. 1991. *Horrible Prettiness: Burlesque and American Culture*. Chapel Hill: University of North Carolina Press.

Alliance Defense Fund (Community Defense Counsel). 2002. *Manual: Protecting Communities from Sexually Oriented Businesses*, 2nd rev. and updated ed.

Amen, Rob. 2007. "Neighbors: Strip Clubs Aren't Such Bad Bedfellows." *Pittsburgh Tribune-Review*, September 21.

American Planning Association. 1997. "Erotic and Exotic Uses." American Planning Association National Planning Conference. APA-7179 (tape recording), Chicago: Teach-em.

Andresen, Jensine, 2001. "Introduction: Towards a Cognitive Science of Religion," in Jensine Andresen, ed. *Religion in Mind: Cognitive Perspectives on Religious Belief, Ritual, and Experience.* Cambridge: Cambridge University Press.

Angier, Roswell. 1976. *"A Kind of Life": Conversations in the Combat Zone.* Danbury, NH: Addison House.

Angioli, Michael D. 1982. *Body Image Perception and Locus of Control in Semi-nude and Nude Female Dancers.* PhD dissertation, United States International University.

Apostolidis, Paul. 2000. *Stations of the Cross: Adorno and Christian Right Radio.* Durham, NC: Duke University Press.

Applebome, Peter. 1996. "Exotic Dancers Follow Olympic Flame to Atlanta." *New York Times,* July 8.

Arnold, Marigene, and Maxine L. Margoli. 1985. "Turning the Tables? Male Strippers and the Gender Hierarchy." Paper presented at the American Anthropological Association Meeting, Washington, DC.

Arterburn, Stephen, and Fred Stoeker. 2000. *Every Man's Battle: Winning the War on Sexual Temptation, One Victory at a Time.* Colorado Springs, CO: WaterBrook Press.

Associated Press. 2001. "Strip Club Vandals Return." *Indianapolis Star,* October 10.

Atkins, Robert, and Svetlana Mintcheva, eds. 2006. *Censoring Culture: Contemporary Threats to Free Expression.* New York: New Press.

Auster, Linda Phyllis, ed. 2000. *Music, Sensation, and Sensuality.* New York: Routledge.

Bader, Michael. 2002. *Arousal: The Secret Logic of Sexual Fantasies.* New York: Thomas Dunne Books/St. Martin's Press.

Bahr, Robert. 2004. "Comment." *Nude & Natural* 24(2): 11.

Baker, Wayne E. 2005. *America's Crisis of Values: Reality and Perception.* Princeton, NJ: Princeton University Press.

Balboni, Jennifer M. 2011. *Clergy Sexual Abuse Litigation: Survivors Seeking Justice.* Boulder, CO: Lynne Reinner Publishers.

Baldas, Tresa. 2011. "Nightclub Owner Headed Back to Detroit to Face Charges of Trafficking Women for Strip Joints." *Detroit Free Press,* February 4.

Balmer, Randall. 2006. *Thy Kingdom Come: How the Religious Right Distorts the Faith and Threatens America: An Evangelical's Lament.* New York: Perseus Books.

Banerjee, Neela. 2006a. "Liberal Denomination Fires Salvos at Right." *New York Times,* April 7.

———. 2006b. "Religious Left Struggles to Find Unifying Message." *New York Times,* May 19.

———. 2006c. "Pastor Chosen to Lead Christian Coalition Steps Down in Dispute over Agenda." *New York Times,* November 28.

———. 2008a. "Soldier Sues Army, Saying His Atheism Led to Threats." *New York Times,* April 26.

———. 2008b "Religion and Its Role Are in Dispute at the Service Academies." *New York Times*, June 25.

Banes, Sally. 1998. *Dancing Women: Female Bodies on Stage.* New York: Routledge.

Bannerman, Henrietta. 2010. "Martha Graham's House of the Pelvic Truth: The Figuration of Sexual Identities and Female Empowerment." *Dance Research Journal* 42(1): 30–45.

Barcan, Ruth. 2004. *Nudity: A Cultural Anatomy.* Oxford: Berg.

Baron, R. A. 1974. "Sexual Arousal and Physical Aggression: The Inhibiting Influence of 'Cheesecake' and Nudes." *Bulletin of the Psychonomic Society* 3: 337–339.

Bartlett, C. S. 2004. *Stripper Shoes.* Bloomington, IN: First Books Library.

Barton, Bernadette. 2006. *Stripped: Inside the Lives of Exotic Dancers.* New York: New York University Press.

Baudrillard, Jean. 1990. *Seduction*, trans. Brian Singer. New York: St. Martin's Press.

Beasley, Juliana. 2003. *Lapdancer.* New York: PowerHouse Books.

Beckford, James A. 2003. *Social Theory and Religion.* Cambridge, UK: Cambridge University Press.

Beckworth, David. 2008. "Praying for a Recession: The Business Cycle and Protestant Religiosity in the United States." http://ssrn.com/abstract=1103142.

Ben-Itzak, Paul. 1998. "Pacific Northwest Ballet's Ariana Lallone: The Triumph of a Patient Mind." *Dance Magazine* 72(1): 70–74.

Bentley, Toni. 2002. *Sisters of Salome.* New Haven: Yale University Press.

Berger, John. 1972. *Ways of Seeing.* London: BBC and Penguin Books.

Bezanson, Randall P. 2009. *Art and Freedom of Speech.* Champaign-Urbana: University of Illinois Press.

Billman, Jeffrey C. 2005. "Operation Overexposed." *Orlando Weekly*, September 22.

Binkley, Collin. 2010. "Churchgoers Reach Out to Strippers After Service, But All Is Not Yet Resolved." *Columbus Dispatch*, August 16.

Black, Rebeckka Sathen. 2005. *Dance to Despair: Memoirs of an Exotic Dancer.* Lincoln, NE: Universe, Inc.

Blair, Elizabeth. 2010. "Strip Clubs: Launch Pads For Hits In Atlanta." *All Things Considered*, December 23.

Blakeslee, Sandra. 2006. "Cells that Read Minds." *New York Times*, January 10.

Boles, Jacqueline Miles. 1973. *The Nightclub Stripper: A Sociological Study of a Deviant Occupation.* PhD dissertation, University of Georgia.

Boodakian, Florence Dee. 2008. *Resisting Nudities: A Study in the Aesthetics of Eroticism.* New York: Peter Lang.

Boston, Rob. 2006. "The Religious Right and American Freedom." *Church & State* 59(6): 4–14.

———. 2007. "Is there a 'War on Christmas'?" *Church & State* 60(11): 244–247.

————. 2011a. "The Art of Censorship." *Church & State* 64(1): 4.

————. 2011b. "Three Years After Being Pronounced 'Dead' by Many Pundits, Fundamentalist Political Groups Are Riding High in Washington and Many State Legislatures." *Church & State* 64(5): 7–10.

————. 2011c. "The Billionaire Boys Club." *Church & State* 64(5):11–14.

Both, Stephanie, Mark Spiering, Walter Everaerd, and Ellen Laan. 2004. "Sexual Behavior and Responsiveness to Sexual Stimuli following Laboratory-induced Sexual Arousal." *Journal of Sex Research* 41(3): 242–258.

Bourdieu, Pierre. 1984. *Distinction: A Social Critique of the Judgment of Taste*, trans. Richard Nice. Cambridge, MA: Harvard University Press.

Brink, Judy, and Joan Mencher, eds. 1997. *Mixed Blessings: Gender and Religious Fundamentalism Cross Culturally*. New York: Routledge.

Brint, Steven, and Jean Reith Schroedel, eds. 2009a. *Evangelicals and Democracy in America, Vol. 1: Religion and Society*. New York: Russell Sage Foundation.

————. 2009b. *Evangelicals and Democracy in America, Vol. 2: Religion and Society*. New York: Russell Sage Foundation.

Brizendin, Louann. 2010. "Love, Sex and the Male Brain." www.cnn.com/2010/OPINION/03/23/brizendine.male.brain/index.html?hpt=C2.

Brown, Jim, and Allie Martin. 2003. "In Honor of Pedophiles and Strippers—What's Next at America's Colleges?" *Agape Press*, February 19.

Bruce, Honey, with Dana Benenson. 1976. *Honey: The Life and Loves of Lenny's Shady Lady*. Chicago: Playboy Press.

Bruckert, Chris. 2002. *Taking It Off, Putting It On: Women in the Strip Trade*. Toronto: Women's Press.

Brustein, Robert. 2005. *Letters to an Actor: A Universal Guide to Performance*. New York: Basic Books.

Bryce, Jennifer. 1997. "The Daisy Chain: The Autobiography of an Activist." *E.D.A. Exotic Dancer's Alliance* 8: 2–3.

Bull, Michael, and Les Back, eds. 2003. *The Auditory Culture Reader*. New York: Berg.

Burana, Lily. 2001. *Strip City: A Stripper's Farewell Journey Across America*. New York: Hyperion.

Burgoon, J. K., D. B. Buller, and W. G. Woodall. 1996. *Nonverbal Communication: The Unspoken Dialogue*. New York: Harper Collins.

Burnham, Terence, and Brian Hare. 2007. "Engineering Human Cooperation: Does Involuntary Neural Activation Increase Public Goods Contribution?" *Human Nature* 18(2): 88–108.

Buss, David M. 1994. *The Evolution of Desire: Strategies of Human Mating*, rev. ed. New York: Basic Books.

Butler, Jennifer S. 2006. *Born Again: The Christian Right Globalized*. Ann Arbor, MI: Pluto Press.

Carey, Benedict. 2010. "Evidence That Little Touches Do Mean So Much." *New York Times*, February 23.

Carter, C. Sue. 1998. "Neuroendocrine Perspectives on Social Attachment and Love." *Psychoneuroendocrinology* 23(8): 779–818.

Chandrasekaran, Rajiv. 1995. "Fair's All-Nude 'Hootchy Show' Is More than Some Can Bear." *Washington Post*, August 30.

Chaplin, Julia. 2000. "New Club Dance Craze: Rear-Ending." *New York Times*, December 31.

Chicago, Judy. 1996. *The Dinner Party*. New York: Viking/Penguin.

Chuku, Gloria. 2005. *Igbo Women and Economic Transformation in Southeastern Nigeria, 1900–1960*. London: Routledge.

*Church & State*. 2007. "Coral Ridge Ministry's New Head Seeks Ties with Reconstructionists" 60(11): 256.

———. 2008. "Ga. Reconstructionist Pleads Guilty to Perjury in Sex-Scandal Lawsuit" 61(2): 41.

———. 2009. "Afghan Video Reveals Problems with Proselytism by U.S. Military" 62(6): 20–21.

———. 2010. "Focus on the Family Affiliates Train Candidates to Run for Office" 63(5): 20.

*Cincinnati Post*. 2005. "Harris Was Right to Call CCV Bluff on Strip Club Bill," November 10.

Clark, Kenneth. 1956. *The Nude: A Study in Ideal Form*. New York: Pantheon.

Classen, Constance. 1993. *World of Sense: Exploring the Senses in History and Across Cultures*. New York: Routledge.

Clipperton, Deborah. 1994. "Liberating the Object: Representations of Class, Gender and High Art in the Work of Two Toronto Strippers." Paper presented at the annual meeting of Congress on Research in Dance.

Coan, James A., Hillary S. Schaefer, and Richard J. Davidson. 2006. "Lending a Hand: Social Regulation of the Neural Response to Threat." *Psychological Science* 17(12): 23–39.

Cody, D. 2005. *Candy Girl: A Year in the Life of an Unlikely Stripper*. New York: Gotham.

Cohen, Adam. 2005. "This Season's War Cry: Commercialize Christmas, or Else." *New York Times*, December 4.

Cohen, Jean L. 2002. *Regulating Intimacy: A New Legal Paradigm*. Princeton, NJ: Princeton University Press.

Conn, Joseph L. 2008. "Americans United Seeks IRS Investigation of Liberty University for Electioneering." *Church & State* 61(1): 12–13.

Cooey, Paula M. 1994. *Religious Imagination and the Body: A Feminist Analysis*. New York: Oxford University Press.

Coogan, Michael. 2010. *God and Sex: What the Bible Really Says*. New York: Twelve.

Cook, Mark, and Robert McHenry. 1978. *Sexual Attraction*. New York: Pergamon Press.

Coontz, Stephanie. 1997. "In Search of Men Who Are in Search of Commitment." *Washington Post*, September 7.

Cooperman, Alan, and Juliet Eilperin. 2006. "On the Religious Right, an Alliance Torn Asunder." *Washington Post*, November 3.

Cranor, Carl F. 2006. *Toxic Torts: Science, Law, and the Possibility of Justice*. New York: Cambridge University Press.

Cressey, Paul G. 1932. *The Taxi-Dance Hall*. Chicago: University of Chicago Press.

Crier, Catherine. 2005. *Contempt: How the Right Is Wronging American Justice*. New York: Rugged Land Books.

Cunningham, Jim C., ed. 2006. *Nudity and Christianity*. Bloomington, IN: Authorhouse.

Davies, J. G. 1984. *Liturgical Dance: An Historical, Theological, and Practical Handbook*. London: SCM Press.

Dee, Tonya. 2002. *The Definitive Manual for Topless Dancers or "Hey Mister, Why Are You Sitting There with My Money in Your Pocket?"* 8th ed. Boca Raton, FL.

de Moraes, Lisa. 2009. "Ted Haggard's Saving Grace: The House Speaker's Daughter." *The Washington Post*, January 10.

Demovic, Angela. 1993. "Strippers in New Orleans: A Preliminary Study." *Human Mosaic* 27(1–2): 19–28.

DeWitt, Clyde. 1995. "Legal Commentary." *AVN* (Adult Video News) 112: 127.

Dionne, E. J. 2008. *Souled Out: Reclaiming Faith and Politics After the Christian Right*. Princeton, NJ: Princeton University Press.

Domke, David, and Kevin Coe. 2008. *The God Strategy: How Religion Became a Political Weapon in America*. New York: Oxford University Press.

Donnerstein, E., and R. Evans. 1975. "Erotic Stimulation and Aggression: Facilitation or Inhibition." *Journal of Personality and Social Psychology* 32: 237–244.

Dragu, Margaret, and A. S. A. Harrison. 1988. *Revelations: Essays on Striptease and Sexuality*. London, Ontario: Nightwood Editions.

Dunn, Bill. 2009. "Kinsey Adds Black Collar Files to Library." *Freethought Today* 26(8): 15.

Dworkin, Shari L., and Lucia F. O'Sullivan. 2006. "It's Less Work for Us and It Shows She Has Good Taste: Masculinity, Sexual Initiation, and Contemporary Sexual Scripts," in Michael Kimmel, ed. *The Sexual Self: The Construction of Sexual Scripts*. Nashville, TN: Vanderbilt University Press, pp. 105–121.

Eaton, Leslie. 2010. "Sin Tax Called Naked Money Grab." *Wall Street Journal*, March 26.

Eaves, Elisabeth. 2002. *Bare: On Women, Dancing, Sex, and Power*. New York: Alfred A. Knopf.

Echterhoff, Gerald, E. Tory Higgins, René Kopietz, and Stephan Groll. 2008. "How Communication Goals Determine when Audience Tuning Biases Memory." *Journal of Experimental Psychology* 137(1): 3–21.

Egan, Paul. 2010. "Strip Club Reps Say Riddle Wanted Bribe." *Detroit News*, January 27.

Egan, R. Danielle. 2006. *Dancing for Dollars and Paying for Love: The Relationships Between Exotic Dancers and Their Regulars*. New York: Palgrave Macmillan.

Ekman, Paul. 2003. *Emotions Revealed*. New York: Times Books.

Eller, Jack David. 2007. *Introduction to Anthropology of Religion: Culture to the Ultimate*. New York: Routledge.

Ellis, Kate, Barbara O'Dair, and Abby Tallmer. 1988. "Introduction," in Kate Ellis, Beth Jaker, Nan D. Hunter, Barbara O'Dair, and Abby Tallmer, eds., *Caught Looking: Feminism, Pornography & Censorship*. Seattle: Real Comet Press.

Emerson, Thomas I. 1963. "Toward a General Theory of First Amendment." *Yale Law Journal* 72(5): 877–956.

Enck, Graves E., and James D. Preston. 1988. "Counterfeit Intimacy: A Dramaturgical Analysis of an Erotic Performance." *Deviant Behavior* 9: 369–381.

Engel, Jonathan. 2008. *American Therapy: The Rise of Psychotherapy in the United States*. New York: Gotham Books.

Enriquez, Roger, Jeffrey Cancino, and Sean Varano. 2006. "A Legal and Empirical Perspective on Crime and Adult Establishments: A Secondary Effects Study in San Antonio, Texas." *American University Journal of Gender, Social Policy and the Law* 15(1): 1–41.

Ensler, Eve. 1998. *Vagina Monologues*. New York: Villard.

Erickson, David John, and Richard Tewksbury. 2000. "The 'Gentlemen' in the Club: A Typology of Patrons." *Deviant Behavior* 21(3).

Feindel, Janet. 1988. *A Particular Class of Women*. Vancouver: Lazara Publications.

Feuer, Alan. 2010. "Sex Business Backs the Party Animal." *New York Times Week in Review*, April 4.

Finan, Chris. 2007. *From the Palmer Raids to the Patriot Act: A History of the Fight for Free Speech in America*. Boston: Beacon Press.

Fine, Gary Alan. 1991. "Justifying Fun: Why We Do Not Teach Exotic Dance in High School." *Play and Culture* 4: 87–99.

Fischer, Carrie Benson. 1996. "Employee Rights in Sex Work: The Struggle for Dancers' Rights as Employees." *Law and Inquiry: A Journal of Theory and Practice* 14(2): 521–554.

Fisher, Helen. 1992. *Anatomy of Love: A Natural History of Mating, Marriage, and Why We Stray*. New York: Fawcett Columbine.

Fisher, Jennifer. 2007. "Tangible Acts: Touch Performances," in Sally Banes and André Lepecki, eds., *The Senses in Performance*. New York: Routledge.

Fisher, Marc. 2004. "Charity's Gaffe Smacks of Burlesque Act." *Washington Post*, June 3.

Fisher, Randy, Daniel Linz, and Bryon Paul. 2004. "Examining the Link Between Sexual Entertainment and Sexual Aggression: The Presence of Adult Businesses and the Prediction of Rape Rates in Florida." Paper presented to the Law and Policy Division at the annual meeting of the International Communication Association, New Orleans.

Foley, Elizabeth Price. 2006. *Liberty for All: Reclaiming Individual Privacy in a New Era of Public Morality*. New Haven: Yale University Press.

304

Ford, Clellan S., and Frank A. Beach. 1951. *Patterns of Sexual Behavior*. New York: Harper and Brothers.

Foster, Susan Leigh. 1996. "The Ballerina's Phallic Pointe," in Susan Leigh Foster, ed. *Corporealities: Body, Knowledge, Culture and Power*. New York: Routledge.

Foucault, Michel. 1977. *Discipline and Punishment: Docile Bodies*. New York: Pantheon Books.

———. 1978. *The History of Sexuality I: An Introduction*, trans. Robert Hurley. New York: Pantheon.

———. 1990. *The Use of Pleasure: The History of Sexuality*, Vol. 2. New York: Vintage Books.

Fountain, Ben. 2011. "Naked Capitalism." *New York Times*, January 8.

Frank, Katherine. 1998. "The Production of Identity and the Negotiation of Intimacy in a 'Gentleman's Club.'" *Sexualities* 1(2): 175–201.

———. 2002. *G-Strings and Sympathy: Strip Club Regulars and Male Desire*. Raleigh, NC: Duke University Press.

———. 2007. "Thinking Critically About Strip Club Research." *Sexualities* 10(4): 501–517.

French, Rose. 2007. "Protestant Sex Abuse: 260 Cases a Year." Associated Press, June 18.

Frenken, Geerte M. N., and Stephen J. Sifaneck. 1998. "Sexworkers and Dope: An Ethnography of Heroin-using Lap Dancers in New York City." *Addiction Research* 6(4): 341–370.

Fruedenberg, Nicholas. 1984. *Not In Our Backyards!* New York: Monthly Review Press.

Fulbright, Yvonne K. 2009. "FoxSexpert: 9 Reasons Strip Clubs Can Spice Up Your Sex Life." Fox News, December 7.

Fuller, Ron, and Sue Miller. 1997. Fulton County [Georgia] Police study of calls for service to adult entertainment establishments that serve alcoholic beverages, January 1995–May 1997, County Attorney's Office, 404 730 5719.

Futterman, Marilyn Suriani. 1992. *Dancing Naked in the Material World*. Buffalo: Prometheus.

Gagnon, John H. 2004. *An Interpretation of Desire: Essays in the Study of Sexuality*. Chicago: University of Chicago Press.

Gardner, Howard. 1983. *Frames of Mind: A Theory of Multiple Intelligences*. New York: Basic Books.

Geary, D. C. 1998. *Male, Female: The Evolution of Human Sex Differences*. Washington, DC: American Psychological Association.

Gellman, Barton. 2005. "Recruits Sought for Porn Squad." *Washington Post*, September 20.

Gilgoff, Dan. 2007. *The Jesus Machine: How James Dobson, Focus on the Family and Evangelical America Are Winning the Culture War*. New York: St. Martin's Press.

Giobbe, Evelina. 1993. "An Analysis of Individual, Institutional, and Cultural Pimping." *Michigan Journal of Gender & Law* 1(1): 33–57.

G. M. D. 2000. "Could Be . . . " *Cannon Falls Beacon*, December 21.

Goffman, Erving. 1959. *The Presentation of Self in Everyday Life*. New York: Anchor Doubleday.

Goldberg, Carey. 1997. "Bellevue Journal: Family Killings Jolt a Tranquil Town." *New York Times*, February 3.

Gomes, Peter J. 2007. *The Scandalous Gospel of Jesus: What's So Good about the Good News?* New York: HarperOne.

Goodstein, Laurie. 2006. "Disowning Conservative Politics, Evangelical Pastor Rattles Flock." *New York Times*, July 30.

———. 2007. "Senator Questioning Ministries on Spending." *New York Times*, November 11.

Grammer, Karl, Kirsten B. Kruck, and Magnus S. Manusson. 1998. "The Courtship Dance: Patterns of Nonverbal Synchronization in Opposite-Sex Encounters." *Journal of Nonverbal Behavior* 22(1): 3–29.

Greeley, Andrew, and Michael Hout. 2006. *The Truth about Conservative Christians: What They Think and What They Believe*. Chicago: University of Chicago Press.

Greenwood, J. R. 2004. "A Public Health Analysis of Rancho Cordova." Submitted to Rancho Cordova Concerning Its Proposed Adult Business Ordinance Number 22–2004.

Griffith, R. Marie. 2004. *Born Again Bodies: Flesh and Spirit in American Christianity*. Berkeley: University of California Press.

Grimsley, Kristin Downey. 1996. "EEOC Says Hundreds of Women Harassed at Auto Plant." *Washington Post*, April 10.

Grossman, Lev. 2003. "What's Next? Trends: The Quest for Cool." *Time Magazine* 162(10): 48–54.

Gruenewald, Paul, and L. Remer. 2006. "Changes in Outlet Densities Affect Violence Rates." *Alcoholism: Clinical and Experimental Research* 7 (July).

Hall, Edward T. 1966. *The Hidden Dimension*. New York: Doubleday.

———. 1976. *Beyond Culture*. Garden City, NY: Anchor Press.

Hall, Jeremy. 2008. "Second Recipient of the Atheist in Foxhole Award: Privileges, Not Rights." *Freethought Today* 25(10): 6–7.

Halperin, Rona Hildy. 1981. *Female Occupational Exhibitionism: An Exploratory Study of Topless and Bottomless Dancers*. PhD dissertation, United States International University, San Diego.

Hamilton, Mari. 2005. *God vs. the Gavel*. New York: Cambridge University Press.

Hanna, Judith Lynne. 1983. *The Performer-Audience Connection: Emotion to Metaphor in Dance and Society*. Austin: University of Texas Press.

———. 1987a. "Dance and Religion (Overview)," in Mircea Eliade, ed. *The Encyclopedia of Religion*, Vol. 4. New York: Macmillan Co.

———. 1987b. *To Dance Is Human: A Theory of Nonverbal Communication*. Chicago: University of Chicago Press.

———. 1988a. "The Representation and Reality of Divinity in Dance." *Journal of the American Academy of Religion* 56(2): 501–526.

———. 1988b. *Dance, Sex, and Gender: Signs of Identity, Dominance, Defiance, and Desire.* Chicago: University of Chicago Press.

———. 1997. "Creativity in Ubakala, Dallas Youth, and Exotic Dance," in R. Keith Sawyer, ed. *Creativity in Performance.* Norwood, NJ: Ablex Publishing Corporation.

———. 1998. "Undressing the First Amendment and Corseting the Striptease Dancer." *Drama Review* 42(2): 38–69.

———. 1999. "Toying with the Striptease Dancer and the First Amendment," in Stuart Reifel, ed. *Play and Culture Studies*, Vol. 2. Greenwich, CT.: Ablex.

———. 2001a. *Reality and Myth: What Neighbors Say about Exotic Dance Clubs: A Case Study in Charlotte, North Carolina.* Presented to City of Charlotte Zoning Board. Charlotte: Tarheel Entertainment Association.

———. 2001b. "Wrapping Nudity in a Cloak of Law." *New York Times*, July 1.

———. 2002a. "Dance Under the Censorship Watch." *Journal of Arts Management Law and Society* 29(1): 1–13.

———. 2002b. "If This Is Stripping, What Is Adult Entertainment?" *Exotic Dancer Bulletin* 7(3): 62.

———. 2003a. "Exotic Dance Adult Entertainment: Ethnography Challenges False Mythology." *City and Society* 15(2): 165–193.

———. 2003b. "Review of Eric Damian Kelly and Connie Cooper, *Everything You Always Wanted to Know about Regulating Sex Businesses.*" *Journal of Planning Literature* 17(3): 45–46.

———. 2003c. "Questions and Answers With . . ." (Ovetta Wiggins interview of Judith Hanna). *Washington Post*, December 7.

———. 2004. "The First Amendment, Artistic Merit and Nudity in Minnesota: Dance, Criminal Public Indecency and Evidence." *Minnesota Law and Politics Web Magazine.* April/May (noted in *Minnesota Law and Politics* 145: 34).

———. 2005a. "Dance and Religion (Overview)," in Lindsay Jones, ed. *The Encyclopedia of Religion*, 2nd ed. New York: Macmillan Co.

———. 2005b. "Adult Entertainment Exotic Dance: A Guide for Planners and Policy Makers." *Journal of Planning Literature* 20(2): 116–134.

———. 2006. *Dancing for Health: Conquering and Preventing Stress.* Lanham, MD: AltaMira Press.

———. 2008a. "Right to Dance: Exotic Dancing in the U.S.," in Naomi Jackson and Toni Shapiro-Phim, eds. *Dance, Human Rights and Social Justice: Dignity in Motion.* Lanham, MD: Scarecrow Press.

———. 2008b. "A Nonverbal Language for Imagining and Learning: Dance Education in K-12 Curriculum." *Educational Researcher* 37(8): 491–506.

———. 2010a. "Dance and Sexuality: Many Moves." *Journal of Sex Research* 47: 1–30.

———. 2010b. "'Toxic' Strip Clubs: The Intersection of Religion, Law and Fantasy." *Theology and Sexuality* 16(1): 19–58.

———. 2011. "Empowerment: The Art of Seduction in Adult Entertainment Exotic Dance," in Frank Kouwenhoven and James Kippen, eds. *Music, Dance and the Art of Seduction*. Delft, The Netherlands: Eburon Academic Publisher.

———. 2012. "Striptease Spectators: Live and Imaginary," in André Helbo, ed. *Spectacle vivant et interdiscipline*. Brussels: de Boeck, forthcoming.

Hansen, Clinton P. 2001. "To Strip or Not to Strip: The Demise of Nude Dancing and Erotic Expression Through Cumulative Regulation." *Valparaiso University Law Review* (Summer), 35 Val. U.L. Rev. 561.

Hanson, F. Allan. 2008. "What Would Jesus Do . . . If He Were a Lawyer?" *Humanist* 68(6): 27–32.

Harding, Susan Friend. 2000. *The Book of Jerry Falwell: Fundamentalist Language and Politics*. Princeton, NJ: Princeton University Press.

Harger, Jim. 2006. "Defense Fund Pushes City to Act on Strip Clubs." *Grand Rapids Press*, February 22.

Hedges, Chris. 2006. *American Fascists: The Christian Right and the War On America*. New York: Simon and Schuster.

Heins, Marjorie. 1993. *Sex, Sin, and Blasphemy: A Guide to America's Censorship Wars*. New York: The New Press.

Hendricks, Obery M. Jr. 2006. *The Politics of Jesus: Rediscovering the True Revolutionary Nature of the Teachings of Jesus and How They Have Been Corrupted*. New York: Doubleday.

Herskovitz, Jon. 2002. "Church Group Leads Strippers Out of Clubs." *Reuters*, July 19.

Hertenstein, Matthew J., Rachel Holmes, Margaret McCullough, and Dacher Keltner. 2009. "The Communication of Emotion via Touch." *Emotion* 9(4): 566–578.

Herzog, Dagmar. 2008. *Sex in Crisis: The New Sexual Revolution and the Future of American Politics*. New York: Basic Books.

Heyman, Steven J. 2008. *Free Speech and Human Dignity*. New Haven: Yale University Press.

Hicks, Thomas, and Harold Leitenberg. 2001. "Sexual Fantasies About One's Partner Versus Someone Else: Gender Differences in Incidence and Frequency." *Journal of Sex Research* 38(1): 43–50.

Higgins, Jenny, and Irene Browne. 2008. "Sexual Need, Control, and Refusal: How 'Doing' Class and Gender Influences Sexual Risk Taking." *Journal of Sex Research* 45(3): 233–245.

Hochschild, Arlie Russell. 1979. "Emotion in Work, Feeling Rules and Social Structure." *American Journal of Sociology* 85: 551–575.

———. 1983. *The Managed Heart: Commercialization of Human Feeling*. Berkeley: University of California Press.

Holsopple, Kelly. 1995. "From the Dressing Room: Women in Strip Clubs Speak Out!" *WHISPER* 9(1): 9.

Hong, Lawrence K., and Robert W. Duff. 1976. "Gentlemen's Social Club: Revival of Taxi Dancing in Los Angeles." *Journal of Popular Culture* 9(4): 827–883.

Howard, Kathryn N. 2004. *The Stripper Diaries.* St. Morris, MN: Tenth Street Press.

Hubbard, Amy S. Ebesu, A. Allen Tsuji, Christine Williams, and Virgilio Seatriz Jr. 2003. "Effects of Touch on Gratuities Received in Same-Gender and Cross-Gender Dyads." *Journal of Applied Social Psychology* 33(11): 2427–2438.

Hudson, David L. Jr. 1997. "The Secondary Effects Doctrine: 'The Evisceration of First Amendment Freedoms.'" *Washburn Law Journal* 37(1): 55–94.

———. 2002. *Adult Entertainment and the Secondary-Effects Doctrine: How a Zoning Regulation May Affect First Amendment Freedoms* (First Reports 2, 1). Nashville: First Amendment Center.

Hunter, James Davison. 1991. *Culture Wars: The Struggle to Define America.* New York: Basic Books.

Ince, John. 2005. *The Politics of Lust.* Amherst, NY: Prometheus Books.

Insel, T. R., B. S. Gingrich, and L. J. Young. 2001. "Oxytocin: Who Needs It?" *Progress in Brain Research* 133: 59–66.

Jamieson, Kathleen Hall, and Joseph N. Cappella. 2008. *Echo Chamber: Rush Limbaugh and the Conservative Media Establishment.* New York: Oxford University Press.

Jarrett, Lucinda. 1997. *Stripping in Time: A History of Erotic Dancing.* London: Pandora.

Jellinek, J. S. 1994. "Perfumes as Signals," in R. Apfelbach, D. Muller-Schwarze, R. Reutter, and E. Weiler, eds. *Chemical Signals in Vertebrates*, Vol. 7. *Advances in the Biosciences* 93. London: Pergamon/Elsevier Science.

Jones, Adam. 1993. "'My Arse for Akou': A Wartime Ritual of Women on the Nineteenth Century Gold Coast." *Cahiers d'Etudes Africaines* 132(4): 545–566.

Joshi, S. T. 2006. *The Angry Right: Why Conservatives Keep Getting It Wrong.* Amherst, NY: Prometheus Books.

Jourard, S. M. 1966. "An Exploratory Study of Body Accessibility." *British Journal of Social and Clinical Psychology* 5(3): 221–231.

Joyce, Kathryn. 2009a. *Quiverfull: Inside the Christian Patriarchy Movement.* Boston, MA: Beacon Press.

———. 2009b. "Biblical Battered Wife Syndrome: Christian Women and Domestic Violence." *Reproductive Justice and Gender*, February 2.

Kahn, Elayne J., and David A. Rudnitsky. 1989. *Love Codes: How to Decipher Men's Secret Signals about Romance.* New York: New American Library.

Kahr, Brett. 2008. *Who's Been Sleeping in Your Head? The Secret World of Sexual Fantasies.* New York: Basic Books.

Katz, R. 1973. "The Egalitarian Waltz." *Comparative Studies in Society and History* 15(3): 365–377.

Kay, Kristofer. 2008. "Business Profile: Cabe & Cato." *Exotic Dancer's Club Bulletin* (January): 62.

308

Kennedy, D. James. 1996. *Evangelism Explosion*, 4th ed. Wheaton, IL: Tyndale House.

Khan, Surina. 2008. "Tying the Not: How the Right Succeeded in Passing Proposition 8." www.publiceye.org/magazine/v23n4/proposition_8.html.

Kimmel, Michael, ed. 2006. *The Sexual Self: The Construction of Sexual Scripts.* Nashville, TN: Vanderbilt University Press.

Kintz, Linda. 1997. *Between Jesus and the Market: The Emotions that Matter in Right-Wing America.* Durham, NC: Duke University Press.

Kirkpatrick, David D. 2006. "Republican Woes Lead to Feuding by Conservatives." *New York Times*, October 20.

———. 2007. "End Times for Evangelicals?" *New York Times Magazine*, October 28.

Klein, Marty. 2006. *America's War on Sex.* Westport, CT: Praeger.

———. 2007. "Americans Search for a Sexual Center." *Sexual Intelligence*, August 19.

Kleinke, Chris L. 1986. "Gaze and Eye Contact: A Research Review." *Psychological Bulletin* 100: 78–100.

Knust, Rebecca Wright. 2011. *Unprotected Texts: The Bible's Surprising Contradictions about Sex and Desire.* New York: HarperOne.

Kolakowski, Leszek. 1971. "An Epistemology of the Striptease." *TriQuarterly* 22 (Fall).

Kroeger, Catherine Clark, and James R. Beck, eds. *Women, Abuse, and the Bible: How Scripture Can Be Used to Hurt or Heal.* Grand Rapids, MI: Baker Books.

Kugel, James L. 2007. *How to Read the Bible: A Guide to Scripture, Then and Now.* New York: Free Press.

Kuo, David. 2006. *Tempting Faith: An Inside Story of Political Seduction.* New York: Free Press.

Kutchinsky, Berl. 1991. "Pornography and Rape: Theory and Practice? Evidence from Crime Data in Four Countries Where Pornography Is Easily Available." *International Journal of Law and Psychiatry* 14: 47–64.

LaHaye, Tim. 1963. *How to Be Happy Though Married.* Wheaton, IL: Tyndale House.

Lane, Frederick S. 2006. *The Decency Wars: The Campaign to Cleanse American Culture.* Amherst, NY: Prometheus Books.

Lane, Lacey. 2004. *Confessions of A Stripper: Tales From The VIP Room.* Las Vegas: Huntington Press.

Leaming, Jeremy. 2007. "Fringe Festival: Christian Reconstructionists Hope To Move Out of the Margins And Take Dominion in America—And They Have Some Powerful Friends." *Church & State* 60(7): 10–13.

Leathers, Dale. 1986. *Successful Nonverbal Communication Principles and Applications.* New York: Macmillan.

Lee, Gypsy Rose. 1957. *Gypsy.* London: Futura.

Leiby, Richard. 1996. "'Striptease' & the Naked Eye." *Washington Post*, June 30.

Leitenberg, H., and K. Henning. 1995. "Sexual Fantasy." *Psychological Bulletin* 117: 469–496.

Leland, John, and Duraid Adnan. 2011. "Mannequins Wear a Message for Iraq's Women." *New York Times*, February 9.

Levav, Jonathan, and Argo, Jennifer J. 2010. "Physical Contact and Financial Risk Taking." *Psychological Science*, April 22 online.

Leventis, Angie. 2007. "Reading, Writing, Risque Two Worlds Coexist in an Uneasy Peace in Tiny Brooklyn." *St. Louis Post-Dispatch*, June 10.

Levine, Mindy. 1994. *Widening the Circle: Toward a New Vision for Dance Education.* Washington, DC: Dance/USA.

Lewin, Lauri. 1984. *Naked Is the Best Disguise: My Life as a Stripper.* New York: William Morrow & Co.

Lewis, Jacqueline. 1998. "Lap Dancing: Personal and Legal Implications for Exotic Dancers," in James E. Elias, Vern L. Bullough, Veronica Elias, and Gwen Brewer, eds. *Prostitution: On Whores, Hustlers and Johns.* Amherst, NY: Prometheus Books.

Lewis, Sarah Katherine. 2006. *Indecent: How I Make It and Fake It as a Girl for Hire.* Berkeley, CA: Seal Press.

Lichtblau, Eric. 2009. "Questions Raised Anew About Religion in Military." *New York Times*, March 1.

Lienesch, Michael. 1993. *Redeeming America: Piety and Politics in the New Christian Right.* Chapel Hill: University of North Carolina Press.

Liepe-Levinson, Katherine. 2002. *Strip Show: Performances of Gender and Desire.* New York: Routledge.

Lindsay, D. Michael. 2007. *Faith in the Halls of Power: How Evangelicals Joined the American Elite.* New York: Oxford University Press.

Linz, Daniel, Eva Blumenthal, Edward Donnerstein, Dale Kunkel, Bradley J. Shafer, and Allen Lichtenstein. 2000. "Testing Legal Assumptions Regarding the Effects of Dancer Nudity and Proximity to Patron on Erotic Expression." *Law and Human Behavior* 24(5): 507–533.

Linz, Daniel, Randy Fisher, and Michael Yao. 2004. "Evaluating Potential Secondary Effects of Adult Cabarets in Daytona Beach Florida: A Study of Calls for Service to the Police Reference to Ordinance 02-496." Report Amending Report of August 30, 2003 (April 7).

Linz, Daniel, Kenneth C. Land, Jay R. Williams, Bryant Paul, and Michael E. Ezell. 2004. "An Examination of the Assumption that Adult Businesses are Associated with Crime in Surrounding Areas: A Secondary Effects Study in Charlotte, North Carolina." *Law and Society Review* 38(1): 69–103.

Linz, Daniel, Michael Yao, and Sahara Byrne. 2007. "Testing Supreme Court Assumptions in *California v. la Rue*: Is there Justification for Prohibiting Sexually Explicit Messages in Establishments that Sell Liquor?" *Communication Law Review* 7(1): 23–53.

Lloyd-Elliott, Martin. 1994. *Secrets of Sexual Body Language.* Berkeley: Ulysses Press.

Luo, Michael. 2006. "Evangelicals Debate the Meaning of 'Evangelical.'" *New York Times,* April 16.

Lynn, Barry W. 2006. *Piety & Politics: The Right-Wing Assault on Religious Freedom.* New York: Harmony Books.

MacDonald, Christine. 2007. "Adult Club War Hits City Coffers," *The Detroit News,* June 22.

————. 2008. "Fight Costs Taxpayers, Detroit, Strip Clubs Battle Heats Up, Lawsuits Against City's Rules Pile Up," *Detroit News,* December 23.

MacFarquhar. Neil. 2008 "Speakers at Academy Said to Make False Claims." *New York Times,* February 7.

MacKinnon, Catharine A. 1987. *Feminism Unmodified: Discourses on Life and Law.* Cambridge, MA: Harvard University Press.

Malley, Brian. 2004. *How the Bible Works: An Anthropological Study of Evangelical Biblicism.* Landover, MD: AltaMira.

Manes, Billy, 2011. "Breasts Out: Winter Park Quietly Slips Secret $250,000 Settlement to Club Harem's Panties." *Orlando Weekly,* June 2–8.

Mann, Lawrence D. 1989. *When NIMBYs Are Really About "Different" People.* Cambridge, MA: Lincoln Institute of Land Policy.

McCullough, Andrew W. 2004. "A New Sort of 'Sin' Tax in Utah." *Exotic Dancer* (April/May): 18.

McElroy, Wendy. 1995. *A Woman's Right to Pornography.* New York: St. Martin's Press.

McEwen, Bruce S. 2002. *The End of Stress As We Know It.* Washington, DC: Joseph Henry Press.

McFadden, Robert D. 2007. "2 Shootings at Church Sites." *New York Times,* December 10.

McGraw, Barbara A. 2003. *Rediscovering America's Sacred Ground: Public Religion and Pursuit of the Good in a Pluralistic America.* Albany: State University of New York Press.

McNair, Brian. 2002. *Striptease Culture: Sex, Media and the Democratization of Desire.* New York: Routledge.

McRobbie, Angela. 1984. "Dance and Social Fantasy," in Angela McRobbie and Mica Nava, eds. *Gender and Generation.* London: Macmillan.

Margolis, Maxine L. 1994. *Little Brazil: An Ethnography of Brazilian Immigrants in New York City.* Princeton, NJ: Princeton University Press.

Marty, Martin E. 1992. "Explaining the Rise of Fundamentalism." *Chronicle of Higher Education* (October 28): A36.

Massey, Joseph E., and Trina L. Hope. 2005. "A Personal Dance: Emotional Labor, Fleeting Relationships, and Social Power in a Strip Bar," in Calvin Morrill, David A. Snow, and Cindy H. White, eds. *Together Alone: Personal Relationships in Public Places.* Berkeley: University of California Press.

Mast, Coleen Kelly. 1997. *Sex Respect: The Option of True Sexual Feeling—Student Handbook 7*, rev. ed. Bradley, IL: Respect Incorporated.

Mathews, Alice P. 1996. "How Evangelical Women Cope with Prescription and Description," in Catherine Clark Kroeger and James R. Beck, eds. *Women, Abuse, and the Bible: How Scripture Can Be Used to Hurt or Heal*. Grand Rapids, MI: Baker Books.

Mattson, Heidi. 1995. *Ivy League Stripper*. New York: Arcade Publishing.

Medvetz, Thomas. 2006. "The Strength of Weekly Ties: Relations of Material and Symbolic Exchange in the Conservative Movement." *Politics and Society* 34(4): 343–369.

Meiselas, Susan. 1975. *Carnival Strippers*. New York: Farrar, Straus and Giroux.

Miles, Margaret. 1989. *Carnal Knowing: Female Nakedness and Religious Meaning in the Christian West*. Boston: Beacon.

Miller, Geoffrey, Joshua M. Tybur, and Brent T. Jordan, 2007. "Ovulatory Cycle Effects on Tip Earnings by Lap Dancers: Economic Evidence for Human Estrus?" *Evolution and Human Behavior* 28: 375–381.

"Misty." 1973. *Strip!* Toronto: New Press Toronto.

Mohney, Jason. 2010. "Good Openings." *Club Bulletin* (September): 28.

Montagu, Ashley. 1971. *Touching: The Human Significance of the Skin*. New York: Columbia University Press.

Moore, Arthur Cotton. 1998. *Powers of Preservation: New Life for Urban Historic Places*. New York: McGraw Hill.

Moore, Monica M. 2010. "Human Nonverbal Courtship Behavior—A Brief Historical Review." *Journal of Sex Research* 47(2): 171–180.

Morris, Desmond. 2005. *Naked Woman: A Study of the Female Body*. New York: Thomas Dunne Books/St. Martin's Press.

Munsil, Len. 1988. *The Preparation and Trial of an Obscenity Case: A Guide for the Prosecuting Attorney*. Scottsdale, AZ: National Family Legal Foundation.

———. 1994. *How to Legally Stop Nude Dancing in your Community*. Scottsdale, AZ: National Family Legal Foundation.

Neu, Jerome. 2002. "An Ethics of Fantasy." *Journal of Theoretical and Philosophical Psychology* 22(2): 133–157.

*New York Times Education Life*. 2007. "Data: Law and Order." January 6.

Novack, Cynthia J. 1990. *Sharing the Dance: Contact Improvisation and American Culture*. Madison: University of Wisconsin Press.

Obourn, Melody. 2003. *The Exotic Entertainer's Bible*. Cabaret D Entertainment LLC.

O'Neal, Kevin. 2000. "Officer Faces Sex, Bribery Charges." *Indianapolis Star*, April 17.

Oppenheimer, Mark. 2007. "The First Dance: One Small Christian College Finds that There May Be Some Redemption in Being Footloose After All." *New York Times Magazine*, January 28.

————. 2011. "A Pole-Dancing Class with a Big Difference: The Clothes Stay On." *New York Times*, April 2.

Oropeza, B. J. 2006. "What Is Sex? Christians and Erotic Boundaries," in C. K. Robertson, ed. *Religion & Sexuality: Passionate Debates*. New York: Peter Lang.

Pasko, Lisa. 2002. "Naked Power: The Practice of Stripping as a Confidence Game." *Sexualities* 5(1): 49–66.

Patrick, K. C. 2003. Editorial. *Dance Magazine*, November 2003: 4.

Patrick, Tera. 2005. "Vivid Girls on the Dance Circuit." *AET (Adult Entertainment Today)* 1(1): 20.

Paul, Bryant, Daniel Linz, and Bradley J. Shafer. 2001. "Government Regulation of Adult Businesses through Zoning and Anti-nudity Ordinances: Debunking the Legal Myth of Negative Secondary Effects." *Communication Law and Policy* 6 (2): 355–391.

Pavela, Gary. 2010. *The Pavela Report: Law and Policy in Higher Education* 15(18).

Paz, Octavio. 1995. *The Double Flame: Love and Eroticism*. New York: Harcourt Brace & Company.

Phifer, Major W. D. 2001. *Adult and Non-Adult Entertainment Establishments, Statistical Analysis from 1/1/98 to 12/31/00*. Fulton County Police Department, Atlanta, GA.

Pierson, David. 2003. "Lap-Dance Decision Cheers Strippers, Patrons." *Los Angeles Times*, November 23.

Piper, John, and Wayne Grudem, eds. 2006. *Recovering Biblical Manhood and Womanhood*. Wheaton, IL: Crossways Books.

Pollard, Alton B. III. 2004. "Teaching the Body: Sexuality and the Black Church," in Anthony B. Pinn and Dwight N. Hopkins, eds. *Loving the Body: Black Religious Studies and the Erotic*. New York: Palgrave Macmillan.

Pollard, Jeff. 2004. *Christian Modesty and the Public Undressing of America*. San Antonio, TX: Vision Forum.

Prewitt, Terry J. 1989. "Like a Virgin: The Semiotics of Illusion in Erotic Performance." *American Journal of Semiotics* 6(4): 137–152.

Ramsay, David. "Eliot Hires Attorney Who Specializes in Fights Against Strip Clubs." www.seacoastonline.com/articles/20110528-NEWS-105280323.

Reed, Stacy. 1997. "All Stripped Off," in Jill Nagle, ed. *Whores and Other Feminists*. New York: Routledge.

Regan, Pamela C., and Ellen Berscheid. 1999. *Lust: What We Know About Human Sexual Desire*. Thousand Oaks, CA: Sage.

Reichert, Tom, and Jacqueline Lambiase, eds. 2003. *Sex in Advertising: Perspectives on the Erotic Appeal*. Mahwah, NJ: Lawrence Erlbaum Associates.

Religion News Service. 2006. "Interfaith Group Wants White House Office Closed." *Washington Post*, April 29.

Renner, Gerald A. 2004. *The Abuse of Power in the Papacy of John Paul II*. New York: Free Press.

Rich, Frank, 2006. "Truthiness 101: From Frey to Alito." *New York Times*, January 22.

Riley, Naomi Schaefer. 2006. "The Press and Patrick Henry College." *Chronicle of Higher Education* (July 14): B12.

Roach, Catherine M. 2007. *Stripping, Sex, and Popular Culture*. New York: Berg.

Robbins, H. Franklin Jr., and Steven G. Mason. 2003. "The Law of Obscenity—Or Absurdity?" *St. Thomas Law Review* 15(3): 517–544.

Rodda, Chris. 2010. *Attitudes Aren't Free: Thinking Deeply about Diversity in the US Armed Forces*. Maxwell Air Force Base, AL: Air University Press.

Roffman, Deborah M. 2006. "What Does 'Boys Will Be Boys' Really Mean?" *Washington Post*, February 5.

Ronai, Carol Rambo, and Carolyn Ellis. 1989. "Turn-ons for Money: Interactional Strategies of the Table Dancer." *Journal of Contemporary Ethnography* 18: 271–298.

Rosin, Hanna. 2007. *God's Harvard. A Christian College on a Mission to Save America*. New York: Harcourt.

Roye, Carole. 2008. "The Hymen Mystique." *Women's eNews*, December 3.

Rudin, James. 2006. *The Baptizing of America: The Religious Right's Plans for the Rest of Us*. New York: Thunder Mouth's Press.

Rupp, Heather A., and Kim Wallen. 2007. "Sex Differences in Viewing Sexual Stimulation: An Eye-Tracking Study in Men and Women." *Hormones and Behavior* 51: 524–533.

Rushdoony, Rousas John. 1973. *The Institutes of Biblical Law*. Dallas, TX: The Craig Press.

Safire, William. 2008. "Long Pole in the Tent." *New York Times Magazine*, January 6.

Salazar, Cristian. 2008. "Women Say NY's Dollar-Dance Clubs Have Darker Side." Associated Press, October 3.

Sanchez, Casey. 2008. "Theocratic Sect Prays for Real Armageddon." *Southern Poverty Law Center*. www.alternet.org/story/96945/theocratic_sect_prays_for_real_armageddon/.

Sandler, Lauren. 2006. *Righteous: Dispatches from the Evangelical Youth Movement*. New York: Viking.

Scheflen, Albert. 1965. "Quasi-Courtship Behavior in Psychotherapy." *Psychiatry* 38: 245–25.

Schlosser, Eric. 1997. "The Business of Pornography." *U.S. News and World Report*, February 10: 43–52.

Schneider. Rebecca. 1997. *The Explicit Body in Performance*. New York: Routledge.

Schwarz, N., L. Sanna, I. Skurnik, and C. Yoon, 2007. "Metacognitive Experiences and the Intricacies of Setting People Straight: Implications for Debiasing and Public Information Campaigns." *Advances in Experimental Social Psychology* 39: 127–161.

Sciolino, Elaine. 2011. "Opération Séduction." *New York Times Style Magazine*, May 22: 63–64, 66, 69.

Scott, David A. 1996. *Behind The G-String: An Exploration of the Stripper's Image, Her Person, Her Meaning.* Jefferson, NC: McFarland & Co.

Scott, Joseph E. 1991. "What Is Obscene? Social Science and the Contemporary Community Standard of Obscenity." *International Journal of Law and Psychiatry* 14: 29–45.

Segerstråle, Ullica, and Peter Molnár, eds. 1997. *Nonverbal Communication.* Mahwah, NJ: Lawrence Erlbaum.

Shafer, Brad. 2011. "Who Holds the Cards If Your Club Gets Hit by a Dancer Class-Action Lawsuit?" *Exotic Dancer's Club Bulletin,* May.

Sharlet, Jeff. 2008. *The Family: The Secret Fundamentalism at the Heart of American Power.* New York: HarperCollins.

Sharp, Elaine B. 2005. *Morality Politics in American Cities.* Lawrence: University Press of Kansas.

Shay, Anthony, and Barbara Sellers-Young. 2005. "Introduction," in Anthony Shay and Barbara Sellers-Young, eds. *Belly Dance: Orientalism, Transnationalism & Harem Fantasy.* Costa Mesa, CA: Mazda Publishers.

Shields, Jon A. 2009. *Democratic Virtues of the Christian Right.* Princeton: Princeton University Press.

Shires, Preston. 2007. *Hippies of the Religious Right.* Waco, TX: Baylor University Press.

Shteir, Rachel. 2004. *Strippers: The Untold History of the Girlie Show.* New York: Oxford University Press.

Simmons, Greg. 2002. "'Freaking' Shakes Up Parents." *Bethesda Gazette,* December 11.

Skipper, James K., and Charles H. McCaghy. 1971. "Stripteasing: A Sex Oriented-Occupation," in James M. Henslin, ed. *Studies in the Sociology of Sex.* New York: Appleton-Century Crofts.

Slade, Joe. 1989. "The American Male: The Naked Truth." *Vogue* (June): 241.

Slevin, Peter. 2006. "'St. Jack' and the Bullies in the Pulpit." *Washington Post,* February 2.

Sloan, Lacey. 1997. *A Qualitative Study of Women Who Work as Topless Dancers.* PhD dissertation, University of Houston.

Smith, Mark M. 2008. "The Touch of an Uncommon Man." *Chronicle Review,* February 22.

Smith, Rogers. 2009. "An Almost-Christian Nation? Constitutional Consequences of the Rise of the Religious Right," in Steven Brint and Jean Reith Schroedel, eds. *Evangelicals and Democracy in America. Vol. 1: Religion and Society.* New York: Russell Sage Foundation.

Snowden, Lynn. 1994. *Nine Lives: From Stripper to Schoolteacher: My Year-long Odyssey in the Workplace.* New York: W. W. Norton & Co.

Solomon, J. 2010. "News Flash: Strip Clubs Could Be Good for Your Health," *Westword,* November 3. www.westword.com/2010-11-04/music/news-flash-strip-clubs-could-be-good-for-your-health.

Spencer, Angelina. 2006. "IRS Complaint in Ohio Alleges Pastors Played Politicians: What Does it Mean for Adult Business?" *ACE National Newsletter* 6(5): 2.

———. 2009. *Political Resources Guide 2009.* Naples, FL: Association of Club Executives.

Spivey, Sue E. 2003. "Bureaucratizing the Erotic: Rationalizing Embodiment in Two Nude Dancing Bars." *Sociological Imagination* 39(2): 93–113.

———. 2005. "Distancing and Solidarity as Resistance to Sexual Objectification in a Nude Dancing Bar." *Deviant Behavior* 26(5): 417–437.

Stamp, Allen. 2004. "Reflections on the Election." *Present Truth*, December.

Steinberg, David. 2004a. "Lap Dancing in San Francisco." *Weekly*, September 8.

———. 2004b. "Comes Naturally" #151. David Steinberg Archives. www.sexuality.org/davids.html.

Stoddart, D. Michael. 1991. *The Scented Ape: The Biology and Culture of Human Odour.* New York: Cambridge University Press.

Stone, Geoffrey R., Louis M. Seidman, Cass R. Sunstein, Mark V. Tushnet and Pamela S. Karlan. 2008. *The First Amendment, Third Edition.* New York: Aspen Publishers Law & Business.

Stoller, Robert J. 1985. *Observing the Erotic Imagination.* New Haven: Yale University Press.

Strossen, Nadine. 1995. *Defending Pornography: Free Speech, Sex, and the Fight for Women's Rights.* New York: Scribners.

Suggs, Donald. 1989. "Private Dancers: Times Square A-Go-Go." *Village Voice*, January 24.

Sulcas, Roslyn. 2011. "Poetry of Stillness, in a Moment Stretched to Infinity." *New York Times*, March 31.

Sundahl, Debi. 1987. "Stripper," in Frédérique Delacoste and Priscilla Alexander, eds. *Sex Work: Writings by Women in the Sex Industry.* San Francisco: Cleiss Press.

Suren, Asuncion, and Robert Stiefvater. 1998. "Topless Dancing: A Case for Recreational Identity," in Martin Oppermann, ed. *Sex Tourism and Prostitution: Aspects of Leisure Recreation, and Work.* Elmsford, NY: Cognizant Communications.

Thayer, Stephen. 1982. "Social Touching," in William Schiff and Emerson Foulke, eds. *Tactual Perception: A Sourcebook.* Cambridge: Cambridge University Press.

———. 1986. "Touch: Frontier of Intimacy." *Journal of Nonverbal Behavior* 1(1): 7–11.

Thomas, Rusty Lee. 2009. *The Kingdom Leadership Institute Manual.* Mustang, OK: Tate Publishing.

Tiersma, Peter Meijes. 1993. "Nonverbal Communication and the Freedom of 'Speech.'" *Wisconsin Law Review* 6: 1525–1589.

Tracey, Lindalee. 1997. *Growing Up Naked: My Years in Bump and Grind.* Vancouver, Canada: Douglas & McIntyre.

Urish, Ben. 2004. "Narrative Striptease in the Nightclub Era." *Journal of American Culture* 27(2): 157–165.

Valdesolo, Piercarlo, and David DeSteno. 2008. "The Duality of Virtue: Deconstructing the Moral Hypocrite." *Journal of Experimental Social Psychology* 44(5): 1334–1338.

Vance, Carole S. 1993. "Feminist Fundamentalism—Women Against Images." *Art in America* (September): 35–37, 39.

Vedantam, Shankar. 2002. "Understanding that Loving Feeling: In a Study of the Brain, Special Nerves Registered the Emotional Context of a Pleasurable Touch." *Washington Post*, July 29.

———. 2007. "Persistence of Myths Could Alter Public Policy Approach." *Washington Post*, September 4.

Vitello, Paul. 2008. An Evangelical Article of Faith: Bad Times Draw Bigger Crowds." *New York Times*, December 14.

Vroon, Piet 1997. *Smell, the Secret Seducer*, trans. Paul Vincent. New York: Farrar Straus Giroux.

Wagner, Ann. 1997. *Adversaries of Dance: From the Puritans to the Present*. Urbana: University of Illinois Press.

Warren, Rick. 2002. *The Purpose-Driven Life: What on Earth Am I Here For?* Grand Rapids, MI: Zondervan.

Watson, Julie. 2010. "Christian Conservatives Target Seated Judges." Associated Press, May 30.

Weinstein, Michael L., and Davin Seay. 2006. *With God on Our Side: One Man's War Against an Evangelical Coup in America's Military*. New York: Thomas Dunne Books.

Weiss, Rick. 2004. "U.S. Scientists Win Nobel Prize in Medicine for Studies on Smell." *Washington Post*, October 5.

Weldon, Glen. 2007. "Macbeth," *City Paper*, June 29.

Weller, Aron. 1998. "Human Pheromones: Communication Through Body Odour." *Nature* 392: 126–127.

Wells, Melanie. 1994. "Woman as Goddess: Camille Paglia Tours Strip Clubs." *Penthouse*, October.

Wesely, Jennifer K. 2002. "Growing Up Sexualized—Issues of Power and Violence in the Lives of Female Exotic Dancers." *Violence Against Women* 8(10): 1182–1207.

West, Darrell J., and Marion Orr. 2007. "Morality and Economics: Public Assessments of the Adult Entertainment Industry." *Economic Development Quarterly* 21(4): 315–324.

West, Traci C. 2004. "A Space for Faith, Sexual Desire, and Ethical Black Ministerial Practices," in Anthony B. Pinn and Dwight N. Hopkins, eds. *Loving the Body: Black Religious Studies and the Erotic*. New York: Palgrave Macmillan.

Wheeler, J. Joshua, and Robert M. O'Neil. 1999. *Amici Curiae Brief of the Thomas Jefferson Center for Protection of Free Expression, Alley Theatre, Association of Per-*

forming Arts Presenters, Kathleen Chalfant, Dance/USA, Tony Kushner, The Looking Glass Theatre Co., Terrence McNally, Oregon Shakespeare Company, Yvonne Rainer, Rachel Rosenthal, Theater Artaud, Theatre Communications Group, and the Walker Art Center, in Support of Pap's A.M. 98–1161 in the Supreme Court of the U.S.

Wilcox, Clyde. 1996. *Onward Christian Soldiers? The Religious Right in American Politics*. Boulder, CO: Westview Press.

Winick, Charles. 1977. "From Deviant to Normative: Changes in the Social Acceptability of Sexually Explicit Material," in Edward Sagarin, ed. *Deviance and Social Change*. Beverly Hills: Sage.

Winters, Jason, Kalina Christoff, and Boris B. Gorzalka. 2009. "Conscious Regulation of Sexual Arousal in Men." *Journal of Sex Research* 46(4): 330–343.

Wolterstorff, Nicholas. 1980. *Art in Action: Toward a Christian Aesthetic*. Grand Rapids, MI: William B. Eerdmans Publishing Co.

Wood, Elizabeth Anne. 2000. "Working in the Fantasy Factory: The Attention Hypothesis and the Enacting of Masculine Power in Strip Clubs." *Journal of Contemporary Ethnography* 29(1): 5–31.

World Archives. Jesus & Strippers. www.worldmag.com/articles/15914.

Yurica, Katherine. 2004. "The Despoiling of America: How George W. Bush Became Head of the New American Dominionist Church/State." *Yurica Report News Intelligence Analysis*, February 11. www.yuricareport.com.

Zelezny, John. 2007. *Communications Law: Liberties, Restraints, and the Modern Media*, 5th ed. Belmont, CA: Thomson/Wadsworth.

Zurbriggen, Eileen L., and Megan R. Yost. 2004. "Power, Desire, and Pleasure in Sexual Fantasies." *Journal of Sex Research* 41(3): 288–300.

# Index

319